THE GLOBAL MANUFACTURING REVOLUTION

Also written by Yoram Koren

Computer Control of Manufacturing Systems
and
Robotics for Engineers

both published by McGraw Hill, New York

and

Numerical Control of Machine Tools

published by Kahana Publishers, Delhi

THE GLOBAL MANUFACTURING REVOLUTION

Product-Process-Business Integration and Reconfigurable Systems

YORAM KOREN

Professor and Director, NSF-Sponsored Engineering Research Center
for Reconfigurable Manufacturing Systems
The University of Michigan, Ann Arbor

RODNEY HILL

Illustration and Technical Cartooning

A JOHN WILEY & SONS, INC., PUBLICATION

Published by John Wiley & Sons, Inc., Hoboken, New Jersey.
Published simultaneously in Canada.

For general information on our other products and services, or technical support, please contact our Customer Care Department within the United States at (800) 762-2974, outside the United States at (317) 572-3993 or fax (317) 572-4002.

Wiley also publishes its books in a variety of electronic formats. Some content that appears in print may not be available in electronic books. For more information about Wiley products, visit our web site at www.wiley.com

Library of Congress Cataloging-in-Publication Data

ISBN: 978-0-470-58377-7

Printed in the United States of America

10 9 8 7 6 5 4 3 2 1

*Dedicated to my loving and supporting wife, Alina,
who encouraged the writing of this book*

In memory of
Professor Shien-Ming (Sam) Wu (1924–1992)
Pioneer in introducing advanced statistical techniques to manufacturing research

Contents

Preface

I began teaching a class on global manufacturing in 1995. Since there were no books on this topic (and prior to this publication, there are still none) I started to write this book in 2002. The first edition of this book was submitted to an NSF review panel in May 2004. This current 2009 edition includes much new data, additional numerical examples, and professionally done drawings.

The book is intended for engineers who desire to pursue managerial careers in the manufacturing industry, to students in business schools who are motivated to lead manufacturing enterprises, as well as to leaders of global enterprises. It provides the tools and knowledge needed for making manufacturing enterprises thrive and ensure their growth in a global environment.

The theme of the book is: "*globalization creates both opportunities and challenges for companies that manufacture durable goods.*" My main challenge in writing a book on globalization is that the pace of events involving the manufacturing industry in the last few years is changing faster than my writing speed. The book aims at helping manufacturing companies to succeed in this turbulent business environment of a newly interconnected world where all competitors have similar opportunities. The book proposes new technologies and new business strategies that can increase an enterprise's responsiveness to volatile markets and enhance the integration of its own engineering and business. Both are crucial for global success.

For manufacturing enterprises to succeed in this current volatile economic environment, a revolution is needed in restructuring all three main components of a manufacturing enterprise: product design, manufacturing, and business model. A company can succeed in globalization if and only if it has (1) a sound strategy for developing new innovative products that fit cultural needs in several world's regions, (2) business models that encompass a global strategy, and (3) factories with reconfigurable manufacturing systems (RMS) that can be rapidly changed to produce new products and quickly respond to changes in market demand. These topics are covered and mathematically analyzed in this book.

I first became concerned about the future impact of globalization on the U.S. manufacturing industry and jobs in the early 1990s. In 1992, the European Union had been formed, and in 1994, the North American Free Trade Agreement (NAFTA) became public. People in the United States were becoming acutely concerned for the future of the domestic automotive industry. We looked for technical solutions and wrote a large proposal to the National Science Foundation (NSF).

On August 1, 1996, we opened the Engineering Research Center (ERC) for RMS with an 11-year grant of $35 million from the NSF to develop and implement reconfigurable systems. Establishing the RMS Center opened the era of reconfigurable manufacturing in which the **speed of responsiveness** is the prime business goal and **reconfiguration** is an important technology enabler for achieving our goal:

"Exactly the capacity and functionality needed, exactly when needed."

To understand the current revolution in global manufacturing enterprises it is necessary to analyze the technical and business dimensions of previous manufacturing paradigms, such as mass production and mass customization. Original models are offered here to study these paradigms. This book introduces many innovations to the whole manufacturing culture: an original approach to the analysis of paradigms; suggested methods for developing creativity in product design; a quantitative analysis of manufacturing system configurations; discussions of the globalization impact on enterprises, and an original approach to the use of information technology for workforce empowerment. The book contains 200 original illustrations and pictures that clarify the topics.

Chapters 2 and 3 of this book deal with **product** design for globalization with emphasis on creativity and developing innovation skills. The topic of Chapters 6 through 10 is **manufacturing systems**, including thorough analysis of RMS. Chapters 11, 12, and 13 focus on **business** issues relevant to manufacturing enterprises: business models, company organization, and enterprise globalization strategies needed in the twenty-first century. The focus of Chapters 1, 4, 5, and 14 is the **integration** of product–manufacturing-system–business. This integration is the systems-view approach that is very essential for leading manufacturing enterprises in the future.

This book is unique in focusing on these globalization issues; as of this printing there have been no others. Thomas Friedman's famous book, *The World is Flat*, deals with the impact of globalization on society and business. Although his work does not discuss manufacturing in detail, it explains how the newly leveled playing field of an integrated world has created a revolution in global business. We have been energized by Friedman's work but we have focused on the manufacturing industry and offered many concrete enterprise and engineering solutions.

This serves as a textbook for a graduate-level class entitled "Global Manufacturing," which is offered at the University of Michigan to graduate engineering students and MBA students. Student's assignments include solving problems, submitting chapter reviews, and a team project that is described in Appendix D. The publisher's website includes material that may help instructors in teaching a similar course. Throughout each chapter we have included the comments of students of previous classes about the material presented. Since the book introduces new ideas, original models, and novel technologies, I asked students (most of whom have had at least some industrial background) to compare their experience with the theories and claims made in the book. I am grateful for their contributions and find them to be very thoughtful and enlightening.

Finally, I would like to thank my wife Alina, who suggested that I write this book and encouraged me through its writing; to Rod Hill for the many professionally prepared illustrations and cartoons and for his editorial support; to my colleagues for their interest and assistance; and to the readers who sent comments, only a small sample of which could be published here.

YORAM KOREN

College of Engineering
The University of Michigan, Ann Arbor
August 1, 2009

Acknowledgments

This book has drawn on the talents of the researchers at the NSF-sponsored Engineering Research Center for Reconfigurable Manufacturing Systems (ERC-RMS), at the University of Michigan, Ann Arbor, as well as the numerous committed industry members of the Center. The generous financial support of the Engineering Directorate at NSF to the ERC-RMS during the years 1996 to 2007 (NSF Grant EEC95–92125) is gratefully acknowledged. Special thanks to Lynn Preston, the director of the ERC program at NSF.

Chapter 1

Globalization and Manufacturing Paradigms

Globalization is the integration and interdependency of world markets and resources in producing consumer goods and services

Globalization has created a new, unprecedented landscape for the manufacturing industry, one of fierce competition, short windows of market opportunity, frequent product introductions, and rapid changes in product demand. Indeed, globalization is challenging, but it presents both threats and opportunities. To capitalize on the opportunities, industry needs to offer products that are innovative and also can be made to appeal to buyers from many cultures so they can be sold all over the globe. The challenge, however, is to succeed in a turbulent business environment where all competitors have similar opportunities.

Success in such a turbulent environment requires a global enterprise structure that can rapidly respond to changing markets and customer's needs. This enterprise should be equipped with a manufacturing system that can be rapidly changed and reconfigured to respond to volatile demand. This new generation of manufacturing systems will need to be reconfigured within two categories: product quantities (changed capacity) and product mix (changed functionality). Capacity reconfiguration is needed to produce exactly the product quantities required by the market at any given time. Manufacturing system and supply-chain functionality must also be reconfigured to support an accelerated pace of product innovation, and to produce the right mix of products required by various regions around the globe.

The Global Manufacturing Revolution: Product-Process-Business Integration and Reconfigurable Systems
By Yoram Koren
Copyright © 2010 John Wiley & Sons, Inc.

In short, a new global manufacturing revolution is needed to succeed in the new global economy; it must be a revolution based on responsive manufacturing systems and responsive business models. Responsive business models should aim at expanding into global markets by developing products that fit the culture of those markets and can be sold there. The business model must encompass not only selling, but also the international buying of components, and establishing global supply chains. The global enterprise should more closely integrate product design with its manufacturing systems and its global business model.

Charles R. Darwin's statement in his book *On the Origin of Species*[*]: "It is not the strongest species that survive, nor the most intelligent, but the ones most **responsive** to change," is now valid for global manufacturing enterprises.

1.1 THE IMPORTANCE OF MANUFACTURING TO SOCIETY

Why are we worried about manufacturing in the twenty-first century? Isn't manufacturing an "old-economy" profession that should be relegated to only poor countries? Is manufacturing really so important for a fully developed nation in the global economy?

Manufacturing is today, as it always has been, a cornerstone of the U.S. economy as it is for other developed nations. Having a strong base of manufacturing is important to any advanced country because it impels and stimulates all the other sectors of the economy. It provides a wide variety of jobs, both blue- and white-collar jobs, which bring higher standards of living to many sectors in society, and builds a strong middle class. Simply put, its most important benefit to society is that **manufacturing creates wealth**.

Think about this:

Only art, agriculture, construction, and manufacturing, and more recently the software industry, create something of value from nothing.

However, there is a big difference in the types of jobs that each industry creates.

> An important advantage of manufacturing is that it creates a whole range of diverse jobs. Whereas agriculture and construction generate lots of low-skilled jobs, and art and software create a few jobs for higher-skilled elites, manufacturing calls on the skills of everyone from entry-level factory workers to scientists, engineers, and business professionals.

---

[*]Charles R. Darwin (1809–1882) developed in England the theory of evolution. His most known book is *On the Origin of Species*, in which he describes the evolution of life on earth and includes this famous quote: "It is not the strongest species that survive, nor the most intelligent, but the ones most responsive to change."

To meet its far-ranging needs, manufacturing stimulates employment in other sectors of the economy. It has been calculated in 2001 by the Association of Manufacturing Technology (AMT) that each $1 million in sales of manufacturing goods produced in the United States supports eight jobs in the manufacturing sector and an additional six jobs in other sectors, such as information technology (IT), transportation, and construction. That means an average of 14 jobs are created by the U.S. manufacturing industry for each $1 million in sales. No other sector comes even close.

American manufacturing has been a strong contributor to the U.S. national economy for generations. In addition, gains in manufacturing productivity pass down to other sectors, building wealth and generating employment through the whole economy. The finished goods amount to only a portion of manufacturing's value. Production of intermediate-level goods (parts included in other products like engines, compressors, pumps, etc.) contributes significantly to the economy. Further, the design and production of manufacturing infrastructure, tooling, and equipment are industries of their own. And this says nothing of the high levels of transportation, information, and communications infrastructure that are all required to support world-class manufacturing. Because of its scale and volume, no other industry can replace manufacturing industry in any nation's economy. While the products America builds may and must change over time, domestic manufacturing continues to play a critical role in U.S. prosperity.

Manufacturing was, is, and shall remain the foundation of a strong economy. No other sector can replace it. Without a solid manufacturing base, the service and finance sectors will collapse.

As shown in Figure 1.1, the percentage of GDP of the U.S. private manufacturing sector has been gradually declining from 32% in 1950 to 13.4% in 2007.[*] From 1950, the manufacturing sector was constantly the highest in GDP percentage until 2005. In 2006, the real-estate sector moved ahead (14.9%) with manufacturing second (13.8%), and, as depicted in Figure 1.2, these sectors were 14.3% (real-estate) and 13.4% (manufacturing). However, even 13% is still a huge portion of the economy. In fact, **manufacturing still remains the largest productive sector in the overall U.S. economy**.

The GDP percentages of several sectors of the economy are shown in Table 1.1. In the late 1980s, "information" emerged as a new sector, which gradually increased to 5% in 2000. It is worth noting that, since 1990, investments in IT on behalf of manufacturing enterprises have contributed significantly to development of the information sector.

---

[*] Source for Figures 1.1 and 1.2 as well as Table 1.3 is U.S. Department of Commerce, Bureau of Economic Analysis, (http://www.bea.gov).

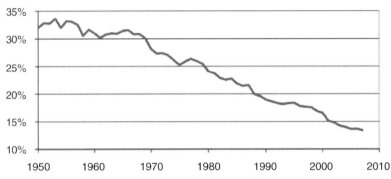

Figure 1.1 Manufacturing share of the U.S. Gross Domestic Product, 1950–2007 (as a percentage of the private industry). *Source*: U.S. Department of Commerce, Bureau of Economic Analysis.

Table 1.1 shows that the productive sectors of the economy halved in 35 years. Simultaneously with the 50% decline in manufacturing in the last 35 years, agriculture also declined at the same percentage. During the same period, the service sectors (including education, health, finance, and insurance) doubled. These data show that the U.S. economy is becoming more of a service economy than an economy that creates tangible wealth. But, is this a healthy trend?

Some renowned economists argue that the future of the United States is in the service industry. However, many portions of the service industry depend on the domestic manufacturing industry—trucking, financing, education, and infrastructure. Furthermore, an export of the service industry is very limited. A balance of export and trade is vital to a nation's economy, and therefore for the economy to thrive, manufacturing must remain healthy.

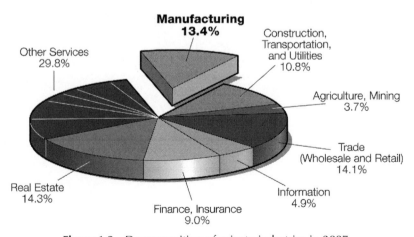

Figure 1.2 Decomposition of private industries in 2007.

TABLE 1.1   Sectors of Private Industries From 1970 to 2006 (in %)

Sector/Year	1970	1980	1990	2000	2007
Manufacturing	28.4	24.5	19.0	16.6	13.4
Agriculture + mining	5.3	4.5	3.6	2.5	3.7
Information	–	–	4.5	5.3	4.9
All services	13.9	16.0	25.9	27.8	29.9
Finance and insurance	5.2	6.1	6.8	8.6	9.0

Advanced industrial countries, including the United States, heavily subsidize agriculture, rendering that sectors benefit to the nation's economy as questionable. And yet, by contrast, manufacturing is not subsidized in the United States, even though its growth directly contributes to the wealth of the country.

Enhancing manufacturing growth depends on increasing productivity and inventing manufacturing technologies. Many major innovations in manufacturing methods originated in the United States—the invention of mass production by Henry Ford at the beginning of the twentieth century, the invention of numerical control (NC) machines of the 1950s, and the invention of reconfigurable manufacturing systems (RMSs) in the late 1990s. Coincidently, these three inventions that contribute to productivity improvements were started in the state of Michigan—the first in Dearborn, the second in Traverse City, and latest in Ann Arbor.

1.2   THE BASICS OF MANUFACTURING IN LARGE QUANTITIES

Manufacturing revolves around the production of quantities of new products. First, the product is developed, then it is manufactured, and finally it is sold to customers. Important factors for product developers to consider include how products look, how they work, and how the user interacts with them. To verify the product design, a product prototype is often constructed and tested to validate the design and product functionality. A prototype is built as a one-of-a-kind, essentially a work of art, and that can take a lot of time and labor. Even so, the prototyping method can be cost-effective when only a handful of copies are ever going to be sold.

When the manufacturer intends to produce large quantities of the product, as in the production of automobiles, refrigerators, or microprocessors, a more economical method is required. If large quantities were produced in the same way as the prototype, each product could be 10–20 times more expensive than the ones produced by a well-designed manufacturing system. For large quantities of products, a manufacturing system capable of mass production has to be developed.

The goal of a manufacturing system is to produce high-quality products at a fraction of what it took to build the prototype, so they can be sold at a marketable price. The manufacturing system achieves "economies of scale" that the prototype shop cannot, neither in output nor in consistency. In a globally competitive environment, designing a cost-effective manufacturing system and operating it efficiently is a key

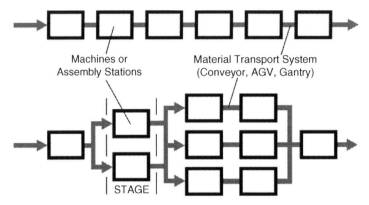

Figure 1.3   Examples of multi-stage manufacturing systems: six stages (top) and five stages (bottom).

competitive challenge especially when competitors have an advantage in countries where labor costs are substantially smaller.

Manufacturing systems typically consist of multiple stages, where each stage contains a machine or an assembly station to perform a given set of operations, as is illustrated in Figure 1.3. The machines are connected with a material transport system.

When the operations in one stage are completed, the raw product is transferred to the next stage, and so forth until all needed operations are completed and the product is finished. When especially large quantities are needed, multiple machines (or assembly stations) can be installed in parallel to perform the same operations at the same time on each machine (Figure 1.3, bottom), which increases the system throughput but makes the system design and operation more complex.

Most manufacturing is applied in multi-stage systems including assembly, such as those used to build automobiles, office chairs, or personal computers from given parts; or they may be systems with chemical processes, such as those on which semiconductor wafers are produced; or they may be machining systems for products that have to be machined, such as engine blocks, motors, pumps, and compressors. In machining systems, the products start out as rough castings that have to be drilled, milled, shaped, and polished using computerized numerically controlled (CNC) machine tools.

1.2.1   Dedicated and Flexible Systems

At the dawn of the twenty-first century, industries around the world used two basic types of manufacturing systems: dedicated manufacturing lines (DMLs) and flexible manufacturing systems (FMSs). Dedicated lines (often referred to as "transfer lines") are designed to produce very large quantities of just one product, and they operate at very high productivity because the machines are simple and robustly designed. For example, engine blocks for cars can be machined on dedicated machining lines at a cycle time of 30 seconds (two engines are produced every minute). Therefore, once the line is properly tuned and calibrated, and as long as the dedicated line operates at its planned high-volume capacity, it produces products very quickly at very attractive prices (but it is only able to produce that one single product per line).

So what happens when there is no longer a need for that many engines, and demand is reduced to say one engine every 3 minutes (1/6 of the line designed capacity)? When that happens the dedicated line is underutilized, and therefore, the cost per product becomes higher. A report published in Italy[1] in 1998 indicated that the average utilization of the surveyed DMLs in the European auto-industry was only 53%. That means that barely half of the potential capacity was being utilized and the lines stood idle for long periods.

Furthermore, DMLs cannot be easily converted to produce new products even if they are similar and of the same product family. In the new global manufacturing paradigm, this is the main drawback of DMLs. With globalization, the marketable life of products is becoming shorter and shorter, and new products are being introduced faster and faster. These realities make DMLs uneconomical, and in fact they are vanishing in many manufacturing industries.

On the other end of the product volume versus variety spectrum (Figure 1.4) are FMSs. Unlike DMLs where each machine does a few simple operations, FMSs include machines that are capable of performing a variety of operations, and by extension can produce a large range of different products. FMSs, however, fit the factory portfolio only when relatively small product volumes are needed because they are slow and expensive (compared to DMLs).

FMS systems are expensive most particularly because the equipment possesses features enabling general flexibility that are expensive to build and maintain. Obtaining general flexibility requires added degrees of freedom, motors, mechanical components, and complex control. They are also expensive in the sense that companies typically purchase machines with more functionality than they really need, because they think they may use them in the future. However, the extra flexibility and functionality that the general-purpose FMS can offer is in many cases

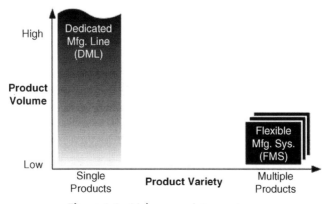

Figure 1.4 Volume–variety spectrum.

a waste of resources, since the extra cost paid for this general functionality equals unrealized capital investment until the extra functionality is actually used. Experience shows these extra resources are rarely utilized.[*]

The spectrum of products that are produced with FMS is quite large, and includes optical parts, missiles, aircrafts, automotive engines, integrated circuit boards, and even shoes. There are even applications in which the FMS is not built for multi-stage operations. In these cases, the FMS consists of a group of identical CNC machines that are arranged in parallel and each machine does the whole set of operations.

1.2.2 Business Models

Products are developed, then manufactured, and finally sold. The business unit of the manufacturing enterprise is in charge of marketing and selling, and the business model actually drives the whole enterprise. Our definition of a business model is:

> A business model is a strategic approach for creating economic value for the company by utilizing the competitive advantage of the company, for enhancing the product value to its customers

A business model considers three essential elements: (1) economic value (e.g., profit from selling products); (2) competitive advantage (over competitors); and (3) value to the customer. The business model should define who the customer is and how to create economic value for the company by providing customers with a product or service from which they can derive benefit.

For some products it is not so easy to define who is the customer, and a thorough understanding of the market may be required. Suppose a manufacturer tries to market a mechanical mini-robot that aids in orthopedic surgery. The customers of this technology are, in the order of importance: (1) orthopedic surgeons, (2) hospitals, (3) insurance companies, and (4) the patients. Yes, the patients come last. If the surgeons don't like the device, it will not be bought; if they do like it, they will recommend it to the hospitals. But only when the hospitals are convinced of the usefulness of the robot for improving surgery results, will they ask for an approval from their insurance companies. Finally, the patients must be convinced that a robotic-aided surgery enhances the success of their surgery. Each one of these four customer groups represents a necessary, but in themselves insufficient condition for the product success. Note that insurance coverage procedures are country-dependent, which makes the global marketing of this device more challenging.

In the business model of the surgery-aid robot, the product (i.e., the robot) may not necessarily generate the full economic value for the manufacturer. It's the consumables! In particular the disposable clamps that connect the mini-robot to the patient's

---

[*]See industry survey in Section 6.5.

spine generate the main economic value. Because of contamination this clamp must be thrown away after every use. Since a sole supplier (a monopoly) provides this clamp at non-competitive prices, it is the primary economic value for the robot manufacturer. Computer printer manufacturers utilize a similar business model: they sell inexpensive printers that consume very expensive ink cartridges.

In many cases, inventing a new business model rather than a new product can generate success. Tom Monaghan, for example, became a billionaire by starting a new firm in Ann Arbor, Michigan—Domino's Pizza. This firm created an economic value not by inventing a new product (the pizza was invented in Italy hundreds of years ago) and not by inventing the process of making the pizza, but rather by inventing a business model of home delivery of his pizza. Home delivery added benefits for the customer, and none of the competition had pizza home delivery when Domino Pizza started. Dominos' competitive advantage was its delivery system and transportation fleet.

Michael Dell also became a billionaire by creating a new business model. By integrating online communication with simple assembly factories for Dell Computers, he created a combination that generates huge economic value. His business model—exactly the computer that you need—benefits the customer, although it required a substantially complex IT infrastructure that Dell built into a competitive advantage.

1.2.3 The Traditional Sequence—Product, Process, Business

Traditionally, the marketing, product design, and manufacturing units work successively on the development of new products. First, the marketing unit conducts research and furnishes the design team with requirements and specifications for a new product, together with its target price and forecasted sales. The product design team must develop a product that includes all the features given by marketing, no matter how much it costs to produce each feature. The real production cost of each feature is not a parameter when marketing makes decisions. The product design team then optimizes for performance versus cost tradeoffs, where material cost is given. Only then is a manufacturing system built to produce the product. This routine substantially increases the product time-to-market, often by many months. By the time the product is manufactured, and the business unit tries to sell it, the customer's requirements and interest may have moved on or been fulfilled by a competitor. In the globalization era, this routine must be changed to speed up the product time-to-market.

1.3 THE 1990s: A DECADE OF INTENSIFIED GLOBALIZATION

Modern globalization means the integration and interdependency of world markets in producing consumer goods and services. But when did the era of globalization begin? Goods have been traded globally for thousands of years; for example, the Silk Road between China and Europe spanned the whole Eurasian supercontinent. And before that, some 4000 years ago, King Solomon in Jerusalem traded with Queen Sheba of Ethiopia in Africa. Nevertheless, globalization, as we know it today, emerged in just the last decade of the twentieth century.

The globalization revolution was shaped mainly by the events that occurred during the 10 years from 1991 to 2001. This decade started with the economic liberalization of India in 1991 that was initiated by Dr. M. Singh, then Indian finance minister, and allowed automatic approval of foreign investment in India. The last landmark in this decade was the inclusion of China as a member of the World Trade Organization (WTO) on December 11, 2001. To do so, China agreed to undertake a series of commitments to open and liberalize its market to foreign products. The WTO, which developed to its current structure in 1995, is a multi-governmental entity (as of July 2008 it had 153 countries as members) that facilitates doing business internationally by (1) formulating rules to govern global trade and capital flows through member consensus and (2) supervising member countries to ensure that the trade rules are implemented.

During that same decade the European Union (EU) and the North America Free Trade Agreement (NAFTA) were also created. The EU was established on November 1, 1993 along with the European Economic Community. The EU is not only a free trade zone, but also an economic and political union of 27 countries, with 500 million people (in 2007), that has its own parliament. NAFTA is a trilateral trade bloc created by the governments of the United States, Canada, and Mexico, which came into effect on January 1, 1994. It is one of the most powerful, wide-reaching treaties in the world.

In addition to these four government initiatives, Russian president Yeltsin initiated changes in 1993 that started to privatize industries in that country that were government controlled prior to that time. These five governmental initiatives are marked **1–5** in Table 1.2.

In parallel to these governmental initiatives, U.S. and European manufacturing industries started to take advantage of the new global conditions. The manufacturing world was shocked when in 1994 GM announced its plan to open factories in China "to penetrate Asia's growing market and to save money by using low-cost Chinese labor."[2] Before then, no one had imagined the fierce competition that was to come across the ocean from China. At the same time, U.S. manufacturing industry, and especially the automotive industry, started to migrate abroad, first to Mexico and later to other parts of Asia as well.

All through that decade, high-capacity fiber-optic cables were laid across the oceans. These cables serve as the information highways of the world and enable Western companies to utilize brainpower in countries where talented professionals can work while we sleep; for example, because of the time difference, GM R&D in Warren, Michigan can send a problem in the late afternoon, to GM R&D in Bangalore, India, and get an answer the next morning; and there are no language barriers. These fiber-optics cables are the blood vessels of globalization, enabling integration of the world's knowledge and markets.

On January 1, 2002, **the Euro currency** was adopted in 12 countries of the EU and stands as a symbolic milestone at the end of this decade of intensified globalization.

TABLE 1.2   Significant Events Marking a Decade of Intensified Globalization

1	1991	**India** was opened to foreign investments by "economic liberalization package," initiated by Dr. Singh, at that time India Finance Minister (he later became Prime Minister)
2	1992	The **European Union** was created
3	1992	**Russia**'s prices were freed and President Yeltsin started enterprise privatization
	1993	**Boeing** Design Center was established in Moscow with 350 engineers
4	1994	**NAFTA** (North America Free Trade Agreement—US, Canada, Mexico) was formed
	1994	**GM** decided to build engine parts in China
	1995	**Ford** India was established as a joint venture with Mahindra to assemble the Ford Escort
	1995	**Delphi** Automotive opened its first factory in China (producing batteries)
	1997	**General Motors Shanghai** (GMS) was established as a 50–50 joint venture partnership with Shanghai Automotive Industry Corp. In 2005, GMS sold 325,000 vehicles in China
	1998	**DaimlerChrysler** was formed by a merger of Daimler–Benz (the manufacturer of Mercedes–Benz, Germany) and the Chrysler Corp. (USA)
	1999	**Ford** India bought out a majority stake from Mahindra and started to produce the Ikon, Fusion, and Fiesta
5	2001	**China** joined the World Trade Organization
a–h	1992– 2001	**High-capacity Transoceanic fiber-optic cable** deployments around the world (see Table 1.3)

From that point forward, globalization rolled like a tsunami, engulfing the entire world economy.

Table 1.2 and Figure 1.5 describe the main events that intensified globalization in the years 1991–2001. Three forces generated these events: governments (marked

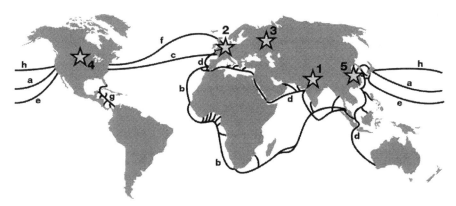

Figure 1.5   The major government initiatives in five global regions that created the modern globalization era (**1–5** on the map) occurred during a single decade (1991–2001); at the same time, high-capacity fiber-optic cables were laid across the oceans (**a–h** on the map).

1–5), manufacturing enterprises (e.g., Boeing, General Motors), and new technology (undersea fiber-optic cables, **a–h**). The synergy among these three forces intensified globalization in an unprecedentedly short period of just 10 years.

Table 1.3 shows examples of fiber-optic cables that were laid across the oceans (**a–h** on the map and in Table 1.3). **The transoceanic bandwidth frequency (in bit/ second) grew by a factor of 1000 in just 10 years**, dramatically increasing overall communication speed over global distances. (Brazil and South America were connected to the United States in 2002.)

TABLE 1.3   Examples of Transoceanic Fiber-optics Cables; Frequency × 1000 Within 10 Years

	Year	Cable	Frequency
a	1992	PC-4 (Trans-Pacific cable 4), connecting United States with Japan	0.56 Gb/second
b	1993	SAT-2 connecting South Africa with West Africa Portugal, and Spain	2 Gb/second
c	1996	Trans-Atlantic (TAT) cable utilizing new fiber-optic technology	20 Gb/second
d	1998	Connecting Australia and Singapore with Germany through the Suez canal	60 Gb/second
e	1999	China–United States cable network (CUCN), over 12,000 km, connecting the U.S. West coast with China, Taiwan, Korea, and Japan	120 Gb/second
f	1999	AC-1 (Atlantic Crossing) new ring-cable, connecting New York with the UK, the Netherlands, Germany, and back to NY	160 Gb/second
g	2000	MAYA-1 connecting Costa Rica and Panama to Mexico and Florida	
h	2001	PC-1 (Pacific Crossing) Japan—U.S. West Coast	640 Gb/second

1.4 THE GLOBAL MANUFACTURING REVOLUTION

The global manufacturing revolution started in the last decade of the twentieth century with evolutionary, and largely independent, developments in three important areas: (1) Governmental policy changed in several regions around the globe opened India, China, and Russia to free trade, and created new multi-country free-trade zones including NAFTA and the EU. (2) Global expansions of the manufacturing industry exponentially increased the potential manufacturing capacity available to all. (3) The laying of a huge network of transoceanic fiber-optics cables increased the volume of inexpensive information flow around the world. The synergy of these fundamental changes has created the global manufacturing revolution (Figure 1.6) and the new global manufacturing paradigm, which erupted at full strength in the first years of the twenty-first century.

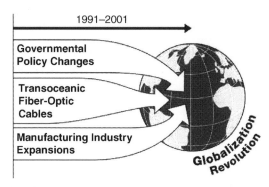

Figure 1.6 The global manufacturing revolution emerged due to changes in governmental policies, global expansion of manufacturing industry, and the development of transoceanic fiber-optics cable networks around the world. The synergy between these three independent forces has created the global manufacturing revolution.

Globalization created a new type of market dynamic driven by fierce worldwide competition among companies that are located in different countries and produce similar products (e.g., cars, furniture, refrigerators, and shoes). When many large corporations produce similar products, a global excess capacity is created. In 2002, the total world automobile production capacity was 80 million units, and actual worldwide sale was 55 million vehicles (69% capacity utilization[3]). A large global excess capacity, with supply much greater than demand, destabilized the market with large fluctuations in product sales per company.

In addition to over-capacity, global enterprises must carefully monitor currency exchange rates. A company's profit margin, say 9%, in one country can be completely wiped out by an equal fluctuation of 9% in the exchange rate of the country in which products are sold. When exchange rates are volatile, this can also have an impact on complex global supply chains that take years to establish.

The fortunes of global manufacturing enterprises are also strongly impacted by changing oil prices, and we are not just talking about the type of cars that people buy. Domestic manufacturers benefit from a rise in oil prices ($140 per barrel in April 2008), because rising ocean freight costs are affected by the cost of fuel, making imports more expensive compared with domestic products. From 2000 to April 2008, the cost of shipping a 40-foot container from East Asia to the United States rose from $3000 to $8000, making the manufacturing of some products in the United States cheaper than importing them. In anticipation of this, global enterprises often build factories in the local markets to minimize transportation costs. For example, IKEA, the world's leading home furnishings retailer, opened its first furniture factory in the United States (in Virginia) in May 2008.

But what happens when shipping prices drop back down to their previous levels? Won't imported cars and other products be suddenly less expensive? This points to the heart of our argument that manufacturing needs to be responsive to such change. Domestic production should be positioned so that it can (a) scale back on excess production volume and (b) introduce new innovations to compete with a resurgent importation. This second tactic includes offering **personalized products**, produced for individual designs and built by domestic manufacturers in closer proximity to these high-end customers who are less willing to wait for products designed and made just for them.[*]

Globalization has created many new opportunities and becoming a global manufacturing enterprise has several benefits:

- Globalization reduces manufacturing costs by utilizing low labor-cost countries.
- Globalization reduces business risk and filters currency exchange fluctuations.
- Globalization is a source for enterprise growth, achieved by accessing new markets.

Globalization means not only that large companies are becoming global in terms of their world-wide sales and the location of their production facilities, but also that they can offer innovative products to satisfy specific customer culture and preferences in different countries and different world regions. A global market with a large number of competing suppliers increases the customer's purchasing power, and these potential consumers now live all over the world. China, for example, now has 1 million millionaires and a large middle class. Many countries in South America also have a strong new middle class with increased purchasing power, and some countries in Eastern Europe (not a part of the EU and economically repressed for decades) have been prospering.

Markets are now global; but competing successfully in the global production paradigm requires reconsideration of the three components of the enterprise: product development, manufacturing system, and business model. These three components have always been in a precarious balance, especially when responding to unanticipated market events, and now these events occur in a much larger arena.

1.4.1 The Way We Are Heading

Increased responsiveness to changing market conditions is crucial for manufacturing enterprises to flourish in a global market and sustain continuous growth. Product development, the manufacturing system, and the business model must all be designed to rapidly respond to unpredictable changes, and be planned by a global strategy that determines issues such as which products to develop, for which regions on the globe, where to locate factories, and how to integrate global supply chains. These issues are the essence of the global manufacturing revolution.

---

[*]See Sections 3.3 and 14.4 for description of personalized products.

1.4.1.1 Product Development   In addition to product development for traditional mass-customization markets, product development in the global manufacturing paradigm will have two new aspects:

1. Producing **regionalized products** that fit customer's culture in different world regions
2. Producing **personalized products** that fit individual needs (aiming at a market of one).

Designers of global products must be responsive to customers who live in different cultures and in dissimilar climate zones, and who have a wide range of purchasing power. To compete in those regional markets their products must be designed for regional customization in mind. To allow cost-effective regionalization and personalization, products should be highly modular, and be designed with changeable functionality within product families.

1.4.1.2 Manufacturing Systems   For global manufacturing systems, responsiveness is an essential feature that can be achieved by developing **RMSs** that have a production capacity that is highly adaptable to market demand. Possession of RMSs enables companies to adjust their capacity (i.e., volume per product variant) to quickly match market demand, rapidly retool for new products, and upgrade with new functionality to produce different product variety. They provide...

...exactly the capacity and functionality needed, exactly when needed.

1.4.1.3 Business Models   In the global manufacturing paradigm, the enterprise must be responsive to volatile markets and capable of rapidly taking advantage of market opportunities. The business model should be of a pull-type, encouraging customers to send their product preferences to the manufacturer via the Internet and receive their products in a timely manner. Industry's marketing must coordinate its actions with the product development team and consider manufacturing costs and constraints earlier in the product development.

As said above, traditionally, the marketing, product design, and manufacturing units work successively on the development of new products. With this approach marketing would often ask for a list of desirable product features to maximize sales, even though manufacturing of these features is very expensive. Marketing is traditionally disconnected from manufacturing and often sets target prices without consideration of the manufacturing costs and capabilities. With globalization this approach must be changed—marketing should consider the manufacturing costs and the capabilities of existing manufacturing systems when deciding upon new product requirements.

1.4.1.4 Globalization Fundamentals   In summary, the three components of the global manufacturing enterprise must adapt to a new age, **age of rapid responsiveness**.

The global manufacturing revolution should stand on four fundamentals:

1. Innovative products for global markets and for personalization in domestic markets
2. Reconfigurable manufacturing systems
3. Global business strategies with rapid responsiveness to customers and markets
4. A solid integration between product, process (i.e., manufacturing system), and business

---

We will elaborate on these topics below.

1.4.2 Innovative Products for Global Markets

In an increasingly competitive global economy, establishing cost leadership over industrial competitors, by itself, is not sufficient to gain prosperity and revenue growth. Leadership in product innovation and in frequent introduction of innovative products is also critical to success in a global economy.

Manufacturing companies must create an environment for creating innovations in existing products and strategies for inventing new products. Inventing products that do not exist today gives one the potential of developing new markets. Past examples include refrigeration, which opened new markets for food, and air conditioning, which enabled increases in population in places like Nevada. New markets of new products will create far more jobs and generate more new wealth in the global economy than simply building things cheaper.

A survey conducted in 2005 by the Deloitte's Global Benchmark Study program[4] of 650 of the world's leading manufacturers revealed that:

- Manufacturers cite launching new products as the No. 1 driver of revenue growth, yet admit that supporting product innovation is one of their least important priorities.
- This is largely because 50–70% of all new product introductions fail.
- And yet, products representing more than 70% of 2005 sales will be obsolete by 2010 due to changing customer demands and competitive offerings.

If new, innovative products are the main source of a company's growth, why is the support of innovation so low, and why do new products fail so frequently? The report shows that many manufacturers were unable to bring new products to market profitably because of several key reasons including:

- Insufficient information on customer needs
- Inferior suppliers unable to provide quality parts on time
- A disjointed approach to innovation across product and supply chain operations.

To capitalize on new products as the main source of revenue and produce them at lowmanufacturing cost, global companies should pay attention to the following points:

New Products—There is a compelling need for developing company strategies aimed at product innovations and, in particular, at new products with global markets in mind. As such, these products will be the main source of growth and revenues.

Shorten Lead time by Developing Supplier Capabilities—New product development must be done simultaneously with developing global supply chains and enhancing supplier capabilities. This will further guarantee low-cost, high-quality products that will generate growth in sales of new products and in new markets.

Product Architecture—Competing within the global manufacturing paradigm requires developing a product platform architecture onto which modular products can be built, each designed to fit a region or a particular culture. This strategy enables the design of products that can be customized and regionalized to fit those sectors and cultures, and still be manufactured at low cost. That same architecture enables manufacturers to produce personalized products at reasonable cost for domestic markets.

Product's Regional Fit—Besides culture and market, regionalization must take into account additional limitations: purchasing power, climate, and legal regulations (e.g., safety, environmental limitations, and driving on the left side of the road). Market research that collects and analyzes information about the habits and needs of customers in the target country is a necessity for the product's success.

Product Personalization—Products that are manufactured to fit the buyer's exact needs are likely to become a new source of revenue in developed countries.

New product release timing is always critical and made more so because of the short windows of opportunity for new products due to global competition. Therefore, a competitive advantage exists for manufacturers who can use existing manufacturing systems that can be rapidly reconfigured to produce new products. To accomplish this, it is essential to add constraints on new product design so they can be made on existing manufacturing systems that currently produce other products. These requirements go well beyond those of existing product design for manufacturability (DFM) methods.

1.4.3 Reconfigurable Manufacturing System (RMS)

The RMS is a modern system that bridges the gap between the DML and the FMS. RMS design is focused on producing a particular family of parts rather than an infinite range of parts limited only by the machine's geometric and operational envelope, as is the case with FMS. The RMS trades a bit of flexibility for higher throughput. While an

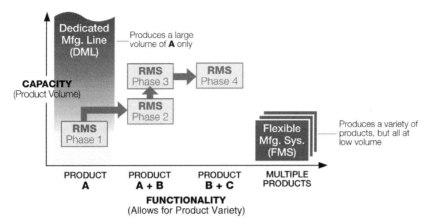

Figure 1.7   Changes in an RMS during its lifetime in response to new products.

RMS does not provide the general flexibility that FMS offers, it can have just enough flexibility (i.e., functionality) to produce the whole part family for which it was designed. Therefore, the RMS has the advantages of both FMS and DMLs without their drawbacks.

More importantly, an RMS includes added advantages that neither of the others possesses. An RMS is designed to "reconfigure," to grow and change within the scope of its lifetime, and so it can respond to market changes quickly. In other words, the RMS is designed for changes in its production capacity (the number of products it can produce) and in its functionality (which provides the capability to produce new parts and products) in ways that do not affect its overall robustness or reliability. Reconfiguration allows an RMS to achieve throughput approaching that of a DML but allows it to produce simultaneously several products.

Figure 1.7 shows the advantages that RMS represents. In this example, the RMS is initially built to produce only Product A. After some time, the system is reconfigured to produce Product B as well. However, since this requires overall higher production output, the system capacity must be higher (phase 2). As the market for Product B grows, more production units are added to the RMS (phase 3). Finally, after a few years, Product A is phased out completely but a new Product C is introduced; the RMS can fulfill all these requirements (phase 4 in Figure 1.7) without a major redesign of the system. The RMS is designed at the outset so that adding capacity can be done cost-effectively, and the system alterations needed to produce new products are done just as easily.

Our definition of an RMS:

> **A reconfigurable manufacturing system (RMS) is one designed for rapid adjustment of production capacity and functionality, across a product family, by rearrangement or change of its components (hardware and software)**

The following anecdote illustrates the risks of fixed production-volume systems and the potential economic benefit of an RMS. In the winter of 1996, the manufacturing lines of Cadillac (a luxury car produced by General Motors Corp.) sat half-idle because of low demand for Cadillac cars. At the same time, an unexpected increase in demand for GM trucks exceeded supply by some 20%. GM considered building new truck manufacturing lines to meet the additional demand but viewed it as a high-risk investment and declined. So, overall, GM lost on both ends. The company lost a portion of their truck market share (for those they could not build), and lost money on their underutilized Cadillac assembly lines (for the capacity they could not use). One solution would be to have the Cadillac manufacturing lines reconfigured for production of small trucks for a few months. However, this required a reconfigurable assembly line, a technology that did not exist in 1996. Imagine the huge economic benefits that a company could gain by being able to build exactly the product needed, at exactly the time that the market demands. That is the manufacturing ideal and the goal of RMS.

1.4.4 Global Business Models

Dell Computers is a global company. The parts for Dell computers (memory, hard disks, etc.) are manufactured in China and Taiwan and shipped to assembly plants in Nashville, TN and Austin, TX in the United States. The company utilizes its mastery of IT (in the early 2000s) to coordinate its complex global supply chain, as well as its customer's orders.

Although the orders of Dell computers are stochastic (customers order computers at random through the Internet), the company avoids both overproduction and shortage by quite accurately forecasting the part quantities that will be needed in the assembly plants, and organizing their shipment exactly on time. This cost-effective global supply-chain model is a competitive advantage for Dell. In fact, like Dell, many types of companies are now restructuring their supply chains to take advantage of globalization. It is difficult, however, to adapt Dell's business model, with its complex information infrastructure, to, for example, the automotive industry, because of the differences in scale and product complexity. In general, a global business model must fit the industry type.

The business model of a manufacturing enterprise must be supported by the company's production capability. With the globalization of manufacturing, hardly a single company, if any, makes their entire product. The successful global manufacturing company focuses on its core competency and shifts production of modules and sub-assemblies to suppliers whose own core competency is to manufacture these sub-assemblies and give them value. Another tier of suppliers produces parts for these sub-assemblies, thus forming a supply chain. Managing the information and material flow within supply chains has become an integral part of the enterprise organization and its business model. Supply chains are now a worldwide operation, since suppliers are globally spread and domestic and international logistics became variables that are critical to success.

1.4.5 Integration of the Global Enterprise—Product–Process–Business

Strategic planning of a global enterprise means not only global production facilities and global sales, but also that the enterprise should:

- Design **products that can be regionalized** to address customers' requirements in several world regions. For example, cars designed for India do not need the luxury and safety features required in the United States, but the chassis and engine may be the same. Global enterprises must be responsive to a diverse customer base—customers with different habits, in dissimilar climate zones, with a wide range of purchasing power.
- Operate **RMS** that have a production capacity **adaptable** to market demand, and thereby are responsive to fluctuations in product demand caused by the global excess production capacity.
- Develop **responsive business models** that take advantage of market opportunities to enhance sales and rapidly penetrate new markets.

These refinements of the three domains are equally important, as illustrated in Figure 1.8.

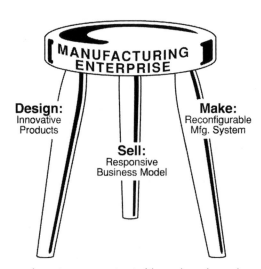

Figure 1.8 The manufacturing enterprise is like a three-legged stool—to be stable, it needs three equally strong legs:

- Innovative, customizable products
- Reconfigurable manufacturing systems, whose capacity and functionality are rapidly adaptable to changing market demands
- Responsive business models to sell, distribute, and maintain a variety of products, as well as form global alliances for new products

It is increasingly important to offer customers as much variety as can be economically justified, and to be able to introduce new goods quickly as technology and customer's demand change. In other words, such enterprises have to achieve **rapid responsiveness** to customers and markets wherever they are on the globe. This responsiveness must encompass all three domains: product design, manufacturing, and the business model.

Manufacturing companies must develop tools in all three components of the manufacturing enterprise to compete under the emerging **global manufacturing paradigm:**

Products designed for regional customization in different market segments, and for personalization for domestic high-end customers.

Manufacturing systems (i.e., **process**) designed for reconfiguration to produce products at volumes needed by the market.

Business models are responsive to volatile markets and to customers.

Globalization has brought a revolution to the enterprise organization as well. The three components are now more interdependent than ever before, as shown in Figure 1.9, and therefore their integration (the ring in Figure 1.9) is essential for an enterprise to succeed. If a company makes products with modular structure, for example, the manufacturing system must be designed to be able to produce the whole family of products based on those modules, and the business model should support personal orders of products that have a modular structure.

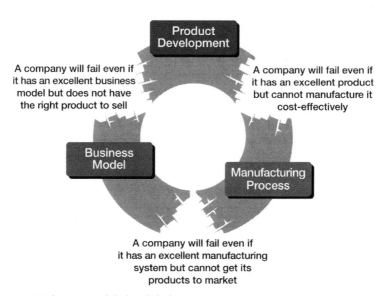

Figure 1.9   To be successful, the global enterprise must integrate its innovative products with its manufacturing system capabilities and a flexible business model.

In globalization, cooperative efforts between marketing, design, and manufacturing should begin during product development. The design team should analyze the product features and determine which specifications are not realistic and must be modified given a business target. This is feedback to the business unit, which must review the product price in response to the new specifications. The new price and modified product features may also change the projected demand and production volume targets, which, in turn, will impact the configuration and reconfiguration plan of the manufacturing system.

This way capacity allocation and manufacturing costs are coordinated with marketing targets during product development. Furthermore, in order to reduce time-to-market and decrease costs, every new product must be produced on available machines and on existing manufacturing systems that can be reconfigured for the new product production.

Remedying a major problem in one component of the enterprise necessitates changes in the other two. Changes in product design affects manufacturing and vice versa; plant productivity relates to the product selling rate, and vice versa. If one of these three components fails, the enterprise will fail.

1.5 THE MANUFACTURING PARADIGM MODEL

Since its birth some two centuries ago[*], manufacturing industry has undergone several revolutionary paradigms induced by (1) new market and economy conditions and (2) emerging societal imperatives driven by customers (Figure 1.10).[5]

Societal needs may arise from the desire to have more products to choose from to satisfy individual tastes and preferences, small purchasing power of a certain population that drives a decrease in product prices, or environmental concerns. Market depends on the economy and may change, for example, because of substantial increase in product supply—making more products than customers buy—or the emergence of new economic powers, like China and India, that change global product prices.

Industry has responded to these market and societal imperatives by developing new types of manufacturing systems to produce products, and new business models to sell them. The integration of the new manufacturing system with the new business model and with the product architecture creates a new manufacturing paradigm. For example, the societal need to reduce automobile cost was realized by the invention of the moving assembly line (which, in 1913, was a new type of manufacturing system). The moving assembly line combined with the technology of interchangeable parts enabled the creation of the mass production paradigm.

---

[*]In the late eighteenth and early nineteenth centuries (two centuries ago), major changes in manufacturing took place, in Britain first, and in all Europe and North America later. In this period, which is called the Industrial Revolution, a move from manual-labor-based economy towards machine-based manufacturing occurred. The introduction of power-driven machinery and the parallel development of factory organization (see Chapter 12) created an enormous increase in the production of many kinds of goods, and is regarded as the birth of modern manufacturing.

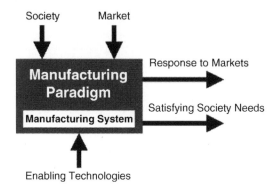

Figure 1.10 The manufacturing paradigm.

We define a manufacturing paradigm as:

A *Manufacturing Paradigm*
A revolutionary integrated production model that arises in response to changing societal and market imperatives, and is enabled by the creation of a new type of manufacturing system

---

Figure 1.11 depicts our manufacturing paradigm generic model. As we said, the goal of each paradigm is driven by new market conditions or by emerging societal needs. Each new manufacturing paradigm is composed of a new type of manufacturing system, a new business model, and appropriate product architecture.

New paradigms become possible as new technology enablers are introduced and subsequently used to create new types of manufacturing systems. For each new paradigm, a new type of manufacturing system is developed—a system that is based on a new technology enabler and addresses the paradigm imperatives. For example, the emergence of the mass customization paradigm was driven by society's demand for expanded product variety. Producing a wider product variety became possible with

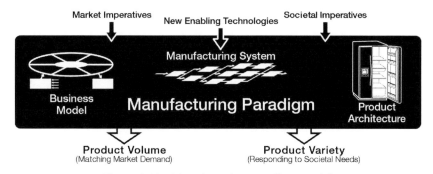

Figure 1.11 Manufacturing paradigm model.

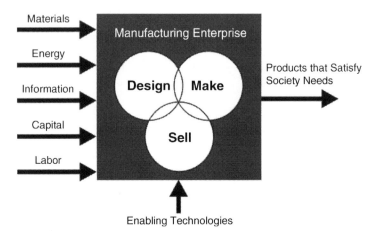

Figure 1.12 A manufacturing enterprise has three basic elements: *Design, Make,* and *Sell.*

the invention of the FMS. The new enabling technology of FMS was the mini-computer that was first integrated in the 1970s into controllers of CNC and industrial automation devices (see Appendix A). Thus, the mass customization paradigm became possible with the invention of the mini-computer.

The **product architecture** also transforms with the paradigm change. As product variety further expanded, product architecture became more and more modular. Each paradigm has its own **business model** that fits its nature and addresses its imperatives—society's needs and market conditions.

Each manufacturing paradigm addresses three basic elements: Design, Make, and Sell, as shown in Figure 1.12.

Design: Designing the product and its functions to satisfy particular societal requirements.

Make: Making the product by a manufacturing system that can quickly respond to the market's needs and opportunities.

Sell: Selling products to customers in order to satisfy their needs and to make a profit for the enterprise.

Is the sequence of these three elements always the same? It turns out that each manufacturing paradigm has a unique business model sequence of the three elements {**Design; Make; Sell**}, a sequence that has changed in each of the four major paradigms in modern manufacturing history.

1.6 FOUR MAJOR MANUFACTURING PARADIGMS

In order to understand the principles of the emerging **global manufacturing paradigm**, one must first understand the imperatives, enablers, and principles of the previous manufacturing paradigms, as well as their basic business-model principles. Today, one may identify four major paradigms in consumer goods manufacturing: (1) craft production, (2) mass production, (3) mass customization, and, most recently, (4) global manufacturing, which points in two directions at once: regionalized and personalized production.

1.6.1 The Craft Production Paradigm

We define craft production as creating exactly the product the customer asks for, on demand, and usually one unique product at a time. Highly customized craft products have been produced since time immemorial but this paradigm reached its zenith both in scale and in complexity with the hand building of coaches and carriages, and then automobiles starting around 1850. By the late 1800s and early 1900s, there were many craft producers of carriages that later turned to automobiles. Like the carriages, each part of an automobile was produced separately in a small machine shop that had general-purpose machine tools. Highly skilled workers that knew how to operate machine tools (such as lathes, drills, and milling machines) took great pains to produce precision parts, especially the complex mechanism like engines and drive trains. These workers also did all the bodywork and assembly.

The principle of the craft production paradigm may be summarized as:

> Skilled workers, using general-purpose machines, make exactly the product that the customer paid for; one product at a time.

Key enablers of this paradigm were:

- Low barriers to entry for new companies.
- A highly skilled work force that was able to produce precision products even with simple machine tools.
- Milling machines, necessary for precision finishing of metal parts, were invented in 1876.
- Development of the electric power station, in 1882 by Thomas Edison, supplied electricity to power the machine tools, making them safer and more reliable, as well as allowing the production of critical parts to take place in many more places, far away from traditional water-powered mills.

To a small but very exclusive market, craft production is still used today to produce exotic sport cars, custom furniture, and other single products. Each of them is literally a work of art.

France was the center of car production by craft methods in the 1880s. By the early 1890s, Panhard et Levassor (P&L) in Paris was building several hundred automobiles per year. Sir Henry Ellis, a member of the English Parliament, was in 1895 the first person in England to drive a car (which was produced by P&L); his car had a maximum speed of 10 miles per hour. In 1896, the first law for a legal speed limit was legislated in England—a maximum speed of 12 miles per hour. We have come a long way since then.

At the end of the nineteenth century, craft production of automobiles flourished in Europe. The total annual production was 1000 automobiles, of which no more than 20–50 were built to the same design. But even those duplicates were not completely identical, since each part was produced separately (not in series). More importantly, each vehicle was customized—it was built to order. By 1905, hundreds of companies existed in Western Europe and the United States, using the craft-production model.[6]

When buying a craft-built product the customer pays in advance, and only then is the product designed (with the customer's input) and produced. Craft production has a **pull-type** business model, with the sequence: $\boxed{\text{Sell} - \text{Design} - \text{Make}}$. First, the customer decides to purchase the product and "pulls" a product design from a variety of possible concepts offered by the manufacturer. Only when the customer orders the product it is designed in detail and then built from scratch. Craft production has the following characteristics:

- **High product variety** because each product is built to order
- **Very low volume per product**
- **Pull-type business model: Sell–Design–Make**
- **General-purpose machines** to perform all the manufacturing operations
- **Highly skilled work force**

1.6.2 The Mass Production Paradigm

Mass production, which flourished for most of the twentieth century, means producing extremely large quantities of identical products. This paradigm is expressed through the synchronized flow of production lines that produce key precision components and assemble the finished product. The moving production line consists of specialized equipment dedicated to assemble, transport, and finish products, and its operations are optimized to create economies of scale. To maintain high production volumes, machinery must take the place of human skill as much as possible, and machines are dedicated to very specific operations to produce the same product over and over without variation. Because extremely large quantities are involved, products can be produced at low cost and this enables a comparable reduction in the sale price. Reducing the cost of manufacturing, and therefore product price, is the main goal of mass production. Note that the two main characteristics of mass production—low product variety and high volume per product—are exactly the opposite of those in craft production.

In contrast to craft production that requires a highly skilled work force, mass production substitutes machinery for most of the human skills. Therefore, compared to craft and other paradigms, the average work force skill level required of mass production is very low.

The invention of the automobile **moving assembly line** in Dearborn, Michigan, by Henry Ford in 1913 is usually viewed as the starting point of the mass production paradigm. Ford's brilliance was that he understood the societal needs of the market—low-cost automobiles, and he invented the manufacturing system that reduced the cost of making them. The cars produced on Ford's 1913 assembly line were of "Model T." With the aid of the moving assembly line, within just 13 years the number of Ford Model T's produced in Dearborn increased from 40,000 to 2 million units annually.

Nevertheless, the availability of high-quality **interchangeable parts** was a main technological enabler for the success of mass production. Prior to interchangeable parts, each piece of a product had to be individually made and fitted in the product assembly. This involved time-consuming precision labor throughout the entire production process. The availability of interchangeable parts technology dramatically reduced production costs and allowed the use of low-skilled workers to build cars.

Mass production succeeded in lowered production cost, which, in turn, enabled reduction of the unit price. As prices lowered, more people could afford to buy the products, increasing the market for cars and resulting in even more sales, and therefore even greater production. More production created greater economies of scale, which lowered costs further; the lower costs enabled a further reduction in prices, and so on. . .

The business model of mass production is of a **push–type** and the business sequence is: Design – Make – Sell . First, the manufacturers design products they can build efficiently with their mass production system, and then they build them assuming there will be always customers to whom the products can be sold. The manufacturer's sales force "pushes" the products to a lot, and eventually the products are sold.

The mass production business model is based on the following principle:

Production of a limited variety of products in high volume reduces production cost, which, in turn, allows price reduction for the benefit of customers. Reduced product price increases customer demand and sales.

The dominant characteristics of mass production are:

- **A very limited product variety**
- **A high volume per product** is produced to achieve economies of scale
- **Push-type business model: Design–Make–Sell**
- **Dedicated machinery and moving assembly lines** reduce costs
- **Relatively unskilled work force**

The mass production era continued from 1913 until the 1980s. Its peak in the USA was around 1955, a year in which the product variety was very small and the volume

TABLE 1.4   Annual Volume and Number of Models (variety) of Four Car Manufacturers

	Ford		GM		Chrysler		Toyota	
Year	Volume	Variety	Volume	Variety	Volume	Variety	Volume	Variety
1950	1,500,000	4	2,700,000	9	1,100,000	12		
1980	2,200,000	16	4,400,000	32	900,000	17	2,400,000	16

per product very high (compared to the United States population at that time). In 1955, six models of GM, Ford, and Chrysler accounted for 80% of all cars sold in the United States. A summary of the automotive industry sales in the United States between 1950 and 1980 is shown in the Table 1.4.

1.6.3   The Mass Customization Paradigm

Mass customization is a society-driven paradigm that started in the 1980s. As the market for a product matures and customers become wealthier, they begin to look for a **larger variety** of products to choose from. Society's need for a larger product selection is the imperative of this paradigm. In response to this imperative, manufacturers start to offer product "options," each comprising a number of extra features that constitute a "package" that is added to their standard product. Consequently, the customer is offered a larger variety to choose from. Increasing product variety at low cost is the goal of the mass customization paradigm.

In the mass customization paradigm, the manufacturers decide on the basic product options they can practically offer, and customers select the package that they prefer, buy it, and only then is the product finished. This allows the manufacturer to draw to the strengths of its mass production assets for the lowest cost production of major components while postponing the customization process to the final assembly with optioned accessories.

The penetration of computers into industrial operations has made the development of flexible automation possible. Flexible automation, in turn, enables inexpensive mass customization—the production of an expanded variety of products of the same product family at low cost. The low cost of production permits the sale of a wide variety of "customized" products based on the same product family at prices comparable to those of standard goods built by mass production methods.

With more variety offered, the probability increases that every customer can get the product he/she prefers. Offering options on cars is an example of mass customization. Types of customization may include dimensional, shape, color, taste, special features, etc.

There are two basic strategies for mass customization:

Strategy 1: Off-the-shelf variety of customized products
Strategy 2: Standard options installed on customized products

Strategy 1 is actually a transition stage from mass production to full mass customization. Pairs of jeans offered in a variety of sizes in a department store are a good example. It is, however, very much still a push-type business model, like mass production. The main economic decision here is how much variety (how many sizes) manufacturers should offer in order to maximize their profit.

Strategy 2 is the real mass customization approach. A typical example of Strategy 2 is the ordering of cars and computers (from Dell, for example) in the United States and Europe. Customers are given a set of possible options (now even on the Internet), and they choose the subset that best fits their needs and wants. Note that the manufacturing system must have a relatively high level of sophistication and flexibility in order to efficiently assemble the product with the correct options at a reasonable cost.

The business sequence of Strategy 2 mass customization is:

1. Design a product that can be enhanced by a variety of options
2. Sell the specific options to specific customers
3. Make (assemble) the product with the options that the customer selected

This is a combination of push (design and, to some extent, make by the manufacturer) and pull (final assembly to produce the customer's selected option). Therefore, we define it as a **Push–Pull type business model**, and the business sequence is: $\boxed{\text{Design} - \text{Make} - \text{Sell}}$.

Mass customization does not mean producing one-of-a-kind products, as in the craft production era. Mass customization develops multiple sets of practical variation (options) that can be produced on a mass production system and offered to potential customers, hoping to satisfy the specific needs of many customers. Therefore, very personalized production does not match with mass customization on one hand, and standard products, produced in the millions, do not fit on the other.

The mass customization business model is, therefore, based on the following principle.

> Production of a wide variety of customized products, at mass production cost, attracts more customers and increases sales.

The key enablers of mass customization are:

- *FMSs* including computerized numerical control (CNC) machine tools and computer-controlled handling equipment as well as welding and assembly robots that can quickly switchover production from one product type to another.
- *Marketing networks and customer–plant direct communications*: The mass customization paradigm started with aggressive direct marketing. The Internet now allows customer's orders that are directly communicated to the manufacturing plant.

> **Lean Production** started around 1960 at Toyota in Japan, with the development of waste reduction methods to reduce product cost and enhance product quality (see Chapter 4). Before implementing "Lean" higher-quality products were produced at a substantially higher cost in effort and investment. Lean proved that high quality could be achieved even at a lower cost to the manufacturer. The principles of lean production started to be implemented in the United States and Europe by the late 1980s, when mass customization was also emerging, and therefore the goal of achieving high-quality products is sometimes associated with the mass customization paradigm. Lean production is not defined here as a new manufacturing paradigm; it just augments the other paradigms—producing higher-quality products at lower cost.

1.6.4 The Global Manufacturing Paradigm

The arrival of manufacturing globalization has intensified worldwide competition to a level not possible anytime in the past. With massive over-capacity in production and the proliferation of advanced communications, the next manufacturing paradigm—global manufacturing—points in two directions at once: regionalized and personalized production. Regionalized production for global markets is stimulated by exactly the same imperatives as mass customization, but directed more by cultural and regional differentiations. Personalized production for domestic markets is stimulated by the desire of customers to have exactly the product that they need (rather than merely settling for options) without paying the price of a craft-built product. Personalized production requires a short delivery time, and therefore fits domestic production that can compete with inexpensive imports.

1.6.4.1 Regionalized Production in the Global Manufacturing Paradigm
Global manufacturing enterprises cannot ignore the customers' desire to have products that fit their specific cultural needs and living conditions. For example, the typical large U.S. washing machine cannot fit into the tiny apartments of Paris, Budapest, and Lima. Products should be designed with the world market in mind, and for regional customization in many specific regions. In the global manufacturing paradigm, regionalized products fit the culture, living conditions, and legal regulations of that region. Nevertheless, regionalized production is based on the principles of mass customization—the manufacturer decides the possible options that fit the region and asks the customers who resides in the region to select an option from those offered. The product features fit the culture of a consumer group, but they are not tailored toward value creation at the individual level.

1.6.4.2 Personalized Production in the Global Manufacturing Paradigm   The
personalized production facet of the global paradigm began to emerge at the close of the twentieth century. In the mass customization paradigm, customers only select

from lists of available options. By contrast, in personalized production, customers are actively involved in the design of the products they want to buy. Personalized production is the next logical step in developing consumer products. "We are moving to a world in which value is determined by one consumer-created experience at a time; $N = 1$."[7]

The product design in the personalized production paradigm has two phases:

1. The *Initial Phase*, Design (A), in which the product architecture and module interfaces are designed, and the envelop of product variety and basic modules are established. This design phase is driven by strategic decisions made by the manufacturer to fit their facilities and strengths.
2. The *Personalized Design Phase*, Design (P), in which the final tailored design takes place with close interaction with the customer.

Although the general product architecture and the basic product modules are designed prior to the sale, the business sequence in this paradigm is such that "Sale" precedes the personal "Design (P)" phase. So, the sequence is $\boxed{\text{Design(A)} - \text{Sell} - \text{Design(P)} - \text{Make}}$ and the business model is of a **Pull** type.

A classic example may be the design, construction, and installation of kitchen cabinets. Initially, the manufacturer makes a series of strategic decisions about the number of modules, their shape, functions, stylistic features, color, and the types of material that they can be made from. The customer's role is to design their own kitchen by selecting modules from a given range of available modules and arranging them to fit their own kitchen dimensions as well as convenient access, functionality, etc. None of the cabinetry is constructed until the personalized design phase is completed and the order is paid off. In the end, each kitchen will eventually be unique—a personal design that fits the customer's needs and price range.

The interior of automobiles could be constructed in the same way if a standard architecture and interfaces were available. Even more personalization can be offered when modules that are beyond the standard range are made available and manufactured not by the auto manufacturer, but by another company.

The business model of the personalized production paradigm is based on make-product-to-customer's design, where modules are selected from a pre-designed, given range. It obeys the following principle.

Cost-effective, timely production of made-to-customer's design products increases sales by exactly tailoring the product's options and features to the customer's needs.

The business model emphasizes timely production. A short delivery time to the customer is an essential component in gaining a competitive advantage in personalized production. Therefore, the personalization paradigm enables shifting production (or at least the product final assembly plants) from low-wage countries to countries in which the product is sold.

1.7 PARADIGM TRANSITIONS OVER TIME

To summarize, we discussed four paradigms:

1. **Craft Production**, in which each product is designed and made for a particular customer, effectively a "Market-of-One."
2. **Mass Production**, in which only a few models are made, assuming there will always be enough buyers.
3. **Mass Customization**, in which customers select a product from a list of available options before production.
4. **Personalized Production**—a segment of Global Manufacturing—in which product options are designed by the customers, sold, and then produced on advanced manufacturing systems.

As we said, each manufacturing paradigm has had a different set of imperatives that came either from societal needs or from market forces, as seen in Table 1.5. These imperatives change the principle of the business model, such that it creates value for the customer and the company.

Over the past two centuries, manufacturing has come nearly full circle: **From focusing on the individual (Craft) to focusing on the product (Mass Production), to focusing on targeted market groups (Customization), and back to the individual customer (Personalization)**. The main principle of the business model originated from a pure pull system in the craft production paradigm and transitioned to a pure push system in mass production, it then transitioned again to a push–pull type for mass customization. The global manufacturing paradigm suggests that the next shift will go almost a full circle with the introduction of personalized products.

TABLE 1.5 Manufacturing Paradigms and Their Drivers

Paradigm	Craft Production	Mass Production	Mass Customization	Personalized Production
Focus	The individual	The product	Market segments	The individual
Societal new needs	Tailored-made products	Low-cost products	Large product variety	Personal-fit products
Business model principle	Pull	Push	Push–Pull	Pull
	Sell– Design–Make	Design– Make–Sell	Design– Sell–Make	Design (A)– Sell–Design (P) –Make

The author perceives the business model shift as a change in the customer's role in relationship with the enterprise's three main basic functions—Design, Make, Sell—as shown in Figure 1.13.

The customer initiates the Sell–Design–Make sequence in craft production (a pull-type model) and drives the design. In the mass production model, the customer is, however, at the back of the sequence (a push-type model). "The customers will always be there to buy products" is the main assumption of mass production. In mass customization, the manufacturer makes the main strategic decisions about the product basic architecture (a "platform" in the auto industry) as well as the number of variants and options offered based on targeted customer groups. The customer can only select the option that best fits his/her preferences and price. The personalized production paradigm promises customers both the greatest fit to their needs with the greatest cost-effectiveness. It is closest to the craft production model but has a more complex sequence, as shown in Figure 1.13.

Although the goal of both the mass customization and personalized production paradigms is to create a better fit between product offering and customer preference, the manufacturer's strategic decisions in each paradigm are different. In mass customization, the strategic economic decision is how many variations and options will provide the highest economic value for the manufacturer. On one hand, more variations will add complexity and cost, but on the other, more variation increases the number of potential customers, and thereby expands sales and market share.

In personalized production, the product has a modular architecture, and the manufacturer's strategic decisions are (1) the product architecture to which modules

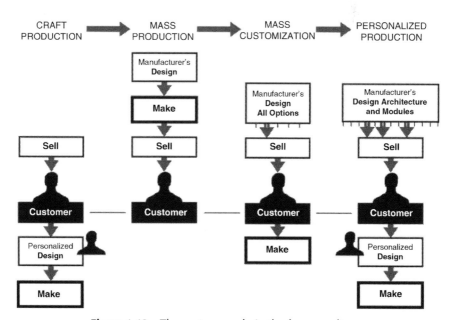

Figure 1.13 The customer role in the four paradigms.

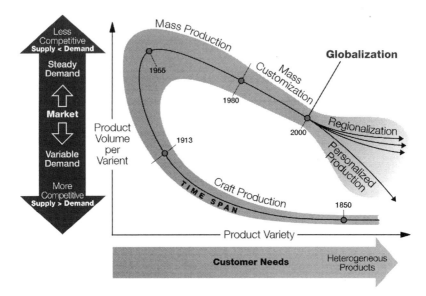

Figure 1.14   The drivers to new paradigms are market and society needs.

will be attached, (2) the type of interfaces to accommodate the modules, and (3) the type and function of modules from which the customers can design their individual product. In the personalized production paradigm, customers are involved in the design of their product, while in mass customization, the customers can only select a best fit to meet their needs.

In a globally competitive world, the customers' role in the Design–Make process is paramount and their involvement is intensified as the paradigm shifts from mass production to mass customization, to the personalized production paradigm. It is maximized in craft production, but there the product cost is highest of all. The personalized production paradigm promises optimal value to the customer when the level of their satisfaction and product price are traded off.

As we have said, new manufacturing paradigms are established by emerging societal needs or by new market conditions. An illustrative model of the four paradigms for automobiles is depicted in Figure 1.14[*]. The years 1850, 1913, and 1955 on the time line in this figure fit the paradigm shifts in automobile production in the Western world.

The paradigm model's inputs are the market and customer's needs. The model's outputs are the number of variants (i.e., models) offered for products with similar functionalities, and the product volume per variant, which reached its peak

---

[*]A different graph that shows the number of products versus the volume per product has been depicted by J. P. Womack, D. T. Jones, and D. Roos in *The Machine that Changed the World*, HaerperPerennials Publishers, New York, 1991, p. 126.

(minimum variants) in automobile production in 1955. From the mid 1950s, the trend in product variety versus volume is toward higher variety and smaller volume per variant, a trend that is applicable not only to automobiles, but also to many consumer goods, such as appliances, office furniture, etc.

The graph shows how changes in the market and consumer's needs propel the paradigm transition. Globalization currently impels regionalization (regional customization) and personalized production, in which society requires a larger variety and smaller volumes per product variant. Market fluctuations, which become larger every day, force manufacturers to produce even smaller volumes per each product variant. This trend in terms of product volume per model is perhaps moving toward those of craft production—a market-of-one.

1.7.1 Paradigms and Types of Manufacturing System

The challenges of each new manufacturing paradigm have always been met by a new type of manufacturing system, which, in turn, was made possible by applying a technological enabler that was new at the time the paradigm started. For example, as depicted in Figure 1.15, the mass customization paradigm was realized by utilizing FMS, since that manufacturing flexibility enabled cost-effective production of a variety of products. And mini-computers (which were a new technology in the 1970s; see Appendix A) enabled the creation of FMS and its basic building blocks—CNC machines and industrial robots.

A wise manufacturer who identifies emerging societal or market needs and knows how to invent a manufacturing system to address these needs will be successful. Henry Ford is a classic example. Ford realized that high product cost was the main obstacle that was keeping people from buying automobiles. He reasoned that if the price could be lowered, many more people could afford to buy cars and the market would flourish. Ford asked himself how product cost could be lowered if the cost of material and labor were constant. His answer was to organize the work differently. He organized the car assembly work sequentially, and later he invented the moving assembly line. The "Ford Method" worked great, but only, as it has been found, in stable markets where demand is greater than supply.

Figure 1.16 shows the relationship between the market and societal needs (e.g., heterogeneous products) on one hand, and the manufacturing systems that work best in responding to these conditions, on the other. In the craft production paradigm, general-purpose machine tools were used. They were replaced in the mass production

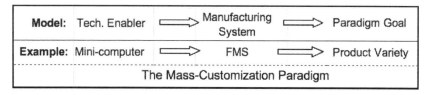

Figure 1.15   The paradigm goal is met by a new manufacturing system.

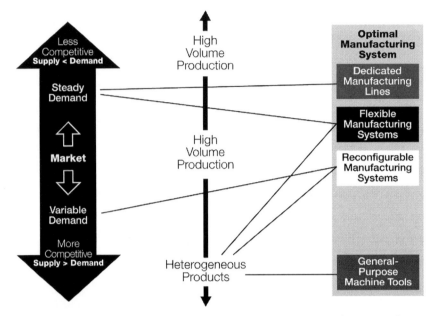

Figure 1.16 Market and society needs are linked to corresponding manufacturing systems.

paradigm by DMLs that utilized fixed automation to manufacture products and parts (e.g., car engines, pump housings, etc.) in very large and stable quantities.

As the balance between supply and demand starts to turn toward Supply > Demand, customers begin to look for products that better fit their preferences, in addition to low prices. The product market gradually stops being homogeneous, and starts to become more and more diverse. In response to this imperative, manufacturing engineers developed the FMS to produce the product mix that the market demands.

The characteristics of FMS perfectly fit markets with stable demand that require systems with fixed capacity. FMS, however, does not fit unstable markets with fluctuations in product demand (rocky markets) as we are witnessing in the globalization era. The engineering response to this new situation is the RMS. The RMS can adjust production capacity (i.e., volume per product) quickly to match market demand, can be rapidly tooled to produce new products, and can be upgraded with new functionalities to produce different varieties of the product. RMS enhances the firm's speed of responsiveness to new market conditions and gives a competitive edge to the enterprise.

Table 1.6 shows how societal needs and market forces have changed over the past two centuries, and the effect this has had on paradigm goals. It shows the corresponding changes in the manufacturing system, the product architecture, and the corresponding business model principle—all aimed at reaching that goal.

TABLE 1.6   Characteristics of Four Manufacturing Paradigms

Paradigm	Craft Production	Mass Production	Mass Customization	Global Manufacturing
Society needs	Unique products	Low-Cost products	Large product variety High quality	Regional products Personalized products
Market demand		Steady	Unstable	Fluctuating
Paradigm goal	Satisfy customer's desire	Product low cost	Wide variety	Rapid speed of responsiveness
Technology enabler	Electricity	Interchangeable parts	Computers	Information tech. and the Internet
Manufacturing system	Electrically powered machine tools	Moving assembly line Dedicated machines	Flexible systems w/Lean operations	Reconfigurable systems
Product architecture		Unified	Modular	Highly modular
Business model principle	Pull	Push	Push–Pull	Pull

The goal of the preceding paradigm is still a goal of the new paradigm, but additional goals divert the paradigm focus. Figure 1.17 conveyed graphically the transition of paradigm goals.

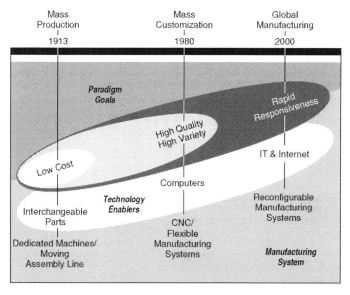

Figure 1.17   Each paradigm was driven by a goal, which was achieved by a new type of manufacturing system, which, in turn, was realized by a technology enabler.

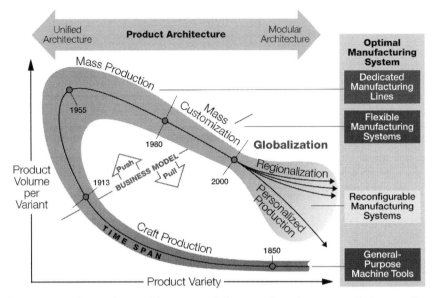

Figure 1.18 The product architecture and the manufacturing system fit the paradigm.

Figure 1.18 illustrates the relationships in the Western world between the type of manufacturing systems, the product architecture, and a simplified business model in four automotive production paradigms. This illustration shows how the paradigms transitioned over time given the changing needs of society, markets, and the emergence of new technological capabilities.

With the emergence of personalized production as an imperative of the global manufacturing paradigm, the time line in Figure 1.18 is moving toward closing the loop with the starting point of the craft production paradigm. The business model of personalized production is again of a pull-type. However, there is some big difference—the manufacturing cost of products in the personalization paradigm is much lower than that in craft production.

The basis of strategic thinking about the future of manufacturing enterprises may be drawn from Table 1.6 and Figure 1.18. Industry leaders must understand the current societal needs and emerging technologies to predict the future direction of manufacturing enterprises. For example, environmental concerns require product's end-of-life solutions, which will impel new life-cycle engineering-business models. For another example—the reduced prices of optical components developed for digital cameras has enabled a new generation of in-line inspection machines that inspect every single mechanical part at the line speed. Integrating these machines into production lines will tremendously increased product quality and reduce warranty costs. Companies have to assess how new technologies can assist in solving burning social imperatives.

Focusing on the marketing of current products may help a company, but only in the short term. Long-term success requires a strategic analysis of business–product–manufacturing relationships as well as an awareness of up and coming technologies that may revolutionize manufacturing operations and product architecture. Studying how past paradigms evolved can also assist in this analysis.

Globalization is causing market fluctuations that have brought serious instability to many manufacturing enterprises that are struggling to survive. Clearly, Darwin's principle—*the species that survive are usually not the smartest or the strongest, but the ones most responsive to change*—is applicable to the twenty-first century manufacturing enterprise! To thrive in the global manufacturing era, manufacturing enterprises must adapt to rapid changes in the new global economic environment. The enterprise's speed of responsiveness is essential to its staying alive in a rapidly changing world.

PROBLEMS

1.1 Compare the manufacturing paradigms in Table 1.5 in terms of (1) work force skills and (2) the level of flexibility of the manufacturing tools.

1.2 We say: "One of the benefits of mass customization is that it has the potential to create a diverse and large customer base. A large and diverse customer base has an advantage beyond market share: the cash flow generated by a large number of customers with diverse tastes is more stable than the cash flow of a large homogeneous customer base." Explain why a diverse customer base provides more stable cash flow relative to a homogenous customer base.

1.3 Is personalized production limited to a certain spectrum of products? Is product complexity a factor in deciding to design a product for personalized production, or is product complexity irrelevant to a product fit to personalized production?

1.4 Do you think customers should be offered as much variety as possible?

1.5 Will the loop in Figure 1.14 be ever closed in terms of variety and volume? What is your prediction?

REFERENCES

1. Y. Koren, F. Jovane, U. Heisel, T. Moriwaki, G. Pritschow, G. Ulsoy, and H. VanBrussel. Reconfigurable manufacturing systems: a keynote paper. *CIRP Annals*, 1999, Vol. 48, No. 2, pp. 6–12.

2. The New York Times, January 7, 1994.

3. http://www.federalreserve.gov/releases/g17/current/default.htm.

4. Deloitte's Global Benchmark Study Program. *3rd Report: Mastering Innovation*, May 2005.

5. F. Jovane, Y. Koren, and C. Boer. Present and future of flexible automation—towards new paradigms: a keynote paper. *CIRP Annals*, November 2003, Vol. **52**, No. 2, pp. 543–560.

6. J. P. Womack, D. T. Jones, and D. Roos. *The Machine that Changed the World*. Harper-Perennials Publishers, New York, 1991, p. 24.

7. C. K. Prahalad and M. S. Krishnan. *The New Age of Innovation*. McGraw Hill, 2008.

Chapter **2**

Product Invention Strategy

Because globalization has brought so many new competitors, manufacturers face a great struggle to hold onto the share of business that they had (their piece of the pie) before the global manufacturing revolution began. Only by enlarging the global economic pie, manufacturers might regain the share of the economic pie that they had before globalization. Creating new markets for new products that do not currently exist can "enlarge the pie." Developing an innovative product in a timely manner and harvesting a huge profit from it is the dream of every manufacturer. But getting to that product is not easy. How does a designer find a product that is needed but hasn't already been invented? There are some even more basic questions: What drives the process of invention? Is it driven by new technologies when they come on line? Or, does a company's management drive it when they decide to go after a competitor's business? Should a product aimed at global markets be designed differently than a product aimed at just one region? Is your company even capable of inventing new products? And what role should the customer play in developing new products? This chapter will explore these questions and more.

Before you make the investment to design, manufacture, and market a product you have examine the market opportunity. How does one recognize a market opportunity in the first place? There have been volumes written on where market opportunities come from new technologies, customers' perceptions, or ideas that can change our daily life. All of these sources and more can create market opportunities. The fundamental question for manufacturers is: *Which opportunities are worth pursuing?*

The Global Manufacturing Revolution: Product-Process-Business Integration and Reconfigurable Systems
By Yoram Koren
Copyright © 2010 John Wiley & Sons, Inc.

Companies recognize three drivers that motivate new product ideas:

- **Technology-driven Products:** Ideas for new innovative products that come from within a firm's own technology, experience, and core-competencies, also called **Company-driven Products**.
- **Customer-driven Products:** Responses to customer testimony based on in-depth market research.
- **Competition-driven Products:** Reaction to successful products already introduced by competitors.

Whatever the motivation, the new product must be perceived as benefiting the customers, that it creates a clear value for them. The new product must deliver economic value to the customer by relating their needs (functional or emotional) to design features of the product.

2.1 TECHNOLOGY-DRIVEN PRODUCTS

Technology-driven products are those made possible by applying new technology that, in many cases, originated within the company. Some legendary examples include the Walkman by Sony, the iPod and i-Phone by Apple, and the mini-van by Chrysler. The Walkman created a whole lifestyle change for users who wanted to listen to recorded sound in new arenas of physical activity. It is hard to remember a time when people did not wear headphones or ear buds as they jogged around the park. When Lee Iacocca, a man famous for driving new products into the market, introduced the Dodge Caravan and Plymouth Voyager, he created an entirely new segment of the auto market. In 1984, Chrysler earned $2.4 billion from its mini-vans, and an additional $3 billion in the next 2 years.

Technology-driven products can radically change the world we live in. The creative genius of product innovators within a company can be a powerful and profitable driver for fulfilling perceived market opportunities and creating new ones of their own. But can employees be taught to innovate? Are there techniques that stimulate creative thinking aimed at product innovation? "At my employer, Ford Motor Company," wrote our student Christopher Mazur in 2004, "the entire organization in both its structure and its culture are being shaped to encourage innovation. Such a strategy raises several questions: In what way does the company define innovation? Is it only in ground breaking new products or does it include business as well? And, how does the company become innovative overnight?"

We will elaborate on six methods that can stimulate ideas for new products.

2.1.1 Paradoxical Products—Products of Creative Thinking

One approach is the concept of "paradoxical products" as a way of inspiring product innovation.[*] Usually, the main function of a product is communicated through its

---

[*]The author coined the term "paradoxical products."

name. If we eliminate the main function of a product, it seems like we would be left with a product that does not make sense. Nonetheless, in some cases we might come up with a new product that has a new application and even a new market. We call this a **Paradoxical Product**.

Consider this example from above. Tape recorders were invented many years ago to record, store, and playback sound. One day, an employee from Sony wondered if there might be a use for a tape recorder that does not record? Sounds paradoxical, doesn't it? And yet, this was the first step toward the invention of the Walkman.

The Walkman lacked the main function of a tape recorder—recording. It created an application different from the original tape recorder. When Sony pursued the idea of the small portable tape "player," they created a paradoxical product that revolutionized the ability to carry recorded sound almost anywhere. By considering commonplace things and then removing (or repurposing) some basic feature, we can sometimes come up with entirely new product ideas, and who knows, perhaps even whole new industries.

A paradoxical product is a product that may seem to be absurd because a main function is missing, but in fact it may be a new, marketable product. Examples of paradoxical products are shown in Figure 2.1.

Can you "invent" a paradoxical product? If you do, try to elaborate on the following points:

1. What is the product good for?
2. What would the product look like?

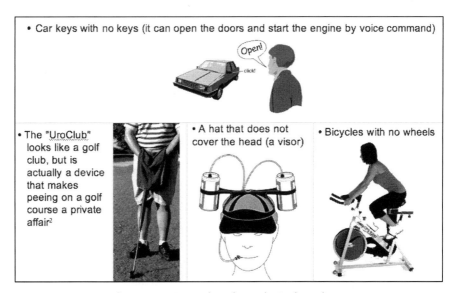

Figure 2.1   Examples of paradoxical products.

3. Would it be cheaper or more expensive to build than the conventional counterpart product?

4. What do you think the market and estimated annual demand would be for your idea?

5. Does the U.S. patent database include similar products? (You'll be surprised what's in there.)

Dreaming up paradoxical products can be an amusing and sometimes profitable exercise.

2.1.2 Products with Supplemental Functionality

We presented paradoxical products as a methodology for generating new product ideas by subtracting obvious, even primary features. Another approach is to think about an existing product and adding a new functionality that is completely unrelated to its main function. This can open another new range of applications.

A profound example of this is the cell phone. Cell phones originated as simply a portable telephone. Now, cell phone manufacturers are integrating cameras web browsers and TV controllers into phone units, and there is no end in sight! In Japan you can buy a soda from a soft-drink machine with your cell phone, and in Israel you can pay for parking. It is clear that your cell phone is gradually becoming some kind of a credit card. Was anyone thinking about such applications in 1990?

Can you think about other current products to which you might add completely new functions that supplement their original use?

2.1.3 Transferring Known Ideas to New Products—Crossover Techniques

A. Hargadon and R. Sutton have studied the innovation process.[1] They have documented that innovators systematically use old ideas as the raw materials for new product ideas. Taking an idea that is commonplace in one area and moving it to a completely new context is another way to spark creativity. This method is a "crossover technique."

Hargadon and Sutton describe that design companies like IDEO in California and Design Continuum in Boston use crossover to create new product ideas by observing users of similar products. This method engendered an innovative surgical skin stapler, as well as other tools used in knee surgery.

Toys can also be a source for serious product ideas. Toys have inspired the external design of laptop computers for Apple and Dell.[2] Toys are cheap and mass-produced, and have many neat things to offer. Among groups of designers, team brainstorming with toys can often generate great ideas.

The U.S. federal R&D budget on defense is larger than all other federal R&D combined. If there were a systematic way to transfer defense technology for the benefit of society, our lives would be continuously enriched with very little investment. The next section elaborates on one such example.

Example: Patients Swallow High-tech Capsules   In May 2000, I read an article in *Nature*[3] describing a new capsule containing a camera that patients can swallow in the morning and have the pictures of their digestive tract displayed on a monitor the next day. It may sound like science fiction, but it is a real capsule being produced by Given Imaging of Israel, and was approved for use by the U.S. Food & Drug Administration in August 2001.

The high-tech capsule is an alternative to the endoscope—the 1–5-m-long tube that is inserted to examine the intestine (the part of the digestive system between the stomach and the anus) for inflammatory bowel diseases or cancerous polyps. The endoscopic exam can be a bit painful and embarrassing so many patients refuse to take it, and risk fatal illness for lack of proper diagnosis.

Although the invention of this high-tech capsule is based on missile technology (see Figure 2.2), it is subject to additional design constraints because of its tiny size and the limited electrical source. The inventor of the high-tech capsule, Dr. Gavriel (Gabi) J. Iddan, was my roommate during my doctoral studies. Prior to this project, he worked for Rafael (a defense company) and worked on missile development. Below is Gabi's story about his invention of the high-tech pill.

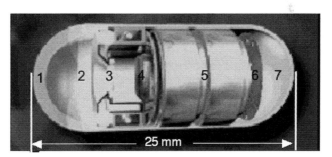

Figure 2.2   The high-tech capsule includes elements of missile technology: an optical dome, lens, digital imager, transmitter, and antenna. The patient swallows the device like a pill. The tiny camera inside the single-use capsule captures two images per second, for a total of 50,000 pictures. The digital imager has a resolution of 0.1 mm. The capsule dimensions are 10 mm in diameter and 25 mm (1 inch) in length.

1. Transparent dome
2. Lens
3. Headlights: Six LEDs emitting white light
4. Digital imager
5. Two batteries (1.5 V, each)
6. Transmitter, operates at 433 MHz
7. Antenna, 1 μW (1% of acell phone's power)

"In the late 1980s, endoscope manufacturers incorporated a small CCD (used in video cameras) in the endoscope to replace the fiber bundle that was used for image transmission until then. In the early 1990s, I started to think about the possibility of separating the CCD head of the endoscope by attaching a mini-transmitter to the CCD head, thus letting the head move free of any physical connection. However, I encountered three main challenges:

- Contamination of the optical window in the intestine
- Long hours of viewing time for the doctor
- Short lifetime of the batteries needed for the CCD, illumination, and transmission

First, I figured out that in order to avoid the optical window contamination and obscuration, the optics will have to be designed in a way that will guarantee constant rubbing of the tissue on an arch-shaped window that is contact imaging and self-wiping of the transparent window. The next problem of long viewing hours was solved by separating the system into three components: a *capsule* containing imager and transmitter; a *recorder* containing antenna and recording medium; and a *workstation* incorporating a reader, processing software, and a monitor. In 1997, I was awarded the first U.S. patent on a video capsule.

In October 1999, the first real capsule was swallowed; clear images were received—the video capsule turned into reality. Given Imaging was issued to the public as the first issue at NASDAQ after the 9/11/2001 disaster."

The product offered by Given Imaging includes the capsule ($450 per capsule), an 8-Gb hard drive worn on the patient's belt, and a workstation with software to which the hard drive is connected for diagnostics. The market for Given Imaging is global; it includes 11 million Americans who endure endoscope exams every year to look for suspicious abnormalities in the small intestine. (See UMHS web site below.)

In 2003, the FDA expanded its approval of the pill to the diagnostics of Crohn's disease. In December 2004, the British National Health Service (NHS) approved the device. (Great Britain has a population of 58 million.) By the end of 2004, Given Imaging was selling 10 thousand capsules globally per month. In 2004–2006, the pill of Given Imaging got substantial Internet and media coverage.

"A short time ago, I was watching Today on NBC and they had a live demonstration of one of the anchors swallowing the exact camera that is discussed above," wrote our student Rachel Krueger in March 2006. "They showed the entire process on TV."

The following story was taken on August 4, 2004 from the University of Michigan Health System (UMHS) web site.

ANN ARBOR, MI[4]—One pill, a glass of water, and about 8 hours is all it takes to produce nearly 60,000 high-resolution digital photos. And patients are finding that the latest in high-tech, digital photography is very easy to swallow. Using this new non-invasive technology, known as a capsule endoscopy system, physicians at the UMHS now have the ability to explore uncharted, and often unseen, territory within a patient's small intestines.

Capsule endoscopy is providing physicians with a clear view of obscure gastrointestinal disorders such as bleeding or Crohn's disease, which were previously difficult to visually detect.

The tiny capsule records its entire journey through the digestive tract while closely examining the 15–18 feet of the small bowel. The capsule sends two images per second to sensors attached to a Walkman-sized digital recording device strapped to the patient's waist. The stored images are transformed into a digital movie. It takes gastroenterologists about 45 minutes to review the series of images.

2.1.4 Disruptive Technologies—Will the World be Changed?

Disruptive technologies—a phrase coined by C.M. Christensen[5]—refer to any new emerging technology that gradually replaces an established, matured technology in the same basic application. Examples include the transistor that replaced the vacuum tube, the digital camera that replaced the conventional film camera, cell phones that are replacing the wired phone, as well as capsule and virtual colonoscopy, which may eventually replace the real colonoscopy. Fuel cells in the automotive industry, which may 1 day replace the internal combustion engine, the personal digital assistant (PDA) or i-Phone that may take a significant market share from laptops and cell phones, may also be defined as disruptive technologies.

In many cases, an innovative replacement technology may emerge at a time when an established company struggles to improve the performance of their current product. If the company ignores the new technology, it may eventually lose its entire share of the market. The transistor came into use in the late 1950s, but its early performance was poorer than that of vacuum tubes that had equivalent functions (e.g., in radios). RCA, Philips, and General Electric controlled the vacuum tube market in the 1960s. RCA does not exist today, and GE is not making microprocessors, the industry that evolved from the transistor industry.

Early digital cameras suffered from poor picture quality and low resolution. Kodak, with more than 60% of the photographic materials industry, did not believe that digital photography performance could improve to a degree that it would replace conventional photography. Therefore, Kodak entered the digital camera business too late, and consequently fell from its pre-eminent position at the top of the photographic industry in 2003.

The dilemma for an established company is whether to invest in a new technology, and how many resources to commit to developing it. If you were the CEO of General Motors in 2001, how much would you want to invest in fuel-cell engine technology, how much in plug-in electric cars, and how much in hybrid cars? Fuel cells do not yet have any national infrastructure (equivalent to gas stations), although electric cars have some. The main obstacle to electric car has been the poor performance and high cost of the battery that runs the electric motor. Earlier, the battery was very heavy and limited the range they could travel. The CEO may know that the market for small electric cars will explode if there is a breakthrough in battery technology within the next 10–15 years, but how can he/she be certain that battery technology will improve. And how could the CEO foresee that oil prices would increase five times between 2001 and 2008? How can a manufacturer know which new ideas will catch on, and when?

The critical decision point for a company is illustrated in Figure 2.3. At the beginning, the performance of a product with the new technology is usually worse than that of the established technology (e.g., the early low-resolution digital camera) and its related products capture only a small share of the market. It may take years to replace the existing product technology and who is to say if a new product's performance will actually surpass that of the existing technology? In some cases, an emerging technology will fade if the expectations never materialize. That investment is lost. For all these reasons, established companies hesitate to invest in disruptive technologies. Some of them prefer to wait until a new product (even a competitor) captures a new market (e.g., Kodak entering to the digital camera market late); but a late entry into an emerging market can be expensive and still may fail.

Even if one comes to the market late, if their product is marketed well, people may buy it. VHS entered the market after Betamax videotapes were introduced. Even though Beta was a more advanced format, VHS was a better fit with customers. VHS tapes were cheaper to make and therefore cost less. More movies were available in VHS, and so more people bought VHS players. VHS became the dominant product. Beta died out.

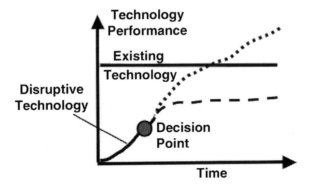

Figure 2.3   The dilemma of investing in a disruptive technology: Will its performance surpass that of the existing technology or will its performance just improve a bit?

2.1.5 Making Lemonade—When the Market Gives You Lemons

Markets Change: That which everyone in the world wanted last year, couldn't get enough of last season, and was willing to pay any price for is now worthless. Overnight, your factory, instead of a vibrant engine of commerce and profit, becomes a museum to an obsolete past. As a manufacturer, you have two choices: install a gift shop and try to sell tickets, or convert your factory to build something that you can sell.

To appreciate the last statement, see if you can answer the following questions:

> A company that sold a product that became obsolete when Thomas Edison invented the light bulb had sales of $1.2 billion in FY 2000.

What is the company?
What is the product?

The company is Blyth Inc. and it makes and markets candles. Blyth is a major producer of home décor and fragrance products, supplying candles, aromatherapy, and even food service heating products all over the world. The company took what they were good at, melting and mixing waxy fluids, and directed it to markets that were previously underserved, and in some regions, did not exist at all.

Many manufacturers think they can learn what customers want by allowing them to determine what products will fill a market niche. The main difficulty in predicting what customers will buy is that...

It's hard to predict which product people will like in the future

2.1.6 Emulating Animal Motions—Fly Like a Bird? Crawl Like a Snake!

Emulating the motions of animals is an exciting variation on the crossover innovation, and a useful approach for inventing new locomotion devices. If you look at the conventional uses of wheels and the way airplanes are propelled, you may think such innovations are impossible. Nevertheless, it may be worthwhile to observe animal motion in nature and try to emulate them. Imagine, for example, if a mechanism that emulates the spring action of a grasshopper's legs was invented—objects that are hundreds of times heavier than the device could be propelled.

An example of emulating animal motions is the mechanical snake robot that was invented at the University of Michigan in the early 1990s by Y. Shan and Y. Koren.[6] The structure of the snake robot enables it to move without wheels. It was constructed of a series of articulated links, each one with a DC motor and a solenoid break. Although each link had only one motor, as shown in Figure 2.4, this structure allowed

Figure 2.4   The mechanical snake invention (Inventors: Y. Koren and Y. Shan).

the robot configuration to be easily controlled, and allowed the snake robot to move in very cluttered environments.

The motion planning system provided the snake robot with a basic movement pattern that can be easily modified for varying tasks and environments. The mechanical snake did not avoid obstacles on its way, but rather "accommodated" them while continuing its motion toward the target even while in contact with those obstacles. In each motion stage the snake used a different number of degrees of freedom, providing the robot with great adaptability.

Such robotic devices may have many applications, especially for crawling into places that are too dangerous or too small for people. Commonly used wheeled robots cannot fulfill many tasks because of their large size. The snake robot demonstrates that emulating animal locomotion may have advantages over conventional locomotion methods—wheels, tracks, and even legs. And, mimicking animal movement can inspire a whole new range of design possibilities.

Yansong Shan (my former Ph.D. student) opened a start-up that implemented the snake principle for medical testing of the small intestine. The snake-like device that he developed utilizes the natural contraction wave of the small intestine to propel the device. The device is equipped with a video camera and illumination source. A communication and power cable is wound within the device and unwinds through an aperture in the rear of the device as it moves through the small intestine.[7]

2.1.7   Adding Complex Features Appalls Consumers

Designers of high-tech products have to be watchful about adding too many "cool" features in the products they offer. An article in the USNWR from January 2001 discussed the December 2000 electronics exhibition in Las Vegas and commented:

> "The technology industry is enduring its first bear market. Many companies are scrambling to find out why consumers aren't falling in love with the latest stuff."

The USNWRs answer was:

"Most folks are trying to figure out how to work the devices they already have."

Companies, eager to bring attention to new products and to differentiate theirs from competitors, often do it by adding and introducing new features. This of course is normal and appropriate, but it can be overdone. Too many superfluous features can frustrate and appall consumers, especially if they are rarely used, cost too much, or the user interface is too complex. Companies should offer products that emphasize ease of use and dependability instead of extravagant lists of rarely used features.

To summarize the section on technology-driven products, here are comments from our former students:

"While technology-driven product might promise tremendous profits, it also carries the greatest amount of risk. Take for example the Segway, which is a technology-driven product that has sold poorly as customers are not willing to pay such a high-price tag." Scott Norby-Cedilio

"An excellent example of a technology-driven product is OnStar. Hughes Electronics possessed most of the innovative technology required to create OnStar. By packaging emergency notification, travel assistance, theft tracking, and satellite phone in one package, OnStar quickly became a success and became the first player in a new market." Jeff Swords

2.2 CUSTOMER-DRIVEN PRODUCTS

A fundamental challenge for a company is to identify market opportunities by gauging customer's needs. In very specific products, like surgical tools, it is possible to develop user-driven, even user-specified, products, since surgeons tend to be exceptionally practical and highly motivated consumers. But in general, this method is of limited value.

Identifying consumer's needs and translating those needs into new products is usually done by implementing a three-step process:

1. **Market Research:** —typically through customer surveys
2. **Interpret:** —the customer survey to understand the customer's intents
3. **Translate:** —the customer's needs and requirements into engineering design features

2.2.1 Market Research

Before launching a new product or penetrating a new market, a firm should do systematic market research to gather data about their potential customers and competitors. Well-performed market research will provide invaluable insights into the company's design team. There are three basic types of market research:

- Primary research (collecting and analyzing new data) can be quantitative (surveys) or qualitative (focus groups, interviews, etc.). Its principal advantage is that it is tailored to the firm's needs. Sample questions include: Which features of the planned product are important? Are the current products meeting customers' needs? If they aren't, why not?
- Secondary research (searching and analyzing published data that is applicable to the new product) is comparably cheaper and easily accessible. Its main disadvantage is that it is usually not specific to the firm's new product and of limited value.
- Quantitative research is expensive and needs to be conducted as thoroughly as a scientific experiment in order to reach meaningful conclusions. Since the subjects are humans and your target answers are specific, you must be careful to precisely craft your questions to avoid biased responses.

To be effective, one should use more than one research technique and look for convergence in your results.

2.2.2 Product Survey Interpretation

The validity of survey results depends on how well the survey is prepared. Detailed analysis and interpretation of the survey results is critical to one's decision of starting a new product development project. Interpreting a survey's results is straightforward when the acquired data show a clear trend. However, when a trend is not obvious, an incorrect interpretation may lead to a failed product and an economic disaster.

Let us look at the challenge of interpreting customer-survey results with the following example. A company has two candidate products: **A** and **B**. One thousand potential customers were surveyed and rated them.

Rating		A	B
I love the product;			
I'll definitely buy it	5	220	50
I think that I'll buy the product	4	100	200
The product is fine	3	60	500
I'm not sure about the product	2	200	200
I hate the product	1	420	50
Average:		**2.5**	**3.0**

Which product, **A** or **B**, would you select for development?

The average reader, we might guess, would say Product **B**, since its overall rating is higher (3.0, compared with just 2.5 for Product **A**). Nevertheless, the right answer is Product **A**. Close to 25% of the surveyed market said they love the product, and almost a third will probably buy it; this is a recipe for success. On the other hand, although Product **B** received a higher overall score, most of the responses were in the middle rating, and few committed to buy the product. Remember that there might be similar products competing in the market, and it is impossible to compare them in this survey. Even if you have established that Product **A** has higher probability of success, you still do not know whether people will buy your new product or something else. The survey results are of limited value.

Robert Lutz, the former president of Chrysler, has been very skeptical of customer surveys. He gave the following example in his book "Guts".[8]

The nice survey taker asked: "Mrs. Ferguson, would you like your next car better if it had a heated cup holder?"

Mrs. Ferguson always wanted a better cup holder.

"And would that more contemporary cup holder be worth to you, say, an extra $40 the next time you buy a car?" I can guarantee she'll answer yes. It's possible, of course, that she really does want a heated cup holder and is prepared to pay for it. But, more often than not, the respondent simply wants to avoid any appearance of being a cheapskate.

The question is whether the survey is asking a specific question: "Would you like to have a heated cup holder?" What do you, the reader, think about asking an open-ended question in order to obtain more reliable results? Let us say that you decide to develop a new digital camera. Your question to potential customers might be:

"Which functions would you like to see in a digital camera?"

Well, such a question might also be tricky. U.S. News & World Report (1/15/2001) had an article that elaborated on this very issue:

You interview a thousand people, and each one says:
"I want these 10 general features plus this specific feature."
So you build a device with 1010 features.
But no one wants 1010 features in a digital camera.

Few people spend their day dreaming about the "ultimate" product; and even if they do, they cannot create them. It is left to visionary engineers to come up with new ideas for tomorrow's breakthrough, ideas that will lead to new technologies and new products.

Nevertheless, manufacturers have to do more than just guess at what will sell. Listening to their customers, and collecting data through surveys, is an essential market research tool. Below, we have an example of a reasonable customer survey (prepared by a team of students) that includes a mix of open questions and rated questions.

2.2.2.1 Car-seat Manufacturing—Customer Survey

- Are you happy with the features currently offered in your vehicle passenger seats?
- Are their any supplemental features that you would suggest?
- What do you (or your passengers) do on long trips for entertainment?
- Are there any features you would desire for your children?
- Please rate the following features from 1 to 5:

	1	2	3	4	5	Comments
Cup holders						
Automatic reclining mechanism						
Reclining mechanism w/footstool						
Heated seats						
Massaging seats						
Lumbar support						
Small cooler for snacks						
Pull-out folding table						
Reading light						
Pull-out screen for DVD or GPS						
Storage drawer						
Laptop power hook-up						
CD player with headphone hook-up						

In any event, a market survey of consumer products is a tool to test customer preferences, but its usefulness in directing new product development should be assessed very carefully. The problem with letting your potential customers direct your new-product plans is that they do not always get it right. And even when they do, their demands and conclusions may not be useful to your situation. Products based on what outsiders think you should do might be a bad fit for your expertise, your production plant, and your corporate structure. However, while surveys may not be the best method for getting customer input on new products, they are a starting point. And, they are very helpful in getting customer feedback on competing products.

2.2.3 Translating Customer's Needs into Engineering Design Features

Translating your customer's desires into a set of features and design requirements is done by a methodology called Quality Function Deployment (QFD). For example,

QFD can translate a customer's statement "I want this door to close easily" into an engineering specification of force and torque. QFD utilizes a series of matrices, each called a House of Quality. The matrices reconcile what customer's want, with what engineers can reasonably build, in a consistent way. (There are many product design books you can consider for reference.)

2.2.4 Industry Leaders on Innovations

Apple, 3M, Oracle, IBM, Canon, General Electric, Intel, and Samsung are just a few examples of companies who have been consistently successful at introducing new products. Business leaders frequently emphasize the necessity of product innovation for company growth; several examples are quoted below:

Larry Ellison CEO, Oracle:

On August 10, 2007, Larry Ellison gave a talk in Tel Aviv, Israel, in which he emphasized the need for innovations: "Innovation is finding the mistake in the common wisdom, and to understand something new when others think differently. If others say that you're crazy, probably you discovered something! Innovation is the only way to get ahead in science and engineering." Ellison said his vision was to store personal medical files. "Almost 75,000 people die every year because doctors are writing prescriptions for drugs contraindicated by other drugs patients take."

Samuel Palmisano CEO, IBM:

"What makes IBM special is its focus on innovation. Innovation needs intellectual talent that is open to change, adaptable, and adjustable."

Bangalore, June 6, 2006

Fujio Mitarai, President and CEO, Canon Inc

"It is essential to create a constant supply of innovative products. We try to replace half of the entire product line every year."

Forbes, January 12, 2004

2.3 COMPETITION-DRIVEN PRODUCTS

There are few things more frustrating than watching a competitor succeed. When your competition introduces a new product, it is almost instinctual to try to create a rival to their success, to take away part of their market, to feast as it were at their banquet.

But if, in pursuit of your rival's product you venture into unknown, or unexpected territory, you may get lost; and, if you go too far, you may lose your company as a consequence.

The company that invents a product and moves first into a new market has usually invested a fortune on the product's invention, development, and marketing. This first mover has taken a great risk, but, if the product is successful, the first mover can earn huge rewards.

A firm that tries to compete through imitation needs less R&D and marketing, since the market has already been created. It can also learn from any obvious mistakes that the first firm made, and avoid them. There are many famous stories of successful competition-driven products. For instance, although Chrysler introduced the mini-van in 1984, it no longer controls the lion's share of this market 20 years later. Apple pioneered the mini-computer market with many unique features and the best operating system in the early 1980s, but 20 years later the PC has over 90% of the market, and Windows is the dominant operating system.

A firm that imitates a successful product can also fail. Follow-on failures can come from many directions, often failing to effectively copy or integrate a competitor's features, or, trying to make your own product better (or at least different) in the market. A big problem is trying to produce the product cost-effectively when your company infrastructure is vastly different from your competitor's. Many companies have failed this way. Remember, it is dangerous to proceed with a competing product unless you have a clear competitive advantage—your experience, facilities, distribution network, access to capital, and infrastructure need to be equal to or better than your rival. Absent that, you'll need to have a uniquely superior product or a truly bright idea how to differentiate your product from competing products.

Another equally fatal risk is that when, although you do succeed in producing a competitive product, your timing might be wrong. You may have even produced the better product, but by the time you get there, the market has moved on and left you holding a very expensive anachronism.

> If a company's strategy is only to copy successful products, it may survive, but it will never become the market leader.

Innovative companies must be always mindful that their competition may be copying their successes, just as they are mindful that competitors are trying to come up with new technologies and new products. In fact, they are foolish to expect otherwise. Either situation will put the company in a crisis state. It is lonely (and scary) at the top. Andy Grove, the CEO of Intel Corporation, wrote a book in the early 1990s, exploring the crisis points that challenge every innovative company. The book title is *Only the Paranoid Survive*.[9]

And on this issue the bible says:

> "Happy is the man that feareth always" [Proverbs 28, 14].

2.4 CLASSIFICATION OF PRODUCT INVENTIONS

Inventors have to ask two basic questions about their new products:

1. What is new in your new product? Is it the whole concept or just a few new functions?
2. How will the product change the buyer's life?

In other words these questions ask: What is the **purpose** of the invention? In Table 2.1, we list seven possibilities for the purpose of a product: a product may increase the customer's productivity—make things run faster, more accurately, or in a more organized way (e.g., Microsoft Excel). Another purpose is a product for fun and entertainment (e.g., computer games). A third is convenience (e.g., the mini-van) or luxury. And still another is personal security or enhancing safety (e.g., safety glasses). Other purposes may include energy generation, mobility, or new "green" products with a reduced-pollution footprint (e.g., hybrid cars). Manufacturers should also be proactive in developing environmentally friendly products. For example, products (even toys) might be able to use a solar array, or be mechanically powered rather than run on batteries or AC adapters. Manufacturers should, as policy, be exploring "green" product options before environmental regulations are even proposed.

Next, the inventor must evaluate the degree to which a product will meet the customer's needs and expectations. The price must be in line with the intended buyer's valuation of the product. A price that is too high will suppress sales volume (remember that only a few people bought the very first video tapes because the price was around $80 per tape!). Every new product must meet the customer's requirements, expectations, and tastes. Personalized products (see Chapter 3) must meet the highest

TABLE 2.1 Mapping Product Invention

A. Invention classification	One of eight classes
B. Purpose	Productivity enhancement Entertainment and fun Comfort, convenience, luxury Security, safety Energy efficiency and generation Mobility "Green," low environmental impact
C. Matching customer's needs	Reasonable price Attractive, aesthetically pleasing Simple to use
D. Influencing factors	Ease of purchase Speed of delivery Recyclable, environmental-friendly Service and warranty

expectation of customer's needs. Finally, the product must be simple to use without a long and complicated training regime. (As said, when you buy a new car you should not have to learn how to drive again.)

Next, delivery and ease of use and service also influence the success of new product. Ease of purchase or rent, especially if it is done through the Internet, is an important factor. Dell computers, as we have described, are ordered via the Internet using a very user-friendly system, and they are delivered within a few days. Imagine how Dell's sales would drop if delivery started to take a couple of months to fulfill! Pizza, fast food, and now computers depend on fast delivery. Lastly, the product service and warranty period also affect sales (e.g., automobiles), although, as products become cheaper, the value of such benefits declines.

2.4.1 Invention Classification

As we have mentioned, product innovations can be classified into eight types. The first four involve original inventions, and the last four describe incremental innovations.

1. Original Products **with completely new functionalities**
   These products do something completely new and provide original solutions to problems that people are facing in life—at home or at work. Examples include electric power, electric light, vacuum tubes, radio, television, photography, movies, telephone, automobile, bicycles, airplanes, trains, laser, xerographic copier, fax, mechanical typewriter, plastics, synthetic fabrics, microprocessor, pharmaceutical products, etc. The above product examples opened new huge markets, and are usually associated with enormous commercial success.

2. Original Products **with new ways of providing known functionalities**
   Examples include jet airplanes, the high-tech diagnostic capsule, the transistor, storage disks (instead of tapes), CD player, VCR, and microwave ovens. Products in this category are often presenting high-risk opportunities, but can also be a huge commercial success.

3. Original Products **that subtract functions from existing products**
   The subtracted functions creat new products or markets. Examples include the Sony Walkman.

4. Original Products **that add new technologies to products in use**
   Examples include electric starter to automobiles (replaced the manual starter of the early automobiles), automatic transmission to cars, transistors (instead of vacuum tubes in radios), DVR (instead of VCR), i-Phone, etc.

5. Modified Products **that change the architecture or size of existing products**
   Examples include the Airbus A-380 airplane with the huge passenger capacity, the mini-van, the personal computer, and personal copier.

6. Modified Products **that better fit the needs of people and society**
   These products respond to evolving challenges with the current products that we use. Examples include hybrid vehicles and recyclable products.

7. Modified Products **that add novel functions to existing products**
   Examples include cell phone cameras, DVD, adding e-mail and PDA functionality to mobile phones, adding CD player for cars, etc.
8. Existing Products **that are repurposed for new markets and uses**:
   Examples include candles that are used for decoration and aroma therapy instead of lighting.

Products from every one of these classes can be a hit. However, any new product becomes a failure if customers do not buy it. As we have said, being at the leading edge of technology and serving a market that does not yet exist brings huge risks. Consider Iridium—a consortium of electronics, aerospace, and telecommunications companies that in 1998 launched 66 satellites into space and initiated the first round of the world telephone service. This high-energy, high-visibility enterprise spent more than $5 billion and filed for bankruptcy within its first year.

2.5 PRODUCT DEVELOPMENT FOR GLOBALIZATION

Developing "Globalized" products is a cornerstone of the global manufacturing paradigm. So how are globally developed products different from conventional design? To begin with, globally competitive products are facing a much larger and diverse range of competition. Innovative design must be based on thorough market research of all potential target markets around the world. Variant product designs can then be tailored to the culture, tastes, needs, and regulatory environment of each target country.

2.5.1 Product Regionalization—Products Designed to Fit Regional Markets

A product that fits one region or country will not necessarily sell in another. To be successful, a product's features and the way that it operates must fit the culture and constraints of the regional market in which it is to be sold. Discovering those regional differences between target markets and cultures, and incorporating those considerations into the product itself, is called "product regionalization". Gone are the days when a manufacturer could rely on their marketing alone to sell the same product all over the world. It has taken U.S. manufacturers a long time to recognize that products that are designed for sale in the United States do not automatically fit the Japanese, European, or Chinese markets.

For example, in the 1980s, U.S. car manufacturers were puzzled that Japanese consumers would not buy the products they imported. It took years for the American car companies to figure out that not only were their cars too big for the average Japanese person, but also the steering wheels on their imported cars were on the wrong side (the left side, as in the United States). Drivers in Japan use the left side of the road (as in Great Britain), and, for years, U.S. manufacturers chose to ignore this essential fact.

However, regionalized products must fit more than just the local traffic regulations and electricity (220 or 110 V). They must also recognize the culture of the consumers in the country where they are to be sold. Another much subtler example is the car door mechanism: Americans like to hear a good solid "bang" when they close their car doors. German drivers hate it, and are willing to pay more for a car whose doors close quietly. When General Motors bought Opel in Germany, GM asked its American engineers to redesign the door assembly for Opel. The resulting "Americanized" product failed in the German market, but it did sell better in the United States.

Another example of cultural difference came when European and American producers tried (and failed) to introduce their vending machines in Japan. The designers could not understand why Japanese people would only buy products (sometimes the same products) from vending machines produced in Japan. Some were sure that this was evidence of Japanese discrimination against foreign manu-facturers. The truth of the matter was completely cultural. Both European and American vending machines use gravity to operate. The product falls to a slot at the bottom of the machine and the person has to bend over to receive it. However, Japanese people are not comfortable bowing to a machine, and so they unconsciously avoided buying products from the foreign vending machines. Japanese vending machines also use gravity but Japanese designers have added a simple mechanism that raises the product up so the buyer can take it from an aperture in the upper part of the machine. The buyer does not have to bow to be served. This original design of a Japanese vending machine is shown in Figure 2.5. Our student Gregory Hawkins wrote "I've worked quite a bit with Japanese engineers at my Mazda-Ford plant, and

Figure 2.5 A Japanese vending machine—a robotic arm hands the soda bottle, and the customer does not have to bow to take it.

I've seen first hand these soda machines and thought them odd until it was explained here in this text."

Keep in mind the rule:

New product development must address multicultural and multi-regional factors.

Each variant of the product should fit the culture and regulations of the target market.

For greatest success, the global product design goal is a line of products with similar basic functionality and key components, but with different features to fit various regional markets. As shown in Figure 2.6, most houses in the United States have a laundry room into which a large washer and dryer fit easily, side by side. In Europe, by contrast, although most cities have infrastructure and lifestyle expectations similar to those in the United States, European houses and apartments are typically much smaller. To save space, the dryer is more commonly positioned on top of the washer. In China, where apartments are even smaller, and where power to run an electric dryer is more expensive (proportional to income), most families just have a washer and they hang their clothes out to be dried in the sun.

"When Unilever and P&G first entered into the market in my country, Peru, they introduced the detergent in big quantities," wrote our student Rocio Diaz. "While these sizes work well in the United States, the experience in Peru is different. Houses are small and people do not have the money to pay for 5lb detergent bag. After getting to know how the Peruvian market really behaves, these companies launched mini-size laundry bags, which resulted in a substantial increase in their sales."

Product pricing is another obvious criterion for product regionalization and must be in line with the purchasing power of customers in each target country. India may want automobiles with similar basic functionality as in the United States or Europe, but they cannot afford to pay U.S. prices and are willing to do

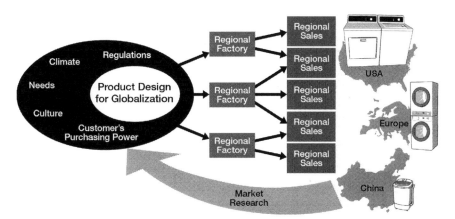

Figure 2.6 Product design for globalization—product variants fit culture and living conditions.

without luxury add-on features that their average buyer cannot afford. For example, the price of the Tata Nano in India is $2500. The price of the Buick LaCross, a typical mid-size American car, is over $25,000 in the United States. Both cars provide the basic mobility function, but, as shown in the table below, they have very different engines, dimensions (in millimeters)[*], and performance expectations.

Car	Engine	Length	Width	Height	Max Speed
Buick LaCross	3800 cc, V6	5032	1854	1458	>200 kmph
Tata Nano	624 cc, 2 cyl	3099	1495	1652	105 kmph

To meet this price, the Tata Nano and other Indian cars that sell below $4000 do not have many luxury features (e.g., air conditioning, adjusting power seats) or safety devices (e.g., airbags) that would be standard on European and American cars. However, for Indian drivers the cars are affordable and they do fit the congested traffic conditions and roads in India.

2.5.2 Manufacturing in the Global Paradigm

To be cost-effective, global products should be manufactured in regionally distributed factories, which can make product design even more challenging. Ideally, factories should be located close to their target customers, especially for products that are large or require long shipping times. Regionally placed factories may supply several regions but to do so they must be able to produce the many variants that fit the region's customers, cultures, and local regulations. To supply the exact quantities needed for each region they serve, these factories will need flexible and reconfigurable manufacturing systems that will allow rapid response to demand changes across the market range, to be able to quickly switch between product variants. For "globalized" product to be successful, all of the above imperatives must be considered.

2.6 THE PRODUCT DEVELOPMENT PROCESS

Products eventually define the mission and success of manufacturing companies, and therefore product development is a critical process. A successful product's marketable lifetime curve has a sigmoid (S) shape consisting of a growth phase period, followed by a high-sale period, and eventually a nearly inevitable phase of decline. If the idea is good and the timing is right, the average product will get to

---

[*]Note the large head clearance of the Nano. It's the "pet" project of Mr. Ratan Tata, Chairman of the Tata Group, who is 183 cm (6 feet) tall.

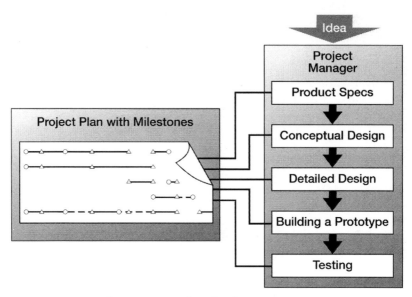

Figure 2.7   Product development stages.

the growth phase, but inevitably, product sales will eventually go into decline. (There are only few exceptions.) In preparation of this, a manufacturer should start to develop the replacing product when the current product is ramping up as shown in Figure 2.7. Successful companies always have a flow of products spread over different phases of the product life cycle. The set of stages of activity required to bring a new product concept to market readiness is called the product development process.

Product development starts with the invention of a new product concept, followed by market analysis, product design process, and eventually preparing manufacturing plans. Competing products already on the market must be analyzed in terms of differentiation and cost. Before resolving to develop a new product, you have to spend time on a pre-design effort—analyzing critical issues that enable you to have a reasonable expectation of success.

2.6.1 Four Critical Issues in Deciding to Develop a New Product

There are four difficult, but critical issues that go into making a decision to develop a new product:

1. **Identifying a Market Opportunity:** The most basic issue is to decide whether there is a real market opportunity and whether a new idea can be translated into revenue. You are making a decision in an uncertain environment, and the window of opportunity will not stay open very long. Therefore, it is imperative

that you effectively calculate whether your efforts fit the time and resources available. To make this decision, some basic critical questions are:

- Is the product unique? What are the advantages of competing products?
- Who are the potential customers?
- Does your firm have the development capability and the skills needed?
- Who are your competitors and what are their technical capabilities?
- What is your risk level? If the product fails, will the company survive?
- Do you have the facilities needed to manufacture the product?
- Do you have the resources to market and sell the product on a global scale?

2. **Product Development Timing:** Design lead-time is a measure of the responsiveness of the firm to a new market opportunity. It is highly dependent on the firm's experience and infrastructure. You cannot afford to risk extending the time to market, and therefore it is critical to have a realistic estimate of the time a team needs to complete the product design and development effort. Remember—not completing the product development on time not only increases your expenses, it may even put the entire project at risk. Some critical questions are:

- How quickly can the firm complete the product development?
- If your product development takes longer than expected, will you lose the market opportunity and risk the whole investment?

3. **Development Cost:** A realistic estimate of a project's development cost is also crucial to success and is usually based on experience. You have to consider both the requirements and any tradeoffs. For example, to increase the car's fuel efficiency it can be made lighter, but the cost of conversion to other materials might be enormous and the resulting fuel saving might be negligible (and sales increase only marginally). Furthermore, changing the material may reduce protection from collisions and this creates new challenges. You have to consider cross-effects of your choices and requirements. Organizing the requirements into a hierarchical list may help in weighing the tradeoffs.[10] The questions are:

- What is the estimated product development cost?
- Are there design tradeoffs (e.g., materials) and what is the associated development cost for each choice?
- If you need to assemble a cross-disciplinary team, will that substantially increase the development cost?

4. **Product Cost:** The final product cost, which includes the material, manufacturing, and development costs per unit, will be the major determinant of the product price. Therefore, it is critical to have a real estimate of the product cost at the outset. You have to take into account the cost of capital equipment, tooling, labor, as well as materials and logistics. Sometimes the choice of a single particular element can make a big difference in your costs, and therefore you have to pay attention to the detailed design. Your checklist should include the following questions:

> - How much will the product cost?
> - How do design tradeoffs affect the product cost?
> - Have you included all manufacturing and overhead costs in your estimate?
> - Will potential customers be able to buy your product at your estimated price?

Self-examination is never a pleasant exercise, but before beginning any major product development process, you must consider the issues that have been highlighted in this section. Enough resources should be committed to the new product development, and even to product marketing on a global scale. The question of risk the project entails and how the company can sustain it are both critical and unavoidable.

As we have said, to have any chance for success you must have a competitive advantage over your competition. You should examine your competitors' products, as well as their manufacturing technology, marketing, and distribution methods. And, it is especially risky, and sometimes economically fatal, to venture into areas that are not in your main area of expertise.

2.6.2 Stages of Product Development

Before proceeding with development of a product, perform market research (Section 2.2.1) to:

- Define the potential market
- Define the characteristics of the product family
- Identify competitive products
- Review available data (consumers reports, etc.) for related products
- Identify potential customers (e.g., interviewing customers, consulting experts, etc.)
- Clarify how customers will use the product and how do they benefit from using it.

The product development process has six basic stages (Figure 2.7):

Stage 1. Establish a Project Plan
Stage 2. Develop product specifications

Stage 3. Create a conceptual product design

Stage 4. Generate detailed product design

Stage 5. Build and test the prototype

Stage 6. Review and address production issues

We will elaborate on each of these stages below.

2.6.2.1 Stage 1. Project Plan Develop a detailed project plan with established subordinate goals (milestones) usually at the completion of major phases of the project's development. Stages 2–6 are based on a project plan and require a project manager (see Figure 2.4) who has to establish milestones and guarantee their accomplishment. Milestone goals are critical to keeping the project on schedule.

Milestones in the project plan may include:

- Important accomplishments and deadlines that define the project critical path
- Demonstrations and reviews
- Delivery of project sub-systems
- Payment schedule

The project manager should keep the project focused on the original goal and make the link between progress and profit clear to the project staff. Insuring the speed to market may bring higher sales early in the product life (e.g., Chrysler earned $2.4 billion from early sales of its innovative mini-van in 1984).

2.6.2.2 Stage 2. Product Specifications Translate customer requirements (such as light weight, small size, and fast performance) to engineering product specifications (such as weight in kg, size in mm, and speed in m/s). Methods, such as QFD can assist in translating the requirements to specifications.

2.6.2.3 Stage 3. Conceptual Product Design This phase is made up of three steps: (1) consider alternative concepts, (2) select the concept to be developed, and (3) develop cost models for the chosen concept.

1. **Concept Alternatives:**
   - Generate alternative concepts that achieve the desired functionality.
   - Analyze tradeoffs between values and cost.
   - Explore the perceived range of product options and product family variants.
   - Evaluate tradeoffs between product architectures: modular versus integrated.
   - Incorporate product modularity to facilitate mass customization.
   - Estimate development time and manufacturing costs for each concept.

2. **Slect the Concept to be Developed:**
   - Define major sub-systems.
   - Identify the manufacturing processes required.
   - Calculate the number of possible product variants in the product family.
   - Consider product-servicing issues (ease of part replacement, specialized tools needed for maintenance, etc.).
   - Identify key suppliers for parts (outsourcing).

3. **Cost Model:**
   - Develop a cost model that includes a rough estimate of the manufacturing cost.
   - Consider product variants switchover strategies in mass-customization manufacturing.

A Preliminary Design Review (PDR) is conducted at the end of Stage 3.

The PDR is a major milestone. Its participants should include the product development team, as well as representatives from manufacturing, marketing, and business units.

2.6.2.4 Stage 4. Detailed Product Design   The detailed product design determines the final features of the product and results in a series of detailed engineering drawings. This stage includes:

Detailed Design of the Selected Concepts:

- Define product geometry.
- Prepare engineering drawings.
- Establish cost-effective levels of customization (for mass-customized products).
- Consider design for delayed differentiation
- Perform analysis and simulation tests.
- Choose materials.
- Assign tolerances.

Bill of Materials (BOM): Develop a BOM. This is a list of all the parts needed and an estimation of their purchase price or fabrication cost.

A Critical Design Review (CDR) milestone is conducted at the end of Stage 4.

2.6.2.5 Stage 5. Prototype and Testing

- Build an experimental prototype.
- Test the performance of the prototype.
- Make design changes
- Prepare field testing program.

2.6.2.6 Stage 6. Production Preparation In this stage, you must make decisions about the type of manufacturing system that will be needed for producing the product. To do this, you must consider all the product variants and options, as well as the customization process and possible product changes indicated by the market or dictated by the designer. Once a manufacturing system has been selected, you can begin to prepare the factory for manufacturing.

The production preparation stage includes selection of the:

- **Manufacturing System:** Dedicated, flexible, reconfigurable; and the level of reconfigurability and flexibility of the equipment and tooling.
- **Material Handling System:** A conveyor, an overhead gantry, and autonomous-guided vehicle (AGV), or robots.

  Selecting the type of manufacturing system is the most important decision in Stage 6 and it impacts the:
  - Skill level of the work force; prepare a training plan.
  - Production throughput and manufacturing system economics.
  - Manufacturability of any product design changes.
  - Ease with which product design changes can be handled.

2.7 HEAD IN THE SKY, FEET ON THE GROUND—BE A DREAMER ON A SOLID FOUNDATION

Product innovation is important to the success for established and start-up companies alike. Inventing ways to improve your current products, as well as periodically introducing new ones, is a vital growth strategy in a competitive market. We have said that, although customers' input is critical, relying only on customer-driven new products is problematic because customers do not always know what they will want to buy in the future. Conversely, a product idea that is merely borrowed from, or incrementally built upon, the idea of a competitor is by definition not new. The company that is first to introduce a truly NEW product can charge the highest prices for it (the Apple iPod and iPhone, for example). And, if they have developed it properly, they will garner profit from their idea for a considerable interval while the competition is forced to develop products of their own.

What is ideal is a consumer who has some knowledge of what is required to produce a product. Therefore, the best method of getting to new and successful products is from the people at your company itself. Characteristics of a true inventor are curiosity, inspiration, and a willingness to reach out for new ideas—the dream of creating new products. But your dreams must have a technologically valid base. To create new practical realities, the dreamer's feet must be on solid ground. Turning these dreams into new products requires a rigorous and systematic approach, as the one described in Section 2.6. The challenge is to get people to think beyond their daily experience, to think "outside of the box" to "dream up" future products.

However, you have to know the boundaries of the box, its requirements and limitations, to move successfully beyond it. Your company needs a lot of common sense, but it also needs to nurture "uncommon wisdom" as well to keep a steady stream of viable new ideas coming. Many companies empower their employees to innovate or at least suggest new product ideas. Without a constant flow of ideas for new products, a company is destined to become obsolete.

Companies, and especially start-ups, should nurture sensitivity for changing needs and seize the opportunity in a timely manner. An entirely new kind of security industry was established in response to 9/11/2001. Companies quickly grabbed the opportunity and formed this new industry bringing a wide range of innovative new products. Remember, the ambitions of the start-up company should reach into the imagination (into dreamland), but its foundations must remain firmly on the ground to be realistic.

As C.D. Jackson[*] said: "Great ideas need landing gear as well as wings"

Our model of a start-up company is taken from **Jacob's Dream** in the Bible [Genesis Chapter 28; #12]: "**And he [Jacob] dreamed, and behold a ladder set up on the earth, and the top of it reached into heaven.**" Jacob's ladder is a good metaphor for innovative product development. The goal (your dream) reaches the sky. However high the ladder goes, it is based on reality and stays on a good engineering foundation.

PROBLEMS

2.1 Imagine a possible paradoxical product, describe it, and answer the five questions in Section 2.1.1 for this new product.

2.2 Can you insert totally new functions to (a) a hat and (b) a boot? See discussion in Section 2.1.2.

2.3 Can the high-tech capsule (Section 2.1.3) be defined as a disruptive technology?

---

[*]C.D. Jackson (Charles Douglas Jackson) served as Special Assistant to President Dwight D. Eisenhower.

2.4 The time is November 2001 and you are the CEO of GM. Having a limited R&D budget, you have to make a decision what percentage of your budget to invest in: (1) conventional combustion engines, (2) hybrid engines, (3) electric cars, and (4) fuel-cell technology. (Based on a true story.)

   (a) How would you divide your budget? Explain why.
   (b) If your budget allows you to invest just in two of these four technologies, which two would you chose?
   (c) Would you define hybrid, electric, and fuel cell as disruptive technologies?

2.5 In response to a new challenge—no electricity source available—the person in Figure 2.8 developed a new way to provide the functionality of a battery charger. How would you classify the invention in this picture? Is it classified as:

   A modified product that better fits the needs of people and society (class 6).

   New functions that are added to existing products (class 7).

   A new application that is achieved by defining new ways to use an existing product (class 8).

Figure 2.8   A new way to charge laptop battery.

2.6 What are the five most important inventions of Thomas Edison?

2.7 What are the five most important inventions of ancient China?

REFERENCES

1. A. Hargadon and R. Sutton. Building innovation factory. *Harvard Business Review*, May-June 2000, pp. 157–166.

2. K. Otto and W. K. Wood. *Product Design*. Prentice-Hall, London, 2001.

3. *Nature*, Vol. 405, 2000, p. 417.

4. http://www.med.umich.edu/opm/newspage/2004/camera.htm (Hi-tech capsule)

5. C. M. Christensen. *The Innovator's Dilemma*. Harvard Business School Press, Boston, 1997.

6. Y. Shan and Y. Koren. Design and motion planning of a mechanical snake. *IEEE Transactions on Systems, Man, and Cybernetics*, Vol. 23, No. 4, July/August 1993, pp. 1091–1100.

7. Y., Shan. Pass-through duodenal enteroscopic device. *US Patent* #5984860, 1999.

8. R. A. Lutz. *Gutz*. John Wiley & Sons, New York, 1998, p. 65.

9. A. Grove. *Only the Paranoid Survive*. Currency Publications, 1996.

10. K. T. Ulrich and S.D. Eppinger. *Product Design and Development*. McGraw Hill, Boston, 2000, p. 71.

Chapter **3**

Customized, Personalized and Reconfigurable Products

Central to the idea of global manufacturing is the premise that the variability of product markets is an ever-intensifying driver of industrial production and profitability. Gone are the days when a manufacturer could dictate to customers "you can have any color you want, as long as it is black." With competition now on a worldwide scale, customers can be sure to find desirable products in almost every color of the rainbow. To stay competitive, manufacturers must develop strategies for cost-effective product customization and personalization. A common strategy is to produce modular product components that can be readily assembled into customized and personalized products. Furthermore, customers often prefer a product that can be adapted to different applications when needed, or that can evolve as a child grows up. Therefore, a popular goal for consumer goods is personalized products that are also reconfigurable according to the changing needs of the customer.

The concept of reconfigurable products is not new, and it is mentioned in the bible in the context of converting weapons into agricultural tools when there will be peace on land [Isaiah, 2; 4]: "*They will beat their swords into ploughshares and their spears into pruning hooks.*"

3.1 INTRODUCTION TO CUSTOMIZATION

Mass customization started in the late 1980s when companies, faced with increased competition in the marketplace, started to look for alternatives to the mass production

The Global Manufacturing Revolution: Product-Process-Business Integration and Reconfigurable Systems
By Yoram Koren
Copyright © 2010 John Wiley & Sons, Inc.

Figure 3.1 Shopping carts.

paradigm. At first, mass production manufacturers simply added minor variations to their normal product output based on assumptions about what customers wanted and what was easy to implement. Later they began to apply information technology to better meet consumer desires. The driving force of mass customization is the consumer, and the driving enabler is information technology.

Mass customization does not mean producing one-of-a-kind products, as in the craft production era but rather to producing relatively large quantities of **varieties** of products from the same **product family** at mass production competitive cost and economies of scale. For example, shopping carts (Figure 3.1) are all of the same product family, but each supermarket chain has its own carts, and there are many variations that are produced in large quantities. Mass customization takes advantage of many if not all mass production strategies. Very personalized products (such as tooth crowns) are not suitable for mass customization production methods.

Our definition of mass customization is as follows.

Mass Customization
A paradigm in which many optional product variants, manufactured at mass production cost, are offered to customers.

The offering of a wide variety of products satisfies the needs and tastes of more customers, and expands the potential market. Producing these products at mass production costs enables manufacturers to offer them at affordable prices, increasing sales and profits.

Mass-customized products can be produced at low cost if the product design is done with the set of options and product variations in mind. The greatest opportunity for minimizing cost is in the product architecture stage. And yet this high-leverage opportunity is virtually ignored in many product development projects, when designers assume the product will have the same architecture as previous or competitive products.[1] Cost is very difficult to reduce after the product architecture and its design are completed.

A Google search for the word "*customized*" in July 2003 turned up more than **21 million** websites, and in July 2008 **42 million**. Companies from a diverse product range are all selling customized products to fit to **your** requirements, **your** taste, and **your** style, as can be seen in the examples below.

A Broad Spectrum of Products are Customized to Your Requirements

Product	Website	Website Slogan
Autos	www2.ford.com	Equipped to **your specifications**
CDs	www.cductive.com	Custom-mixed to **your taste**
Computers	www.dell.com	Configured to **your requirements**
Eyewear	www.paris-miki.com.au	Customized to fit **your face** and personality
Golf clubs	www.golftofit.com	Customized to **your body** and playing style
News lineup	customnews.cnn.com/	Matched to **your interests**
Shoes	www.digitoe.com	Fitted to a precise 3D model of **your foot**
Vitamins	www.acumins.com	Formulated to **your nutritional needs**
Greeting cards	www.americangreetings.com	Personalized with **your look** and sentiment
Shirts	www.shirtcreations.com	Tailored to **your build and taste**
Dolls	www.mytwinn.com	Designed to look like **your child**
Jeans	www.ic3d.com	Tailored to **your shape** and style
Weather forecasts	www.weather.com	Customized to **your location** or trip

Did you know that you had so many personal desires and physical attributes? And can these manufacturers really build products just for you, or will you be buying packages of options?

The definition of a product family and the architecture phase will determine how many useful options can be offered and to what extent the products can actually be personalized. This phase determines the optimal balance between modularity, variety, and cost.

Consumer goods that do fit the mass customization profile include bicycles, wheelchairs, in-line skates, scooters, watches, backpacks, certain classes of cars, office furniture, comfort chairs, kitchen cabinets, toys, rearview mirrors, computer keyboard, golf clubs, shopping carts, cosmetics, jeans, suits, boots, to name just a few.

3.2 DESIGN FOR MASS CUSTOMIZATION

On one level, mass customization may be as simple as a pair of blue jeans of the right size. That is not to say that blue jeans are simple to make, but once having developed a system for making them, customization can be as simple as manufacturing a range of sizes of the very same product. By adding this **size range**, manufacturers greatly expand the market for the same product—no one likes jeans that are too loose or that fit too tight.

At this level all the products look the same, and with the exception of the amount of material involved, they are the same. They have the same stitching, the same accessories, and more importantly they require essentially the same number of operational steps in their manufacturing.

The key to this level of customization (**Strategy 1**) is that it accommodates only one or two variations (waist size and length) based on the variety of anatomy of the customer base. Customization at this level is simple but critical to the widespread marketing of some products. The sales approach of this level of customization is a **push-type business model**—products are sent ("pushed") to the stores and the customers purchase them off the shelves with zero delivery time. Strategy 1 is actually a transition stage between mass production and mass customization.

A more sophisticated model of mass customization (**Strategy 2**) is known as the "**option package.**" Again returning to the automotive industry for an example, once the initial auto manufacturing market leveled out from its extreme supply-driven mode, designers began looking for ways to offer products that were different from the norm but not so different as to significantly alter their costs or their manufacturing schemes. Carmakers started offering sets or "packages" of options to appeal to various driving markets. There remained the "standard" option of a fully functional vehicle, but in addition, there now appeared a "sports model" and typically, a "luxury" edition as well. The sports model might offer a more powerful engine; different transmission, tires, wheels, and seats. The luxury edition attended more to comfort features such as furniture wood and metal finished interiors as well as better sound-dampened interiors and powered controls.

One of the main issues with option packages is that customers often do not get the exact features that they need. This issue was articulated by two of our students:

"My father bought a Toyota Camry in Israel. He wanted the model with a sunroof. But he had to pay also for heated seats—this is the option that Toyota offers in Israel: A Sunroof + Heated Seats. But who needs heated seats in a hot country like Israel? Why cannot Toyota create a product with features that are more precisely tuned to customer's needs?" Tamar Erlich, 2007.

"In the US auto industry selling 'option packages' is the form of mass customization. Customers are sometimes pushed to purchase items that they wouldn't normally choose. An example is the moon and tunes' package, where a deluxe stereo system is paired with a moonroof. Each of these items can be purchased separately for a higher cost than to purchase the whole package. In this case, a customer may only want one, but must choose both. So the customers aren't truly getting what they want." Cindie Niemann, 2004.

The marketing of options packages focuses more on the unique features being offered, and these may or may not actually add significant cost to the product. But options packages do add to a manufacturers menu of offerings enabling them to reach markets that they otherwise could not without creating whole new product lines. And, manufacturers are able to sell the packaged models at much higher markups to customers who want and are willing to pay for the novelty of those unique features. The computer industry (e.g., Dell Computers) offers hundreds of packages for laptops and desktop computers.

The difference between the two strategies of mass customization is significant in terms of both manufacturing and marketing. At the first level (Strategy 1) products that include all options are made and sent to the stores and dealerships for sale—a push-type business model. Products that are not sold amount to a loss of sales.

In a real mass customization (Strategy 2), all options are designed (e.g., car package options, computer packages, etc.), but only the product with the option being ordered is made. The financial transaction with the customer (i.e., the Sell phase) occurs between the product design phase and the manufacturing phase (Make), as shown in Figure 3.2. From the product design standpoint this is still a push-type business model, but from the manufacturing aspect it is a pull-type model (i.e., built-to-order). The combined design and manufacturing aspects create a **push–pull type business model**.

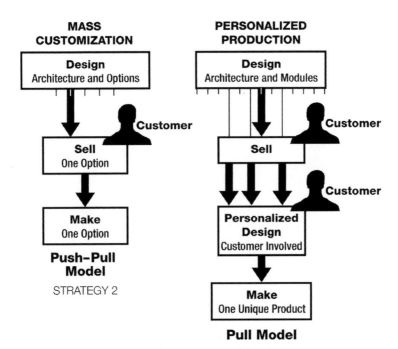

Figure 3.2 The Design–Make–Sell sequence models of mass customization and personalized production.

Offering a range of options is a significant step up in the marketing of the product, but at this stage the option packages are just that—packages. A customer cannot choose features from one package and mix them with features of other packages because it would cause significant strain on the marketing, distribution, and manufacturing systems that provide them. Most manufacturers do not or choose not to try to accommodate them, since doing so increases the complexity of their operations and reduces their profit on the product.

Over time, and as markets continue to exert pressure on manufacturers, smaller, more discrete packages of options have been made available. Some single features: climate control systems, tinted windows, window defoggers, leather interiors to name but a few, can be gotten without committing to full "luxury" packages and their exceptional pricing. As product design and manufacturing systems develop, more and more of these single options become available and simpler to install.

In fact, the ease of applying some of these options has become so simple that they are now "**dealer options.**" Dealer options are those that can be applied at the finish stages of final assembly, where auto dealers can handle simple customization projects for individual customers at the point of sale. The **point-of-delivery customization** (or **point-of-delivery personalization**) is actually the simplest level of personalized products. Our student in Australia sent us a comment about a shortcoming of this strategy.

"I live in Adelaide, Australia, where two auto-manufacturing plants are located," Steve Pratt wrote us in 2006. "In Australia, personalized production comes in the form of after-market modifications offered by a subsidiary company at a premium price. However, these modifications are still merely options offered for customers to 'personalize' their vehicles."

3.3 PERSONALIZED PRODUCTS

The evolution of mass customization has led eventually to some levels of personalization. Like mass customization, personalized production may be as simple as a pair of blue jeans, but these jeans would be of exactly the right size. With personalized production, the jeans are made exclusively for a particular customer at exactly the size that they need. A longer version of the following article, written by Rose-Marie Turk, appeared in the New York Times in the winter of 1996.

"If the Levi's Fit, will people order them?"

Would you pay an extra $10 to let a computer choose your next pair of Levi's?
And why not? The customer would get "individually tailored goods," while the manufacturer would avoid costly over-production. "You're not mass-producing product and hoping it sells. You've already got a sale," a Levi Strauss & Co. executive told the New York Times. Everyone, seemingly, would win.

> A woman who visited a selected Original Levi's Store, had her measurements fed into a computer and paid the $10 fee could have a pair of jeans custom-made for her particular body.
>
> After two months, the program's title was revised to '**personal fit**,' rather than 'custom fit.' But the "personal fit" jeans are limited to the approximately 400 samples contained in each store. A salesperson measures the customer's waist, hips, inseam and rise. She punches the information into a computer, which suggests a sample for the customer to try.
>
> If the first sample doesn't fit perfectly, the customer can indicate where she wants improvement. The salesperson then either feeds the new data into the computer or simply pulls another sample off the rack.
>
> **Even then a woman might not find her Personal Pair (the trademark name)**. "We hope to fit a lot of women, but you can't fit everyone," said Kates, the director of Original Levi's Stores.
>
> Levi's is targeting two consumer groups. The first contains "a small percentage of women who feel they never received a pair of jeans that fit," said company spokesman Sean Fitzgerald. "The second group is those women who have to have the ultimate **pair of jeans**."

With personalized production, products are cost-effectively made or assembled to fit the exact personal needs of individual customers. A very basic example is custom kitchen design; considering room shape, window location, size, and illumination, each kitchen starts out being different. A different individual customer who has his/her needs, preferences, and taste will use each kitchen—which adds another level of difference. However, kitchens are made with a technique in which customers select preferred modules from a large list of possible modules that eventually allows offering "personalized" kitchens at affordable prices.

The low-cost production of personalized products is accomplished by dividing the product design process into two phases. The first phase, which is done by the manufacturer, includes the design of the building blocks, or modules, of the product (type, function, shape, material, etc.), and the general architecture that specifies how modules will be connected, interfaced, and integrated with each other when considering three aspects: (1) mechanical (e.g., brackets, bolts, grooves, etc.), (2) power (electrical, hydraulic, water, etc.), and (3) information (sensor signals and controls).

Then the financial transaction—the sale to a customer—occurs, and the customer starts to be involved in the personalized design phase (see Figure 3.2). Based on the modules offered, the physical constraints, and the customer's body measurements and preferences, the personalized design is finalized. Only then are the modules (the cabinets and accessories, for example) manufactured and the product is assembled.

Indeed, both mass customization and personalized production are supplying products that fit the customer's needs and preferences. The basic difference between the two is that in mass customization the customer selects options packages and get what they want combined with things they may not want or need. By contrast, in personalized production **the customer is involved in the design process** and selects individual modules that once combined create a personalized product. The modular product design methodology enables the low-cost manufacturing of personalized product.

You can find the three main paradigms of manufacturing when you go to a restaurant. Fast food is basically mass-produced. In a regular restaurant, you order a particular dish from the menu — the fish comes with mashed potatoes and asparagus; this is the package. If you want to replace the asparagus with rice, it is impossible — you are experiencing "mass customization." But, if you go to a restaurant that has a large list of side-items ("modules") that can be added in any combination to the main entrée, and you decide the combination of "modules" served personally to you, you have truly experienced personalization.

"No alcohol, extra sugar, please." Rony, here is your personalized drink—just for you!

Products that are produced for personalized production may require measuring the customer at the point-of-order (e.g., in the store). One example is the Levi's personalized jeans mentioned above. Similarly, the company VSUITO (Ann Arbor, 2003) manufactured tailored suits, with 14,000 ways to personalize a suit to fit customer preferences, based on customer's seven measurements (Figure 3.3).

VSUITO developed two special measurement systems to take the needed measurements of the customer, either in stores located at targeted sale markets, or with the aid of the Internet. The customer sends the measurements to the factory online.

Another small start-up company in Ann Arbor worked to manufacture personalized backpacks based on a person's body shape and size. This required simple measurements of a few dimensions of the customer's back in the store, or supplying these measurements over the Internet.

To achieve these levels of mini-customization and personalized production, and do it cost-effectively, industry must pursue a whole new paradigm in the design and operations of manufacturing systems. Manufacturing systems must be reconfigurable and flexible enough to provide acceptable levels of response to customer's demand.

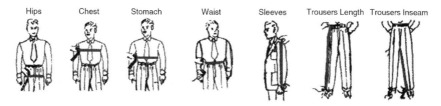

Figure 3.3 Customer's seven measurements.

3.3.1 Airplane Interior Personalization

For years the interior of airplanes have been designed with the customers (i.e., the airlines) in mind. The main modules are the passenger seats and the galleys (the kitchen on the aircraft). The airlines make decisions regarding the spacing between rows, the size of each cabin, the location of the kitchen, etc. Some airlines have special security requirements that also change the interior design. El-Al airlines for example, has a small, one-person-fit secured corridor with doors on each end between the cockpit and the passenger cabin to protect the pilots. Each airline chooses the color of the cabins. At the end of the day, the interior of the plane does not look so different from one airline to another, but still the airplane interior is designed exactly as the customer, the airline, wants it.

Our student Rachel Krueger wrote the following description of airplane personalization: "I'm working in the airline industry. In addition to the interior personalization of the plane, the exterior—the engines and almost every feature on an aircraft—is customized or personalized. Each aircraft manufacturer will offer an airframe that can be configured with up to three different engine types. The wings and nacelle casing are customized depending on the engine that is chosen. Next, the customer can determine the thrust rating that the engine has. Each engine will be rated in an engine class with a range. Each plane ordered has a purpose: Short flights, long flights, or cargo—which is a major decision-maker for the engine. Next, some of the parts installed in the engine are interchangeable depending on where the aircraft will operate. Aircraft that operate in sandy conditions, such as desert operators, require different hardware installed to account for the additional sand ingestion that will occur during each takeoff and landing."

3.3.2 Personalized and Reconfigurable Displays for Automobiles

Future automobiles will have reconfigurable digital displays, which can be configured by the driver, thereby making them personal. The driver will be able to select the information to be shown on the display, such as the fuel tank level, speed, navigation instructions, various warnings, etc. It will be possible for cars to recognize a driver's display preferences based on their individual keys or fingerprints and automatically adjust according to those parameters. These parameters depend on the recorded driving style of the individual, and his/her preferences (e.g., voice instructions or visual displays).

The operation of these displays will be based on software with embedded intelligence that contains information about the individual's driving habits, age, and desires. For example, a car could have sensors measuring the distance to the vehicles in front and back, and suggest when to break safely (by voice or displayed warnings). The distances from the cars in front and back that evoke the warning signal could be adjustable by the driver, but perhaps be fine-tuned based on the car's speed, the driver's age, and accumulated data about their breaking habits. This intelligent system might also sense (by using fuzzy-logic algorithms) whether the driver is tired (for example, based on the driver's reaction time) and adjust the warning signals accordingly.

3.3.3 Vehicle Personalization at Ford Motor Company

In 1999, Ford Motor Company began "Vehicle Personalization" on their products. Ford's Mass Customization Department runs the vehicle personalization program. This indicates some confusion in industry between the two terms. By our definition, Ford's personalized vehicles are actually mass-customized vehicles that are more differentiated than other Ford vehicles. Vehicles involved in Ford's 2002 vehicle personalization program included the Mondeo, Focus, and Mustang. Ford utilized their assembly plants or "modification centers" next to the plants to install "packages" of unique trim and accessories. Examples of personalization features on these Ford vehicles were unique interior and exterior color as well as trim, body styling, in-car entertainment systems, and special paint. In 2002, Ford's personalized vehicle order-to-delivery time was between 3 and 6 months!

At that time, Ford also offered "personalization by dealer installation," which included: luggage racks, rear window, spoilers, remote start, fog lamps, projector beam headlamps, rocker panel molding, front and rear bumper balance, hitch mount bike rack, hands-free cell phone, rear seat TV, and wheels and tires.

Below is an excerpt of a speech that was delivered by Ms. Christine Feuell, Manager of Ford Vehicle Personalization, at the 40th annual Specialty Equipment Market Association (SEMA) show in October 2006.[2]

"Ford's Vehicle Personalization business is growing faster ... as customers demand more choice. Truck owners are some of the biggest customizers. Seventy percent of them personalize their vehicles within a year of purchase, spending an average of more than $1500. Last year, we introduced a mobile office concept for Ford trucks. Based on the great reception it received, it is now on sale across the country.

People are turned on by what looks cool and different, and if they can make their vehicles look different even by just changing a headlamp or putting on a different grille, then it's a pretty cost-effective way to make their vehicle more theirs. **And that's really what personalization is all about.**"

3.3.4 Personalization of Vehicle Interior

We predict that, by 2020, customers will be offered the opportunity to design the interior of their new cars in Europe and the United States in a way similar to that of airplanes. This will be an alternative to buying conventional options packages. There will be a set of modules (e.g., different car seats, storage, entertainment equipment, microwaves, small refrigerators, cloth hangers, armchairs, etc.) that the customers could select from and compose according to their preferences, subject to safety and manufacturing constraints. As a result, the interior of cars of the exact same model will look very different from one another.

Figure 3.4 A design of car interior.

The requirements of a parent, with two small children sitting in the back of the car, driving in the city are different than those of salesperson going on long trips and who would like a small fridge within reach. An elderly person, who usually sits in the back, may prefer a more comfortable seat in place of a three-passenger bench. A short person would like a different instrument panel arrangement (selected from a set of given modules) from a tall one that can reach further. Some people may prefer to have a car seat with a folding shelf, like in airplanes, so they can work with a laptop during long trips while somebody else is driving.

The interior of the car will be an open space. The customers will look at a computer monitor and design the interior of their car (see an example in Figure 3.4). The input will be some physical dimensions, such as the length of the hand and the driver's effective reach. The computer will show the virtual interior space, and lead the customer through a step-by-step selection of desired modules from a given database (seats, computer monitors, cabinets, dog baskets, exercise equipment, etc.).

Similar to the software and open computer architecture that allows adding and swapping components on PCs, car manufacturers will develop an open architecture platform for auto interior (e.g., installing rails to which components can be safely attached and defining the space between bolts where modules may be attached). The open architecture platform will define the mechanical, electrical and information interfaces for compatibility of modules. The car manufacturer will also

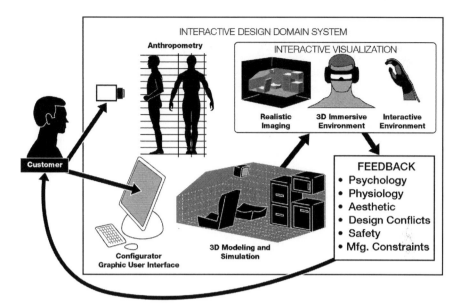

Figure 3.5 A interactive design system to assist in interior module arrangement.

create the module database and a set of allowed usage constraints. These constraints are of three types: safety (such as unsafe seat position), design conflicts that may be either functional (such as not enough electric power to support combination of devices), or geometry (such as not enough leg room), as well as manufacturing constraints.

In addition to established auto suppliers, numerous new small companies will invent and supply modules designed to be compatible with the open automobile platform. The interior integration will be done by the original car manufacturer or by licensed module installer.

Customers will be able to design the interior of their cars with the aid of a new Interactive Design System (IDS), as depicted in Figure 3.5.[3] The IDS will allow a customer to design the interior of their automobile before purchasing it, such that it is tailored exactly to the buyer's personal preferences, yet conforms to predefined safety and vehicular constraints.

The IDS will allow customers to select a car model and its displayed interior space. The customers will generate their personalized car design by selecting components from the database and placing them around the interior of the automobile in a preferred location and arrangement. A fit to the buyer's physical attributes is also tested (physiology feedback).

The buyer will be able to view the results in both stationary and in simulated motion environments (virtual reality). This design process is repeated until the buyer's final approval is achieved. The final design is then stored digitally and sent to the manufacturer where it is used to assemble the vehicle.

At first, the interiors of each person's ideal vehicle may not look much different from one to the next but as the culture changes and people become accustomed to the idea, difference may vary in surprising ways. In either case, the customers will have the perception they have designed their own vehicles. Perception counts, and will be a driver for the sale of personalized products.

Society's perception of automobiles will be revolutionized. The automobile's interior will be able to change to fit the customer's evolving life style. For example when the customer's children grow up, they may swap modules to fit their new transportation needs. Replacing a car seat with a small fridge for long trips in hot days may become the norm instead of a fantasy. And trading of used cars will be partially replaced by trading used modules on e-Bay.

We can vividly see how the car interior design will create whole new industries of module producers, module installers, and module trading markets. Because the car delivery time must be short (transshipment alone takes months by containership), the final assembly will probably always be done in proximity to the sale location, no matter what the prices of cars produced overseas. This will, therefore, create new domestic jobs.

To summarize, trends in the interior design of the auto industry will be towards:

- **Products tailored exactly to customer needs and preferences**
- **Open-ended products that can be reconfigurable by users**

3.3.5 Personalized Shoes

Paradigm shifts are also taking place in industries that produce less complex products. Take, for example, the shoe and footwear industry. The shoe industry has gone through the same market history as other products: from a work-of-art manufacturing model—all hand-made—to machine-aided and mass production in the 1960s.

Because shoe manufacturing still requires a high degree of handwork, particularly in the final assembly, the mass production paradigm that existed in this industry until the 1980s pushed a de-localization of shoe manufacturing to low-wage countries.

In order to protect their world market position, by the middle of the 1990s the Italian shoe industry has developed production systems composed of innovative machines with increased flexibility that could produce small lot sizes, but with limited product variety that still did not attract wealthier customers.

By the late 1990s, the personalization paradigm started to take hold of the Italian shoe industry. Developing the knowledge-embedded software that enabled to design shoes for consumers' individual needs became the center of the footwear sector's research activities. Highly flexible and reconfigurable machines and production systems were also developed at this time.[*4]

---

[*]Personalized shoes are made according to the very specific shape of the customer's feet. The customer's feet are first scanned digitally for measurements using a laser optical scanner. Based on the scans, 3-D models of the customer's feet are constructed, and utilized to produce the personalized shoes.

Figure 3.6   Personalized shoes.

As a result, Senora DaVinci can go today to an experimental shoe factory at Vigevano, Italy, to buy a pair of personalized shoes. The weight of her foot is measured while standing, as well as her foot dimensions. She selects the color, style, and material from a variety of options. Within a couple of hours her personalized fitted shoes are ready (Figure 3.6). This short turnaround time, from personalized order to delivery, is a competitive advantage that will return portions of the shoe industry from the Far East back to Italy.

A schematic layout of the personalized shoe factory in Vigevano is shown in Figure 3.7. It shows the part flow and return paths of the production system. A square box represents each machine (three to five machines around each index table). The curved line shows the shoe-making path through the factory. The shoes are delivered to Senora DaVinci, and the shoe fixtures are returned to the warehouse through the "return path."

3.3.6 Mr. Johnson Needs This Fridge

How might refrigerators be ordered in the personalized production paradigm? We made a small survey among married men, and 80% of them wanted to see swivel, "Lazy-Susan" type shelves in their refrigerators, so they could reach the stuff behind the milk. Why not design the inside architecture of refrigerators according to the customer's need?

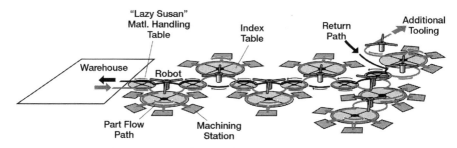

Figure 3.7   A schematic layout of a shoe factory.

Imagine the following scenario: The customer, Mr. Johnson, comes to the store to buy a new fridge. He selects the refrigerator volume (cubic ft), and then looks at a computer monitor to design the interior of his fridge. The computer shows him a virtual reality image of the interior compartment of the model that he has just selected. Within the given interior compartment, Mr. Johnson can specify: the spacing between shelves and their width, the size and shape of the container bins on the door, the location of the egg box, the number of drawers and shelves, and the Lazy-Susan carousel diameter (Figure 3.8).

Now the computer displays a virtual image of his new fridge with the eggs in their special chamber, some fruit, and a few beer bottles and a jug of milk on the Lazy-Susan shelf. Mr. Johnson is able to "rotate" the Lazy Susan and find his beer behind the milk (although he will not be able to drink the virtual beer). He can even change the location of the door shelves and adapt them to his particular needs. A week later, Mr. Johnson's new personalized fridge is delivered to his home from a plant that began working on his order as soon as he placed it.

3.3.7 Personalized Medicines

In fact, the personalized production model will extend beyond mere consumer products to whole regimes of human behavior. For instance, a recent customization

Figure 3.8   Personalized refrigerator.

trend is to produce customized pharmaceutical products. Researchers have discovered therapeutic advantages in customizing medicinal formulas or food supplement compositions so that they are tailored to each individual patient. An article by Samantha Levine titled "Tailor-made Treatments" (U.S. News & World Report, November 16, 2002) elaborates on the applied research that aimed at solving the problems that women suffer at menopause.

Menopause, the article says, "has at least 32 million ways to experience it. That is how many women in the United States are between the ages of 45 and 64—the years when, for most women, menopause becomes keenly felt. In every one of these people, the nagging issues associated with menopause vary." A woman may suffer from a severe hot flash or a mild flush. A woman's night sweats may keep her awake. A woman may forget her ATM password. And other women may develop heart disease. Despite the wide spectrum of symptoms and risks, the traditional therapy has been to reach for one prescription—Prempro, a standard, two-hormone pill. Today, the article says, the medical community is changing its thinking. The main conclusion of the article is:

One-size-fits-all therapy is not working for menopause-related problems.

Individualized care must be the new treatment trend.

Since early 2004, the FDA has begun to support the principles of personalized medicine. The era of blockbuster drugs that can generate annual sales of $1 billion or more are almost over. "Large pharmaceutical companies have little choice but to change. Those that stick with blockbuster models face a future of declining sales and profits."[5] However, there is a major gap between knowing the optimal medical composition in a personalized pill and the manufacturing of individual pills at affordable price. A major challenge that the pharmaceutical industry is facing is how to cost-effectively manufacture individual pills. As always, the product design challenge and its cost-effective manufacturing challenge must be addressed simultaneously.

3.4   PRODUCT MODULARITY

Product modularity is an enabler of customizable products that is the core of mass customization and personalized production. Modularity arises from the division of a product into modules or components. The utilization of standardized modules to assemble different products allows a company to create product variety at lower cost. The design of modular architecture follows principles that enable the low-cost manufacturing of products.

3.4.1   Product Architecture

Any product design study should start with an analysis of the product architecture, which is defined as follows:

> **The architecture of a product is the scheme by which the physical elements interact to achieve the desired operations and performance.**

The physical elements are the architectural building blocks of the product. The two common types of product architectures are:

1. **Integral Architecture:** The product functions are all contained in **a single structure**, or in a very small number of physical units, each implementing multiple functions, with rigid connections among units, such that **the boundaries between the units are not distinguishable**. That means that each physical unit, or element, performs a large number of functions. Integral product architectures are cost-effective for very high volume products, where the cost of the product can be reduced by economies of scale.
2. **Modular Architecture:** The product consists of interchangeable elements, or modules, to create and/or alter product functions, where each module implements one or only a few functions. The interfaces between modules are well defined and simple. Interfaces may be mechanical, hydraulic, electrical, information, and control signals.

For example, if the engine and transmission of an automobile powertrain system were implemented as a single physical unit (as is done in many motorcycles), then the powertrain architecture would be an integral architecture.[6] Another example of a modular architecture is a computer, display, and keyboard that are sold as separate components. An integral architecture exists in laptops, in which the keyboard, display, and computer are integrated into a single unit.

Modular architectures are typically more complex and expensive than integrated architectures, but they enable mass customization and personalized production as well as product upgrade, and ease of reuse. The manufacturer of mass-customized products should invest in developing versatile modules and components to be utilized in many products. The distinctive characteristic of a modular architecture is the well-defined interactions and interfaces between the modules that enable the rapid integration of the product. We call this characteristic **Integrability**.

3.4.2 Principles of Design-for-Modularity

The components from which modular products (that belong to the same product family) are composed may be categorized as either differentiating components or base components.

Base components: are those generic parts that provide function or structure without differentiating or influencing the product's uniqueness (special functions, quality, etc.).

Differentiating components: are specifically designed for the product and directly contribute to the product's performance, features, safety, esthetic appeal, or reliability.

A product platform: consists of the base components common to the whole product family.

A product variant: incorporates the product platform with a selected set of differentiating components (also called instances).[7]

Three principles guide the Design-for-Modularity:

1. *Similarity between physical and functional elements*
   The functionally of a product can be described as a collection of functional elements linked together by exchange of signals, power, or mechanism. In a good modular architecture, the physical elements and the functions correspond, and are often the mirror image of each other. An ideal modular design embodies a one-to-one correspondence between each physical component and a functional element.
2. *Minimization of the interactions between physical modules*
   To the highest degree possible, the functional elements of modules should remain inside the module. The designer should minimize the functional interactions between physical modules and limit them to only those interactions that are critical to the function of the whole product. Applying this principle reduces the number of interfaces and facilitates the product as a whole. The reduction in interfaces should apply to all three types of interfaces: mechanical, power, and communications.
3. *Maximize the number of base components shared across the product family*
   Maximizing the number of base components that are shared across the product family reduces the production cost. However, an abundance of standard components can make differentiating between variants difficult, even if they are meant to appeal to different groups of consumers. In other words, the designer should pay attention to avoid excessive product similarity (with too

many base components). It is therefore advisable that the differentiating components be those most visible to the consumer.[8]

3.4.3 Design of a Product Family with Modular Architecture

To reduce the overall cost (R&D, engineering, and manufacturing), each manufacturer has to strike the balance between maximizing component commonality while maintaining the right level of differentiation between product variants. The design of a product family requires (1) the determination of the product's platform, i.e., the base components of the product family, (2) the formulation of product variants that consist of base modules and differentiating modules, and (3) the economic selection of product variants that will be produced. We elaborate below on these three requirements.

1. Product platform design involves a balance between a high degree of component commonality and a sufficient performance differentiation among the product variants of the product family. An iterative procedure in which base modules are defined and the performance of individual product variants are measured against the targets for each market segment may be used to determine the optimal product platform. The product commonality index (PCI)[9] measures the degree of component commonality in the product family.

$$\text{PCI} = 1 - \frac{u - \max p_j}{\sum_{j=1}^{v_n} p_j - \max p_j} \qquad (3.1)$$

   where u is the number of unique parts, p_j is the number of parts in product variant j, and v_n is the final number of product variants offered.

2. Product variants are derived from the product's platform and at least one alternative (called an instance) of each differentiating component. Figure 3.9 shows the product family architecture of an office chair and two product variants that can be achieved from this architecture. As shown in the product family architecture, the differentiating components are the arms, wheels, and lumbar support. The remaining components constitute the office chair's product platform. Each differentiating component shown has two alternatives, to include or not include the differentiating component. One possible product variant of the office chair would have arms and wheels but no lumbar, while the other product variant has a lumbar but no arms or wheels. In general, if a product architecture has n differentiating modules and each differentiating module has d_i alternatives (instances), the total number of possible product variants (v_n) is computed by:

$$v_n = \prod_{i=1}^{n} d_i \qquad (3.2)$$

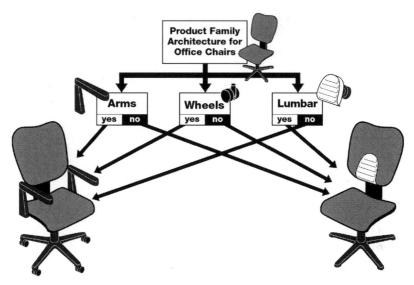

Figure 3.9   Product family architecture and two possible product variants of an office chair.

3. The selection of product variants is the final step in the design of a product family. This selection of product variants is critical for determining the profitability of the product family. By increasing the number of product variants, a manufacturer may increase the product family's sales. However, an increase in the number of product variants also leads to increased production costs. Therefore, a manufacturer must employ strategies to determine which combination of product variants would lead to optimal product family profits.[10]

Maximizing the number of base components that are shared across the same family, but still providing unique functions to each variant, impacts the ability of companies to offer product variety at low cost. S. Kota et al. conducted research that studied the product family design of Walkman®-type cassette players.[11] A relevant example of this study is depicted in Figure 3.10. In Sony EX122, a single flexible guide is present at the lower left-hand portion of the component, whereas two such guides are present in FX321. This minor difference, which can be added easily in the assembly process, adds a new function—auto-reverse—in the FX321, whereas the EX122 has just auto-stop.

Example: *A manufacturer wishes to produce a family of disposable cameras, and to capture the greatest possible market share. Every variant of the product family (the product's platform) must have **five** base components: (1) an interior body, (2) a six-part shutter mechanism, (3) inner lens, (4) outer lens, and (5) camshaft.

---

*Dr. April Bryan (the author's former Ph. D. student) wrote this example and its solution.

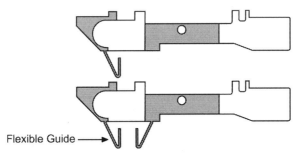

Flexible Guide

Figure 3.10 Single and double flexible guides employed to serve different functions in Sony EX122 (top) and FX321 (bottom) models.

There are **six** differentiating components:

1. Three different versions of front and back covers, which are offered as a combination.
2. Two different film holder/advance mechanisms (six parts in each).
3. Three different lens holders.
4. Two different viewfinders.
5. A washer.
6. A circuit board and battery for the flash.

Each camera must have either a washer, or a circuit board and battery. Cameras with the washer also have the front and back exterior covers and outer film advance. These latter components are not in the cameras with the circuit board and battery.

(a) What is the maximum possible number of product variants that the manufacturer can offer in the disposable camera product family?

(b) The manufacturer selects **three** variants of disposable cameras for the product family. One of these variants will be used in water. The camera that will be used in water has the washer, the outer film advance, and the front and back exterior covers. The other two variants do not have these components. The water camera also has a different version of the viewfinder than the other two cameras. The camera that will be used in water and one other camera have the same film holder/advance mechanism. Each camera has a unique lens holder and front and back cover. **Calculate the CPI**.

Solution

Let us start by arranging the various alternatives in a tabular format.

Module #	Base Components	Number of Alternatives
1	Interior body	1
2	Shutter mechanism	1
3	Inner lens	1
4	Outer lens	1
5	Camshaft	1
	Differentiating Components	
1	Front cover and back cover	$d_1 = 3$
2	Film holder/advance mechanisms	$d_2 = 2$
3	Lens holder	$d_3 = 3$
4	Viewfinder	$d_4 = 2$
5	Circuit board with battery	$d_5 = 2$
6	Washer	
	Front and back exterior cover	
	Outer film advance	$d_6 = 2$

a. Using $v_6 = (d_1 \times d_2 \times d_3 \times d_4 \times d_5 \times d_6)/d_6 = $ **72**. There are 72 possible variants.

b.

Sub-assembly/ Components	Number of Alternatives	Number of parts/ Components	Total Number of Unique Components
Front cover	3	1	3
Back cover	3	1	3
Film holder/advance Mechanism	2	6	12
Lens holder	3	1	3
Viewfinder	2	1	2
Circuit board	1	1	1
Battery	1	1	1
Front exterior cover	1	1	1
Back exterior cover	1	1	1
Washer	1	1	1
Outer film advance	1	1	1
Interior body	1	1	1
Shutter mechanism	1	6	6
Inner lens	1	1	1
Outer lens	1	1	1
Camshaft	1	1	1

Summarizing the total of the right column yields the number of unique components—**39**.

3.4.3.1 Camera Variant 1   Components: Base components, washer, outer film advance, front exterior cover, back exterior cover, viewfinder (instance 1), film holder/advance mechanism (instance 1), front cover (instance 1), back cover (instance 1), lens holder (instance 1).

$$\text{Number of Components } (p_1) = 24$$

3.4.3.2 Camera Variant 2   Components: Base components, circuit board, battery, viewfinder (instance 2), film holder/advance mechanism (instance 1), front cover (instance 2), back cover (instance 2), lens holder (instance 2).

$$\text{Number of Components } (p_2) = 22$$

3.4.3.3 Camera Variant 3   Components: Base components, circuit board, battery, viewfinder (instance 2), film holder/advance mechanism (instance 2), front cover (instance 3), back cover (instance 3), lens holder (instance 3).

$$\text{Number of Components } (p_3) = 22.$$

$\Sigma p_j = 24 + 22 + 22 = 68$ $\max p_j = 24$ Number of unique components: $u = 39$.

$$\textbf{The commonality index:} \quad \text{C.I.} = 1 - \frac{u - \max(p_j)}{\sum\limits_{j=1}^{v_n} p_j - \max(p_j)} = 1 - \frac{39 - 24}{68 - 24} = 0.66$$

where u is the number of unique components, which is 39 in this example; p_j is the number of components in product variant j; v_n is the final number of product variants offered, which is 3 in this case; note that $24 + 22 + 22 = 68$.

3.4.4 Benefits and Drawbacks of Product Modularity

Product modularity requires developing product platform architecture on which the modular products can be built. A modular architecture may also be built on a bus (similar to computer interfaces) to which different components are attached, depending on the desired functionality of the product. Modularity requires interfaces, which make the product more expensive (especially the mechanical interfaces). Additional cost is associated with testing the product integration at assembly.[12] By contrast, integral design is less expensive, since there is no need for interfaces, but an integral design reduces the possible variety of products in the family.

On the other hand, product modularity offers value by providing a broader range of products. Value can be gained, for example, by designing products that can be customized to fit various population sectors or different regional cultures, and still be manufactured at low cost. Modularity offers the option of building reconfigurable products, which may add value to an enterprise. Still, modularity may be more expensive, and, in some cases, even delay the product's time to market.

We summarize below several benefits and drawbacks of product modular architecture.

3.4.4.1 Benefits of Modularity

1. **Design for globalization:** Different market segments around the globe have different requirements, and modularity enables companies to offer products tailored to the target market. This is especially important in globalization where target markets are in different countries. Modularity enables providing products that fit a region or a particular culture at short leadtime and reasonable price.

2. **Design for variety:** Even when considering the same particular market, offering product variety is adding value. Different consumers have different tastes and modularity allows tailoring product options to customer's needs and price range. Modularity supports the concepts of mass customization and personalization.

3. **Reconfigurable products:** Product modularity enables offering reconfigurable products. Modularity also allows a reconfigurable product to be designed for upgrading.

4. **Component economies of scale:** When applying modularity, the same basic components are used across different products of the family. When a component is used in many product lines, its production volume is higher than if a component is designed just for a particular product.

5. **Differential consumption:** Not all components have the same lifetime. Modular design enables upgrading some of the components, without having to change out the whole product.

6. **Ease of product diagnosis, maintenance, service, and repair:** Modularity simplifies problem identification and repair.

7. **Decoupling the design tasks:** The design of the modules can be done simultaneously, thereby reducing the time to market.

8. **Response to markets:** A modular structure allows a firm to respond quickly to changes in product design and to rapidly integrate new technology.

9. **Rapid product changes:** Product changes can be made without affecting the entire design. A functional change can be achieved with minimal physical change to the product.

3.4.4.2 Drawbacks of Modularity

1. **Ease of reverse engineering:** By making different components, it is more vulnerable to copy a modular product.

2. **Increased product costs:** The interfaces add intrinsic costs in material and detail design time, as well as the testing for integration of modules.

3. **Excessive product similarity:** Modularity may make products in the family look too similar.

3.5 RECONFIGURABLE PRODUCTS

Reconfigurable products can alter their shape during their lifetime to adapt to new applications, additional emerging needs, and changing customer preferences. A well-known biblical example of product reconfiguration is: "*They will beat their swords into ploughshares and their spears into pruning hooks.*" However, the test for a truly reconfigurable product is whether one can also change that pruning hook back into a spear at will, and how easily it is accomplished.

Product **modularity** is a sufficient, but not necessary condition to create reconfigurable products. Reconfigurable products must be **convertible** from one shape to another (see example in Figure 3.11), and/or **scalable** from one size to another (bigger or smaller). For example, reconfigurable children bicycles could be adapted (i.e., scaled) to the child's height. A reconfigurable chair may be placed upside down and modified to become a stepladder. Well-designed reconfigurable products are easily modifiable by the end-user, the customer. Such products can be reconfigured over and over as the end-user sees fit.

Another familiar example is the rear automobile seat. For years, automobile seats have been made that could be repositioned to allow easier access from one part of the passenger compartment to another. Then, an innovation was introduced, particularly in hatchback style cars; where a rear seat back could be folded down to provide a flat surface to increase cargo space. And when the user again needed more seating, the seat back could be returned with minimal effort. The earlier seat back function was merely repositionable, since the seat was still a seat. The innovation changed the seat into

Figure 3.11　A reconfigurable chair is modified to become a stepladder.

Figure 3.12   Reconfigurable tricycles (http://www.fisherprice.com/).

something else entirely. The car seat has become reconfigurable into two modes: an extended deck for storing cargo and an equally usable rear passenger seat.

What if a car seat could be completely removed to make space for customer-specified accessories, such as a mini-desk, small fridge, dog basket, etc.? If such an accessory is not attached correctly, it will become dangerous during a collision or even a severe braking event, and could lead to a serious injury. The legal implications in cases like that could be significant for a product manufacturer. Nevertheless, similar debates about legal consequences happened before air bags became a standard accessory in vehicles. Similarly, we believe that vehicle interior reconfigurability will become a reality in the near future, despite possible legal consequences, because the market will demand it.

Since the turn of the last century, a broad range of reconfigurable products have appeared on the market, from furniture to toys that can be reconfigured from robots to racecars and back again. One more recent example of a reconfigurable product—the reconfigurable tricycles—is shown in Figure 3.12.[*]

The reconfigurable tricycles product has three possible configurations. First, the base is locked under the unit for rocking fun by very young toddlers, as (shown at left)—this is Position 1. As the child grows, the tricycle can be reconfigured to Position 2—the rocking base is converted to a long push handle so an adult can stroll behind while the child learns to pedal. When the kids are ready to ride on their own, the handle is removed completely and the seat is adjusted to their height, so they can reach the foot peddles (Position 3). This is a reconfigurable product that demonstrates three core characteristics:

- Modular
- Integratable
- Convertible

How about having these characteristics in automobiles, so that customers are able to change their vehicle according to their needs? The invention of the automobile significantly changed our lives in the first part of the twentieth century. But how

[*]This photo was taken from a sales magazine in 2001.

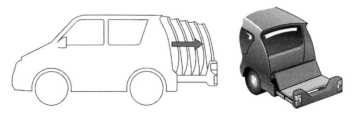

Figure 3.13   Reconfigurable automobile cargo (artist Rod Hill).

little the sedan style has changed over the past 50 years. Why are not there reconfigurable add-on trunks offered for cars? A trunk that is shorter and allows for easier parking in a crowded city, where parallel parking is a necessity, can be made longer for a luggage/storage space when going on vacation or shopping (Figure 3.13).

Why cannot we see more reconfiguration in back seats? How about seats that can be arranged for comfortable conversation? And how about the front passenger seat? Can it be built with a tray (as in airplanes)? How about reconfiguring the passenger seat into a convenient bed for long trips, or made so that it can invert into a rear-facing seat to join in the conversation with passengers sitting in the back of the car?

3.6   DESIGN OF CUSTOMIZED AND RECONFIGURABLE PRODUCTS

Customized and reconfigurable products have basic features in common.

1. Both are defined around product families
2. Both obey a set of design principles that fit this product category
3. Both share a set of core characteristics

3.6.1   Product Families

Fundamental to the mass customization paradigm is the concept of part families and product families. From a manufacturing point of view, any parts that serve a similar function within a comparable range of sizes and made from the same sort of materials using the same methods belong to a **part family**. Conceptually, all customized finished products with similar form and function belong to a **product family**. All products from the same family possess the same basic functionality, and play essentially the same product role. A basic office chair, for example, must have a seat and legs, although some members of the product family may have armrests and wheels, as depicted in Figure 3.14.

The concept of a part or product family is essential for mass customization and personalization. The rationale is double fold. First, it is less expensive to design variety into a product family by using the principles of modularity, and second, if the production is done on a manufacturing system that is designed to produce a part family, or a product family, the production cost is much less expensive and similar to that of mass production.

Figure 3.14   A product family of office chairs.

The reconfigurable manufacturing systems that will be discussed later in the book are designed to produce product families or part families, and thereby become important enablers to reduce manufacturing costs in mass customization and personalization.

Similar to the base and differentiating components of modularization, when designing and identifying members of a part/product family one should distinguish between two basic groups of features:

Core family features: define the functions that are required in all products within a part/product family, and thus define the family.

Augmenting features: help to satisfy different market needs and are *not* essential for defining membership in the part/product family.

3.6.2 Design Principles for Customized Products

Both customized and reconfigurable products must obey a set of basic design principles:

- **Core functionality must remain unchanged across all products within a family:** The core functionality and features define the product family. If that core functionality is missing, it is a different product. Note that a Walkman that does not have resistance to vibration cannot serve its main mission.

- **Minimize non-value-added variations across variants within a product family:** Non-value-added variation does not actually extend the range of products offered. It amounts to a marketing trick to attract customers. Product variety should benefit the customer, and adding unimportant variety that confuses the customer can reduce sales.

- **Key design characteristics must be embedded in the product architecture:** Basic design features that enable cost-effective production of customized, personalized, and reconfigurable products must appear in all members of the product family.

3.6.3 Core Characteristics of Customized and Reconfigurable Products

There is a set of six product characteristics that make a product suitable for mass customization, personalization, and reconfiguration.

Modularity	Product modularity enables the change of product shape to fit various customers and utilizations
Integrability	Integrability refers to defined module interfaces (mechanical, electrical, and information) for ease of product reconfiguration and customization
Customization	Customization provides customers with just the product functions they need, and not features that they will not use
Convertibility	Convertibility enables products to be changed to fulfill various utilizations of the same product
Scalability	Scalability allows a product to be scaled up or down to fit to the user's body or applications
Diagnosibility	Diagnosibility means that a product is designed with embedded diagnostic functions, for easy service and maintenance

The table below and Figure 3.9 show the key characteristics that should be embedded in customized and reconfigurable products.

Product Type	Modularity	Integrability	Customization	Convertibility	Scalability	Diagnosability
Customized	v	v	v			v
Reconfigurable	v	v		v	v	

When implementing the characteristics, the designer should distinguish between necessary and sufficient conditions. Modularity is a necessary condition to achieve variety within families of customized and personalized products. Product modularity is not, however, a necessary condition for creating reconfigurable products, although it is sufficient to achieve product reconfiguration (e.g., lego).

With the characteristics of modularity, integrability, convertibility, and scalability, reconfigurable products can be designed for easy modification as the customer's needs change over time. The characteristics of convertibility and scalability (with a child's age and development) are demonstrated in the reconfigurable tricycle depicted in Figure 3.15.

Customized products can be designed with cost-effective variety by embedding the characteristics of modularity, integrability, and customization. Diagnosibility is needed in more complex products, such as cars.

The example of the customized digital camera in Chapter 2 describes the dilemma of implementing customization: "You interview a thousand people, and each one says

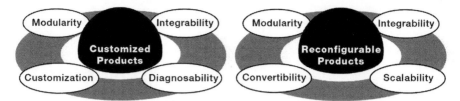

Figure 3.15 Successfully reconfigurable and customized products possess a set of key characteristics.

'I want 10 general features plus this one specific feature'. So you build a device with 1010 features. But no one wants 1010 features." [USNWR 1/15/2001]. On the other hand, it is not economical for a manufacturer to offer 1000 product variants (models), each with 11 features. Therefore, the manufacturer has two choices: (1) offer several variants, each with a package of features (options) or (2) offer personalized products, in which camera platforms, with basic features, are produced first, and special features are offered later, to be installed when the product is ordered and paid for (see delayed differentiation in Chapters 6 and 11).

PROBLEMS

3.1 A family of toy cars is built from six different modules. Three of the modules are the same in every variant of the toy car. Two of the remaining modules have three alternatives (i.e., instances). The remaining sixth module is optional.

(a) What is the maximum number of possible product variants in this product family?

(b) What is the product commonality index (PCI)?

3.2 A product family consists of four product variants. All of the differentiating modules have two instances. Exactly one instance of each differentiating

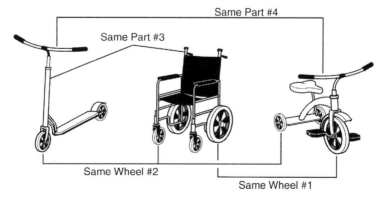

Figure 3.16 Three products with some similar components.

module must be in every product variant. How many base modules are in the product family if the product commonality index is 0.944?

3.3 Figure 3.16 shows three products: a scooter, a wheelchair, and a tricycle. A manufacturer defines them as a product family, and would like to produce all three products.

(a) Make a list of parts (components) needed in each product. In addition to the four parts that are marked, which parts may be identical (common) in at least two products?

(b) Calculate the product commonality index.

(c) Suggest modifications in these products that increase the number of common components that are non-differentiating (e.g., wheel chair seat and tricycle seat are differentiating and they are supposed to be different).

3.4 Suggest product modifications aimed at making the tricycles reconfigured to scooters as the child grow.

REFERENCES

1. D. Anderson. *Agile Product Development for Mass Customization*. Irwin, Chicago, 1997.

2. http://www.conceptcarz.com/vehicle/z12589/default.aspx.

3. Y. Koren, J. Barhak, and Z. Pasek. Interior Design of Automobiles, *US patent pending*.

4. C.R. Boër and F. Jovane. Towards a new model of sustainable production: manuFuturing. *Annals of the CIRP*, Vol. 45, No. 1, 1996.

5. M. A. Aspinall and R. A. Hamermesh.Realizing the promise of personalized medicine. *Harvard Business Review*, October 2007, pp. 109–117.

6. K. Ulrich and K. Tung. Fundamental of product modularity. *Proceedings of ASME Annual Meeting Symposium on Issues in Design/Manufacturing Integration*, Atlanta, 1991.

7. M. V. Martin and K. Ishii. Design for variety: development of complexity indices and design charts. *Proceedings of the ASME Design Engineering Technical Conferences*, Sacramento, CA, September 1997.

8. S. Kota. Managing variety in product families through design for commonality. *Proceedings of ASME Design Engineering Technical Conference*, Atlanta, GA, September 1998.

9. S. Kota, K. Sethuraman, and R. Miller. A metric for evaluating design commonality in product families. *ASME Transactions Journal of Mechanical Design*, December 2000, Vol. **122**, pp. 403–410. (The paper introduces the PCI definition.)

10. A. Bryan, S. J. Hu, and Y. Koren. Concurrent design of product families and assembly systems. *Proceedings of ASME International Manufacturing and Science Engineering Conference*, Atlanta, GA, October 2007, pp. 803–813.

11. S. Kota, K. Sthuraman, and R. Miller. A metric for evaluating design commonality in product families. *ASME Journal of Mechanical Design*, December 2000, Vol. **122**, pp. 403–410.

12. C.Y. Baldwin and K.B. Clark. Modularity-in-design: an analysis based on the theory of real options. *Harvard Business Review*, September–October 1994.

Chapter 4

Mass Production and Lean Manufacturing

Mr. Henry Ford's desire to make his "Model-T" affordable to a much larger number of potential customers was the driver for the mass production paradigm. To accomplish this, he had to invent a new production method that would dramatically reduce the manufacturing cost of the product by increasing the production output. This method, which is based on a moving assembly line, became the enabler of the mass production paradigm. To appreciate the impact of mass production on product prices let us look at the history of Ford Motor Company as summarized in the following table.

1896	Ford's first automobile prototype
1903	Ford Motor Co. established
1905	95 car manufacturers in the United States
1909	Model-T: **$825**
	Minimum salary: $2/day
1913	Ford's moving assembly line introduced
	Ford manufactures ~50% of automobiles in the United States
1914	Model-T: **$440**
	Minimum salary: **$5**/day

The 1908 "Model-T" is depicted in Figure 4.1. The most striking contradiction between the "Model-T" price and the wages of the workers who built it occurred during the 5 years from 1909 to 1914. In that period **wages increased by 2.5 times, and the Model-T's price was cut in half!**

The Global Manufacturing Revolution: Product-Process-Business Integration and Reconfigurable Systems
By Yoram Koren
Copyright © 2010 John Wiley & Sons, Inc.

1908 T

Figure 4.1 Ford Model T. 1908: "*You can have any color of a car you want, as long as it's black.*" Henry Ford

- How could the price of the Model-T be reduced so dramatically in 5 years?
- How can it be that wages went up so high, and at the same time the product price went down?
- How did Ford manage this "miracle?"

We have to thoroughly understand the principles of mass production and develop its mathematical model in order to explain what appears as a paradox when first observed.

4.1 THE PRINCIPLES OF MASS PRODUCTION

In craft production, one-of-a-kind parts are individually made to fit together for each product. Mass production, however, could not exist without the invention of interchangeable parts.

Interchangeable Parts—The manufacture of interchangeable parts was an idea that originated in the early 1700s, in the making of clock gears. By the end of that century it had become a military necessity for the manufacture and maintenance of firearms. Soldiers needed to be able to replace parts on their weapons to stay in the fight. The first demonstration of the interchangeability ideal came at the Harpers Ferry Arsenal in 1827 when muskets (long guns) were assembled from pieces selected at random from boxes of parts. It took almost 100 years for that idea to propagate to the manufacturing of consumer products and to make the mass production paradigm possible.

Under the craft production paradigm, flawed or irregular parts were discarded (or improved) by craftsmen as they assembled one-of-a-kind products on an assembly stage. Only when large quantities of identical, truly interchangeable parts were available, could Henry Ford's mass production scheme be successful. As product progressed from station to station, assemblers had to have parts that would fit and could be added without alteration. Interchangeable parts made it possible for the system to move and maintain the desired output. The availability of interchangeable parts is a key enabler of mass production.

The opening of the moving automobile assembly line in Dearborn by the Ford Motor Co. in 1913 is regarded as the starting point of the mass production era. The car that Ford produced on this line was the famous Ford Model T.

The contribution the moving assembly line made can be seen in the data below. From 1911 to 1914 the number of cars produced increased from 40,000 to 260,000 units annually. And, in the next 10 years Ford's annual production increased **eightfold**, to 2 million units. But it is also worth noting that an earlier **sevenfold increase,** from 1908 to 1911, resulted from simply organizing the assembly work sequentially—the assembled cars were stationary and the workers moved from one car to the next, with each group doing just a limited set of operations on each car.

Ford Model T

1908 - 6000

1911 - 40,000

Moving Assembly Line

1914 - 260,000

1916 - 580,000

1924 - 2,000,000

Ford's assembly scheme essentially converted a **parallel process**, where small teams of workers performed multiple tasks on a single unit, into a **sequential (serial) process**, where workers perform only a small set of tasks, and then transfer the work-in-progress to the next worker team who performed another set (approximately the same amount of work effort in each step).

Henry Ford did this conversion from parallel to sequential assembly before introducing the moving assembly line, and cut the time that a worker spent on a car, from 9 hours to 2.3 minutes per car (i.e., the worker did the same task, taking about 2.3 minutes, and therefore became more efficient). With the moving assembly line, which brought the car to a stationary worker, the time per car was cut again, from 2.3 to 1.2 minutes. This was a direct saving of almost another 50% on labor, achieved just by implementing the moving assembly line.

The cars that Ford produced were identical. His statement "*You can have any color you want, as long as it's black*" symbolizes the limited variety of cars offered. However, at that time, consumers were not as picky as today, needing a car just for transportation (not as a status symbol), and they were happy just to be able to buy a car. In 1909, wages were low—just $2 per day, and this money was needed for food, clothes, and lodging. Only a small percentage of the U.S. population could afford a car (similar to the situation in China in 2000).

The introduction of the sequential process, and later the moving assembly line, was complementary to Ford's mass production business strategy: Increased production at low cost enabled a consequent reduction in the product price; by lowering the product price, more people could afford to buy cars, which, in turn, expanded the market for Ford's cars.

Henry Ford expanded the market by reducing the price of the car from $825 to $440. This allowed more people to afford to buy one. Instead of selling some 12,000 cars per year at $825 per car (in 1909)—revenues of $10 million—he reduced the selling price by about 50% and sold 260,000 vehicles in 1914—a revenue of $115 million, which is 11 times larger. This huge price decrease was enabled by increased production capacity.

The capacity (i.e., maximum possible production volume) of the moving assembly line was enormous compared with that of the parallel assembly method. The cost benefits were also huge even though the innovation required new and expensive hardware because those costs were distributed over the whole production run.

The main principle of the **mass production paradigm** is, therefore, as follows:

> Producing a limited variety of standardized products at low cost as a strategy that increases customer demand and allows market expansion.

But the reduction in the car price alone was not enough to create the big market expansion that Ford envisioned. He was also concerned about the small number of people who were currently in the car buying market. Earning a common salary of just $2 per day, Ford's workers were not able to buy new cars. Paying his workers more than the prevailing wage, about $5 a day, was the second part of Ford's strategy. He needed to expand the market for all the cars he could make, and so he increased his **customers' purchasing power**. By increasing his workers' salary to more than twice what they were accustomed to earning, they saw that they could actually own one of the cars they were building. Because of equity across industries, an increase in salaries at Ford eventually caused an overall increase in all U.S. salaries, and Ford's car market doubled again (from 260,000 units annually to 580,000 units) in just more 2 years. It is ironic that Henry Ford, an icon of American capitalism, contributed to his workers' wealth more than anybody else ever did.

The mass production era continued from 1913 until the mid-1980s. Its peak in the USA was around 1955, the year in which product variety was the lowest and the volume per product was at its maximum (compared to the U.S. population at that time).

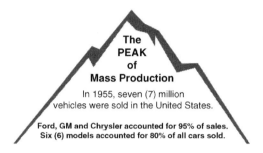

The **PEAK** of **Mass Production**

In 1955, seven (7) million vehicles were sold in the United States.

Ford, GM and Chrysler accounted for 95% of sales. Six (6) models accounted for 80% of all cars sold.

The mass production business model may be summarized as follows:

> Production of standardized products in very high volume reduces production cost, which, in turn, allows price reduction to the benefit of the customers. Reduced product price increases demand and sales.

Low price per unit is the focus of mass production. Mass production is not much concerned with the customer's preferences and needs. The mass production paradigm assumes that as product prices are lowered, more people that can afford to buy the products will enter the market resulting in more sales. This in turn, encourages greater production that can be done at even lower costs, and therefore the product prices can be further lowered, and so on.

In the mass production paradigm both product and process changes come very slowly, at a snail's pace. But mass production manufacturers do not care where the customers come from. They just assume they will always be there to buy their products. The product is designed with limited variety and the manufacturing system is designed to produce a limited product variety (see Figure 4.2).

The two most expensive elements of a manufacturing system for automotive production are machining systems that produce the powertrain components (engine blocks, transmission cases, etc.), and assembly systems that assemble the various parts to a complete automobile. When automobiles are produced in mass production, both the machining systems and the assembly systems are **dedicated** to produce that one product (model), and they are doing it at very high quantities. Mass production is based on economies of scale. Economists calculate that economies of scale reduce the variable manufacturing costs by approximately 15–25% for every doubling of the produced volume. If the system produces the planned quantities, the product cost is inexpensive. We see, therefore, a strong link between this type of manufacturing system and the business model goal, as defined above.

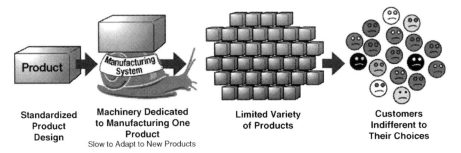

| Standardized Product Design | Machinery Dedicated to Manufacturing One Product Slow to Adapt to New Products | Limited Variety of Products | Customers Indifferent to Their Choices |

Figure 4.2 In mass production the product variety is limited; the manufacturing system is dedicated to produce just this limited variety and can be changed at only a snail's pace.

To summarize, the goal of mass production is **low-cost manufacturing**. Three enablers contribute to the achievement of this goal: (1) interchangeable parts, (2) the moving assembly line, and (3) dedicated machinery and manufacturing systems. Dedicated machines and systems enable cost-effective production, especially of powertrain components, which require the most effort to produce and the most expensive machinery, and therefore are the most expensive parts in automobiles.

4.2 SUPPLY AND DEMAND

The way supply and demand influence the price of a product in the market can be shown graphically in Figure 4.3:

- The buyers' demand for the product is modeled on a demand curve that shows what buyers are willing to pay relative to all buyer wishes and not related to sellers. The demand curve is modeled for fixed conditions, such as a certain buyer's purchasing power (i.e., their income) and unchanged people's tastes.
- The seller's willingness to supply the product is modeled by a supply curve. The supply curve represents solely the seller's (not the buyer's) attitudes. A supply curve shows that the price at which a supplier would be willing and able to deliver the indicated quantity of a product to the market.

The demand and the supply curves are usually drawn just for one product (e.g., Ford Model T). In Figure 4.3, the demand curve, α, indicates that if the product price were equal to AO, then consumers would want to buy a quantity AC' (or OC) of this product. Should the price fall to BO, the quantity demanded by consumers would increase to BD' (or OD) because more people would be able to buy the product at the lower price. The quantity read from the demand curve does not indicate whether or not that quantity could be supplied at the given price. It reflects only what the consumers want to buy and what they can afford.

Figure 4.3 also includes a supply curve β that illustrates, for example, if prices were equal to AO, then quantity AF' (or OF) would be supplied. If the price falls to BO, it

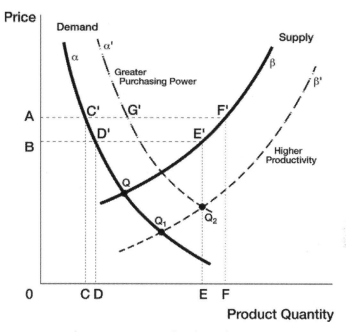

Figure 4.3 Demand and supply curves

will be less attractive to produce the product, and therefore the quantity that suppliers will be willing to supply would fall to BE' (or OE). These quantities are based only upon the consideration of the suppliers' decisions; they are not related to the willingness of consumers to purchase the indicated quantities at the indicated prices.

The equilibrium in the marketplace is achieved at point Q, at which there is just one price for which the product quantity demanded equals the quantity supplied.

Price is, of course, not the only factor that influences suppliers to sell. If the costs of production climb, then suppliers will want to produce and sell fewer units. By contrast, if, for example, technology increases productivity, and the cost of producing the product goes down, then prices may be lowered and the entire supply curve is shifted to a new position β'. The equilibrium in the marketplace is now achieved at point Q_1, which indicates that a larger quantity could be bought, but at a lower price than before.

Alternatively, if a buyer's purchasing power (i.e., income) increases, the entire demand curve shifts to a new position, α' When the demand curve was at position α, the product price had been AO, and the consumers would have been buying quantity OC. Now, with higher incomes, they want to increase their purchases to AG' on curve α'. This does not mean they will succeed in buying quantity AG' at price AO. The supply curve will influence that. The point is that because of the income rise, consumers will want to buy larger quantities than they would previously have wanted. The equilibrium in the marketplace between curves α' and β' is achieved at point Q_2.

Henry Ford used the principles described above to increase his profits. His invention of the moving assembly line boosted productivity and shifted the demand–supply equilibrium point from point Q to point Q_1 at which the product price is lower. Then he increased the purchasing power of consumers by increasing the wages of his workers, which, in turn, caused an overall increase in U.S. salaries. This created a new equilibrium point Q_2, which further increased the quantities bought by customers, who were even willing to pay a modest increase in the vehicle price. This shift in both the demand and supply curves increased the quantity of cars sold and boosted Ford's profits tremendously. This answers the question that we posed at the beginning of this chapter: Is it not a paradox that when wages at Ford went up, its product prices went down?

4.3   THE MATHEMATICAL MODEL OF MASS PRODUCTION

Below we present an original mathematical model for mass production. The model shows that the mass production process behaves as a closed-loop system with positive feedback. To understand this, we first start by defining two pricing methods, that, although they may look similar, they provide very different perspectives.

4.3.1   Pricing

There are two perspectives on how the price of a product is derived: either (1) by adding a profit margin to actual production costs or (2) by the marketplace. Calculation by the first method is typically associated with mass production, and the latter fits the philosophy of lean production.

In the mass production mindset, companies have held the perspective that adding a profit to their costs dictates the selling price in the market.

Product selling price = Profit + Fixed cost + Variable costs

where the fixed cost includes the investment cost (machines, factory) plus other fixed costs prorated per product (e.g., health insurance for employees and retirees), and the variable cost includes the direct cost per product: material, labor, tools, distribution, etc. Under this assumption, desired levels of profit are maintained, and any increase in cost results in an increased price to the consumer. This pricing method is best applicable in a mass production environment, characterized by low competition and high volume per product, and is the basis for the mathematical analysis presented in this section.

In the alternative—market-pricing method—competition determines the selling price. Profit is a result of subtracting costs from the selling price, i.e., what the market will bear:

Profit = Product selling price − Fixed cost − Variable costs

Under this premise, the only way to increase profitability is to reduce the manufacturing cost. This is usually done by changes in non-value-added operations, by eliminating waste, and by increased productivity (see Section 4.4). This pricing method is utilized in competitive markets, and it is applicable today by global companies.

4.3.2 Mass production Closed-loop Representation and Principles

The mass production model is applicable when the market satisfies two conditions:

> (I) **A product can be supplied by a small number of suppliers**.
>
> (II) **Homogeneous products** are purchased by consumers (no product variety).

Under these two conditions, and because fixed costs are high and variable costs are relatively low, a positive feedback loop model is created (Figure 4.4).[1] The positive feedback loop follows four principles:

1. Higher product volumes reduce the manufacturing costs per product.
2. If costs are lower, product price may be reduced.
3. Lower prices expand the market and increase demand.
4. Higher demand generates higher product volumes—back to point 1 above

This positive feedback loop feeds itself and will stabilize only if it encounters a constraint—product price cannot be smaller than the variable costs in order to maintain profit.

4.3.3 Mass Production Cost Model

From now on in this section we will use the car as an example of a product. In the mathematical model developed below we use the relationship:

Car cost = Fixed cost per car + Variable costs of each car

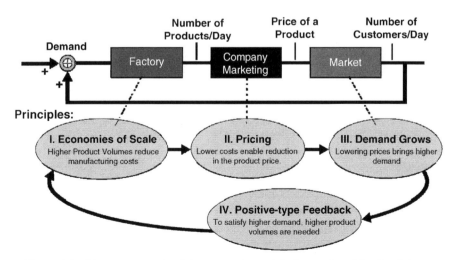

Figure 4.4   The mass -production process is modeled as a closed feedback loop.

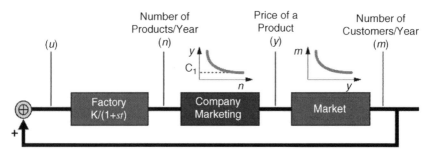

Figure 4.5   A block diagram mathematical representation of mass production.

To determine the total cost per car, the fixed cost should be divided by the total number of cars produced. This equation is the basis for the company pricing strategy.

The block diagram of Figure 4.5 depicts the **mathematical model** of mass production. The terms K and τ in Figure 4.5 are explained below.

$K = 1$ means that the factory production capacity is larger than the number of car orders per year, u, and therefore the number of cars produced, n, is equal to u. The condition $K < 1$ means that the factory is working at full capacity and demand cannot be supplied. For the model developed here we assume $K = 1$.

τ means that it takes some time from when an order is placed to the time that the product is supplied. For simplicity we assume $\tau = 0$.

The car cost, y, is the sum of the fixed and variable costs per car.

$$y = C_1 + C_0/n \tag{4.1}$$

where C_0 = fixed costs (investment cost + maintenance cost, etc.) prorated **per year**,
$\quad C_1$ = variable cost/car,
$\quad n$ = the number of cars produced per year.

In the early mass production era, because the machinery was expensive (compared with labor cost), C_0 was very high compared to the variable costs. Since in our model C_0 is the invested cost prorated per year, C_0 becomes smaller as the same product is produced over more years.

Note that Eq. (4.1) expresses the car price as a function of the quantity produced solely from the manufacturer economic viewpoint, and it does not reflect the market. This curve is plotted in Figure 4.6 as the manufacturer curve.

When the price of a car is lower, more people will buy cars, as depicted by the demand curve in Figure 4.3. We assume that the number of customers purchasing cars, m, is inversely proportional (with an exponential function a, where $a \geq 2$) to the car price (z):

$$m = C_2/z^a \tag{4.2}$$

u is the number of people who want to buy a car (i.e., number of car orders), and it is equal to the number of people who buy cars, m (assuming no loss of sales).

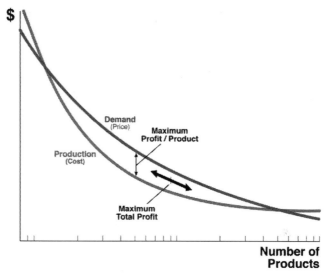

Figure 4.6 To be profitable, the manufacturer production curve must be below the demand curve.

The closed-loop principle yields

$$n = K \cdot u = K \cdot m \tag{4.3}$$

Substituting Eq. (4.2) into (4.3) yields

$$n = K \cdot C_2/z^a \tag{4.4}$$

Eq. (4.4) expresses the demand curve, and is shown in Figure 4.6. For $y = z$ substituting Eq. (4.1) into (4.4) gives us the closed-loop equation

$$n = K \cdot C_2/(C_1 + C_0/n)^a \tag{4.5}$$

Since under the mass production conditions $K = 1$, the final equation is

$$n = C_2/(C_1 + C_0/n)^a \tag{4.6}$$

For a given C_0, C_1, C_2, and a, Eq. (4.6) can be solved by numerical methods for n. For $a = 2$ this equation becomes quadratic and can be solved analytically. Solving Eq. (4.6) yields the two intersection points in Figure 4.6.

The production cost curve is given by Eq. (4.1), and the market demand curve is based on Eq. (4.4). To be profitable the manufacturer's production cost must be below the market price, as depicted in Figure 4.6. The number of products at which the maximum profit per product is obtained, n_{max}, is between the two intersection points solved by Eq. (4.6). If more products are produced, although the profit/product diminishes, the total overall profit to the company is larger. Therefore, the optimal number of products that should be produced for maximum profit is on the right side of n_{max}, as shown in Figure 4.6.

To evaluate the company's position in the marketplace, the supply curve should be added to Figure 4.6. If the intersection between the supply and demand curves (which reflects the equilibrium in the marketplace) is on the left side of the right intersection point between the demand and production curves, then the company can take the lead in the market.

If the supply curve intersects the demand on the right side of the right intersection point between the demand and production curves, then the company is not competitive and must take steps to cut waste, reduce non-value-added expenses, and find ways to increase its productivity. Otherwise, it will have to take steps to improve its position such as offer incentives to the buyers.

4.4 LEAN PRODUCTION—GOALS AND BENEFITS

In the mass production era, high-quality products were more costly to produce. Also, in the early days of mass production, machines were expensive and labor and space were cheap. Manufacturing systems were designed to use more people, extra space, and large buffers between machines to ensure smooth operations. Over the years, however, the cost of people and space has increased. The extra people, space, and the buffers that stockpile huge numbers of in-process products have made manufacturing expensive. In the early 1960s Japanese manufacturers, led by Toyota, began manufacturing cars by applying more efficient production systems that focused on eliminating waste of time and material. These practices reduced costs substantially. Not only were their cars less expensive, in many cases, because process errors were eliminated quicker, but their standard products were also of higher quality.

Better Quality at Lower Price: When Japanese automotive manufacturers started to export in the mid-1960s, their U.S. and European competitors treated them with disrespect. (I vividly remember how in 1970 everyone in my neighborhood wondered when my neighbor's new Subaru would break down; it didn't happen for 4 years! Not a big deal today, but it was unheard of at that time.) Western manufacturers completely ignored this competition, assuming that the Japanese products were cheap and of low quality. Things changed 180° as consumers began to understand that, dollar for dollar, the Japanese products were consistently of higher quality than their Western counterparts. Consumers realized that high quality did not have to come at a higher price. This was a revelation for both manufacturers and consumers. In the mid-1970s consumer goods manufacturers in both the United States and Europe began very busy travel schedules to Japan—they wanted to study this "miracle" first hand.

How did Japanese manufacturers do it? It was not a miracle—just rigorously implemented operations management methods that they had developed over time. This set of methods and principles came to be known as "Lean Production"—a term coined by the authors of the book "The Machine that Changed the World" in 1990.[2] The book was based upon the results of a 5-year study by the Massachusetts Institute of Technology (MIT) on the future of the automobile, and documented the evolution of manufacturing in the automobile industry from craft production, to mass production, and to lean production.

4.4.1 Sources of Waste

Lean production systems can economically produce high-quality products even at relatively low volumes. This is achieved by both reducing cost and improving quality and productivity through the absolute elimination of waste. For example, excess inventory, manpower, and equipment are all wastes that increase manufacturing costs. Excess inventory increases manufacturing costs because of the extra floor space required, the people needed to handle it, the masking of potential quality problems, and the cost of holding the parts in process. Lean manufacturing reduces production costs by eliminating waste in the production system through the implementation of improvement activities.

Waste is defined in lean production as

Waste = anything beyond the minimum amount of equipment, materials, parts,
space, and workers time that is essential to add value to the product

The eight classic sources of waste are

1. **Overproduction:** Making more than is required by the market, or the next process; making it earlier than required by the next process; or making it faster than is required by the next process. Overproduction is viewed as the worst type of waste because it not only increases inventory (holding cost), but also increases labor cost and the facility cost.

2. **Product defects:** Producing defective products not only forces product scraping (that wastes material and all the effort expended prior to the defect) but also inserts many non-value-added activities into the system including increased delay for good products downstream, to say nothing of inspection activities.

3. **Inventory:** Excess inventories that are maintained "just-in-case" something goes wrong, or as a result of overproduction, tie up space and work effort. In a lean system, inventories are kept at a minimum by applying the principles of a pull system (i.e., producing "just-in-time (JIT)" for a downstream customer's request).

4. **Transportation (Conveyance):** Long or complicated transportation routes between operations, due to poor factory layout, can double or triple handling costs.

5. **Unnecessary motion:** Moving parts on the production floor, when not really needed, do not add value. Motions should be limited to actions that add value.

6. **Waiting:** Parts to be processed held in buffers; machines waiting for parts (machines starving); and operators idly watching machines run or being idle when the required work is finished.

7. **Under-utilized personnel:** People who are either idling or not utilized effectively comparable to their skills and knowledge.

8. **Inefficient processing:** Operations that require excess labor due to poor maintenance, unnecessary process steps for meeting product requirements, or excess operational capacity or capability for the production requirements.

In summary, waste is any production resource (e.g., machines, buffers, people) or operation (e.g., long transportation) that is expended but does not add value to the product. The elimination of waste is vital to increasing profitability, especially in a market-driven pricing model. A systematic approach to examining the production flow, and application of lean production principles can minimize waste. Products can be produced in greater variety, at higher quality using less resources, in less time.

4.4.2   The Benefit and Objectives of a Lean Production System

The goal of lean manufacturing is the absolute elimination of waste in the production system through a discipline of continuous improvement. The relentless pursuit of waste in all facets of the manufacturing process results in two major outcomes: reduced overall cost and improved quality in the baseline product. Therefore, we may say that lean production's main benefits are reduced production cost and enhanced product quality. Reducing product cost has always been at the heart of mass production but mass production as expressed in the earlier model traded higher quality for greater cost. Lean production has proven that it is possible to have both.

As we have described, an important way to eliminate waste in the system is to reduce the number of defective products, preferably to zero. With lean production, quality problems are either prevented through mistake proofing as the system is installed, or being detected early within the process, instead of at the end of the production line. Detecting and diagnosing errors in real time and immediately fixing them is a valuable asset. It minimizes the number of defective finished goods that must be scrapped, and reduces the need for re-work and repair of the production line. Both of these significantly reduce production costs. Thus, lean manufacturing improves product quality and reduces product cost simultaneously.

In-process quality means that each piece of machinery in the process supplies only good parts to the next stage of manufacturing, thus eliminating work that is expended on defective parts in future stages—a non-value-added operation that increases cost. Since producing defective products increases the average time needed to produce good products, it reduces system productivity as well. Avoiding this problem, standardizing the way the work is performed and the monitoring of product quality at every stage, enhances overall product quality and ultimately improves customer satisfaction.

In summary, implementation of a lean production system results in two benefits:

1. **Reduced cost** by focusing on the elimination of waste and all non-value-added activities.
2. **Improved quality** by concentrating on defect prevention and the in-process identification and repair of defective parts/products, not allowing them to continue through the process.

4.5 THE PRINCIPLES OF LEAN PRODUCTION

Lean production evolved to facilitate the lean manufacturing ideal: the elimination of waste in all aspects of the operation. Toyota was the first to apply the principles, to their low-volume/high-variety production, by the early 1960s, and developed the Toyota Production System (TPS). During the next decade (to the mid-1970s) the other Japanese auto companies adopted the lean production principles.[3] The rest of the world has been working to implement them since the 1980s. Before we can appreciate the principles of lean production we must understand the process of "implementing Lean."

The first step is developing an understanding of the current state of the process by creating a map of the value stream of the entire production flow. In analyzing the current state of production flow, **operational availability** (which is defined below) is a key factor in value stream mapping.

$$\text{Operational Availability} = \frac{\textbf{Actual Run-time}}{\textbf{Scheduled Run-time}}$$

where

Scheduled run-time = Minutes per shift − Planned (scheduled) downtime.

Actual run-time = Scheduled run-time − Equipment breakdowns − Changeover time − Lost time (people, material).

Operational availability (OA) is usually expressed as a percentage (higher is better) with a maximum of 1.0 or 100%. The definition recognizes that the actual run-time is a function of scheduled run-time, which includes planned downtime, and an unscheduled downtime. Basically OA is the percentage of time the system is actually available to run compared with the maximum time the manufacturer might plan to run it.

Of course, the actual run-time of the system is smaller than the scheduled run-time. Reasons include:

- **Unscheduled equipment downtime** because of breakdowns or extensive repairs
- **Changeover time** needed to switch production between product models
- **Unavailability of parts** when needed, machinery starving, and personnel idle time
- **Unavailability of people** when needed to service machines, machinery starving

4.5.1 Takt Time and Cycle Time

Takt time is the total time available during a production period divided by the demand for that period. The takt time is the **desired time** between units (of production output) synchronized to the rate of customer demand. Improving operational availability is important in meeting the takt time.

Cycle time is the inverse of the line production rate; namely, it is the **actual time** interval for products coming off the production line. Due to process reliability problems, the cycle time is usually set at 0.85 to 0.9 of the takt time.

Defective products impinge on the frequency of good products being produced and increase the average cycle time, essentially, the average time required to produce a good product. This impacts the ability to meet takt time. If the system is producing products that require re-work, the time between good output products is increased, and the manufacturer will not be able to meet the customer demand.

Based on this information, production flow is analyzed in a systematic way to compare the value-added and non-value-added operations or activities. The principles of lean production (on which we elaborate below) are based on management operations methods, and aim at minimizing the non-value-added activities and minimizing sources of waste.

4.5.1.1 Principle 1: Waste-less Continuous Process Flow by Value-Stream Mapping, Eliminating Non-value-added Process Steps, Stable Flow Manufacturing and a Leveled Production Schedule

We have to analyze which steps and operations in the process are adding value to the product, and cut off or reduce the non-value-added steps. For example, drilling a part on a machine tool is a value-added step. Putting parts into a buffer, waiting to be drilled is not adding value to the product. A process step is adding value if:

1. The process step makes a physical improvement to the product being manufactured.
2. The customer is benefiting from the step and is willing to pay for it.

Ideally, we should eliminate or reduce buffers, since parts waiting are not adding value. However, if a buffer is eliminated, a machine in the system may wait for parts (is starving), and adding a buffer in this case extends the system's average cycle time. Thus, an analysis is needed to decide the appropriate buffer size that guarantees a smooth and continuous operational flow of the line while minimizing non-value-added operations.

As a rule, all non-value-added steps are either "waiting" or "moving" steps. Examples include parts waiting in a buffer, products waiting to be taken to customers, new cutting tools waiting to replace worn tools, etc. Moving parts from one machine to another for subsequent processing, or moving parts to inventory, are non-value-added steps. In this case, the physical distance between machines doing successive operations must be kept as small as possible. Similarly, the distance between a supplier and a customer should be as short as possible. For example, a car seat manufacturer must be in close geographic proximity to the car final assembly plant because the travel time between the two plants does not add value to the product and travel interruptions in supply of one will directly impact the production schedule of the other plant.

Stable continuous process flow is established and maintained by leveling the production schedule (i.e., the workload) so that it has as little fluctuation as possible.

This is accomplished by eliminating bottlenecks in the line, and with as little inventory as possible. Line balancing operations are conducted throughout all the stages of the line so that the flow of manufactured products continues with minimum delays.

On a system that produces two products, or more, that have small lot-size production runs, balanced operations are important also between products. Otherwise, the system must be purged when the product type is switched over, which will cause production delays.

4.5.1.2 Principle 2: Built-in Quality—Team Responsibility

A traditional assembly line moves products continuously from one assembly station to the next and the product is partially assembled one operation at a time. In each station, a team of people does the assembly while the product is moving. During a typical stage, perhaps 30–60 seconds long, several parts are installed into the same product by the team. There is not a lot of time for spotting errors or fixing mistakes, and so defective products are usually just passed to the end of the line where they are either repaired or scrapped.

In lean production each person on the line has quality checking responsibilities. Team responsibility and ownership of the team's assembly operation is a key principle of lean manufacturing. If a defect is encountered, either it is fixed in the station during the normal station interval, or the team leader stops the line by pulling a cord. This practice of stopping the line to fix quality problems reduces defects, enhances product quality, and eliminates the rework area, since quality products are achieved every time. Consistently producing quality products the first time reduces costs. The end result is better baseline quality at lower price.

The team also has the responsibility of improving their tasks of the assembly operation. This may include doing the assembly in a more efficient way, changing the order of steps, reducing inventories, etc. In the end, the team takes ownership and responsibility on incremental, continuous improvement (referred to by Toyota as *kaizen*) that is constantly seeking to optimize the system (see also Principle 4).

4.5.1.3 Principle 3: Just-in-time—"The Right Parts at the Right Time in the Right Amount"

Just-in-time (JIT) is a methodology of lean production that coordinates the flow of parts within the supply chain, and within the factory between processes (e.g., between a machining system and an assembly line). JIT means supplying each process with the parts and material needed, exactly when they are needed, and in the exact quantity that is needed. Production quantities are adjusted constantly to produce only what is required by the customer (or the next supplier in a supply chain) so as to avoid overproduction. JIT is the archetype of a pull system.

To manage their JIT organization Toyota implemented a *kanban* system. Kanban means, "*a card used as a sign*" in Japanese. At every station, the product quantities that the next station requires are written on placards and the current process is expected to supply exactly those quantities, exactly when needed. There are also cards that show the exact quantities that the previous process was to supply to the current process, in order to coordinate the process, station-to-station, and keep the line running at its takt time. The *kanban* information system coordinates the quantities supplied to every process in the entire production system. Its goal is to always manufacture products with an absolute minimum of excess inventory.

JIT is a pull system—The quantity of parts to be supplied is determined solely by the demand at the next production stage. This is in contrast to the push system in which parts are supplied to stations based on generalized production schedules, with no consideration of the actual processing rate.

There are at least two segments of a manufacturing enterprise where JIT should be implemented: inside the company—between successive processes; and in managing a supply chain. These aspects are illustrated in Figure 4.7, which depicts a supply chain within and outside the enterprise. Inside the enterprise, engine block castings are machined and transferred to the engine assembly line, and then the assembled engines are supplied to the final automobile assembly line. Outside suppliers provide engine block castings to the manufacturer's machining line. Other suppliers provide a variety of parts to the automobile final assembly line: car seats, door mechanisms, instrumentation panels, etc. (See details in Chapter 6.)

JIT Management of the Supply Chain—The key to JIT is that suppliers synchronize their delivery directly in coordination with their customer's production schedule, dramatically impacting the customer's inventory needs. In the past, for example, a 1980s automobile assembly plant maintained inventories to guarantee 2 weeks (10 days) supply of production covering two shifts. Today, the inventories are geared for only 2 hours! If automobiles are assembled at a rate of 50 per hour, the inventory for each part has been reduced from 8000 to 100, namely by a factor of 80. Since a car has over 10,000 parts, this is an enormous saving in inventory cost (including parts and the space and personnel to store them).

Time is a critical issue in JIT management. The supplier must be able to deliver their parts on time regardless of disruptions such as changes in orders, production

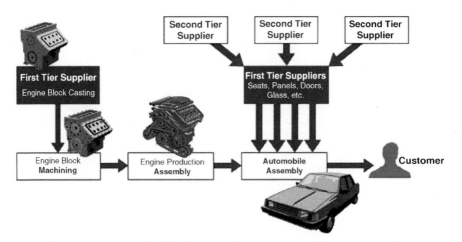

Figure 4.7 JIT is applied both inside the company and in its supply chain.

failures, and delays in transportation. Because delivery times are so critical, geographic proximity to the supplier's customer can give a competitive advantage to nearby supplier. Unanticipated disruptions require buffers; but buffers add no value to the customer, which contradicts the JIT philosophy. Real factory operations are different than the ideal world described in textbooks.

Obtaining high-quality parts consistently from suppliers is another challenge for JIT. There are many historic cases where assembly lines have been shut down because of part quality issues coming from suppliers. In January 2010 Toyota recalled 2.3 million vehicles for sticking accelerator pedals caused by a part that was manufactured by a supplier. This shows the vulnerability of the manufacturer to quality problems caused by its suppliers. Implementation of JIT is not trivial; it took 20 years to fully implement these principles within the Toyota supply chain.[2]

Summary: Advantages of JIT	Drawbacks of JIT
• Less cost of high inventory of parts	• Dependency on suppliers that must supply parts in a coordinated, timely manner
• Less inventory space	• Vulnerability to problems outside the manufacturer's system
• Less equipment to handle inventories	

4.5.1.4 Principle 4: Flexible, Highly Motivated People Who Believe in the Lean Philosophy

Workers that are motivated and empowered by management to perform above and beyond traditional laborer's duties are the foundation of lean production. Teams, to be effective, must take ownership for identifying quality defects and striving for continuous improvement. With the authority to stop a running production line (called *jidoka* in Japanese), workers have responsibility that goes all the way to the enterprise level of the company. Team members must be flexible and support each other, since the effort of the whole team is needed to successfully implement the system, so much so that they are cross-trained in the jobs of other teams. There is no question that multifunctional workers, who can help exactly where needed, facilitate the factory workflow.

4.5.1.5 Principle 5: A Single Operator to Control Several Operations

Assigning one operator to control multiple operations, as illustrated in Figure 4.8, is another example of how to improve manpower efficiency with lean methods. When a person is in charge of only loading and unloading one machine, there is a repetitive cycle in which the person does nothing as the machine works on the part. This wasted time is eliminated if the person is in charge of two adjacent machines and alternates from one to the other. There are many operations in a factory where a person can take on additional responsibility and improve the system, but personnel have to be educated in lean methods and take ownership of their work.

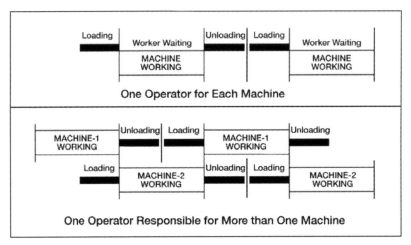

Figure 4.8 Efficient manpower utilization.

Three of our students shared their work experience in implementing lean methodologies with us.

"I have experienced first-hand both mass production and lean production. The cultural methods of mass production discussed in this chapter do not seem to go away [2006]. I have yet to see the 'many buffers to ensure smooth production' go away and replaced with one-piece flow, as Lean would suggest." Greg Wood

"The idea of Just-in-Time may be over-simplified. For example, at GM Pontiac Assembly Center, the plant was shut down for 1.5 days [in 2003] due to a union issue at one of GM suppliers. Even though the issue was resolved quickly, the limited supply in the pipeline caused the assembly line to shut down." Cindie Niemann

"I work in a new facility that uses Lean principles in a mass-production environment [2006]. Most of the machines at the site are flexible machining centers. The plant is closely tied with another plant that is an old mass-production facility, but makes the same product. As we work to implement different product changes in both plants, it is amazing to see how much faster and cheaper that my site can handle new (or updated) products." Dan Gulledge

4.5.2 Summary of Lean Production System

Lean production principles are **operations management methods** that have two goals: **reduce cost** and **enhance product quality**. Both goals are achieved through the identification and elimination of waste. Principles 2 and 3 of lean production constitute the **two pillars of Lean**, as depicted in Figure 4.8: built-in product quality, which is embedded in the manufacturing process (rather than checking quality at the end of the production line), and JIT, as described in Principle 3. When implementing lean production, quality problems are identified and remedied before they build up and create waste.[4]

JIT produces only what is needed, when it is needed, in the amount needed, meeting the exact current demand of the customer. JIT should be synchronized with the takt time—the time that should be taken to produce a product based on customer demand (calculated as: total daily operating time/total daily customer demand). JIT is a pull system, which eliminates overproduction and minimizes holding costs.

The three Japanese concepts that are useful when studying lean production are

Kanban (a placard that documents the materials needed to pass from one process to the next, which is the basis of a pull system)

Kaizen (actively taking responsibility for continuous improvements in the system)

Jidoka (the authority to stop a production line when a quality problem is detected)

Implementation of lean production principles and methods requires a **cultural change in the company**; this is the basis for lean production, as is illustrated in Figure 4.9. Cultural changes includes management willingness to assign authority to worker teams on the production line to make decisions (empowerment of the workforce), where empowerment means that teams take ownership and responsibility for identifying quality defects and strive for continuous improvement. Ownership involves team members being flexible in their task assignments and support of each other.

A culture of empowerment also means suppliers are involved in the flow of process management and are a constant part of the decision-making process. A successful lean production system requires serious commitment from top management and workers as well as from suppliers. An enterprise can only achieve the lean goals of lowering

Figure 4.9 Lean production goals and tools.

costs and enhance quality when the two pillars of lean production, JIT and built-in quality, are firmly established.

PROBLEMS

4.1 A manufacturer is producing a high-volume product for a mass production market.

(a) Given, the fixed costs per year $C_0 = \$3000$ M/year, and $C_1 = \$6000$. Plot the car price $y = f(n)$ using Eq. (4.1): $y = C_1 + C_0/n$ in the range $n = 100,000$–$1,500,000$ cars per year. (Draw price on the vertical axis and quantity on the horizontal axis to obtain the production curve.) What are your conclusions?

(b) If the number of customers who purchased a car is $m = 500,000$, $y = \$16,000$, and $a = 2$, calculate C_2 from the demand curve expressed by Eq. (4.2): $m = C_2/y^a$. Repeat for $a = 3$. Plot the demand curves on the same scale as the production curve in item a.

(c) Solve Eq. (4.6) analytically for $a = 2$ and define the relationship between C_0, C_1, and C_2

(d) Use the values of C_2 obtained in item b. For $a = 3$, solve Eq. (4.6) using numerical methods.

4.2 Assume that a modified Eq. (4.2) is given by $m = C_2 - ay$, where C_2 denotes the total market size and a is the price sensitivity of demand. Let $C_1 = 3 \times 10^9$ and $C_0 = 5000$ in Eq. (4.1), and $C_2 = 450,000$ and $a = 10$ in the modified Eq. (4.2).

(a) For the range of 50,000–350,000 cars produced, plot the number of cars produced versus (i) selling price per car and (ii) production cost per car. Let the number of cars produced be on the x-axis and the price/cost per unit shown on the y-axis.

(b) How many cars should be produced to maximize the profit per car?

4.3 Compare in a tabular format traditional mass production and lean production.

	Traditional Mass Production	Lean Production
Manufacturing cost		
Product quality		
Product variety		
Tool flexibility		
Workforce skills		

REFERENCES

1. J. PineII. *Mass Customization—The New Frontier in Business Competition.* Harvard Business School Press, 1993.

2. J. P. Womack, D. T. Jones, and D. Roos. *The Machine That Changed the World.* Harper-Perennials Publishers, New York, 1991.

3. J. P. Womack and D. T. Jones. *Lean Thinking.* Simon & Schuster, 1996.

4. J. K. Liker. *The Toyota Way.* McGraw Hill, 2004.

Chapter 5

Analysis of Mass Customization

The mass customization era, which started with automobiles around 1980, has blossomed so that today consumer products (e.g., kitchen appliances, computers, and office furniture) are produced by mass customization methods. Compared to mass production (that peaked in 1955), the variety of each product in mass customization is large and the volume per product variant is relatively small, as seen in Figure 5.1. Due to increased customer purchasing power, as it is expected to continue in the globalization era, the trend toward larger variety will intensify, especially with the emergence of the personalized production paradigm. In this chapter, we analyze the relationships between product variety and mass customization business models.

5.1 INTRODUCTION TO MASS CUSTOMIZATION

Global competition has created a market in which supply is much greater than demand for many consumer goods. These market conditions allow more consumers to be more selective in buying products that fit their various needs; at the same time it is forcing companies to look for new ways to gain a competitive advantage. Finding ways to offer more cost-effective mass customization is a way to create a competitive advantage. Even considering recent contractions, all indicators support the overall trend that global mass customization will continue to expand and flourish. The list of products that are suitable for mass customization is broad and can include bicycles, wheelchairs, scooters, watches, backpacks, automobiles, furniture, toys, clothing,

The Global Manufacturing Revolution: Product-Process-Business Integration and Reconfigurable Systems
By Yoram Koren
Copyright © 2010 John Wiley & Sons, Inc.

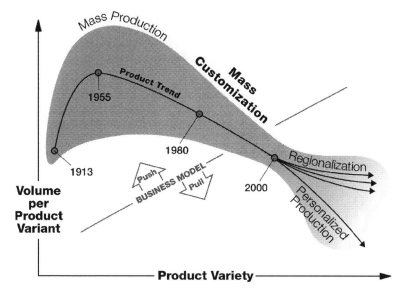

Figure 5.1 Mass customizations is characterized by large product variety and small volume per product variant (model).

refrigerators, computers, keyboards, air-conditioners, golf clubs, shopping carts, cosmetics, shoes, and blue jeans to name but a few.

Table 5.1 (composed by Dr. Z. Pasek) clearly demonstrates that between the early 1970s and the end of the twentieth century our society witnessed a revolutionary increase in the variety of products that we use on a daily basis. With this increased variety, consumers have been better able to select products that fit their needs and wants (be it running shoes or TV screens) or their tastes (e.g., 340 breakfast cereals).

Ever more selective consumers are purchasing products because they believe that they are getting a better value for their money, which is the mass customization goal.

TABLE 5.1 An Increase in Product Variety

Item	Early 70s	Late 90s
Vehicle models	140	260
SUV models	8	38
TV screen sizes	5	15
McDonald's menu items	13	43
Breakfast cereals	160	340
Milk varieties	4	19
Running shoe styles	5	285
Bicycle styles	8	31
Pain relievers	17	141

The goal of mass customization is to increase customer's value of a product by adding a range of product variations that fit specific customer's taste and needs while maintaining low prices.

Mass-customized products with similar function belong to a **product family**, and mass-customized parts of a similar form and function belong to a **part family** (see examples in Figure 5.2).

In mass customization, manufacturers continue to produce large quantities, but now of a **variety** of products from the same **family,** at close to mass-production competitive cost. We have previously described a product family as including a set of products that possess core functions that are common to all products within that family. In addition to the core functions, each product model (i.e., variant) within the family possesses augmenting features that differentiate it from the other members of its family.

The concept of a product family is essential for mass customization to be economically viable. One can achieve at least partial economies of scale by producing many or most members of the part family on a single manufacturing system. Manufacturing systems that are reconfigurable can be designed to produce up to every feature encountered in a part/product family using a system that adjusts to accommodate all features of all members.

Our definition of the mass customization methodology is as follows:

> Mass Customization
> Production of a wide product variety of customized products at mass production efficiencies as a strategy that generates competitive advantage. A wider product variety increases demand and sales.

Figure 5.2 Three part families.

The basic challenge that mass customization manufacturers face is:

How much variety to offer, and how much customization to put forward?

Too much customization is not only expensive; but also complicates service and confuses buyers. To illustrate this point we go to example from the book *Guts* by Robert Lutz[1].

"Lincoln-Mercury [was] bringing out an all-new Continental sedan in 1996.

It featured a high-tech, high-performance V-8. But, Lincoln decided to make steering programmable: customers could select any feel they liked, from pinky-finger-blue-haired-little-old-lady effortlessness to NASCAR-tattooed-ham-fisted bubba. And programmable suspension! Everything from floating-on-clouds to a ride guaranteed to loosen fillings. Most other features of the car were programmable as well.

Yet buyers failed to flock to the Continental.

Its fatal flaw, I think, was best summed up in Lincoln's own brochure: 'If you experience difficulty in selecting the modes that best suit you, your local Lincoln-Mercury dealer will be happy to tailor your Continental to the characteristics of your choice.'

Lincoln was saying: 'We don't know what you want you decide!' it's the manufacturer who's supposed to decide, and don't leave the creative work to the consumer!"

Is Mr. Lutz right?

5.2 BUSINESS STRATEGIES OF MASS CUSTOMIZATION

Any business model for mass customization must offer solutions to two basic issues:

- **Variety Management**: How does a manufacturer cope with product variety, and what is the economic upper boundary of product variety.
- **Rapid Response Time**: How does a manufacturer supply the buyer's customized orders quickly, accurately, and in a cost-effective way.

We will discuss four business strategies for mass customization. They yield different levels of the upper boundary of product variety. We will see, however, that at higher levels of variety, delivery time and cost may increase, reducing their attractiveness to customers.

5.2.1 Strategy 1: Off-The-Shelf Product Variety

Offering off-the-shelf variety is the simplest approach to mass customization—a standardized range of products is manufactured with economically calculated variations (see example in Section 5.4). The whole range is distributed to stores and sold directly to consumers. Customers choose whatever best fits their needs, "off-the-shelf"

Figure 5.3   Strategy 1—Off-the-shelf product variety.

(see Figure 5.3). Some common examples of this product strategy include breakfast cereals, running shoes, blue jeans, etc. Variety is limited primarily by display space and manufacturing costs. Because of the limited variety, consumers frequently have to compromise their exact preference in favor of cost and availability. Any particular size or brand that does not sell as expected amounts to a loss for the manufacturer, since the merchandise is returned to the manufacturer. So, although this strategy may seem to be the least expensive, it has drawbacks for both the customer and the manufacturer.

The mass customization of Strategy 1 is a transition phase from mass production and also represents a **Push Business Model**—products are pushed to customers; they are manufactured, put on shelves at department stores or parked in dealership lots, and offered directly to customers. The customer's only role is to pick out their selection. However, there is a difference between this model and the mass production push model—in the latter there is no quick feedback to the manufacturer. Ideally, in mass customization once a product is bought, the store immediately orders a new product, so its stock is always adequate for customers' needs, and the manufacturer has a quick feedback about the sales. Although Strategy 1 represents the lowest level of mass customization, it has two advantages:

- The product price is cheaper than more highly customized products.
- The delivery lag time is zero, since the whole range is offered at the same time and place.

5.2.2 Strategy 2: Intense Options of Products

Strategy 2 represents true mass customization. In this strategy, customers order products with the options that fit their needs and preferences, and only then the product is made. Examples include ordering a pizza, or a computer (at least from Dell Computers), or cars (see Figure 5.4). The manufacturers make decisions regarding the type and number of option packages they offer; from this viewpoint it is a **push model**. From the product-manufacturing (or assembly) viewpoint, however, this strategy represents a **pull model**, because each product is made only in response to a confirmed customer's order. This is a combination of push (design phase) and pull (assembly to produce the selected option). Therefore, Strategy 2 represents as a **Push–Pull Business Model**, with a business sequence of $\boxed{\text{Design} - \text{Sell} - \text{Make}}$. Note that the financial transaction (Sell) is executed before the product is made. Products of Strategy 2 are more expensive than those of Strategy 1.

LEVELS OF SELECTION

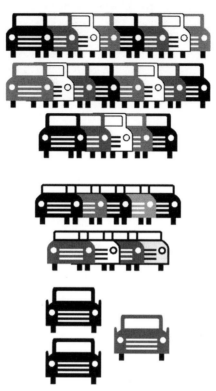

Figure 5.4 Strategy 2—many options are offered by the manufacturer. Through a gradual selection process, the customers narrow down their list of selected options until they reach the desired product, which is then manufactured.

Dell Computers offers its customers a huge number of customizable options and the customer can select every feasible combination of features. Within each product line, the buyer can select features such as screen size, system weight, and the number of drive bays as well as the processor, memory, hard drive, battery size, graphics card, operating system, software, peripherals, and warranty/service options. All of these options are established ahead of time by Dell, the manufacturer, and "pushed" to the buyer. Dell utilizes a pull-based procurement and manufacturing system to offer this mass customization, and since every one of their products is assembled to order, there is no cost premium for customization.

5.2.3 Strategy 3: Point-of-Delivery Personalization

Strategy 3 is different from the above options approach because standardized (and even options package) products can be further adjusted to the customer's exact needs at the delivery point. It is actually a primitive version of personalization. Examples include alterations to clothes in department stores or adjustments on bicycles bought in bicycle shops. Even more sophisticated customization is being offered by automobile dealerships when adding special accessories, such as fog lights, sound systems, DVD players, trailer hitches, bike racks, spoilers, etc.

The manufacturer "pulls" the type of accessories they offer from customer's desires. Then the manufacturer "pushes" the product with those accessory offers. This is why we classify this strategy as a **Pull–Push business model**.

Products bought using the point-of-delivery strategy are more expensive than those of the previous two strategies. This is true of course due to the cost of the alterations, adjustments, or the extra devices themselves, but also because of the increased complexity in the up front product design and manufacturing phase, the complexity that allows the added features. This is especially true in more complex products, such as automobiles. In order to add features like air-conditioning, fog lights, or advanced sound systems to a car at the point-of-delivery, all the related controls, electrical, and mechanical interfaces must be installed during the general product manufacturing phase, whether the added features are ever used or not. This additional layer of design and production makes the product more expensive for both the manufacturer and the consumer.

5.2.4 Strategy 4—Personalized Products

In Strategy 2, the manufacturer designs product options, and customers buy pre-established "packages," of those options, each package containing desired features plus (typically) a few that are not really needed. By contrast, in personalized production, **the buyer designs the product option set** and gets a truly personalized product. Strategy 4 requires products that are designed to be customized during the manufacturing or the assembly process, very flexible and reconfigurable manufacturing systems, and do it within a very rapid response time (Figure 5.5). Products sold under this strategy are more expensive than any of the previous strategies presented

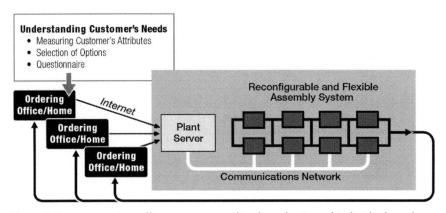

Figure 5.5 Strategy 4—pull system: personalized production of individual products.

above. The customers, however, get exactly the product that they want. Here the focus is on the individual rather than on the product.

Strategy 4 represents a **pull business model**. With this strategy, supply self-adjusts to demand. This means that despite the elevated per unit cost, there is no waste, since each product is built to order ("Pulled" by the customer) and typically even paid for in advance. With this strategy, the manufacturing companies do not accumulate undesired inventories and are not stuck with products that they cannot sell. Note that Dell, for example, does not really offer personalized products. But because of the large number of combinations offered, the customers' perception is that they are getting a personalized computer.

Strategy 4 requires a highly responsive manufacturing system. It also requires accurate understanding of the customer's need and a means of feeding that into the production. For example, a factory for personalized backpacks needs a measurement device to quickly measure dimensions of the customer's back and transfer those via the Internet to the factory. A manufacturer of Internet-order personalized suits must develop a website for the critical body measurements needed to tailor the suit for the customer. Automobile dealers may some day measure the way a customer fits into their car so that its instrument panel and safety belts can be custom-fit to the buyer. Such measurement devices and methods will one day be integral components of the product personalization strategy.

5.2.5 Product Variety and Delivery Time

As we have stated, the business model of mass customization must present solutions to two basic issues: (1) product variety management and (2) short delivery time of customer's orders. The four business strategies presented above are the core of four business models that deal with these two issues. The **product variety** offered to the customer increases at each level, but at each step **product delivery time** increases as well. The **product price range** (or the cost for the manufacturer) also increases along with the effort of providing richer variety. We compare these variables—product variety, delivery time, and cost range—in Figure 5.6.

Figure 5.6 also shows that the number of identical products (volume per model) is reduced as we move from Strategy 1 to Strategy 4. With Strategy 4, it is possible to have even just one-of-a-kind product with the features that exactly fit just one customer's preferences—a market of one.

Moving toward personalized products comprises a major challenge for manufacturing companies. Their success depends on the type of manufacturing system they can employ in the enterprise, and even on the location of the manufacturing plant in relation to the customers. Reducing delivery time of highly personalized products requires the final product assembly and many of the component manufacturing plants to be in close proximity to the customer market. Customers of personalized products will not wait 2–3 months for their products to be shipped over the ocean. The manufacturing plant must be able to deal, on a daily basis, with variable product quantities and large product mix, and be able to incorporate different options in each product produced.

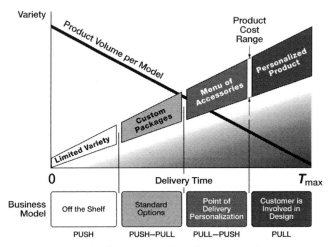

Figure 5.6 Business models of four strategies of customization and personalization.

5.3 MANUFACTURING SYSTEM CHARACTERISTICS

The two major inputs for manufacturing plants are **product volume** and **product mix** (i.e., variety) that have to be produced on a given manufacturing system at any given time. Producing products for mass customization and personalization presents a challenge because of the abrupt and substantial changes in the operation:

- **Product mix** is high (to accommodate the offered variety) and changes very often.
- **Product volume** (per model or variant) is small relative to mass production.

5.3.1 Scalability and Convertibility

To respond to frequent changes in volume and mix, the manufacturing systems that produce products for mass customization and personalization must possess two important characteristics: convertibility and scalability.

Convertibility expresses the **Mix** flexibility and is defined as: The ability to change the system functionality to produce different types of products.

Scalability expresses the **Volume** flexibility and is defined as: The ability to change the system capacity to produce different product volumes.

Convertibility is achieved by rapidly switching the system's task software, the fixtures that hold parts, and the tooling (manual tools, cutting tools, grippers, etc.). The manufacturing system that fits the mass customization paradigm must be scalable, convertible, and preferably reconfigurable.

5.3.2 Design Manufacturing Systems for Delayed Differentiation

A manufacturing system for mass customization can produce several members of a product family. Since many basic functions and features within a product family are shared among all members of the family, manufacturing the common features first, and adding those features that define the product variants in the later stages of production, often results in a substantial operational and cost savings.

Our student, Robert Rudolf, who worked at Dell Computers in 2005, describes a simpler process of delayed differentiation: "At Dell, laser-etching letters onto the keyboards is done according to the language character-set of the region to which that product is being shipped. This allows Dell to stock only one type of keyboard, and be flexible to fluctuations in demand from any of its markets across the globe."

Designing for delayed differentiation, or postponed differentiation, involves designs both the product and the process of a product family in such a way that the point where the product's differentiating functions are added is delayed to the very last possible stage of the manufacturing process (be it assembly or machining).

Usually the method is to move manufacturing operations of all the common functions to the initial steps of the manufacturing process, and adding the specified, differentiating functions (to form the product variants) to the last stages of the system. In this way, dedicated machinery might be used at the initial stages, and reconfigurable or flexible equipment as well as skilled product assemblers can be reserved for the later stages, as depicted in Figure 5.7. Progressive differentiation may be also utilized, in which the more popular differentiating features are built first, and those that are ordered seldom are added later.

Our student, Alex SJ Kang, described a very useful application of delayed differentiation: "I worked for Production Engineering Research Center at LG Electronics for four years. One of my projects was to develop a methodology for mass-customized refrigerators. In most countries in Asia, houses are not as big as those in the United States, and consequently the kitchen is a part of the living room. Therefore, customers want refrigerator to blend into their living room and furniture. To satisfy this need, we developed a manufacturing system, which allows buyers to customize the outer panels of refrigerator to match their house. However, meeting this

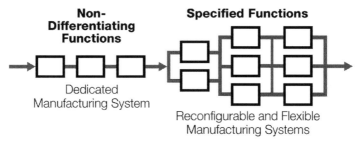

Figure 5.7 To accomplish delayed differentiation the customization is deferred to the flexible/reconfigurable stages of the manufacturing system.

need by holding inventory of differently colored refrigerators does not make economic sense. Our solution was a postponement production system. Refrigerators are first assembled without the outer panel. When a buyer finalizes an order, the factory attaches the outer panel and its accessories (e.g., ice dispenser, LCD TV), and delivers the product overnight. The project was a great success. Customers can choose 16 different colors and textures and 6 types of control units. LG was able to meet various customer demands without increasing its finished good inventory."

In an environment where customized product demands are stochastic, implementing delayed differentiation reduces overproduction of unwanted products and smoothes changes in product demand. Additional benefits include reduced cost of product handling in the factory, reduced manufacturing costs, and reduced inventories. For similar reasons, global supply chains are often designed with delayed differentiation. The common modules (e.g., a computer mother board) of products are assembled in low-labor-cost countries and shipped to the countries in which the product is to be sold, where final assembly takes place.

5.4 ECONOMICS OF PRODUCT VARIATION

How many product variations can a firm offer and still maximize its profit margin? More variations mean more customers. However, there are costs associated with more variation: manufacturing cost, handling cost, and the cost of space in the store that sells the product.

5.4.1 The Tradeoff

On one hand, when more product variations are offered the firm will sell more products and more customers will get exactly what they need and be satisfied. However, too many product variations may be very expensive to the manufacturer because

- Manufacturing complexity increases.
- Product development expends resources.
- Inventory control and handling cost at the point of delivery is more expensive.
- After-sale support is more complex.

Therefore

> The decision about the optimal number of product variations offered is a tradeoff between manufacturing cost and customer satisfaction.

The following two examples clarify the issue of the excessive cost associated with handling a large number of variations. Mass-customized shirts are sold in five sizes: S, M, L, XL, and XXL, and in four colors. The number of products that the store should handle is $5 \times 4 = 20$. The store needs 20 shelves to display that many shirts. Jeans are sold in 10 waist sizes, in 6 length sizes, from 4 manufacturers. The number of products that the store should handle is $10 \times 6 \times 4 = 240$. The store needs 240 shelves to display the jeans. Is this practical?

Note that the number of product differentiating features increases the total number of product types very fast. The number of the product differentiating features is a measure of the product complexity. Product complexity is a burden on the manufacturing system, and may cause assembly errors. Herman Miller, for example, offers a variety of office chairs. The customer may select the following options: two (2) height adjustments, three (3) tilt positions, five (5) arm options (including no arms, two fixed pad finished arms, and two options of adjustable arms), two (2) seat types, two (2) options of back support, six (6) options of seat finish, six (6) options of back finish, two (2) chair-base types, five (5) options of casters and glides, 20 fabrics for the seat, and 20 fabrics for the back. The number of office chair options offered by Herman Miller is:

$$2 \times 3 \times 5 \times 2 \times 2 \times 6 \times 6 \times 2 \times 5 \times 20 \times 20 = 17,280,000$$

Namely, Herman Miller offers over 17 million product variations. The workers on the chair assembly line have to handle an enormous product complexity. Moreover, line rebalancing, required because of frequent volume changes, is a major challenge for Herman Miller's operations engineers. However, even with these frequent rebalancing operations and the large variety, the number of human errors in the chair assembly process (which is done manually) is small, and the errors are identified at the inspection station at the end of the assembly line.

In the above example, it is obvious that there is no store that will display 240 types of pants, because it is not economically justified. If a store tries to handle computers and sells them off the shelf, the number of computers to be carried is huge (different memory size, different speed, different hard disks, different built-in accessories, etc.). Storing a huge number of product variations is absolutely not a cost-effective marketing strategy. Like the manufacturer, a store must determine the optimal number of variations that it can handle by looking at it as a tradeoff between customer satisfaction and store handling costs.

Given that a basic challenge is "how much variety should we offer," the following example demonstrates a simple method of calculating the optimal number of variations in storing products when applying Strategy 1 of mass customization.

5.4.2 Example: Selling Pants in a Store

Imagine that the entire market requires pants of only waist sizes 30–36, and that the length is irrelevant, since the product can be altered at the store. Assume a sole source manufacturer of pants, and that v is the number of product variations.

Let us start the analysis by assuming that only waist size 32 is available, that means an offering of $v = 1$. Let us assume the distribution model for pants that is depicted in Figure 5.8.

The distribution model assumes that 50% of the potential customers will buy the product because it perfectly fit their size. We can further assume that an additional 40% of the customers need a smaller size (i.e., a different variation of the product), but will compromise and will buy size 32 pants and use a belt. In addition, another 10% will buy a smaller size than they really need, since the right size is not available.

If m is the total number of pants sold, we assume $m = 100$ in this case (when only size 32 is available). If there had to be a perfect fit between the customer size needs and the available pants, the manufacturer could only sell 50 pairs of pants. Since we assume that the entire population needs seven (7) sizes of pants (30–36), the maximum potential market is 350: $50 \times 7 = 350$. This means that if only one size is available, the manufacturer can sell only 100 pairs of pants, which is $100/350 \times 100\% = 29\%$; namely, only 29% of the potential market is captured.

Let us continue the example by adding also size 35 (sizes 32 and 35 are now available). The number of product variations is increased to $v = 2$. The distribution in

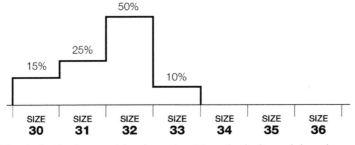

Figure 5.8 A distribution model, where size 32 perfectly fit, and the other customers compromise and buy products that almost fit their needs.

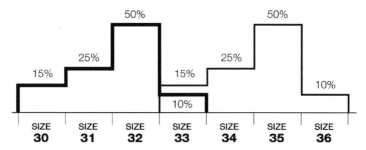

Figure 5.9 A distribution model with two product variations.

this case is depicted in Figure 5.9. Now, as shown, customers who need size 33 may select either a smaller size (32) or a larger size (35). We guess that at least most of these customers will buy size 35 and use a belt, rather than buy the more narrow size. This means that the added size is sold to only an additional 90 people. The sales now are to 190 customers (and not to 200, as one may think). The number of customers is $m = 15 + 25 + 50 + 15 + 25 + 50 + 10 = 190$.

We see that when a new size is introduced, the net gain depends on the difference between the sale potential of the new size and what was already captured by the other sizes introduced earlier. This statement is correct also for the introduction of a new product from a product family that already exists in the market.

We can now repeat the calculations that were demonstrated for sizes 32 and 35 and continue to introduce waist sizes in the following order: 36, 30, 31, 33, and 34 (which is the optimal order if we started with 32 and 35). The results are shown in Table 5.2. In this table, Δm means the market incremental increase as a result of the increase in v, and $m\%$ means the percentage of the market share for a given v.

5.4.2.1 The Handling Cost

The revenues, z, are proportional to the number of pants sold. For simplicity, we assume that each pair of pants is sold for \$1. In order to calculate the profit, we have to make an assumption about the handling cost y. We assume a linear mathematical model with constant fixed expenses to prepare the

TABLE 5.2   The Effect of Increasing the Number of Variations on the Market Share ($m\%$)

V	Size	m	Δm	$m\%$	z (\$)	y (\$)	Profit
1	32	100	100	28.6	100	60	40
2	35	190	90	52.8	190	90	100
3	36	230	40	65.7	230	120	110
4	30	265	35	75.7	265	150	115
5	31	**300**	35	**85.7**	**300**	180	**120**
6	33	325	25	92.9	325	210	115
7	34	350	25	100.0	350	240	110

In bold are the optimal values that yield maximum profit.

location in the store where the products will be displayed, plus a variable cost, which is proportional to the number of variations (shelves to display the pants).

$$y = 30 + 30v \qquad (5.1)$$

5.4.2.2 Maximum Profit   As seen in Table 5.2, the highest profit is achieved for $v = 5$, when the captured market share is 85.7%. When additional variations are introduced, although the total revenues are slightly higher, the net profit becomes lower.

The data from Table 5.2 are plotted in Figure 5.10. As seen, the profit becomes larger with the increase in the number of variations up to $v = 5$, and then starts to decline (although revenues continue to increase).

When the revenue data points are connected, the resulted graph can be approximated by an exponential curve as shown in Figure 5.10. For this example, the equation is

$$z = 350(1 - e^{-0.3v}) \qquad (5.2)$$

This exponential equation is a solution of the following first-order differential equation:

$$\frac{\Delta m}{\Delta v} \cong (350 - m).\alpha \qquad (5.3)$$

where, in this case, $\alpha = 0.3$. A larger α means that a larger segment of the market can be captured with a smaller number of variations.

The consequent question is whether the order in which product variations are introduced into the market makes a difference in the value of α, and consequently moves the optimal profit point. For example, we know that most stores carries only even numbers for men's pants: 30, 32, 34, and 36.

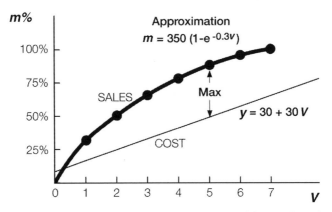

Figure 5.10   The captured market share $m\%$ as a function of the number of variations v.

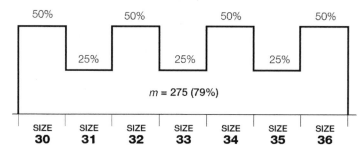

Figure 5.11   The captured market share $m\%$ as a function of the product size.

The market share with these four (4) sizes is shown in Figure 5.11. The market share is now 275 of a potential of 350, namely 79%.

If an additional size, 31, is added, the distribution is shown in Figure 5.12. The market is now 300, or 86%. It is not economical to add the size 31 just to capture additional 7% of the market, since the incremental additional handling cost is larger. The calculation that proves this point is shown below:

Assuming the same cost model as before, $y = 30 + 30v$, one may calculate the expansion of the market share for this example. The results are shown in Table 5.3.

The results of Table 5.3 are drawn in Figure 5.13. From the table and Figure 5.13, one can see that the maximum profit is achieved at $v = 4$, namely when all the even sizes (30, 32, 34, and 36) are stored, and after that the profit starts to go down. This result verifies what the stores are doing in practice—carrying only the even sizes of men's pants.

The differential equation in this case is

$$\frac{\Delta m}{\Delta v} \cong 0.35(350 - m) \tag{5.4}$$

This means that $\alpha = 0.35$ whereas in the first part of the example, when sizes were introduced by a different strategy, the coefficient was $\alpha = 0.3$. We see that larger α is reaching the maximum profit with a smaller number of variations.

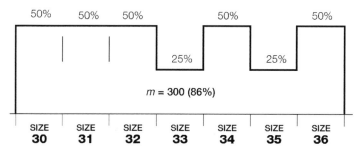

Figure 5.12   The captured market share for five sizes.

TABLE 5.3   The Captured Market Share _m_% and the Profit as a Function of _v_

V	Size	m	Δm	m%	z	y	Profit
1	32	100	100	28.6	100	60	40
2	36	190	90	52.8	190	90	100
3	34	240	50	68.6	240	120	120
4	30	275	35	78.6	275	150	**125**
5	31	300	25	85.7	300	180	120
6	33	325	25	92.9	325	210	115
7	35	350	25	100	350	240	110

In bold: four variations ($v = 4$) yield the maximum profit (125).

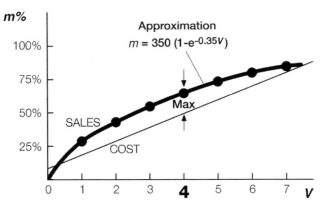

Figure 5.13   The captured market share as a function of the number of variations.

We see by this example that the company profit is affected by the order in which the product variety is introduced to the market.

> "I have never thought of the economies of product variations. However, this explains why I always had such a difficult time finding size 33 jeans (before I gained weight to force me to buy 34!)" BJ Baker (a student).

5.5 MATHEMATICAL ANALYSIS OF MASS CUSTOMIZATION

In this section, we offer a simple mathematical analysis of the relationships between cost and the number of product variations that are needed to expand a company's sales.

5.5.1 Cost of Complexity Associated with Variety

It is true that increased variety with mass customization methods expands markets and sales. Nevertheless, mass customization, and especially product personalization, is adding complexity to the firm, and handling complexity costs money. Product and process complexity also adds cost due to management of the portfolio of products over their entire **life cycle**. Specifically, the added cost and confusion arise from the effort required and potential errors arising out of the need to switch from one product variant or option to another, during

- Product development
- Product manufacturing
- Logistics and product distribution
- After-sales service and warranty support
- Disposal of the products

To be more specific, product variety increases the cost because of the following reasons:

1. Increased variety increases the product development cost because the product has to be designed differently, for example, with a modular architecture.
2. Increased variety increases the manufacturing cost because
   - Cost increases due to small-batch operation.
   - Downtime for conversion between products may be needed.
   - People who are doing the final assembly make more mistakes when the number of variations or options is larger.
   - Machinery cannot be the inexpensive dedicated type, and flexible-reconfigurable equipment is needed.
3. Increased variety increases the marketing, logistics, and product distribution cost. More manuals are needed. Larger display spaces are needed. More effort and coordination is needed to send the right product to the right customer.
4. Service given to more product versions requires workers with more skill, which also increases the cost.
5. Disassembly for disposal of the products at the end of their lifetime may be more complex when more product versions are produced.

5.5.2 Variety-based Feedback Model

Figure 5.14 shows a block diagram of a market model. Here we assume that offering new product variants of a product family allows the manufacturer to penetrate new market segments—the customers that did not buy the existing product variants. The total market size can continue to grow as new product variants, with their own varieties, penetrate to new market segments and increase the total demand for the product. In order to penetrate to even more market segments, what is needed are more product varieties. This creates a positive feedback loop as shown in the figure.

According to the variety-based positive feedback model in Figure 5.14, demand can always grow if new variants of the product family are offered, because there will always be customers to whom the new variants will offer a better fit to their needs.

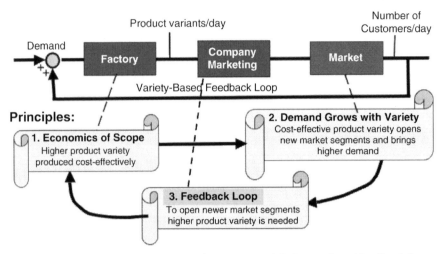

Figure 5.14   Mass customization production is modeled as a closed feedback loop.

The major difference between the positive feedback loop of mass production and the one shown here for mass customization is that the former is a volume-based loop whereas the latter is a variety-based loop. Alternatively, we can say that the mass production loop is based on economies of scale, and the mass customization loop is based on economies of scope.

5.5.3   Calculating the Number of Variations for Maximum Profit

The drawback of the feedback model is that it does not take into account the costs associated with handling the expanded variety and the growing number of product variants and versions. The simplistic variety versus cost model that was introduced in Section 5.4 assumes that the manufacturer (or retailer) costs increase linearly with the number of product variations offered. It also assumes that the total market size has an upper boundary ($m = 100\%$). According to this model an optimal point can be calculated in which the profit is maximum. For example, in Figure 5.15 the optimal point is achieved for offering four variants, namely $v = 4$.

Although revenues continue to increase beyond the optimal point, the extra costs associated with manufacturing and handling the variations are larger than the sale profit margin, and therefore it is not economical to offer a larger number of product variations beyond the optimal point. Based on our simplified mathematical model, we below offer a simple method to calculate the number of variations that will result in the maximum profit.

We have shown that the number of variations, v, that will result in the maximum profit may be calculated by the following simplified mathematical model:

$$\text{Profit} = C.(1 - e^{-\alpha v}) - A - Bv \tag{5.5}$$

where α is a parameter that depends on the type of variations that are introduced and the buyers' attitude toward them, C is the maximum potential revenues with an infinite

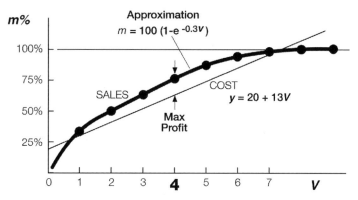

Figure 5.15   The captured market share $m\%$ as function of the number of variations v.

number of variations (i.e., market size), and A and B are parameters that depend on the costs associated with manufacturing and handling the product variations. The optimal product variety, v_m, is

$$v_m = (1/\alpha).\ln[\alpha C/B] \qquad (5.6)$$

Calculating the optimal product variety is a critical business decision. Manufacturers should be mindful of the number of product variations that will bring the maximum profit margin.

The above analysis does not and cannot take into consideration the new market segments, both locally and globally, that may open when competing product varieties and options are introduced. As long as products can penetrate new market segments, and do it before competition arises, there can be additional profit for the company. With increased global competition, the windows of opportunity are getting smaller and companies must act very quickly in penetrating any new market segments.

5.6 SUMMARY

The goal and the enablers that make mass customization possible are
   Goal: Offering product variety at affordable prices

   Enablers:
- Modular products.
- Fulfillment system for getting customer orders directly to the manufacturing plants.
- Flexible/reconfigurable manufacturing machines and systems that allow rapid changes in product mix and volume.

TABLE 5.4 Comparison of Two Major Manufacturing Paradigms

	Mass production	Mass customization
Market	Demand > Supply	Demand < Supply
Conditions	Homogeneous markets	Fragmented markets
Product	A few products	Variety of products
	Long product lifespan	Short product lifespan
Business strategy	Economies of scale	Economies of scope
	Ignore niche markets	Sell to niche markets
Mfg. system	Dedicated lines	Flexible and reconfigurable

> A major strategic decision in mass customization relates to variety versus cost.

Manufacturing companies should establish the number of cost-effective product variants or options at which their profit margin is at its maximum. Companies should also bear in mind that profit is affected by the order in which variety is introduced, namely, which options or sizes should be introduced first, which should come second, and the sequence in which options and sizes affect the total profit. Similarly, it is important to determine which options and sizes should not be offered at all because incremental costs associated with the offer may be larger than the profit from additional market share. Products must always stay in sync with the ever-changing desires of customers. Also, a company's manufacturing facilities must be able to respond quickly to take advantage of new market opportunities.

As a summary, Table 5.4 compares mass production with mass customization in terms of market type, product variety and lifespan, and the type of manufacturing system needed to cope with the paradigm requirements.

Finally, note that if the firm's business model is for mass customization...

- The product design
- The manufacturing system, and
- The business model

...should all accommodate cost-effective product variety.

PROBLEMS

5.1 Do you agree with the following statement by Mr. Lutz (see Section 5.1): "It's the manufacturer who's supposed to decide, and don't leave the creative work to the consumer!"

5.2 Determine mathematically the number of variations that result in the maximum profit in Figures 5.10 and 5.13.

5.3 Dishes and Silverware Company (D&S) needs to determine the number of variations of a popular dish set to sell in their store. The plates come in four sizes: 6, 8, 10, and 12 inches. Demand for each size is equal at 100 units. Revenue from each plate is $10.

Sixty percent (60%) of customers, not being able to find their preferred size, will buy one size larger and 40% of customers will buy one size smaller if the exact size of their preference is not available. For example, if only 6 and 10 inches are offered, in addition to the normal demand of 100 units for each of these sizes, 60 people initially requiring 8-in. plates and 40 people initially requesting for 12 in.-plates will also buy the 10–in. plate. Regardless of the number of variations, the fixed cost is $750 and there is an additional $500 cost per variety offered.

Determine the number of variations (1, 2, 3, or 4) and which plate sizes D&S should offer in order to maximize its profits.

Chapter **6**

Traditional Manufacturing Systems

Manufacturing companies in the twenty-first century face increasingly frequently changing and unpredictable market imperatives caused by increased competition and globalization. These include rapid introduction of new products, constantly varying product demand, and changing government regulations. To stay competitive, companies must use manufacturing systems that not only produce their goods with high productivity but also allow for rapid response to market pressures and changing consumer needs. Can traditional manufacturing systems, many of them designed in the 1980s, cope with these new requirements?

6.1 MANUFACTURING SYSTEMS

A manufacturing system is defined as a collection of manufacturing machines (or stations) that are integrated to perform a controlled set of repeatable operations on raw materials, which alter that material to achieve a desired final form, or to assemble a final product (Figure 6.1). Assembly systems and machining systems are particular cases of manufacturing systems. In machining systems every operation is done by a machine tool that has many cutting tools deployed from either large tool holders or a tool magazine. In assembly systems, the manipulative operations may be performed by robots, people, or combinations of both.

Examples of manufacturing machines include milling, turning, drilling, and grinding machines for machining, robots and welders for assembly, presses for

The Global Manufacturing Revolution: Product-Process-Business Integration and Reconfigurable Systems
By Yoram Koren
Copyright © 2010 John Wiley & Sons, Inc.

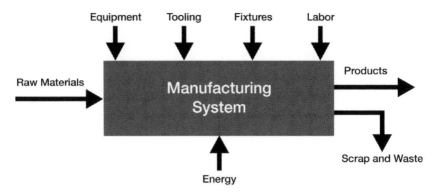

Figure 6.1 A manufacturing system converts raw material to a useful part or product.

metal forming, laser processing equipment for metal cutting and heat treatment, injection molding for plastic manufacturing, and more. Machining systems typically remove material in order to shape parts into a finished or refined state. Examples of machined parts include engine blocks, pump housings, and compressors. Assembly systems are used to fit parts together in order to make a finished product. They are utilized, for example, to assemble computers or build automobiles from given sets of parts and sub-assemblies. Chemical manufacturing systems apply complex chemical processes to produce, for example, pharmaceuticals and semi-conductors wafers.

When building complex products, many manufacturing processes are needed. For example, one machining system will receive rough castings of transmission cases as input and mill and bore the finished shells. These are then transferred to an assembly system where the various gears, shafts, and other components are installed into the transmission case. The assembled transmission is then sent to a car assembly system that assembles the whole car.

Multi-stage Manufacturing Systems: Manufacturing systems for production at medium and high quantities are composed of multiple stages, with each stage containing a piece of equipment that performs a given set of operations. When the operations in one stage are completed, the partially processed product is transferred to the next stage, and so forth until all needed operations are completed and the product is finished. Examples of multi-stage systems may be for machining, assembly, semi-conductor fabrication, paper production, etc.

Multi-stage manufacturing systems can be configured in many different ways, defined by (1) the way that the machines are arranged in the stages and (2) the way that the part is transferred between machines (with the aid of material transport systems, such as conveyors or overhead gantries). Many manufacturing systems are arranged sequentially, in serial lines, as depicted at the top of Figure 6.2. Serial assembly lines are very common in many industries. When large quantities of the product are needed, or when a set of operations takes an especially long time to complete, multiple machines (or assembly stations) may be installed at a stage to perform identical operations (Fig. 6.2, bottom).

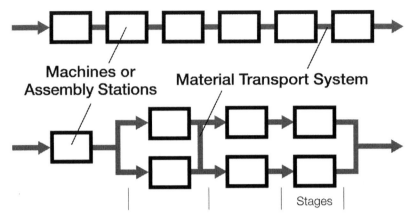

Figure 6.2 Examples of multi-stage manufacturing systems: a serial line (top), and a four-stage hybrid system (bottom).

6.2 PRODUCTION OF COMPLEX PRODUCTS

In this section, we present two examples of manufacturing operations flow in the production of complex products. Both examples involve several manufacturing processes that must be synchronized to avoid large buffers (inventories) between operations and between processes.

6.2.1 Production of Automobiles

Your car or truck is the most complex product that ordinary people buy. It is by far more complex than your computer or TV set. The production of automobiles is multifaceted and requires expertise in a variety of manufacturing areas: stamping, casting, injection molding, welding, machining and assembly, as shown in Figure 6.3.[*]

Automobile production begins at the stamping plant where huge presses stamp sheet metal into metal dies to create the panels that make up the automobile. The various panels are shipped to an auto-body automated assembly plant, in which welding robots join the metal panels and create the overall shape of the car, what is called the body-in-white. In parallel, the doors are manufactured in another stamping plant and then transferred to the auto-body assembly plant and assembled manually onto the body-in-white. The automobile is then sent on a moving line for spray painting, which is performed by robots.

Simultaneous with the auto-body fabrication, powertrain plants manufacture the major drive components—engine blocks, cylinder heads, crankshafts, and transmission cases—by machining operations (the left side of Figure 6.3). The raw parts for the machining operations arrive from casting plants. The powertrain plant primarily uses high-precision machine tools arranged in multi-stage systems (often 50–100

[*]The flowchart of automobile production was composed by the author.

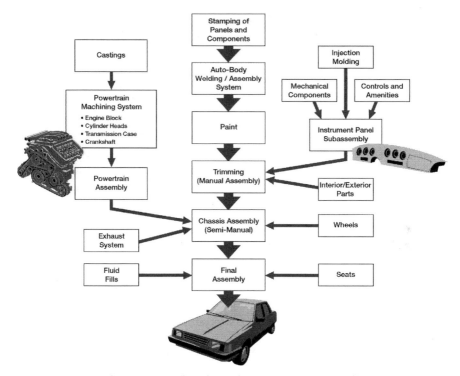

Figure 6.3   A flowchart of automobile production.

machines per system), and inspection equipment to measure the machined parts to tolerances as precise as $10 \,\mu m$. The powertrain plants are the most expensive plants in the auto industry, more expensive than assembly plants by far. In parallel to the manufacturing of the major powertrain components, first-tier suppliers make other powertrain components, such as pistons. These parts are added to the engine block, together with the electrical wiring, fuel lines, and belts, in the powertrain assembly section of the engine production plant.

At the same time, other first-tier suppliers build the entire front instrument panel (IP) sub-assembly, including air-conditioning and temperature control, audio system, airbags, gauges, etc. The components in the IP are supplied to the first-tier supplier by second-tier suppliers. Other first-tier suppliers build the car seats, the exhaust system, etc.

After painting, the vehicle shell enters the assembly shop. A typical assembly shop has three sections: trimming, chassis assembly, and final assembly. The cars enter trimming on moving platforms, each car on a separate platform, which travel one after another in a line. Trimming is a manually intensive assembly process; workers, arranged in teams, stand on the slowly moving platform and assemble various parts in the car interior, such as the IP and steering column, as well as the windshield, lamps, bumpers, and exterior molding. Each team of workers is responsible for a limited set of tasks that takes about 50 seconds. They are doing these tasks repetitively all day.

Note that the (quite complex) IP, for example, is shipped from the first-tier supplier as one sub-assembly and installed in the car at the line cycle speed of about 50 seconds including all of its various connections.

Next, the chassis assembly is done. In chassis assembly, the bottom of the car is put together. There are plants in which the whole chassis, including all of the powertrain and exhaust system components, is pre-assembled and attached to the car at the line cycle speed, again within 50 seconds. Finally, the car moves to the final assembly section where the car seats and wheels are installed, and fluids are added. The engine starts, and the car rolls off the assembly line on its own power, at an average rate of one car per minute. Keep in mind that cars rolling out at a rate of one per minute must also be sold at a rate of one per minute.

Our student, Craig Ashmore, described the manufacturing process of the IP.

"I was recently at an IP manufacturing plant and saw this process first hand. The IP being built was a skin and foam panel. The skins were created about every 3–4 minutes. The skins then went over to the next line where foam was put between the retainer and skin and then sent to a water jet line. The water jet cut out all the extra skin material. The IP was then sent to an area where AC vents were installed. Immediately the top panel was sent to a line where it was mated to the cross-car beam and all the other items were added. The complete IP was then loaded onto racks and loaded on a truck to be shipped that day to the plant. The IP is then installed into a car the day it is received at the manufacturing plant. I was very impressed at the efficiency that was used in the plant. The whole IP line was contained in an area about 1000 square feet."

6.2.2 Production of Appliances

The appliance industry is a growing global manufacturing sector. It includes the production of washers and dryers, refrigerators, freezers, dishwashers, ranges, compactors, room air conditioners, and microwaves, together with portable appliances such as stand mixers, hand mixers, and blenders. The 100 top global appliance companies earned combined sale revenues of more than $900 billion U.S. in 2005.[1] Whirlpool Corporation, for example, accounts for over $14.3 billion of these sales, and its brand names are marketed in more than 170 countries worldwide.[*]

One of the most common appliances in the global market place is the refrigerator. In 2007 there were 10 million refrigerators exported from the United States by domestic home appliance manufacturers. The manufacturing of a refrigerator is a multifaceted process and requires the expertise of many skilled workers as well as manufacturing processes such as extrusion, thermoforming, stamping, welding, and injection molding.

---

[*]This section was written by Kate Presnell, Lukasz Skalski, and Katherine Warner, former students of the global manufacturing class, who are Whirlpool's employees; see also www.whirlpoolcorp.com.

Like most manufacturing processes, the refrigerator begins with raw materials; most notably in the form of plastic pellets and coils of steel. A number of preparation steps and sub-assemblies occur before the product enters the final assembly line. The first of these sub-assemblies is the door and can be found on the left side of Figure 6.4. The plastic pellets are extruded into a sheet, which is then thermoformed. The thermoforming process includes heating up the plastic liner sheet, forming it over a mold, and cooling the product in a temperature-controlled environment. The liner is then assembled to the metal doors. The doors are formed by straightening the coils of steel into flat sheets, then cutting, stamping, and welding them accordingly.

Between the plastic liner and the metal door, the appropriate internal ice and water sub-system components are attached. These components typically consist of conduits for the wiring harness and water inlet, as well as the reinforcing structure for the exterior elements of the system added later in the assembly process. Expanding adhesive foam insulation is then sprayed into the vacant space between

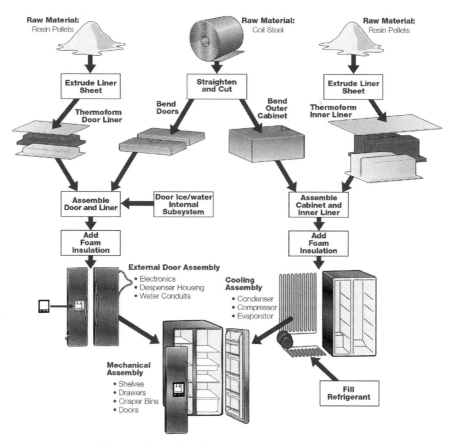

Figure 6.4 A flowchart of refrigerator production.

the inner and outer doors. This foam serves as the insulating agent as well as adds to the structural stability of the door. This sub-assembly then proceeds down a conveyor to where the external door features including dispenser electronics and housing, handles, and water inlet hose are added.

The other major sub-assembly consists of the main refrigerator cabinet and its components. The cabinet is formed much like that of the door described earlier, of an inner liner and metal exterior. These two parts are assembled and foam insulation is again injected into the vacant space between the two pieces and allowed to expand. Once again, the foam serves to both insulate the cabinet and add structural reinforcement. The cabinet is then equipped with the cooling system that consists of a condenser, compressor, evaporator, and necessary conduits. These conduits are then charged with refrigerant.

The cabinet then travels to the main assembly line. Here, the remaining features are installed: shelves, drawers, bins, etc. Once the inside of the refrigerator is assembled, the doors are attached. There is then a quality check to ensure the refrigeration system is sealed with no leaks. Some refrigerators may proceed to performance testing for an additional quality check while the majority of finished goods are packaged and sent to the distribution centers.

6.3   THE STATE OF ART AT THE END OF THE TWENTIETH CENTURY

Multi-stage manufacturing systems are made up of many machines or assembly stations connected via a material transfer mechanism. The transfer mechanism may be an overhead gantry system, a conveyor, or an autonomous-guided vehicle (AGV). The machines may be dedicated to one fixed set of operations, flexible such as robots in an assembly system, or programmable computerized numerically controlled (CNC) machine tools. CNC controllers are very versatile and can be easily applied in milling, turning, drilling, grinding, shaping, laser processing, etc.

To be regarded as a true manufacturing "system," the operation of at least the critical elements of the line must be coordinated through a supervising central command station where a computer controls and synchronizes the operations of the machines. The two most common manufacturing system types that were available at the end of the twentieth century were the dedicated manufacturing line (DML) and flexible manufacturing system (FMS). Many manufacturing industries combine a portfolio of dedicated and FMSs to produce their products. This approach has evolved because neither approach, on its own, is adequate to meet the ever-expanding challenges of a global economy of rapidly changing demands and consumer tastes while maintaining low prices.

6.3.1   Dedicated Manufacturing Lines

Dedicated lines (also referred to as "transfer lines") are designed to produce just one product, but at very high throughput. (*The average output of a production machine or*

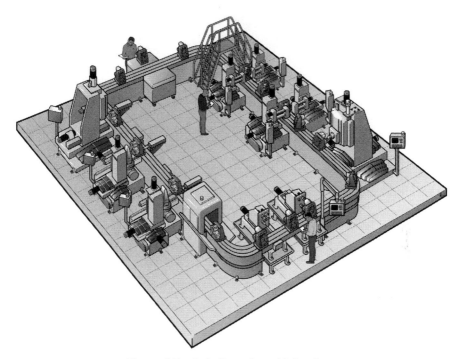

Figure 6.5   A dedicated machining line.

system, measured in parts per time unit, is called **throughput**.) The DML is based on a collection of relatively simple machines arranged sequentially in a line, where the processed part moves in a synchronous manner from one machine (or station) to the next. The high throughput of DML is cost-effective when very large quantities of the product are needed.

An example of a dedicated machining line composed of 10 dedicated machining stations is shown in Figure 6.5. This system was built to produce just one part. An operator loads the raw parts and unloads the finished parts. The part moves along the conveyor and stops at each station for processing. In some stations several tools work on the part simultaneously. Two stations in the system of Figure 6.5 even have machines that do machining operations on both sides of the part simultaneously. The DML control is done by fixed automation (called hard automation) that in practice cannot be changed. This production line has very high throughput of identical parts. Once in place, DMLs operate reliably and are well suited to produce high volumes of identical parts at great efficiency.

Each station or machine in a DML performs a single unchangeable operation on every part passing through. Special multi-spindle tools that drill or tap a fixed pattern of several holes at one stroke contribute to the high throughput of DMLs that produce machined parts. The pattern of holes fits only certain part geometry, as shown in Figure 6.6.

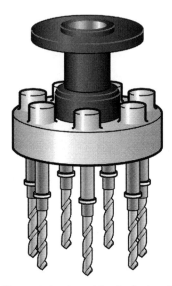

Figure 6.6   A multi-spindle head.

DMLs have been a basic element of high-volume manufacturing for generations. True to the mass production paradigm, since their output volume is high, the cost per part is relatively low. Once fully in place, DMLs perform at a constant designed rate, outputting identical high-quality parts at large quantities. However, with increasing pressure from global competition, the demand for specific parts can vary widely. Situations often occur where dedicated lines do not operate at full capacity, and when that happens the cost per part is much higher.

For example, a dedicated line can produce an engine block every 30 seconds. As long as the dedicated line operates at its planned capacity, it produces many parts at very attractive costs. However, if engines are produced at a rate of 30 seconds each, it stands to reason that they have to be assembled into corresponding numbers of vehicles that will be sold at a rate of a car every 30 seconds. What happens when cars cannot be sold at a rate of one every 30 seconds? Then the rate needed has been reduced, say to one every three minutes. When that happens the dedicated line is underutilized, and loses its economy of scale. The cost per product becomes higher. In fact, because of increased market volatility and competitive pressures, DMLs are increasingly underutilized. A report published in Italy in 1998[2] indicated that the average utilization of the surveyed DMLs in a European auto manufacturer was only 53%! One common reason for this low average utilization is that in the introductory stages of new products, or at the end of a product life cycle, fewer parts are required, considerably lower than optimal volumes. But because of global competition, even products in the mature phase do not always reach the production volumes forecast when the line was designed.

At the other extreme, DMLs also fail when demand goes above the design capacity (Figure 6.7). If a product's popularity exceeds all market expectations, or when new

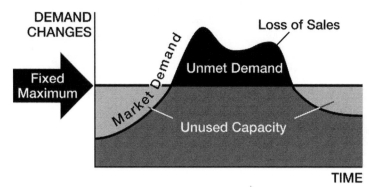

Figure 6.7 A DML system is an excellent choice when it is operating at its designed throughput capacity, which cannot be easily changed. Losses can occur in unmet demand when a product is popular, as well as in unused capacity as its popularity wanes.

uses are found for existing products, the DML is powerless to respond, resulting in a loss of sales.

If market demand for a product increases quickly, the fixed maximum capacity of the DML does not allow the manufacturer to grab the opportunity to produce and sell more products. This results in substantial losses in potential sales and actually entails much larger economic losses than those from unused capacity.

In the quote below we cite Ronald Zarrella, a former President of General Motors (GM), who described how a shortage of engine blocks (a component produced largely on DMLs) caused a loss in sales of entire vehicles.

General Motors Corp.'s top executive said that a sharp rebound in market share would not be possible if the industry sales continue at their torrid pace because GM could not produce enough full-sized pickup trucks to meet demand. "GM simply cannot make enough big V8 engines to build all the full-sized pickup trucks it needs to meet the market share goal," said Ronald Zarrella, the president of GM's North American Operations. But Zarrella said low gasoline prices, which help sales of sport utility vehicles and pickup trucks, were still better than high gasoline prices, which help sales GM's low-profit cars, for which it has extra production capacity. "If gasoline prices rose, he said, there'd been positive in terms of market share and lots of negative in terms of profitability." (*The New York Times*, February 12, 1999).

The main drawback of DMLs in the globalization era is that these lines are not designed to change, and therefore they cannot be converted to produce new products easily. In the globalization era, the marketable lifespan of a product becomes shorter and shorter with competing products being introduced faster and faster. This all makes the building of DMLs uneconomical, and for this reason they are vanishing in many manufacturing industries.

6.3.2 Flexible Manufacturing Systems

As we have said, DMLs cover the high-volume/low-variety work and stand-alone computer numerically controlled (CNC) machines are for low- to medium-volume, high-variety production on the other end of the spectrum. The middle ground (mid-volume/mid-variety manufacturing) is taken by FMS and by reconfigurable manufacturing systems. The FMS is defined as: *An integrated group of processing units, such as CNC machine tools, linked by an automated material handling system, whose operation is controlled by a supervisory computer.*

History of Flexible Manufacturing Systems: One of the first firms to develop an integrated manufacturing system was Molins Company in the United Kingdom. In 1967 this company presented the "Molins System 24," a flexible and integrated system demonstrating a novel way to increase productivity. In this system several machining stations were linked by an automated handling system for transferring parts that were mounted on pallets.

Four years later, in 1971, Sundstrand (in Illinois, USA) developed the "Shuttle Car System", a rail-type pallet transfer system on which parts flow to and from the machining stations, located along the rail track.[3] This system, however, was suitable only for long and variable machining times.

At the Leipzig Spring Fair in 1972, Auerbach, a German machine tool builder, presented their manufacturing system "M250/02 CNC". It was quipped with two three-axis machining centers, three two-arm changers, and one four-arm robot; this system enabled a complete five-face machining of prismatic parts. A central computer was used to control the machining centers, but the part handling was done manually from an operator's station.

In the mid-1970s FMS emerged for producing small batches of many different parts. Cincinnati Milacron, a machine tool builder in Ohio, was an industry pioneer in the development of FMSs.[4] Production cells linked with automated material handling systems emerged in the 1980s (e.g., by Max Müller and Fritz Werner). In the last 20 years of the twentieth century FMSs proliferated throughout the industrialized world, although the trend in some industries has been to utilize smaller, less expensive flexible manufacturing cells.

FMS is a major enabler of mass customization because it can produce a variety of components or products within its stated capability. FMS also enables the redesign of products to meet new market requirements without adding substantial investments in the manufacturing system. Most of the experience gained with FMS installations has been with machining systems.[5,6]

The building blocks of FMSs are CNC machines (in machining systems), or robots (in assembly systems and automatic welding lines). Both have sophisticated operational controllers integrated with a material handling system that transfers the parts between machines and/or assembly stations. CNC machines in flexible machining systems include machining centers, drilling machines, and laser cutters, and

Figure 6.8 A machining center with a chain-type tool magazine and an automatic tool changer.

sometimes automated inspection machines. Typical material handling systems are conveyors, overhead gantries, and AGVs. The successful operation of a whole FMS is based on coordinating the operation of its flexible pieces of equipment.

In order to perform various operations quickly, CNC machines are equipped with rotating tool magazines and automatic tool changers (ATCs), as depicted in Figure 6.8. The variety of tools in the magazine enables CNC machine tools to perform different milling and drilling operations on the part on one machine. If the tool magazine of the CNC machine is large enough to contain all the tools needed to produce several parts, the CNC can even be programmed to produce a variety of parts.

In machining systems parts are located and clamped on fixtures, which allows transferring the part for succeeding machining operations. The fixtures are built to precisely fit the part geometry, and their clamps must be located such that they allow for cutting tool accessibility. The fixtures with their parts are mounted on pallets, which are transferred between machines through the whole system.

The data stream sent to the CNCs, and the robots that constitute the FMS, is a sequence of tasks that they have to perform (e.g., drill, change tool, mill, weld, move a part, etc.) in order to manufacture a particular part. This data stream is called a part program. The machines and robots are designed to accurately follow the series of numerically defined steps over and over. Producing a new part type requires loading a new part program as well as having the right tools in the tool magazine and using the proper fixtures to hold the new parts.

If the tool magazine of each CNC machine contains the tools needed to produce several types of parts, the FMS can rapidly switch its production from one part type to another. The operation of an FMS produces several types of parts, each type in a batch of multiple identical parts. For example, if three parts A, B, and C have to be produced, then a certain number (called the lot size, or batch) of parts A are produced first, then a batch of part B, followed by a batch of part C, and then a batch of part A is produced again.

The size of the tool magazine and the total number of operations needed on each part are the two important factors in deciding the number of parts that a machine can produce without replacing tools in the magazine. However, when the tool magazines in a system are too small to contain all the tools needed to produce all types of parts, an optimization algorithm that balances the workload per machine can be utilized to allocate the operations (and their cutting tools) of a selected subset of the parts that will be processed.[7]

Adding sensors to the machines, and transmitting their data continuously to the CNC controller, greatly enhances machine diagnostics. Typically, accelerometers and vibration sensors are used, although other sensor types such as acoustic emission monitoring and force/torque sensors are sometimes utilized. Cutting tools may be changed out based on these sensor readings, the number of parts cut by the tool, or at the end of each work shift.

6.3.3 Is a Pure-parallel FMS Practical?

It is a common assumption that FMS should be able to produce (1) any part (within the machine envelope), or (2) any mix of parts produced at any sequence (namely, non-batch operation). But only a purely parallel FMS can fulfill these requirements effectively without losing time because of balancing processing-time issues between stages. A purely parallel FMS, however, is not designed for multi-stage operations; it is rather a group of CNC machines arranged in parallel, where each machine produces the entire part (Figure 6.9).

This parallel configuration provides the highest flexibility and efficiency in producing a variety of parts or products simultaneously. Parallel FMS may be found in the aerospace and opto-mechanical industries, for example.

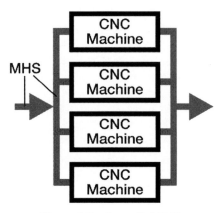

Figure 6.9 A parallel FMS.

However, significantly increasing the number of fully equipped CNC machines connected in parallel creates a reverse economy of scale in the system. First, **each CNC machine must include the entire set of tools** needed to produce the whole part even though only one tool operates at a time, meaning that many expensive tools sit idle as they wait their turn to be used. Second, **large magazines of tools** must be attached to each CNC, which increases each machine's cost. These two points are amplified when the machines produce several different parts that each requires its own set of cutting tools.

Paying for **unused machining horsepower** can also be a cost issue. While high horsepower might be required for a few operations (e.g., large surface milling), it is wasted on all the others where it is not needed (such as drilling of holes in the casting, which requires low power). An additional cost factor is that every CNC machine in the system must be designed with **a wide geometric range of motions** to accommodate the largest and most complex operation needed. These four reasons (a large number of tools, large tool magazines, high machine power, and machine geometric size) increase the cost of each CNC machine, and thus the entire cost of the parallel FMS can become very large.

Case Study—Parallel FMS: At the 1996 International Machine Tool Show (IMTS) in Chicago, Makino demonstrated the full machining of a GM engine block with a single five-axis CNC machining center. After the initial machining in this demonstration, the semi-machined block was taken automatically out of the machine, flipped 90°, or 180°, (by a special mechanism), and then inserted back to the machine worktable for continued machining. The Makino staff in the booth told me that GM bought 96 five-axes CNC machines, to be installed at GM plants in a pure-parallel arrangement. Each machine, they said, could produce an entire engine block or an engine head (except for line boring operations) in the same way that was demonstrated at IMTS.

These 96 machines were installed at a GM engine plant in Michigan to produce both engine blocks and heads of a particular six-cylinder engine. That machining system went into production in early 1998, and had a capacity of 600 engines/day with a very good uptime. However, the machines were not installed in a purely parallel configuration, as the Makino folks announced at IMTS. GM concluded that it was not practical to machine an entire block or entire head on a single machine in one setup. For one thing, the part has to be gripped somewhere, and therefore all of its sides cannot be accessed in one setup.

A single machine doing two setups that are switched using a special dedicated mechanism is also impractical. In fact, it is actually impossible to do it and still achieve the required precision. Although the fewest possible stations (or setups) required for machining an entire block or head would be two, this is still only possible if one can perform engine assembly operations (e.g., inserting valves) as well as machining operations in the same setup. But performing machining and assembly on a single station is very impractical and risky because one has to find a way to wash the part and keep it free of contamination before the assembly.

Furthermore, when a complex part is machined, some operations must come after others. In cylinder heads, for example, one must machine a valve seat pocket before pressing in a powdered-metal valve seat. But machining the valve seat itself can only be finished after it has been pressed in place. This means that the cylinder head must be taken off the machine for valve seat insertion, and then put back on a machine for finish valve machining.

For all these reasons, the GM cylinder machining system was installed in six parallel lines, each with eight machines to run eight different machining operations (i.e., eight stages). This system contained 48 of the Makino machines. GM could run the system with or without crossover among these parallel lines. Throughput increased tremendously, however, when crossover was allowed. The engine block machining system had a similar structure.

The conclusion is that for complex parts with several faces to be machined, a purely parallel system of CNC machines is absolutely impractical. The GM system produced these engines (blocks and heads) until 2002, when the product was phased out.

To conclude, whether arranged in parallel or not, FMSs are expensive. They are expensive for several reasons; most particularly because the equipment, which possesses features enabling general flexibility, is expensive to build and maintain. They are also expensive in the sense that companies sometimes purchase more functionality than they really need and the extra functionality is never utilized, or is only used after several years (see the survey in Section 6.5). Nevertheless, due to dramatic reductions in the price of CNC equipment in recent years, FMS is still a frequent optimal choice for producing parts in medium to high quantities.

6.3.4 Comparing DML and FMS

DMLs are based on fixed (or hard) automation and produce a single part in very large quantities. Dedicated equipment tends to be relatively inexpensive to buy and simple to maintain. However, altering any element of a DML in order to add a new operation requires a lot of downtime and expense to return the line to optimal efficiency. Changing the line in order to make a new product will take a couple of years and is completely uneconomical for runs shorter than several years.

On the other end of the spectrum FMSs are composed of computer numerically controlled (CNC) machines and other programmable automation, and are able to perform many different operations. FMSs can produce a variety of products on the same system. The production capacity of FMSs is much lower than that of dedicated lines and their initial capital cost is higher. The spectrum of products that are being produced on FMS is quite large, from optical parts for missiles, to aircrafts, car engine blocks, and even mass-customized shoes.

The common denominator for both DML and FMS-type systems is that they use fixed hardware. FMS and CNC operate with fixed software. Although part programs can be changed on CNC machines, neither the core software nor the control algorithms can be altered by the user.

The one practical advantage the DML has over FMSs is throughput. Flexible machining systems composed of CNC machines are more expensive and slower compared to dedicated machines, to produce the same number of parts. Consider, as an example, that on a CNC, a cluster of drilling operations is preformed with a **single tool** rather than applying a multi-tool "gang" drilling device such as a dedicated machine could use. Furthermore, even though the CNC is capable of different machining operations, each one requires a different tool and there is a delay for each tool change. The distances each tool must travel to and from the tool changer (i.e., tool positioning) are not a value-added operation and add time to complete production. These extra motions needed for tool positioning and tool changes make the CNC much slower than dedicated equipment. In contrast, in a DML, a whole block full of tools might be operating at the same time, performing the process at very high rates of speed. Because they are slow, more CNC machines are needed and the entire FMS becomes more expensive than the DML.

In summary, typical DMLs can produce a single part at very high production volume, and for this reason they can still be efficient for basic work on core products of the company. In the spectrum of manufacturing systems, DMLs are at the highest volume per product and the lowest functionality position, as depicted in Figure 6.10. High functionality means a system includes many functions (and tools) that enable it to move very quickly from the production of one product to another. This is the area where FMSs excel. FMSs are highly flexible in converting from one part operation to another, but because of their slower throughput and higher cost, they are better applied to those operations that change frequently.

The comparison between the dedicated and flexible systems, shown in Table 6.1, identifies key limitations in both types of systems.

The workforce skill level required by the two systems is very different. Dedicated, transfer lines require basic skills from most of the operators. CNC machines (used in FMS and RMS) require much higher skill levels. FMSs require skilled labor for (1) loading part programs, (2) changing worn cutting tools in the tool magazines of the machining centers, and (3) performing maintenance, diagnostics, and repairs on all components. The operators must possess some familiarity in computers and a knowledge in operating machines via computer screens, including reading basic trouble-shooting instructions and reacting accordingly.

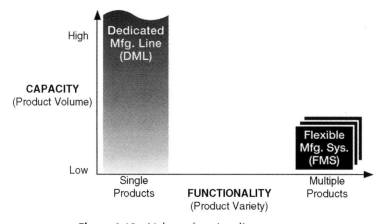

Figure 6.10   Volume-functionality spectrum.

TABLE 6.1 Comparison Between DML and FMS

	DML	FMS
Limitations	Not flexible—*for a single part*	Expensive
	Fixed capacity—*not scalable*	Slow—single-tool operation
Advantages	Low cost	Convertible for new products
	Fast—multi-tool operation	Scalable capacity
Workforce skills	Basic	Require computer knowledge
Hardware	Fixed	Fixed
Software	None	Fixed

The system design focus is perhaps the most important difference between DML and FMS. A designer cannot just design a dedicated line if the part to be processed is not given. That means that when considering a DML, the system design focus is on the part first and foremost. The focus on the part at the design stage enables opportunities for simultaneous multiple-tool operation (e.g., gang drilling) that, in turn, enhances system productivity, which creates even more cost-effective DML systems.

In contrast, the design efforts for most FMS are focus on the equipment—standard CNC machines and robots. Unlike DML stations, **CNC machines are not designed around the part** or even a part family. Rather, general-purpose CNCs are built around a generalized operational envelope, designed before the manufacturer determines the product to be built. Only when CNCs are selected to make up a system, is process planning undertaken to adapt the process to the part. In most cases, CNC machine builders do not know ahead of time what specific applications their machines will be used for when they design them. That is why flexible systems and machines are typically constructed with more features than are ever really needed to produce the parts they will manufacture. Customers, in turn, pay for things that they do not really need and the extra functionality amounts to a waste of capital.

A serious drawback of the DML system comes from the lead time required for product design. Basically, a specific product design needs to freeze many months before production is to begin so that there is time to design and tune the DML. With product development times shrinking, implementing a DML becomes problematic.

To conclude, Table 6.2 summarizes the main features of DML and FMS as we have discussed above. Further discussion on convertibility and scalability is presented below.

System Convertibility is defined as the ease of rapidly adjusting a system's production functionality, changing the production of one product to a new one being introduced to the market. System convertibility must take into account (1) the range of convertibility of the machines in the system, (2) the arrangement of the machines in the system, and (3) the material handling devices that connect the machines. As a rule, better convertibility usually makes the capital investment in a system more expensive.

Deprived convertibility is a major limiting factor of how quickly new products can be introduced. For example, in a serial line (Figure 6.11a) the configuration has a

TABLE 6.2   Features of DML and FMS

	Dedicated	FMS/CNC
Structure	Fixed	Fixed
System design focus	Part	Machine
Convertibility/flexibility	No	Yes (general flexibility)
Volume scalability	No	Yes in parallel FMS
Multi-tool operation	Yes	No
Productivity	High	Low
Lifetime investment cost	Low	Reasonable
	when fully utilized	for production of many parts

minimum increment of conversion of 1.00 or 100%. That is, in order to introduce a new product, the entire line must be shut down, changed over, reconfigured (if possible at all), and restarted. The configuration in Figure 6.11(b), however, can be partially converted to a new product after only 50% of the machines have been shut down and reconfigured (a conversion factor of 0.50).

The convertibility of the completely parallel configuration (Figure 6.11e) is the best; this one can be converted to a little production of a new product after only 16% of the machines have been shut down and reconfigured. This pure parallel configuration is valuable when a company wants to introduce new products to the market as quickly as possible, and then later ramp up to full production. In contrast, DMLs do not have any degree of cost-effective convertibility because they are not designed for change.

System Scalability is defined as the ease of rapidly adjusting production capacity, or changing a given system's throughput from one yield to another as needed to meet changes in market demand. We define system scalability as

System scalability = 100 − smallest incremental capacity in percentage

Scalability is the capacity increment by which the system output can be adjusted to meet new market demand. For example, in configuration (a) in Figure 6.11 the

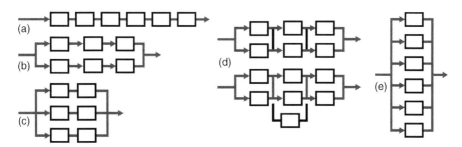

Figure 6.11   Five scalable configurations.

minimum increment of adding production capacity is 100% of the system (i.e., adding a whole new line); we define its increment as: **Scalability $= 100 - 100 = 0\%$**. Thus, zero scalability means that in order to increase the system capacity beyond its maximum, the entire line must be duplicated.

Similar calculations show that Configuration b has a scalability of 50%, Configuration c has 67%, and Configurations d and e have a scalability of 84%. That means that a minimum increment of one sixth of the system—in this case, one machine—can be added to increase the system capacity (e.g., a machine can be added to stage 2 of configuration d).

Scalable Capacity: Dedicated lines do not have scalable capacity and cannot cope with large fluctuations in product demand. This challenge can theoretically be met by FMSs that are scalable, when designed with CNC machines that operate in parallel, but the economics of implementing a parallel FMS is questionable.

The system designers have to weigh the amount of capacity they need to add. For example, to add capacity to Configuration a, 100% of the equipment would need to be duplicated. To add to Configuration e, only 16% of the equipment needs to be duplicated. However, adding any capacity to Configuration a doubles the actual output. Instantly doubling capacity is rarely appropriate and so, in most cases, is not justified.

In summary, one can see how system responsiveness—convertibility and scalability—is a critical concern in a manufacturing system. It plays a key role in gaining a competitive advantage for a company in the globalization era.

Two of our students, who work at the auto industry, shared their practical experience:

"The discussion on dedicated manufacturing lines and the comparison to flexible manufacturing systems matches exactly to my own experience (in 2003). I am working with three plants to implement a product change. Two sites have FMS-type equipment, and one site has a dedicated manufacturing line. The difference in cost and time to implement a change is significant! What can be accomplished in six months on the FMS equipment will take 18 months on the DML equipment, and cost much more. But the cost per unit produced is lowest at the DML site. Therefore, the DML site generates high profits, but only if the market is stable. The longer changeover could result in lower profit from lost sales."
—Dan Gulledge

"I have good experience with flexible manufacturing systems and it's odd to hear of an FMS as being traditional. But then, if you look into dedicated lines, there is somewhat a factor of flexibility about them today. I currently (2004) supervise a dedicated line that produces lost-foam engine block and head castings, and even though that is all we produce, the tooling can be switched from block to head on each machine. Although the casting sector is dedicated, it too can be outfitted with the others tooling to produce the opposite product. Even engine block machining lines are flexible enough to be altered for different blocks and are just as capable as putting up the numbers as dedicated lines do. I suppose the differences would be in the tooling to accomplish, such as gorge to mill, but other than that, systems even 15-20 years old now are flexible somewhat." Greg Wood

6.4 ASSEMBLY SYSTEMS

Assembly systems are utilized in virtually all types of durable goods manufacturing. There are three basic types of assembly systems: (1) manual assembly, which is carried out by human assemblers, usually with the aid of simple power tools. This is the most flexible assembly system, since humans are very "flexible" and can easily adapt to perform new tasks. This type of assembly is the norm in assembly of any complex products and especially in automotive final assembly. (2) Assembly systems that combine human assemblers and automated mechanisms. This type is common in assembly of mass-customized personal computers as described below. (3) Fully automated assembly systems for mass-produced parts, and particularly in hazardous environments such as in welding of auto body panels (an assembly operation).

The invention of programmable industrial robots in the early 1980s accelerated the development of automated assembly systems.[8] Assembly robots are equipped with various "end effectors" that can perform simple operations such as inserting screws and grasping and placing parts. Simple grippers containing two or three fingers can hold parts and place them in the assembly; more complex end effectors may include an automatic bolt screwing device or a fast tool-changing device. The geometry and working-envelope of the robot must fit all members of the particular product family for which the assembly system is designed. Because robots have CNC-type controllers, multiple task programs may be stored in the controller, and that program is executed when a particular product of the family is assembled. The robot end effecter typically must be changed to assemble each different product, similar to tool changes in CNC machining centers.

A typical automated assembly station has two basic functions: (1) the transfer and feeding of components into the assembly station and (2) the insertion of components into the product assembly. In fully automated assembly systems the feeding mechanisms usually consist of magazines (or buffers) into which the components are staged, and multiple material-flow sub-systems that feed the components automatically to the assembly station. The actual insertion of the components (i.e., the assembly itself) is done by assembly robots and automated (often pneumatic) equipment, aided by sensors. The types of sensors used depend on the application and include computer vision, force sensing, proximity, and photoelectric sensing.

The design features of the product and its components determine if it can be assembled on an automated assembly system or if it must be assembled manually. Note that many products require at least some insertion operations that are too complex to be automated. Such products must be at least partially assembled manually.

In multi-station automated assembly systems, pallets carry the product through all assembly stations (one pallet for each product). The pallets ride on a conveyor along the conveyor until encountering a stop gate at an assembly station or another pallet. The product assembly is done sequentially in the stations along the conveyor. An automated assembly station for an engine is shown in Figure 6.12.

Assembly systems are designed in stages where each stage rigidly transmits its output to the immediate successor stage. There are serial, **synchronous** assembly

Figure 6.12   An engine assembly station (courtesy of GM R&D Center).

systems, in which the product is partially assembled at each stage, allocating exactly the same amount of time at every stage. Office chairs, for instance, are assembled manually on serial synchronous lines of about 20 stations, and the chair stays for 30 seconds at each assembly stage. That means that the line throughput is two chairs per minute.

But there are other multi-stage assembly systems in which each stage requires parts that have been assembled from several preceding stages. These complex systems are asynchronous and usually require buffers between the stages. Figure 6.13 shows a typical assembly line[*] with assembly stations, M, and buffers, B. The highlighted stations form the main assembly line, and the others are sub-assemblies that provide components to the main line stations. For example, three sub-assembly lines feed three different components to station Ma. The output of station Ma moves to buffer Ba awaiting transfer to station Mb, where new parts as well as a component from another sub-assembly line (Mb1-Bb1) are added on. Station Mb1 is an automated station that assembles two parts and places the sub-assembly in buffer Bb1. The assembly tasks on station Mc take very long time. To balance the assembly line flow and ensure even throughput, three identical assembly stations are arranged in parallel at this stage (Mc1, Mc2, Mc3). A second buffer Bb distributes output to all three, and buffer Bc collects them again for the next stage Md. The final assembly station, Me, completes the product and moves it off the line.

It is common now for personal computers to be custom assembled to satisfy a customer's particular order. The assembly line for these consists of robots and automated mechanisms for kitting, testing, and packaging, but people still perform the actual computer assembly. Because of the huge variety of customer's orders, human assemblers are the most practical option to accommodate the various needs.

---

[*]This example, brought by Dr. Wencai Wang, is from the auto industry. Station Mb1 is an automated station that puts a needle bearing onto a shaft. The other stations in this example are all manual.

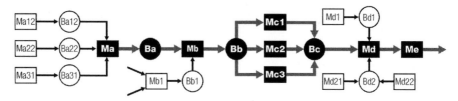

Figure 6.13   A typical multi-stage assembly system.

Figure 6.14, depicts the computer assembly line starting with a series of kitting stations where trays move along a line and amass the components for each computer order. Each order has its own tray. A robot selects the desired component at each station and puts it on the tray in the appropriate order. For example, a robot picks a particular hard disk from a magazine of several choices and places it on the tray. All components are selected in the same way. At the end of the kitting line, all the parts needed for a given order are on the tray, arranged appropriately for assembly. Each tray is then conveyed to a manual assembly station where two workers, facing each other, assemble the computer. The topmost component, the computer shell, comes off first and then each internal component is inserted as required. The time required for the assembly of each computer order is different depending on the number and type of components required. To meet demand and to maintain the pace of the serial portion of the line, there may be 10–20 assembly tables arranged in parallel. When each assembly is completed, the computer is sent for automated software loading and testing stations. When that phase is successfully completed, the computer is put back on a conveyor, sent to the automated packaging station, and then shipped to the customer who ordered it. Typically, computers are rolled out of the assembly system at a rate of 4 seconds each.

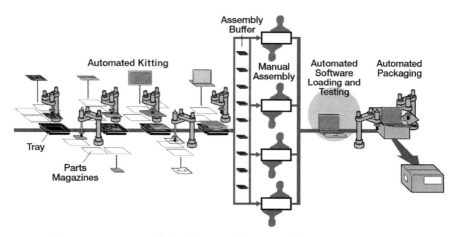

Figure 6.14   A typical flexible assembly system for personal computers.

There are also reconfigurable assembly systems. A key feature of these systems is a modular conveyor system that can operate asynchronously, and is reconfigurable to accommodate a large variety of component choices according to the application and the product being assembled. A reconfigurable conveyor allows quick rearrangement to alter process flow, adding or bypassing assembly stations according to the desired product. It also allows for serial–parallel configurations to balance the assembly line flow as necessary to ensure even throughput. An example of this type of conveyor can be seen at this reference website.[9]

6.5 INDUSTRY EXPERIENCE WITH FMS—A SURVEY

The development of flexible automation enablers (e.g., robots and CNC machining centers) during the 1970s has resulted in many successful FMS systems since the 1980s.[10] Nevertheless, in the early 1990s we also began to hear about cases of FMS failure. These stories were not popular, and information about them was not easily available. One case was reported in Japan, where a large manufacturing company decided to get rid of its FMS because it was too complex to operate, and its productivity was much lower than expected. An engine manufacturer in Michigan bought a flexible machining system composed of 12 CNC machines to augment its dedicated lines, but after 2 years of unsuccessful attempts to operate the system, the company got rid of the whole FMS. In another case in Michigan, a well-known system integrator sold a FMS consisting of 15 machining centers to an engine producer, but could not achieve the required part quality. It also suffered from greater than expected downtimes due to operator's training issues. The system integrator finally had to take back its system, and the case was settled out of court.

These stories motivated us to investigate the reasons for success and failures of FMS in the mechanical industries (machine builders, automobile producers, engine manufacturers, etc.). Our research was based on a survey that was conducted by a CIRP* Working Group on *"Flexible Automaton—Assessment and Future"* held jointly with the ERC for reconfigurable manufacturing systems during fall 2001 through summer 2002.

At that time the manufacturing industry was just starting to face new challenges of fluctuating markets and the need for production of high quantities of a mix of products from the same product family on a single FMS. In our study, industry experts were asked to evaluate their current FMSs and suggest enabling technologies that were needed to improve the performance of flexible manufacturing. The survey findings indicated some valuable results, the most important of which was that reconfigurable manufacturing systems had emerged as the major operational priority across the board.

We received 27 responses to our questionnaire; 14 responses from companies in the United States, and 13 from Europe (seven from Germany, four from Italy, and two

*CIRP is *the International Academy for Production Engineering* that has headquarters in Paris, France. The survey was conducted by the *Manufacturing Paradigms Working Group* of CIRP. The survey leaders were: Y. Koren in the United States, U. Heisel in Germany, C. Boer in Italy, and D. Dumor in France.

from France). The range of respondents covered a wide spectrum from Vice Presidents and Executive Directors in the auto industry, to R&D Managers and system designers in the machine tool industry.

The objectives of the survey were to

- Understand the reasons for success and failures of FMS in the mechanical industry.
- Evaluate possible technologies that may contribute to the success of FMS.

The system configuration types utilized by the surveyed industry, as reported to us, are shown in Figure 6.15.

Regarding the system design phase, the survey conclusions were

- New flexible systems should be designed to produce both existing and future products.
- In many cases, the purchased systems had over-capacity and excess functionality. Purchasing over-capacity is more common than purchasing over-functionality. That extra capacity was never utilized in 20% of all cases, and the extra functionality was never utilized in 30% of them.

The time to design and install (ramp up) large manufacturing systems is considered very critical by most experts. Regarding the system utilization phase, the survey concluded that:

- In most cases systems were utilized for the activities they were purchased for, indicating coherence between design and use.
- High satisfaction with the FMS was reported in all cases in which systems were utilized to increase the product variety.

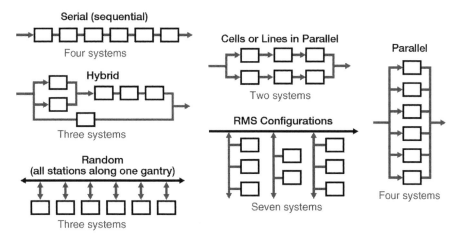

Figure 6.15 Types of system configurations reported in the survey.

- The reports were equally divided between cases in which systems are operated as expected and cases in which systems were not to operate at their full potential.

The main conclusions of the survey were

System Cost **is by far the most important factor in future success of large flexible manufacturing systems**. The main cost factors are (ranked in the order of importance)

- Maintenance cost
- Floor space
- Capital investment cost
- Manpower cost to operate the systems

System Reconfiguration **capability and ease of upgrading system capacity is the second most important issue.**

Workforce Training **is extremely important to effectively operate FMSs.**

Machine and control reconfiguration **capabilities are important features, but they are at lower priority than the items listed above.**

The major findings of the survey are summarized below.

- Respondents were equally divided whether FMSs are being operated at their potential performance (41% YES; 41% NO) and whether FMSs performance has met their expectations (35% YES; 25% NO)
- 20% of the FMSs that were installed in the 1990s failed, and were not used in 2001/2002
- 70% of FMS users plan to purchase additional FMS
- The FMS experience in the United States is consistent with that in Europe
- RMS configuration (Figure 6.15) is the most popular configuration being used
- There are no inherent problems in product quality when using FMSs
- The industry is very dissatisfied with the large initial capital investment in FMSs
- Industry is not pleased with the high cost of maintenance of FMS
- In the United States, the actual system productive uptime is 25% lower than expected
- 90% of all respondents assumed an FMS expected lifetime of 14–15 years in their economic analysis
- Industry is installing systems with more capacity and functionality than initially needed; this extra capacity was never utilized in 20% of these cases, and the extra functionality was never utilized in 30% of these cases

A student in our class with substantial experience in operating manufacturing systems expressed his thoughts about the survey:

"The survey of manufacturing industry professionals gave valuable insight into the thoughts and practices of flexible manufacturing systems. The most surprising finding on the survey is that manufacturers typically purchase additional machine functionality that is usually not used. I can relate to this since the manufacturing line that I work with was purchased with the ability to manufacture V6 and V8 crankshafts. The manufacturing line has never machined a V6 crankshaft in its 10-year life."
—Andy Jacobson

PROBLEMS

6.1 Rank the convertibility of the five systems in Figure 6.11.

6.2 The rate at which parts are assembled in station Mb in Figure 6.13 is T seconds, and in stations Mci is $3T$ seconds. Buffer Bb has 10 parts. Station Mc2 stopped to operate for a period of $9T$. How many parts are in the buffer when this station starts to operate?

6.3 The automated kitting line in Figure 6.14 is adding a tray to the assembly buffer every 10 seconds. The manual assembly time in the four parallel stations may vary between 30 and 60 seconds, depending upon the number of components being assembled. The buffer contained 10 trays when the following assembly cycles started:

Station 1	30	40	50	60
Station 2	50	30	40	60
Station 3	40	60	40	40
Station 4	60	50	30	50

How many trays are in the buffer after 130 seconds, and how many after 170 seconds?

6.4 A part (cylinder head) has to be machined before manual assembly (see Figure 6.16). The machining and assembly operations are not balanced: machining takes 60 seconds per part and assembly takes 40 seconds per part. Therefore, the machining system works 12 hours a day, and the assembly line 8 hours per day. During the 4 hours in which assembly is not operational, the machined parts are stored in a buffer and later used by the assembly when needed. The buffer can store machined parts also during the 8 hours in which assembly is operational.

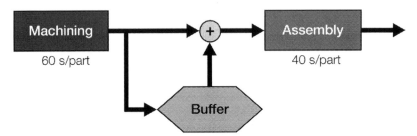

Figure 6.16   A factory that includes machining and assembly lines.

(a) How many parts are machined per day (assume no machine failures), and how many parts can be assembled per day?

(b) Explain the steady-state operation of the factory (i.e., flow of parts) during 6 minutes of normal production of machining and assembly.

(c) What is the needed buffer maximum capacity?

(d) What happens if the transfer mechanism (e.g., a robot) between the buffer and the assembly line ceases operation for 30 minutes?

(e) What happens if the machining system stops for 30 minutes during the operation time of the assembly line?

REFERENCES

1. World Appliance Companies, 4th edn. Appliance Magazine and Industry Statistics, Ltd., July 2006.

2. T. Tolio and A. Matta. A method for performance evaluation of automated flow lines. *CIRP Annals*, 1998, Vol. **47/1**.

3. Y. Koren, F. Jovane, U. Heisel, T. Moriwaki, G. Pritschow, G. Ulsoy, and H. VanBrussel. Reconfigurable manufacturing systems. *CIRP Annals*, November 1999, Vol. **48**, No. 2, pp. 6–12.

4. Y. Koren. *Computer Control of Manufacturing Systems*. McGraw Hill, New York, 1983.

5. J. Browne, D. Dubois, K. Rathmill, S. P. Sethi, and K. E.Stecke. Classification of flexible manufacturing systems. *FMS Magazine*, 1984, Vol. **2**, No. 2.

6. A. K. Sethi and S. P. Sethi. Flexibility in manufacturing. *International Journal of Flexible Manufacturing*, 1990, Vol. **2**, pp. 289–326.

7. K. E. Stecke. Formulation and solution of nonlinear integer production planning problems for flexible manufacturing systems, *Management Science*, 1983, Vol. **29**, No. 3, pp. 273–288.

8. Y. Koren. *Robotics for Engineers*. McGraw Hill, New York, 1985.

9. http://www.crux-engineering.com/Automation/Solutions/

10. G. Chryssolouris. Flexibility and its measurement. *CIRP Annals*, 1996, Vol. **45**, No. 2, pp. 581–587.

Chapter 7

Economics of System Design

The cost of building a new manufacturing system may be between $50 million to over $2 billion (a microprocessor fabrication facility), and its average lifetime is 12–15 years. Such substantial investment that may impact several product generations requires a rigorous planning that includes a sequence of important decisions:

1. Decide whether to invest at all in a new production system, and, if to invest, in which type of system.
2. Based on product sale forecasting and estimated capital investment, determine whether to invest in dedicated, flexible, or portfolio capacity.
3. Calculate the cycle time of each operation and the total time needed for the whole process to produce one product.[1]
4. Optimize the system configuration such that a proper line balancing maximizes system throughput, and tooling cost is minimized to reduce capital investment (a methodology to optimize configurations is offered in Chapter 10).
5. Find out the buffer capacity that optimizes the system throughput.
6. Determine the projected operations costs; it is more challenging when flexible systems that produce several products are employed.
7. Consider system responsiveness to changing orders of customers; responsiveness impacts the system throughput.
8. Calculate the optimal speed of each machine; it will impact the whole system throughput.

The Global Manufacturing Revolution: Product-Process-Business Integration and Reconfigurable Systems
By Yoram Koren
Copyright © 2010 John Wiley & Sons, Inc.

Designing a system is not a sequential process that follows the above-mentioned steps. For example, the system configuration affects the tooling cost, which, in turn, has an effect on the capital cost, but the latter is needed to determine the system type; the system operations cost impacts profit, and may change decisions about the total installed capacity. Therefore, the system design is an iterative process that iterates among the above eight points (and perhaps takes into account more considerations) until converging gradually to the optimal economic solution.

7.1 LIFE-CYCLE ECONOMICS

Making investment decisions in new manufacturing systems requires knowledge in engineering as well as in finance and economics. We start, therefore, by defining some basic economics terms.

7.1.1 Basic Economics Terms

Capital (money) used for building a new manufacturing system should earn returns for the invested capital. For a new manufacturing system to be economically viable, the projected sales of the products that the system will produce during its lifetime must be higher than the cost of the capital invested in building the system. The cost of the capital should include the rate of interest paid on the invested capital in building the system.

Return on investment (ROI) is the ratio of money gained (or lost) relative to the amount of money invested. ROI is given as a percent and usually does not indicate how long the investment is held. For example, a $10,000 investment that earns $500 generates a 5% ROI. The ROI may be also stated as an annual rate of return.

Cash flow is the balance of the amounts of cash being received by a company during a given time period. In the context of this chapter, measurement of cash flow can be used to evaluate the performance of a manufacturing system and validate whether it generates net income.

Net present value (NPV) is defined as the total present value of an investment project, found by discounting all present and future receipts and outgoings at an appropriate rate of interest. If the NPV is positive, it is worthwhile investing in a project.[2] NPV is an indicator of how much value an investment in a new manufacturing system adds to the firm, and it measures the excess or shortfall of cash flows, in present value (PV) terms.

NPV > 0 means that the investment in a new manufacturing system would add value to the firm. It is worthwhile to build the system.

NPV < 0 means that the investment in a new manufacturing system would create loss to the firm, and the project should be rejected.

Example 7.1 A corporation must decide whether to introduce a new production line. The new product will have startup costs, operational costs, and incoming cash flows from selling the manufactured products over 6 years. This project will have an immediate ($t = 0$) cash outflow of $100,000 (which includes machinery and employee training costs). Other cash outflows for years 1–6 are the operation costs that are expected to be $5,000 per year. Cash inflows are expected to be $30,000 per year for years 1–6 and there are no cash flows expected after year 6. The interest rate is 10%. The PV can be calculated for each year:

$$T = 0 : \ -\$100,000/1.10^0 = -\$100,000 \, \text{PV}$$
$$T = 1 : \ (\$30,000 - \$5000)/1.10^1 = \$22,727 \, \text{PV}$$
$$T = 2 : \ (\$30,000 - \$5000)/1.10^2 = \$20,661 \, \text{PV}$$
$$T = 3 : \ (\$30,000 - \$5000)/1.10^3 = \$18,783 \, \text{PV}$$
$$T = 4 : \ (\$30,000 - \$5000)/1.10^4 = \$17,075 \, \text{PV}$$
$$T = 5 : \ (\$30,000 - \$5000)/1.10^5 = \$15,523 \, \text{PV}$$
$$T = 6 : \ (\$30,000 - \$5000)/1.10^6 = \$14,112 \, \text{PV}$$

The sum of all these PVs is the NPV, which equals $8881. Since the NPV is greater than zero, the corporation will have a profit by investing in the new product line.

7.1.2 Life-cycle Economics of Manufacturing Systems

The dedicated manufacturing line (DML) is an ideal solution when a part design is fixed, the change in its design is not imminent, and demand is fixed. A Flexible manufacturing system, although more expensive than DML, enables the production of new members of the same part family on an existing system, which, in turn, expands the lifetime of the system.

In the example below, we use NPV to evaluate the life-cycle investments in DML and FMS when producing a single product. By using a simple economic model, we study the effects of product life cycle and equipment reusability of each production system on the investment strategy of a manufacturing firm. The results illuminate some basic concerns regarding the fast-changing products and the need to reconfigure the production line frequently.

Example 7.2[3] Consider an engine block manufacturer planning to fulfill demand of three (3) product generations over the next 12 years where each product generation lasts **4 years**. The demand volume is assumed to be 300,000 engine blocks per year, and the profit per part is $120. The manufacturer may invest in either DML or FMS. The DML capital cost is $100 million, and that of FMS is $130 million. Once the next product generation arrives the same FMS can be reutilized, but there is a need for new fixtures, new tools, and ramp-up that cost **$25** million. At the end of its lifetime (12 years), the salvage value of the FMS (selling used CNC machining centers) is **$17** million. Each time a new product generation is manu-factured a new DML must be built, but certain parts of the existing DML, which is worth **$20** million, can be either reutilized for the new line or sold (have a salvage value). The annual interest rate is 10%.

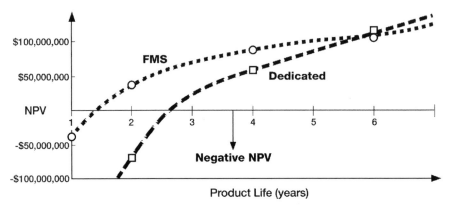

Figure 7.1   An economic comparison of two systems: dedicated and FMS.

Table 7.1 shows the cash flow forecast and PV of using DML and FMS. Since the FMS NPV is greater than the DML NPV, building the FMS is more economical.

Now let us examine the case for different product lifetimes—of 2 years and of 6 years. The results are shown in Tables 7.2 and 7.3, accordingly. We see that if the expected product lifetime is 6 years, the two systems create equal values.

A similar calculation was done for a product life cycle of 1 year, which yields an NPV of −$42 million for FMS, and −$367 million for DML.

Figure 7.1 shows the NPV comparison between the two systems, with the following conclusions (for the data given above):

1. If the expected product lifetime is less than 1.5 years, building any system is a loss.
2. If the expected product lifetime is more than 6 years, install a dedicated machining line.
3. If the expected product lifetime is between 2 and 6 years, install the FMS.

Although these conclusions are drawn for a particular example, they may be considered as general rules for system life-cycle economic planning.

7.2 CAPACITY PLANNING STRATEGIES

When planning a new manufacturing system for producing several products, the optimal investment in the system capacity is a major decision to make. This decision, which has long-term economic consequences, addresses two major issues: (1) How much capacity to build? (2) Whether to invest in dedicated or flexible resources, or a portfolio consisting of both dedicated and flexible systems. Flexible systems possess the ability to produce multiple types of products very economically and quickly. Therefore, by switching from one product to another, they may alleviate unfavorable effects of demand uncertainties. However, the versatility to produce multiple products

TABLE 7.1 Cash Flow (in $ million) and Net Present Value for DML and FMS for Product Life Cycle of 4 Years

	Year	0	1	2	3	4	5	6	7	8	9	10	11	12	NPV
DML	Cash flow	−100	36	36	36	36 +20 −100	36	36	36	36 +20 −100	36	36	36	36 +20	NPV
	PV	−100	32.7	29.8	27	−30	22.3	20.3	18.5	−20.5	15.3	13.9	12.6	17.8	**59.7**
FMS	Cash flow	−130	36	36	36	36 −25	36	36	36	36 −25	36	36	36	36 +17	NPV
	PV	−130	32.7	29.8	27	7.5	22.3	20.3	18.5	5.1	15.3	13.9	12.6	16.9	**92**

DML(NPV) = $59.7 million FMS(NPV) = $92.0 million.

TABLE 7.2 NPV for Product Life Cycle of 2 Years

Year	0	1	2	3	4	5	6	7	8	9	10	11	12	NPV
DML PV	**−100**	32.7	−36.4	27	−30	22.4	−24.8	18.5	−20.5	15.3	−17	12.6	17.8	**−82.4**
FMS PV	**−130**	32.7	9.1	27	7.5	22.4	6.2	18.5	5.1	15.3	4.2	12.6	16.9	47.5

TABLE 7.3 NPV for Product Life Cycle of 6 Years

Year	0	1	2	3	4	5	6	7	8	9	10	11	12	NPV
DML PV	**−100**	32.7	29.8	27	24.6	22.4	−24.9	18.5	16.8	15.3	13.9	12.6	17.8	106.5
FMS PV	**−130**	32.7	29.7	27	24.6	22.3	6.2	18.5	16.8	15.3	13.9	12.6	16.9	106.5

often requires higher investment costs compared to dedicated systems that can only produce one type of product.

In most industries, capacity investment decisions are made before demand is observed and the optimal capacity choices may vary from one firm to another even in the same industry. The investment decision on the amount and type of capacity—dedicated, flexible, or a portfolio of dedicated and flexible systems—is mainly influenced by the following factors:

1. The number of products to be produced simultaneously in the plant.
2. Investment costs in dedicated versus flexible systems.
3. Product marginal revenues.
4. Product demand volatility during the planning horizon.
5. The frequency of product changes and the expected lifetime of products.

The Number of Products to be Produced Simultaneously: Flexible technology can deal with changes or uncertainty in demand mix. It enables to change the mix of products manufactured in a plant, and produce more of highly profitable products when their demand surges. Usually, if a plant produces more than four, five products simultaneously, the decision will be to invest in flexible capacity.

Investment Costs of Dedicated Versus Flexible Systems: When producing large quantities, the investment cost in flexible systems is always larger than that in dedicated lines. The margin may be 10–100% in large machining systems. Flexible capacities are usually favored more when their investment costs are closer to those of dedicated lines. When the manufactured quantities are small, dedicated lines are not cheaper than flexible systems, and the latter is the optimal solution.

Product Revenues: Higher profit margins and higher prices of the product produced warrant a higher investment level, since losing sales of products causes a significant financial loss. Installing flexible capacity in such cases is economically justified.

Product Demand Volatility During the Planning Horizon: Investment in flexible capacity hedges against uncertainty in future demand, since production can be easily shifted from a product with diminishing demand to a product with rising demand. Therefore, when market volatilities are high, an investment in flexible capacity is the right economic choice.

The Frequency of Product Changes and the Expected Lifetime of Products: When a firm plans to rapidly introduce new product models in the near future and expanding its product scope, the firm should invest in flexible capacity.

When the above-mentioned considerations are not conclusive beyond all doubt, a firm may invest in a portfolio consisting of both dedicated and flexible systems.

To gain further insights, we provide below a formulation for the optimal capacity investment problem and demonstrate a solution for numerical examples. The examples show at what circumstances profits are maximized when considering three investment strategies: dedicated capacity only, flexible capacity only, and a portfolio.

7.2.1 Capacity Investment Problem Formulation

Product Demand: Consider a manufacturing firm that produces two types of products (A and B) over a time horizon consisting of several periods. Marginal revenues of p_A and p_B are received for each unit of type A and type B product, respectively. For planning purposes, the firm employs demand forecasts for each type of product. For example, if the forecast for the sales of a product is: 100% confidence that at least 300,000 units will be sold, 70% confidence that at least 400,000 units will be sold, and 20% confidence that 500,000 units will be sold, a discrete probability density function, as given in Table 7.4, may be calculated.

As future periods possess higher levels of uncertainty, the forecasting accuracy decreases with time. In this analysis, we consider a scenario where an existing product A is gradually replaced by a new product—product B. Figure 7.2(a) illustrates typical demand distributions for the products where Ψ_i^t and $\bar{d}_i^t$ denote, respectively, the probability density function and mean demand in period t for product i, $i = A, B$. For a three-period analysis, we let $\mathbf{d} = (\mathbf{d}_A, \mathbf{d}_B)$ denote the realization of all product demands, where $\mathbf{d}_A = (d_A^1, d_A^2, d_A^3)$ and $\mathbf{d}_B = (d_B^1, d_B^2, d_B^3)$.

Manufacturing Capacity: The investment decision is carried out at the beginning of the planning horizon (before demand is actually observed) based on the demand forecasts for both products. Let $\mathbf{k} = (k_A, k_B, k_{AB})$ denote the variables expressing the size of the capacity, where k_A, k_B, and k_{AB} are the dedicated capacities for products A and B, and the flexible capacity, respectively. In terms of investment costs, let $\mathbf{c} = (c_A, c_B, c_{AB})$ denote the investment cost per unit capacity in dedicated line for product A, dedicated line for product B, and flexible (for A and B), respectively. It is assumed that $c_A, c_B \leq c_{AB} \leq c_A + c_B$. The right term, $c_{AB} \leq c_A + c_B$, gives the upper bound on the cost of a flexible system. As an example, if dedicated lines cost $100K each, we would only invest in a flexible system if it costs less than $200K.

To define the additional cost of a unit of flexible capacity compared to that of a dedicated capacity, we use the term "flexible premium." For example, a flexible premium of 30% indicates that a unit of flexible capacity costs 30% more than a unit of dedicated capacity.

The capacities are purchased in discrete batches where the increments of the dedicated capacity are always larger than that of the flexible capacity. However, a capacity below a given lower bound will not be purchased. The reason is that firms may incur additional costs to simultaneously operate and maintain dedicated and flexible systems. Therefore, it is worthwhile to possess a portfolio of system types at the same plant only if the capacity purchased of a certain type exceeds its lower bound.

TABLE 7.4 An Example Discrete Probability Density Function for Product Demand

Product Demand	Probability Density Function
300,000	0.3
400,000	0.5
500,000	0.2

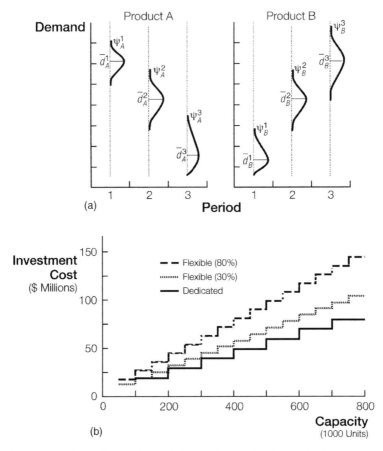

Figure 7.2   Example: (a) demand distributions and (b) capacity investments.

The lower bound for flexible capacity is lower than that of dedicated. Figure 7.2(b) represents an example cost structure for dedicated and flexible capacity investments, for flexible premium of 30 and 80%.[4]

Optimization Model: At the beginning of the planning horizon, the firm first makes a **strategic** investment decision on the quantity and types of manufacturing systems to purchase. Once the initial investment decisions are given, the firm continually makes tactical, **operating** decisions every period on how to allocate its resources in the most profitable way across products.

We need to solve the problem in two stages. First, assuming that a **strategic** investment decision is already given, we compute the maximum possible **operating** revenue during the entire lifetime of all products (i.e., the planning horizon). Next, we make the **strategic** capacity decision by choosing the recommended installed capacities that will generate the maximum profit that is corresponding to the highest operating revenue minus investment costs.[5]

The problem may be formulated as a linear program with an optimization cost index $R(\mathbf{d},k)$, which expresses the revenue that can be achieved for a given capacity investment decision k, and for any fulfillment of product demands $\mathbf{d}$ over the planning horizon.

$$R(\mathbf{d},k) = \max_{x,y} \sum_{t=1}^{T} \beta^{t-1} \left[p_A(x_A^t + y_A^t) + p_B(x_B^t + y_B^t) \right]$$

subject to constraints

(a) $x_A^t \leq k_A$ $\forall t = 1,\ldots,T$

(b) $x_B^t \leq k_B$ $\forall t = 1,\ldots,T$

(c) $y_A^t + y_B^t \leq k_{AB}$ $\forall t = 1,\ldots,T$

(d) $x_A^t + y_A^t \leq d_A^t$ $\forall t = 1,\ldots,T$

(e) $x_B^t + y_B^t \leq d_B^t$ $\forall t = 1,\ldots,T$

The decision variables x_A^t and x_B^t denote, respectively, how many units of dedicated capacity A and B are needed to fill period t demand, whereas the decision variables y_A^t and y_B^t denote the optimal allocation of the flexible capacity between products. In addition, β is the discount factor per period that is used to calculate the NPV of the revenues, $\beta = 1/(1 + r)$, where r is the annual rate of return as defined in Section 7.1. Constraints (a)–(e) guarantee that one will assign neither more capacity than the maximum available, nor more capacity than demand (i.e., the production quantities within a period do not exceed available capacity and are bound by the demand).

Having obtained the maximum operating revenue, we can now write the strategic decision problem of determining the optimal capacity investments, k.

$$\max_{k} \; E_{\mathbf{d}}(R(\mathbf{d},k)) - c \cdot k'$$

In the above formulation, $E_{\mathbf{d}}[R(\mathbf{d},k)]$ is the expected value of the operating revenue where the expectation is taken over demand distributions and $c \cdot k'$ represents the total investment costs. The firm's objective is to maximize $E_{\mathbf{d}}$.

7.2.2 Numerical Examples

We will now solve the above formulated optimization problem for a planning horizon of three periods. The objective is to explore how investment costs, product revenues, and demand volatilities affect optimal capacity investment decisions.[6]

Optimal Capacity Investment: In order to analyze the effects of the relative investment costs on optimal capacity investment decisions, we first consider a base case constructed by the following problem parameters. Assume demands for products A and B generate revenues of $p_A = p_B = 75$ and, for a three-period horizon, they have mean values (600, 350, 100) and (125, 450, 700), and standard deviations (50, 70, 70)

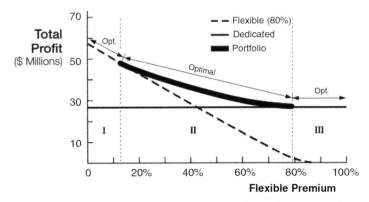

Figure 7.3   Profits obtained by pure flexible, pure dedicated, and portfolio strategies.

for A and (25, 70, 70) for B. The investment costs for dedicated capacity are $c_A = c_B = 100$, and the unit cost for the flexible capacity varies from 100 to 200 corresponding to a flexible premium of 0–100%. To calculate the NPV of the revenues, we assume a discount factor of $\beta = 0.8$.

Figure 7.3 shows profits obtained from three different investment strategies: (1) dedicated capacity only, (2) flexible capacity only, and (3) a portfolio consisting of both dedicated and flexible systems. The decision space has three distinct regions. In region I—invest in flexible capacity only. In region III, install only dedicated lines. In region II, however, a portfolio strategy results in strictly higher profits.

Figure 7.4 depicts the quantities of capacity purchases that lead to the optimal profits shown in Figure 7.3. Specifically, we observe that as the unit cost for the flexible capacity increases, a portfolio consisting of gradually increasing share of dedicated capacities becomes optimal.

Product Revenue: Next, we consider the effects of product revenues on optimal capacity investments. Figure 7.5 displays the optimal investment decisions for various product revenues ranging from $30 to $150 per unit. As shown by the figure, higher

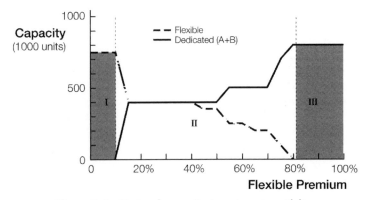

Figure 7.4   Optimal capacity investment portfolio.

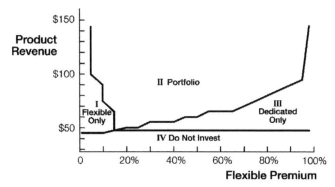

Figure 7.5   Effects of product revenues.

product revenues enlarge the range over which the optimal strategy is of a portfolio type. The rationale for this interesting conclusion is explained below.

As product revenues get higher, it is more profitable for firms to increase production in order to reduce missed demand opportunities. Since dedicated capacity costs less, it makes sense to build the increased level of total capacity partially by dedicated systems. On the other hand, employing flexible capacity is also crucial as it allows allocating capacity when needed and hence enables a higher demand fill rate and revenues in the presence of demand uncertainties. Therefore a portfolio of flexible and dedicated systems is optimal over a larger flexible premium range.

Demand Variance: Lastly, we analyze the effect of demand variance on optimal capacity investment decisions. Figure 7.6 displays the constituents of the optimal capacity investments when demands exhibit lower volatility. We observe that the value of the pure flexible investment strategy diminishes (compare to Figure 7.4). In other words, when market is more predictable, an optimal investment strategy favors dedicated systems.

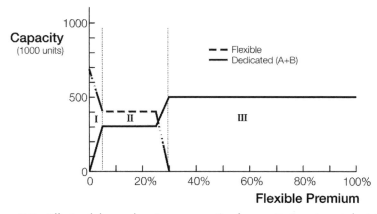

Figure 7.6   Effects of demand variance on optimal capacity investment decisions.

7.3 ECONOMICS OF SYSTEM CONFIGURATIONS

The designer of a new manufacturing system should comply a design process that starts with high-level strategic decisions—which system type is needed: a dedicated, a flexible-reconfigurable, or a portfolio consisting of both. The deliberations on choosing the right system have been described and analyzed in Sections 7.1 and 7.2. Forecasting, as mentioned in Section 7.2, provides the required capacity of the system.

The next step is to calculate the individual operation times that are needed to produce the part, where the total production time, *t*, is given. Producing a part may be, for example, machining a part by a system composed of machining centers and lathes, or assembling a part by automation or by workers. Machining a part requires the calculation of the machine optimal cutting speeds (an example is presented below), which will affect the total machining time per part, and will eventually affect the number of machines needed in the system. If the system capacity (which is based on forecasted demand) and the total time needed to produce a part are given, it is possible to calculate the minimum number of machines or stations needed in the system.

If the daily demand is Q (parts/day), and the total production time per part is t (minute/part), the minimum number of machines, N, needed in the system is calculated by the equation

$$N = \frac{Q \times t}{\text{Minutes/day available} \times \text{Machine reliability}} \tag{7.1}$$

When the number N of machines is given, the next step is to decide upon the right configuration of a system that is composed of N machines. There may be several ways to configure a multi-stage manufacturing system with a given number of machines. Figure 7.7, for example, shows three possible configurations, each with six machines, and each produces two parts A and B. There are configurations that require a large investment in tooling (e.g., Figure 7.7c); in others, a complex material handling

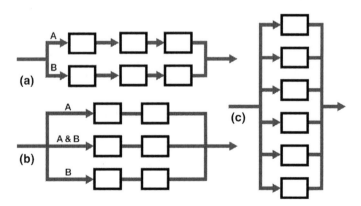

Figure 7.7   Three system configurations, all with six machines.

system increases the investment cost. Note that in the configuration in Figure 7.7a, each machine performs about one third of the operations needed to complete the part, and therefore the total number of tools in this system is smaller than that in the other two configurations.

The selected configuration of the system not only affects the investment cost, but also has a significant impact on the system throughput and on the system responsiveness to market changes. Responsiveness includes not only the daily operational responsiveness of the system to changes in unexpected customers' orders, but also convertibility and capacity scalability. All these considerations are part of the system design process.

There are also operation considerations in selecting a configuration. If the demand for Part A increases by 33% and at the same day the demand for Part B decreases by 33%, the configuration in Figure 7.7c can supply the new demand (four machines produce A and two produce B). Satisfying the new demand with the other two systems will not be that simple and will require tool changes during the day, which will reduce the daily throughput. Therefore, the configuration in Figure 7.7c has the best operational responsiveness of these three systems. This system, however, requires more tools and machines with larger tool magazines, and therefore its capital investment cost is higher.

7.3.1 Tooling Cost

Let us compare the number of cutting tools needed to place in the tool magazines of each system configuration in Figure 7.7. Assume that 30 different cutting tools are needed to produce Part A, and an additional 30 tools (different than those for Part A) are needed for Part B. In configuration 7.7a, product A is produced by three machines, and product B is produced by the other three machines. The total number of cutting tools in system 7.7a is **60** (an average of 10 tools in the tool-magazine of each machine).

In system 7.7c, if three machines produce part A and three produce part B, then each machine requires 30 tools (these machines need tool magazines that are three times larger than the machines in configuration 7.7a) and the total number of tools for six machines is **180**.

In Figure 7.7b, two lines have machines with 15 tools each (namely, 60 tools in four machines) and two machines in the middle line have 30 tools in each tool magazine (because they produce both parts A and B). Altogether configuration 7.7b contains **120** tools. Alternatively, if a higher degree of responsiveness is needed, each line must be able to produce both Part A and B, and then the total number of tools loaded in the system's tool magazines is given in Table 7.5.

7.3.2 Impact of Configuration on System Throughput

In the above scenario, from a tooling cost viewpoint, the optimal system is obtained by configuration 7.7a. However, there are other aspects than just tooling cost assessing when looking at the operational cost. Let us consider the impact of a single machine

TABLE 7.5   The Number of Cutting Tools Needed in the Systems Depicted in Figure 7.7

	Number of Cutting Tools		
	7.7a	**7.7b**	**7.7c**
System as shown in Figure 7.7	60	120	180
Each machine can produce both Part A and Part B	120	180	360
Loss of throughput if one machine is down	50%	33%	16%

failure that continues more than a few hours, for example. In systems (a) and (b) above, the machining sequence is interrupted, and the whole line loses productivity. If such an event causes the system, or a significant portion of it, to shut down, the system is not adequately responsive. The bottom row of Table 7.5 shows the percentage of throughput lost when such an event happens. (Note that in Figure 7.7a, 50% is a loss of the total production; it is 100% for one of the products. Similarly, in Figure 7.7b, 33% is a loss of the total production; it may be 66% for one of the products.)

The system throughput is impacted not only by machine failures, but also by the configuration itself. A simple example that demonstrates the impact of configuration on throughput is shown in Figure 7.8. To be completed, the part requires three operations of 90, 150, and 120 seconds. In a serial dedicated line, the slowest operation (in the second stage) dictates the throughput. The second configuration has two parallel machines that perform the first two operations, and thereby the system throughput is increased by 25% (150/120).

When selecting a configuration, two measures of responsiveness—system convertibility and scalability—should be considered as well. This issue and others that influence the selection of the appropriate configuration are analyzed in Chapter 10.

7.4 THE ECONOMICS OF BUFFERS

Having buffers to store parts between stations, or machines, in manufacturing systems is controversial. On one hand, buffers are not value-added-operations, and therefore adding buffers is a waste according to the Lean principles. However, adding buffers between unreliable machines increases the system throughput in cases of unpredictable events, such as operation time variations, machine failures, and the time required to repair them. The buffers isolate such disruptive events from propagating in the line.

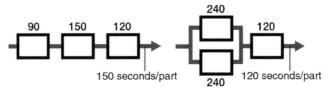

Figure 7.8 Two configurations with the same number of machines but different throughputs.

Having infinite-size buffers between operations is an extreme case that completely decouples the operations, such that a failure of a particular machine does not affect the others in the system. In this case, the slowest machine in the line determines the system throughput. We will study the issue of a cost-effective buffer size in the case of serial lines.

The expected throughput of a single isolated machine is proportional to the machine reliability R that is calculated by

$$R = \mathrm{MTBF}/(\mathrm{MTBF} + \mathrm{MTTR}) \tag{7.2}$$

where MTBF is the mean time between failures of the machine and MTTR is the mean time to repair a machine failure. Both machine breakdowns and machine repairs occur at random.

Serial manufacturing lines may be either **synchronous** or **asynchronous**. In a synchronous machining line, all machined parts are moving exactly at the same time from each machine to the next, and all machines start to operate simultaneously. These lines cannot have buffers between machines. If one machine stops—the entire line stops.

Building a synchronous machining line is less expensive than building an asynchronous line, but its reliability is much lower. If the average machine reliability is R, the line average expected throughput is R^n of the planned throughput of a fully operational line with n machines. For example, in a line of six machines with an average machine reliability of $R = 0.9$, the average expected throughput is only 0.53%.

In asynchronous serial lines, it is not necessarily that all machines start and stop simultaneously. Machines may stop working because of three reasons: (a) the machine failed because of a fault or a malfunction; (b) the machine is "starved," namely, parts are not available from the upstream buffer or machine (which apparently stopped to operate); and (c) the machine is "blocked," namely, it cannot send the finished part downstream because the output buffer is full, or (if there is no buffer) the next machine failed.

In typical asynchronous serial lines, the machines are connected with a material transfer device, such as a long conveyor, on which parts may be accumulated (up to a certain maximum quantity) and wait to be processed on the next machine (see example in Figure 7.9). This means that between the machines there are buffers that have maximum part capacity. In other types of asynchronous lines, special buffers are added between the machines, for example in a form of small closed-loop conveyors, which also have maximum capacity.

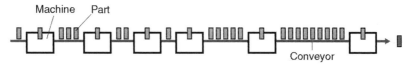

Figure 7.9   Asynchronous serial line with buffer spaces on the conveyor.

In asynchronous serial lines without buffers, if one machine fails to operate, the entire line does not stop immediately—the upstream and downstream machines continue to operate until either the failed machine is repaired or the line is purged (all downstream parts were processed). Asynchronous serial lines with buffers will continue to operate as long as there are parts in the upstream buffers and empty spaces in the downstream buffers. Therefore, asynchronous lines have higher throughput than synchronous serial lines.

The line designer's dilemma is that adding buffers increases throughput, but adding buffers creates waste, because it increases the in-process inventory and contradicts the principles of lean manufacturing. Considering the tradeoff between throughput gain and inventory increase, buffer space should be limited.

Example: Given an asynchronous serial line with six machines and equal buffers between machines. The maximum possible throughput (i.e., production rate without failures) is 20 parts per hour (cycle time $T = 3$ minutes). The machines have equal reliability, with MTBF $= 9$ minutes and MTTR $= 1$ minute. Namely, the average machine reliability, R, is 0.9. The buffers between the machines are equal. What are the line production rates (in % of the maximum throughput) as function of the buffer space?

The solution (solved by PAMS software[*]) is given in the table below:

Buffer size	0	1	2	3	4	5	6	10	100
Throughput (%)	71.3	83.7	86.1	87.3	87.9	88.2	88.5	89.1	90

Note that even when the asynchronous line does not have buffers, the throughput is 71%, compared with just 53% of a synchronous line with an average machine reliability of $R = 0.9$. The reason is that in the asynchronous line if a machine is down, the other machines continue to operate and can transfer parts to consecutive operating machines. The capital investment in a synchronous serial line is lower, but its average downtime is higher.

A buffer of 1 yields a large marginal increase in the line throughput, and then the marginal gain becomes smaller as the buffer size increases. If the buffer size is infinite, every machine is completely decoupled, and the line reliability becomes equal to the machine reliability. In this example, the line designer will probably add buffers with a capacity of 4 or 5 parts; the throughput gained with larger buffers than 5 starts to be marginal.

In the above example, we assumed that the line is balanced, namely, every machine in the line has an equal operation time. In reality, however, lines are usually not balanced. In these cases, one of the machines in the line is the slowest, and it is the bottleneck machine for achieving higher throughput.

---

[*]Dr. Sam Yang developed the software PAMS at our ERC/RMS. This software utilizes original mathematic methods (rather than simulation) to calculate the throughput, inventory, and bottlenecks of manufacturing systems and to optimize their design.

When the line is not balanced, the bottleneck machine limits the system throughput. In this case, larger buffers are needed before and after the bottleneck machine to reduce its probability of being blocked or starved.

Principles of Buffer Design: In order to obtain a certain throughput when the machine failures occur at random, larger buffer spaces are needed in the following cases:

1. When there are more unreliable machines in the line
2. When the reliability of the machines is lower
3. When a machine's MTBF and MTTR are much longer than its operation time
4. On both sides of a bottleneck machine in unbalanced lines
5. In the middle of the line in balanced lines.

The five examples below correspond to these five principles.

Example 1: Consider a four-machine asynchronous serial line in which all machines have the same operation speed and identical reliability data: MTBF $= 9$ minutes, MTTR $= 1$ minute, and the machine operation time is $T = 1$ minute. According to Eq. (7.2), each machine has a reliability $R = 0.9$ (90%). Our PAMS software shows that without any buffers the system throughput is 0.72 parts/minute. To reach an expected throughput of 0.8 parts/minute, a total of four buffer spaces are required in the system: B1 $= 1$; B2 $= 2$; B3 $= 1$. (B1 is the buffer between the first and second machine, B2 is the buffer between the second and the third machine, etc.) However, if the line is expanded to eight machines with all other data unchanged, without any buffer the system throughput is decreased from 0.72 to 0.60 parts/minute. To reach the expected throughput of 0.8 parts/minute, the system requires 15 buffer spaces that are spread as follows: B1 $= 1$; B2 $= 2$; B3 $= 3$; B4 $= 3$; B5 $= 3$; B6 $= 2$; B7 $= 1$.

Example 2: The reliability of the machines in Example 1 is lower. Given: MTBF $= 5.6667$ minute and MTTR $= 1$ minute, so according to Eq. (7.2)$R = 0.85$ (85%). The machine operation time is $T = 1$ minute. Without any buffers the four-machine system can only reach a throughput of 0.62 parts/minute. To reach the expected throughput of 0.8 parts/minute, 17 buffer spaces are required: B1 $= 5$; B2 $= 7$; B3 $= 5$. Note that a decrease in the machine reliability requires a substantial increase in the buffer total capacity from 4 to 17 spaces.

Example 3: Consider again the four-machine case in Example 1 with reliability $R = 0.9$ (90%). Without any buffers the system has an integrated throughput of 0.72 parts/minute. Now let us keep the reliability of each machine at $R = 90\%$, but expand MTBF and MTTR by 10 times. Namely, MTBF $= 90$ minutes and MTTR $= 10$ minutes. Now the system throughput is reduced to 0.696 parts/minute when no buffers exist in the system. Furthermore, if we expand MTBF and MTTR by 100 times so that MTBF $= 900$ minutes and MTTR $= 100$ minutes (the machine reliability is still 90%), the system throughput becomes only 0.693 parts/minute.

Principle 3 states that if the machines in the system maintain a constant reliability, but MTBF and MTTR are increased, the system throughput is decreased. The system reaches a higher throughput when the breakdowns and repairs occur more frequently.

Example 4: Consider the four-machine system in Example 1, but with a machine operation time of $t = 1.1$ minute on the second machine. The operation time of the other three machines remains $t = 1$ minute. All machines still have the same reliability data: MTBF $= 9$ minutes, MTTR $= 1$ minute such that $R = 0.9$. The computation with PAMS shows that to reach the expected throughput of 0.8 parts/minute, the system requires nine buffer spaces in total, which are spread as follows: B1 $= 4$; B2 $= 4$; B3 $= 1$. Note that when the line was balanced the total buffer space was 4 units, and now, with 10% increase in the operation time of one machine it is 9 units. The total buffer space is very sensitive to imbalanced lines.

Example 5: Given a line of nine identical machines with identical reliability data and operation speed: MTBF $= 7$ minutes, MTTR $= 3$ minute, and the machine operation time is $t = 1$ minute. According to Eq. (7.2), each machine has a reliability $R = 0.7$. The total given buffer capacity is 64. If the eight buffers are spread evenly among the nine machines, their capacity between adjacent machines is 8, and the throughput is 32.16 parts/hour. If, however, the buffers are spread as in Figure 7.10, the throughput is 33.87 parts/hour—an improvement of 5.3%. The buffers at the two ends are small, because the first machine will be never starved and the last machine will be never blocked.

7.5   BATCH PRODUCTION

In large manufacturing systems, the production is done in operational stages. A stage may be a machine, several machines in parallel, an assembly station, a chemical

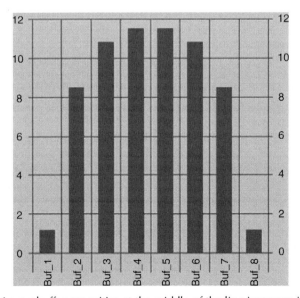

Figure 7.10   Larger buffer capacities at the middle of the line increases its throughput.

process, etc. At each stage several manufacturing tasks are performed. When the tasks in a stage are completed, the product is transferred to the next stage, and simultaneously the product that was in the previous stage is transferred forward. In the last stage, the finished products (or parts) are exiting the system at an average time, T.

Ideally, the processing times in all stages should be equal, and then the manufacturing system (or line) is perfectly balanced. A perfectly balanced system has the highest throughput, since time is not wasted on products occupying machines and waiting ("blocked") to be processed in the next stage, and machines are not waiting for parts ("starving"). The calculations in which various manufacturing tasks are assigned to stages with the aim to balance the system are called line balancing.

In flexible manufacturing systems that produce more than one product type, the processing is done in batches, where each batch produces one type of identical products that need equal processing times. Switching from one product type to another requires time to change tools and fixtures, and in many cases, time is also needed to purge the manufacturing system from the old products. The sum of all these times is the switchover time (t_s).

We define below basic terms utilized in operations planning of manufacturing system.

Throughput	The average output of a production machine or system, measured in parts per unit time
Cycle time (T)	The actual average time interval between successive parts exiting a manufacturing system, measured in time units **Cycle time = 1/Throughput**
Switchover time	The total time needed to switch production on a flexible system from a batch of one part to a batch of another part
Makespan	The total amount of time needed to produce a fixed number of jobs (which may consist of several products)
Holding cost	Sum of all inventory costs (physical storage space + possible part breakage + possible product obsolescence) that are proportional to the amount of inventory
Shortage cost	The cost of losing sales; it typically occurs when demand exceeds the capacity (namely, the rate of demand exceeds the system throughput). However, it may also occur when products orders are changed between the time the production plan is made and the time its implementation is completed
Takt time	The total time available during a production period, divided by the demand for that period. It is the **desired time** between output units synchronized to the rate of customer demand
WIP	Work-in-process, which is the sum of all parts present in a manufacturing system between its start and end points
Throughput time	The average time it takes one part to move all the way through a manufacturing system from start to exit (also called lead time)

7.5.1 Flexible System Makespan

A typical flexible manufacturing system produces multiple types of products of the same product family. The time to complete the production of all products is called makespan. The products are produced in batches; the number of products in the batch is the lot size. Switching from one type of batch to another requires a switchover time.

To be more flexible there is a need to switch between product types at high frequency. However, in each switchover a production time is lost, so, in the end of the production period (e.g., a day) a smaller number of products is manufactured, and therefore the cost per product becomes higher. The calculation of this cost is presented below.

Notations:

T = total given time period for production and switchovers (e.g., 16 hours)
t_c = cycle time (time to complete production of one product)
t_s = switchover time between product types
m = number of switchovers within the given time period T
L = lot size

We assume equal cycle time for products in the family and equal lot size for each product type. The time spent on all switchovers during T is mt_s and therefore the production time is $T - mt_s$. The number of products, n, produced during the time is

$$n = \frac{T - mt_s}{t_c} \tag{7.3}$$

The lot size is

$$L = \frac{n}{m+1} = \frac{T - mt_s}{(m+1)t_c} \tag{7.4}$$

We assume production of two types of products. The maximum lot size is obtained with one switchover, namely for $m = 1$,

$$L_{max} = \frac{T - t_s}{2t_c} \tag{7.5}$$

From Eq. (7.4), we can obtain

$$m = \frac{T - Lt_c}{t_s + Lt_c} \tag{7.6}$$

and therefore

$$m + 1 = \frac{T + t_s}{t_s + Lt_c} \tag{7.7}$$

The product manufacturing cost, y, is the sum of the fixed costs (C_0) per product and the variable costs (C_1).

$$y = C_1 + C_0/n \tag{7.8}$$

where, from Eq. (7.4), $n = L(m+1)$. Substituting $(m+1)$ from Eq. (7.7) into Eq. (7.8) yields

$$y = C_1 + \frac{C_0}{L}\left(\frac{t_s + Lt_c}{T + t_s}\right) \tag{7.9}$$

To obtain the cost as function of the relative lot size, $L_r = L/L_{max}$, we divide the numerator and denominator of Eq. (7.9) by L_{max}, which yields

$$y = C_1 + \frac{t_c L_r + 2t_s t_c/(T-t_s)}{(T+t_s)L_r} C_0 \tag{7.10}$$

Eq. (7.10) is valuable at the design stage of flexible systems that will produce multiple products. If the system is designed for the minimum number of switchovers, the lot size is the maximum possible according to Eq. (7.5), and the cost is minimal. However, if because of practical operations requirements there will be a need for additional switchovers, the system capacity would not be able to meet demand. Therefore, it is more economical to design the capacity of flexible systems with lot sizes smaller than the maximum as long as it does not increase substantially the cost of producing the products.

Figure 7.11 shows an example of a part that requires a cycle time of 2 minutes for its production, and required switchover times between product types (sot or t_s) of 10, 20, 30, and 40 minutes (typical values in the powertrain industry). In this example $T = 960$ minutes (equals 16 hours or two shifts), $C_0 = 2000$, and $C_1 = 10$. If the switchover time is small (10 minutes) compared with the cycle time, designing the system capacity with lot sizes of $0.25\,L_{max}$ has a very insignificant impact on the cost, but allows more flexibility when operating the system. However, when the switchover time is large (40 minutes) compared with the cycle time, a lot size of $0.75\,L_{max}$ is recommended for designing the system capacity.

7.5.2 Minimizing Irresponsiveness to Customer's Demand

When producing simultaneously multiple product types, a typical optimization measure for the sequencing of products is minimizing makespan, which is achieved by the production of large lot sizes.[7] This operation policy assumes that customer's orders will not change after the production started, and that severe disruptions will not occur. However, in "lean" environments, where customer orders are typically filled through new production rather than from inventory, minimizing makespan by

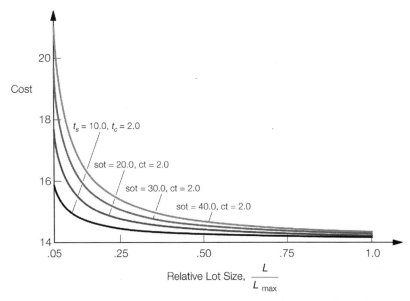

Figure 7.11 Product manufacturing cost as function of the lot size and switchover times.

producing large lot sizes may create a product shortage. As a result, manufacturers are losing sales, and consequently might also lose their customers.

We observed a shortage issue in which products were not ready to be supplied when needed in an engine machining line that produced two types of engine blocks, A and B, in large lot sizes with one switchover (which takes about 40 minutes) during the working period. The line scheduled to produce part A in the first 8 hours, switch over, and continue to produce part B. Because of disruptions upstream in the car assembly process, the order was changed during the day—the line was instructed to supply immediately type B engine blocks, which had to be produced later in the day. Since engine blocks of type B were not available, a shortage occurred. This sort of changes in orders during production is becoming more common in a variety of industries.

Customer's orders may change even after the production has already begun. We observed such production environment in a 1999 visit to Intel's Fab-8, which produced simultaneously 40–60 types of wafers. The production of a wafer takes about 6–7 weeks. During this long period customers are changing their order quantities; but even though, Intel supplies the modified ordered quantities on time.

Manufacturing systems cannot be primarily designed based on demand forecasts without concern for changes in customer orders. The competitiveness of today's global economy necessitates focusing on the manufacturing system responsiveness to customers. To be responsive to customer's needs, the manufacturing system should be designed with enough capacity to operate with policies that satisfy customers' demand (e.g., adjusting lot sizing, and allowing an optimal number of switchovers).

The manufacturer's dilemma is to determine an optimal lot size. On one hand, if the lot size is too small, many switchovers occur, and potential production time is lost, which may create a shortage of products. On the other hand, if the lot size is too large and the customer changes orders, a shortage cost may occur, since the system cannot produce the new orders on time, thus it is not responsive to the customer's need.

System Responsiveness: Matson defines responsiveness as "the ability of a production system to respond to disturbances that impact upon production goals."[8] Shafaei and Brunn define customer responsiveness as whether or not the customer demands are *fully satisfied* by the due date.[9] However, an analytical expression could not be found in the literature.

We present below a calculation of a shortage cost caused by the irresponsiveness of the manufacturing system.[*] The shortage cost that relates to system irresponsiveness has two components, and a third cost component affects the product cost.

1. If the lot size is very large, a shortage, as described above in the engine block example, may occur (i.e., a sales shortage).
2. If the lot size is very small there are many switchovers, the net production time is smaller, and a smaller number of products is manufactured, which may also cause a shortage (i.e., a production shortage).
3. When there are many switchovers (i.e., small lot sizes), the fixed costs are divided by a smaller number of actual produced products, which, in turn, increases the average cost per product. This cost is expressed in Eq. (7.10).

The challenge is to determine a reasonable optimal lot size that trade offs these costs.

A very large lot size will cause a sales shortage cost, C_l, due to lack of responsiveness to order changes. The cost C_l is zero when the lot size is 1 (e.g., the manufacturing system is producing products in the sequence ABAB...); at lot size of 1 the system has its maximum responsiveness. We assume that the sales shortage cost caused by the slow responsiveness is given by

$$C_l = C_L (L-1)^2 \qquad (7.11)$$

where C_L is a cost coefficient.

Substituting $L = L_r L_{max}$ in Eq. (7.11), with L_{max} substituted from Eq. (7.5), yields

$$C_l = C_L \left(L_r \frac{T-t_s}{2t_c} - 1 \right)^2 \qquad (7.12)$$

On the other hand, we calculate the shortage cost component that is caused by producing in small lot sizes, which requires many switchovers. If the system produces two products, there must be at least one switchover. The production shortage cost caused by one switchover is 0. If the lot size is small, there are many switchovers and a production time mt_s is lost. The number of products that could be

---

[*]Dr. Wencai Wang developed the calculations in this section.

produced during this time is mt_s/t_c, and if the cost of a shortage of each product is C_s, then the total production shortage cost is

$$C_t = C_s (m-1)^2 \frac{t_s}{t_c} \tag{7.13}$$

Substituting m from Eq. (7.6) yields

$$C_t = C_s \left(\frac{(T-Lt_c)}{(t_s+Lt_c)} - 1 \right)^2 \frac{t_s}{t_c} = C_s \frac{t_s}{t_c} \left(\frac{T-L_r L_{\max} t_c}{t_s + L_r L_{\max} t_c} - 1 \right)^2 \tag{7.14}$$

Substituting $L_{\max}$ from Eq. (7.5) yields

$$C_t = C_s \frac{t_s}{t_c} \left(\frac{2T - L_r(T-t_s)}{2t_s + L_r(T-t_s)} - 1 \right)^2 \tag{7.15}$$

The overall cost C is obtained by adding Eqs (7.10), (7.15), and (7.12):

$$
\begin{aligned}
C &= y + C_t + C_l \\
&= C_1 + \frac{t_c L_r + 2t_s t_c/(T-t_s)}{(T+t_s)L_r} C_0 + C_s \frac{t_s}{t_c} \left(\frac{2T - L_r(T-t_s)}{2t_s + L_r(T-t_s)} - 1 \right)^2 + C_L \left(L_r \frac{T-t_s}{2t_c} - 1 \right)^2
\end{aligned}
\tag{7.16}
$$

Figure 7.12 shows the changes of product cost C with the relative lot size L_r. where $L_r = L/L_{\max}$ and the maximum lot size, $L_{\max}$, is the lot size with one switchover during the working period. We can see that the cost tradeoffs cause an almost flat minimum cost that is insensitive to the lot size in the range: $0.75 L_{\max} > $ lot size $> 0.25 L_{\max}$.

When the system produces two products, A and B:

- An average lot size of $0.75 L_{\max}$, actually means operating with **two** switchovers (SWO), and the producing schedule is: half As, SWO, all Bs, SWO, half As.
- A lot size of $0.5 L_{\max}$ means operating with **three** switchovers, and the producing schedule is: half As, SWO, half Bs, SWO, half As, SWO, half Bs.
- A lot size of $0.25 L_{\max}$ means operating with **seven** switchovers, and the producing schedule is: 1/4 As, SWO, 1/4 Bs, SWO, 1/4 As, SWO, 1/4 Bs, SWO, 1/4 As, SWO, 1/4 Bs, SWO, 1/4 As, SWO, 1/4 Bs.

When planning the capacity of a new manufacturing system and the switchover time is long, the capacity should be designed to accommodate at least two daily switchovers. When the switchover time is short, the system's planned capacity should allow for not more than seven daily switchovers. There is no substantial benefit in operating a system with more than seven switchovers.

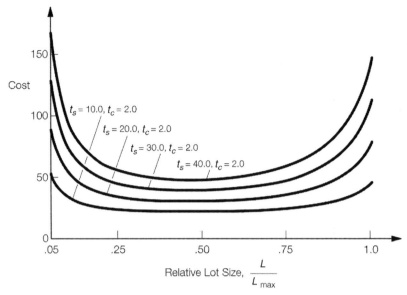

Figure 7.12 Cost as function of the lot size for various switchover times. Parameters used to obtain the chart are: $C_0 = 2000$, $C_1 = 10$, $C_2 = 80$, $C_3 = 150$, $k_s = 0.9$.

A short switchover time is defined around one hundredth of a production period (e.g., 10 minutes when the planned production period is 16 hours). A long switchover time is about four times longer.

7.6 OPTIMAL CUTTING SPEEDS

Determining the right machine speed of each machine in a system has a profound effect on the system throughput. The following example demonstrates that the considerations in selecting machine speeds are different when a stand-alone machine is operated and when the machine is integrated into a system (of two machines in this case).

A part has to be machined on a single machine tool and you have to recommend a cutting speed. If the cutting speed is higher, more parts are machined before a tool change, but the tool life deteriorates exponentially as the speed becomes higher. The tool life data are given in the table below.

Cutting speed (m/minute)	150	238	300	513	600
Tool life (minute)	480	120	60	12	7.5
Time to machine one part	12	7.5	6	3.5	3

The tool changing time of worn tools is on average 5 minutes.

The plant is working in two shifts, each of 8 hours, with 1-hour break between shifts.

(a) *Calculate the number of tools needed and the number of parts machined in 8 hours at each of the above five speeds. What is your recommendation for a cutting speed?*

At speed of **150** m/minute, the number of tools needed in 8 hours is $\frac{8\times60}{480} = 1$.

The number of parts machined is $1 \times \frac{480}{12} = 40$.

At speed of **238** m/minute, the number of tools needed is $\left[\frac{8\times60}{120+5}\right] = 3$.

The remaining time to the end of the shift after the last tool change is $8 \times 60-3 \times 125 = 105$ minutes.

The number of parts machined is $3 \times \left[\frac{120}{7.5}\right] + \left[\frac{8\times60-3\times125}{7.5}\right] = 48 + 14 = 62$.

At speed of **300** m/minute, the number of tools needed is $\left[\frac{8\times60}{60+5}\right] = 7$.

The remaining time to the end of the shift after the last tool change is $8 \times 60-7 \times 65$ minutes.

The number of parts machined is $7 \times \frac{60}{6} + \left[\frac{8\times60-7\times65}{6}\right] = 70+4 = 74$.

At speed of **513** m/minute the number of tools needed is $\left[\frac{8\times60}{12+5}\right] = 28$.

The remaining time to the end of the shift after the last tool change is $8 \times 60-28 \times 17$ minutes.

The number of parts machined is $28 \times \left[\frac{12}{3.5}\right] + \left[\frac{8\times60-28\times17}{3.5}\right] = 84 + 1 = 85$.

At speed of **600** m/minutes the number of tools needed is $\left[\frac{8\times60}{7.5+5}\right] = 38$.

The remaining time to the end of the shift after the last tool change is $8 \times 60-38 \times 12.5$ minutes.

The number of parts machined is $38 \times \left[\frac{7.5}{3}\right] + \left[\frac{8\times60-38\times12.5}{3.5}\right] = 76+1 = 77$.

The results are summarized in the table below:

Cutting speed (m/minute)	150	238	300	513	600
Number of tools needed	1	3	7	28	38
Number of parts machined	40	62	74	85	77

If tooling cost is not considered, the speed that provides the highest throughput, 85 parts per shift, is 513 m/minute. However, note that 28 tools are changed during the 8-hour shift.

Now, let us see how this recommended speed changes when the machine is part of a small system composed of two machines. The machined parts are transferred to the next manufacturing operation that requires 6.5 minutes per part. The machine of this operation is fully automatic and tools are changed on this machine once per day.

(b) *What is the recommended cutting speed for the first machine in this two-machine system?*

The speed of first machine should produce parts at the similar rate of the second machine. In an 8-hour shift, the second machine produces

$$\left[\frac{8 \times 60}{6.5}\right] = 73 \text{ parts.}$$

From the answer of question a, we see that at a cutting speed 300 m/minute, the number of parts produced on the first machine, 74, is the closest to 73. Therefore, the recommended cutting speed on the first machine for two-machine operation is 300 m/minute. In this case the system will produce 73 parts per shift, and only seven tools will have to be changed during the shift.

Conclusion: The optimal cutting speed on each machine in a system (or the operation speed in assembly systems) depends on the system configuration. The goal is to maximize the whole system throughput, rather than the individual machine throughput.

PROBLEMS

7.1 A VP of a manufacturing firm that produces two products has to decide (1) How much capacity to build? (2) Whether to invest in dedicated or flexible resources, or a portfolio consisting of both dedicated and flexible systems.

The VP received the following forecasting for the demand of each product.

	Year 1–2	Year 3–6	
	Volume	Volume	Probability
Product A	500,000	200,000	0.7
		600,000	0.3
Product B	200,000	200,000	0.3
		600,000	0.7

A dedicated line can produce 300,000 annually and its cost is $30 million. Flexible systems are supplied at chunks; each has an annual production capacity of 50,000 units and costs $7 million. The revenues from each product sold are $40.

(a) Calculate the optimal capacity—type and quantity.

(b) What is the optimal solution if the cost of a dedicated line that can produce 200,000 annually is $15 million?

(c) What is the optimal solution if the cost of a dedicated line that can produce 300,000 annually is $40 million?

7.2   A factory manufactures two products A and B on a flexible system during 15 hours every day for 5 days per week. The cycle time of part A is 9 minutes, and that of B is 12 minutes. The switchover time from one product to the other is 20 minutes.

The customer requires shipping equal quantities of A and B once a day in containers of 10 parts each (separate containers for part A and for B). Only full containers with 10 parts are being shipped. A few parts may be stored overnight for next day delivery.

(a) How many parts are shipped to the customer every week if the system operates with n switchovers per day, where $n = 1, 2, 3, 4,$ and 5. Calculate the lot sizes in each case.

(b) If the customer requires shipping parts twice a day (not necessarily at certain times), what is the recommended n?

(c) In emergency situations the customer unexpectedly requires shipping containers of A and B every 4 hours. What is the recommended number of daily switchovers (n) to satisfy this requirement?

7.3   Calculate the total number of tools in the tool magazines of all machines in the three systems depicted in Figure 7.9, if each machine is capable of producing both part A and part B. Which of three systems in Figure 7.9 is the most economical in your opinion?

7.4   A part has to be machined on a single machine tool and you have to recommend a cutting speed. If the cutting speed is higher, more parts are machined, but the tool life deteriorates exponentially, as shown in the table below:

Cutting speed (m/minute)	150	240	300	480	600
Tool life (minute)	240	80	60	20	15
Time to machine one part	16	10	8	5	4

The tool-changing time of worn tools is on average 8 minutes.

The plant is working in two shifts, each of 8 hours, with 1-hour break between shifts.

(a) Calculate the number of parts machined in 8 hours at each of the above speeds (remember to include the tool changing time in your calculations).

(b) Calculate the number of tools needed in 8 hours at each speed.

(c) If tool-changing cost is not considered, of these five speeds, what is your recommended cutting speed?

7.5   Assuming that two machines are needed to complete a part, a robot transfers the semi-machined part from one machine to the next in 30 seconds (see Figure 7.13). If identical cutting speeds are used on both machines, the

Machine 1   Machine 2

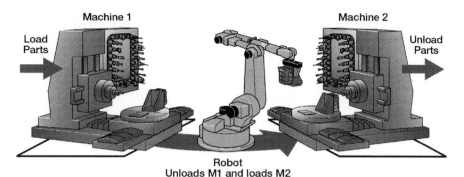

Load   Unload
Parts   Parts

Robot
Unloads M1 and loads M2

Figure 7.13   A machining system of two machines.

cutting time per part on Machine 1 is 40 seconds and the cutting time on Machine 2 is 50 seconds.

(a) What is the throughput of the line (assuming machine reliability 100%) in parts per 8-hour shift?

(b) Can you recommend a change (in %) in the cutting speed of the machines in order to increase the system throughput?

REFERENCES

1. The cycle time is calculated with the aid of process plans. A process plan determines the sequence of individual manufacturing operations needed to produce a given part or product, in which the machining parameters for each opearion are given. We do not discuss this topic in the book. For reference you may see: W. Wencai and D. Yip-Hoi: Modeling and identification of feed drive kinematics and cycle time calculation. *ASME International Mechanical Engineering Congress*, Washington, DC, 2003.

2. J. Black. *Oxford Dictionary of Economics*. Oxford University Press, 2003.

3. R. Katz, I. Duenyas, W. Norongwanich, and Y. Koren. Economic benefits of reconfigurable manufacturing systems (RMS). *Global Powertrain Conference*, Ann Arbor, MI, September 2002.

4. Y. Koren, F. Jovane, U. Heisel, T. Moriwaki, G. Pritschow, AG. Ulsoy, and H. VanBrussel. Reconfigurable manufacturing systems. *Annals of the CIRP*, 1999, Vol. 48, No. 2, pp. 6–12.

5. J. A. Van Mieghem. Investment strategies for flexible resources. *Management Science*, 1998, Vol. 44, No. 8, pp. 1071–1078.

6. O. Ceryan and Y. Koren. Manufacturing capacity planning strategies. *Annals of the CIRP*, August 2009, Vol. 58, No. 1.

7. P. Damodaran, K. Srihari, and S. Lam. Scheduling a capacitated batch-processing machine to minimize makespan. *Robotics and Computer-Integrated Manufacturing*, April 2007, Vol. 23, No. 2, pp. 208–216.

8. J. B. Matson and D. McFarlane. Assessing the responsiveness of existing production operations. *International Journal of Operations and Production Management*, 1999, Vol. 19, No. 8, pp. 765–784.

9. R. Shafaei and P. Brunn. Workshop scheduling using practical (inaccurate) data—part 1: the performance of heuristic scheduling rules in a dynamic job shop environment using a rolling time horizon approach. *International Journal of Production Research*, 1999, Vol. 37, No. 17, pp. 3913–3925.

Chapter **8**

Reconfigurable Machines

To illustrate the concept of reconfigurable machines (RMs) let us look at mechanical wrenches (Figure 8.1). An open-end wrench that is dedicated to grip just one-size bolt (fixed part geometry), the adjustable wrench that is a flexible tool (fits any part geometry), and the reconfigurable, modular socket wrench, which can turn bolts whose geometry fits a bolt family. The perfect fit between the socket and the part geometry enables quicker working speeds, and the changing sockets enable a functionality fit to a whole part family of bolts.

The modular tool with its sockets represents one type of reconfigurability that depends on modularity. But modularity is not a necessary condition for reconfigurability. A structure may be reconfigurable without being modular as the following example illustrates.

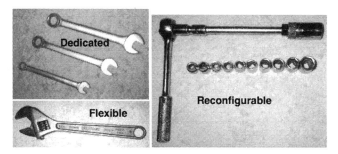

Figure 8.1   Reconfigurable tools fill the gap between dedicated tools and flexible tools.

The Global Manufacturing Revolution: Product-Process-Business Integration and Reconfigurable Systems
By Yoram Koren
Copyright © 2010 John Wiley & Sons, Inc.

An excellent demonstration of what we mean by reconfigurable structures are toy action figures that are transformable (from a robot to a truck, for example). The capability of transformation is always present in the toy whatever configuration is desired at the time. By simply applying a series of manipulations, the child modifies the toy from one form to the other without adding or subtracting anything. Likewise, with one class of non-modular reconfigurable machines, just modifying the structure can change functionality without additional parts.

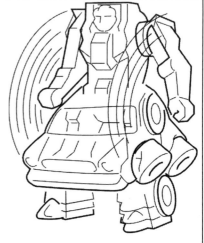

Illustration by R. Hill

8.1 THE RATIONALE FOR RECONFIGURABLE MACHINES

A RM is a machine whose structures can be altered to provide either alternative functionality or incremental increase in its production rate in order to meet changing demand. The RM can be continuously returned to its original state, or modified to provide new functionality or production capacity as needed. **RM design has, therefore, two basic objectives:**

1. **To adapt the machine functionality to fit a new member of a family of parts**
   (...*exactly the functionality needed*)
2. **To increase the machine production rate by adding resources**
   (...*exactly the capacity needed*)

RMs are designed around the common characteristics of part families, and this feature differentiates them from dedicated or flexible machines. For example, while there might be major differences between various engine cylinder heads, the basic configuration of all of them is quite similar, as depicted in Figure 8.2. A reconfigurable machine tool (RMT) can therefore be designed to perform the necessary machining operations common to all the members of the part family with reconfiguration to the machine itself. Similarly, a reconfigurable inspection machine (RIM) can be designed to perform the appropriate inspections on a set of features for members of the part family and then reconfigure to inspect another set of features. The RM concept can cost-effectively produce or inspect a whole family of parts, even part styles that have not yet been called for.

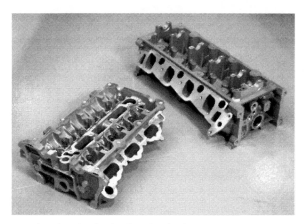

Figure 8.2   A part family of cylinder heads: the basic machining features are similar.

RMs constitute a new class of production and inspection machines that fill the gap between dedicated machines and flexible machines, as shown in Table 8.1

The RM sacrifices some general flexibility for faster throughput speed in performing the task. To create an RM, the part family (including all potential members) must be understood before the machine is designed. This allows the RM to be designed for repetitive, fast operation like dedicated tools. But unlike dedicated tools, RMs have features that allow enough flexibility (extending the envelop reach, changing whole tool magazines, adding functions) that they can produce any of the part family members, in quantity and on demand. RM performance in an environment of volatile markets makes them superior to flexible machines that are, by contrast, built with the widest range of flexibility possible, (like coordinate measuring machine, CMM), and only then the application is made suitable for a specific part (usually by programming).

The RM paradigm is driven primarily by economic considerations. Rather than custom-build a multi-spindle dedicated machine, for example, a manufacturer could purchase a single-spindle reconfigurable machine and then add spindles to it; allowing it to cut several parts at the same time as market demand justified the investment (an adjustable-capacity RM). Also, rather than invest in a highly complex, general-purpose computerized numerical control (CNC) machine tool, it would be more economical to have a simpler machine with enough functionality to produce a whole

TABLE 8.1   Machine Types

Machine Type	Dedicated	Reconfigurable	Flexible
Given part geometry	Fixed part geometry	Part geometry fits a part family	Any part geometry
Operation speed	Very fast	Fast	Slow
Flexibility	Not flexible	Customized flexibility for a part family	Full flexibility

family of parts without buying a lot of extra unused functionality (an adjustable functionality RM). Focusing one's purchase on only the capacity and functionality needed for a desired part family gives the RM an advantage.

The primary aim of a RM is to cope with changes in the products or parts to be manufactured. The possible changes that are considered:[1]

- Part geometry
- Production volume and production rate
- Required processes
- Material property, such as kind of material, hardness, etc.

8.1.1 Convertibility—Fitting Functionality to the Part Geometry

Adding new motion units to increase the number of axes-of-motion, or changing out one unit for another having a different degree of freedom (DOF), may change machine functionality for different part geometries in the same family. Figure 8.3 shows a schematic of a possible reconfigurable five-axis machining center that includes two optional rotary axes for rotational motions.

8.1.2 Scalability—Changing Production Volume and Rate

In order to increase the rate of production, the capacity of a machine spindle unit can be increased by changing from a single-, dual-, or even multi-spindle unit. The multi-

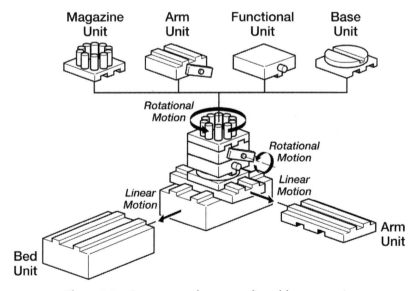

Figure 8.3   Components for a reconfigurable rotary axis.

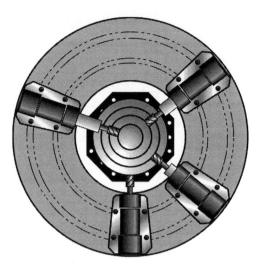

Figure 8.4   Top view of a vertical turning–milling center with multiple spindles.

spindle unit is a very powerful tool to increase productivity, performing multiple operations simultaneously. Modularized spindle units capable of different speed ranges and horsepower are another good use of RMTs. Figure 8.4 shows an example of a RMT where a part mounted on a rotary table is being machined simultaneously by four spindles.

The number of spindles in the example of Figure 8.4 can be varied to accommodate the desired production rate. Each spindle is a Z-axis module. Two additional manual axes are the location of the spindle and its cutting angle.

8.1.3   Reconfigurability for Changes in the Machining Process

More than just the cutting tool, sometimes the spindle type, or even the machine tool configuration can be changed to cope with changes in the machining process. In some applications turning can be performed not only on a turning center but also on a milling machine, and milling and drilling operations can be performed on a lathe by using a milling spindle that replaces the fixed tool post. Another example is the machine in Figure 8.4 that can be converted to a vertical turning center, in which parts are machined simultaneously with multiple tools for drilling, and turning operations.

8.1.4   Reconfigurability for Material Properties

Milling titanium, for example, requires high torque at low speed, while milling aluminum requires the opposite—low torque at high speed. That is why there are milling machines in the aerospace industry that were designed for changeable spindles. Spindles are rapidly changed according to the workpiece material.

8.2 CHARACTERISTICS AND PRINCIPLES OF RECONFIGURABLE MACHINES

A RM is designed around a defined part family. Approaching machine design from this point of view creates a less complex, albeit less flexible machine. Still it is a machine that contains all the functionality and flexibility needed to produce (or inspect) a whole part family. This characteristic is called Customization or Customized Flexibility; it is in contrast to the general flexibility characteristic of a CNC or a CMM that is commonly used in inspection.

We define a RM as follows:

> A RM is a machine designed for rapid change in its structure in order to quickly adjust production capacity and/or functionality within a part family.

RMs can be easily switched from handling (i.e., machining, assembly, or inspection) one part of the family to another part. This is called machine responsiveness. To enhance the RM responsiveness, there is a set of core characteristics that should be embedded in the machine system, both in the mechanical structure and in its controls. In general, RMs possess the six core characteristics that are defined below.

Customization	The ability to apply a customized flexibility to production or inspection machines to meet new requirements within a part family.
Scalability	The ability to efficiently change the machine's production throughput by altering or augmenting the components in the machine.
Convertibility	The ability to efficiently redirect the functionality of the machine and its controls to suit new production requirements.
Modularity	The compartmentalization of operational functions and hardware into units that can be manipulated between alternate machine configurations.
Integrability	The ability to integrate machine modules rapidly and precisely by a set of mechanical, informational, and control interfaces.
Diagnosability	The capability of monitoring the current state of a machine and controls so as to detect and diagnose the root cause of output product defects.

The first three characteristics: customization, scalability, and convertibility are critical to creating cost-effective machines. An RM with customized flexibility will be less expensive to build and operate than a comparable CNC machine that has general flexibility. Similarly, an RIM with customized flexibility will be less expensive and much more rapid to accomplish the inspection job than a comparable CMM with general flexibility. Every RM should be convertible (to handle part changes), or scalable (to handle demand changes), or both.

Modularity and integrability are characteristics that are sufficient to constitute an RM. Diagnosability, when embedded in the machine and its control structure, provides the means for quick and accurate reconfiguration.

8.2.1 Design Principles of Reconfigurable Machines

RMs can be altered in response to part or product changes as well as to market demand changes (for example, adding more spindles increases the machine throughput). RMs are designed according to three primary principles.[2]

---

1. The RM is designed with an **adjustable structure** that enables either machine scalability in response to market demands, or machine convertibility to adapt to new products.
2. The RM is designed around a **part family** with just the customized flexibility needed for producing all members of this part family.
3. The RM embeds a set of **core characteristics** in both its hardware and control structures.

Adjustable structure may be achieved by machine modularity, changing the configuration of mechanical links in the machine, or adding/subtracting resources to/from the machine. Resources may be spindles, sensors, assembly arms, etc. The part family focus is the essence of the RM; it allows the design of the machine with customized flexibility—just the flexibility needed to handle all the members of the family.

An RM may be built for various manufacturing applications:

Machining—reconfigurable machine tool (RMT)[3]

Assembly—reconfigurable assembly machine (RAM)

Fixtures—reconfigurable fixtures

Inspection—reconfigurable inspection machine (RIM)[4]

We will describe below several types of RMTs, as well as reconfigurable fixtures and inspection machines.

8.3 RECONFIGURABLE MACHINE TOOLS

RMTs are cost-effective because they are designed for a specific range of operation requirements, and can be economically converted from one to the other. The challenge

TABLE 8.2   RMT Combines Features of Dedicated and CNC Machines

	Dedicated	RMT	CNC Machine
Machine structure	Fixed	**Adjustable**	Fixed
Design focus	Part	**Partfamily**	Machine
Scalability	No	**Yes**	Yes
Flexibility	No	**Customized**	General
Simultaneously operating tools	Yes	**Yes**	No

is to focus the machine design effort on a specific part family and create an adjustable machine that is capable of machining features of every part of this part family, and do so rapidly. Every DOF of an RMT is designed after the operation set of all parts of the family has been determined. As operational requirements change, the RMT needs to be mechanically modified to adapt to these changes.

As summarized in Table 8.2, machines with adjustable structures constrained to a part family create responsive machines and constitute the new class of machines that have customized flexibility and scalable throughput.

We will describe three types of RMTs: modular, multi-tool, and arch-type RMT.

8.3.1   Modular Machine Tools

One might naturally associate the term "reconfigurable machine" with modular machine tools. It is true that modularity of machine components is a sufficient condition for reconfigurability, but a machine may be reconfigurable without being modular. Nevertheless, modular machines are an important class of RMs. Some projects on designing modular machines have already been carried out within the framework of the international Intelligent Manufacturing Systems (IMS) initiative.[5] Figure 8.5 shows examples of three-axis modular machining centers.*

The motion and drive units of modular machines are powered with electricity and are connected with the controller by wires. Some modules also require hydraulics or compressed air. Integrating the modules to an operating machine requires interfaces to transfer the electricity, hydraulic power, etc. Interfaces may be divided into three main classes: mechanical, power, and information or control (see Figure 8.6). Mechanical interfaces define the machine geometry and kinematics. The power and energy interfaces dictate requirements that limit the overall size and dynamics. Information interfaces connect the various controllers and sensors via communication networks to computers and transmit data. To fulfill the requirements of an open, modular machine structure, these interfaces must be specified in detail.

Interfacing the module's wiring and piping with an external energy source can be an obstacle for reconfiguration. The absence of adequate mechanical interfaces that

---

*Professor T. Moriwaki brought the example of modular machine tools.

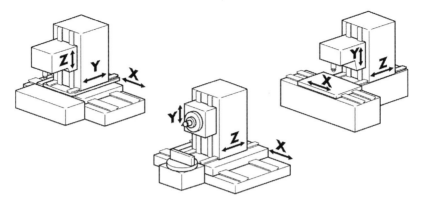

Figure 8.5 Modular machining centers.

can facilitate rapid setup and alignment is an additional major barrier impeding machine modularity.[6] Another barrier to the common use of modular machines is the lack of methods to rapidly calibrate and adjust the alignment of modular components. For all these reasons changing the configuration of modular machines while still achieving effective operations is sometimes impractical. To deploy practical modular machines it is therefore necessary for each module to be autonomous and independently functional, and standardization of the module connecting interfaces needs to be established. All these requirements do not exist today.

8.3.2 Multi-tool RMT

Although built with just "customized flexibility," RMTs provide all the flexibility needed to process a specific part family. One example of customized flexibility is a variant of a gang drill, common to dedicated lines. A gang drill includes multiple spindles holding drill-bits (see Figure 6.6) that can simultaneously drill a pattern of

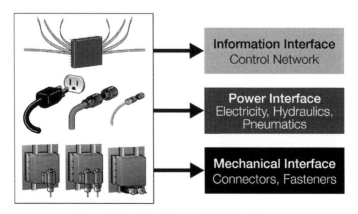

Figure 8.6 Machine modules interfaces.

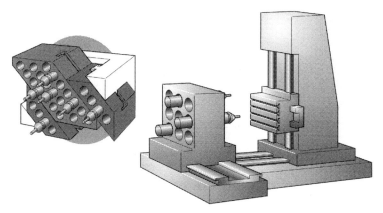

Figure 8.7   Reconfigurable machine tool—RMT.

holes in a part. A reconfigurable multi-spindle gang drill can cut all the holes needed by a part family member and then quickly reconfigure to drill a different pattern of holes in the next member part, as needed. An example of an RMT that can drill holes in one plane of a part is depicted in Figure 8.7. This RMT is capable of drilling multiple holes simultaneously. It can drill some 10, 20, and even 50 holes with a single motion of the Z-axis. When a different part is needed, the spindle head may need to be changed as well or the spindle head itself may be reconfigurable.[7] In a more sophisticated RMT, the spindle heads are on a 80° index table, and it rotates to fit the part entering the machine for processing. The index-type spindle head can accommodate up to four members of the part family.

The comparison between the RMT of Figure 8.7 and its two counterparts is presented in Table 8.3.

Other practical examples of how single-axis drive modules can change machine functionality are shown in Figure 8.8. In these examples the reconfigurable modules can allow for single or multiple spindles in either a vertical or horizontal configuration.

Figure 8.9 shows a conceptual design of a multi-tool RMT based on the patent of Koren and Kota[8]. Single-axis drive modules may be mounted to operate at different angles simultaneously. As the part size and features change, the spindles can be relocated to perform the same operation in a different location or replaced with another spindle to perform a different operation. Note that spindles can also be added or removed to optimize resources.

TABLE 8.3   Machine Tools

Dedicated	Multi-tool RMT	Flexible (CNC)
Very fast	Fast	Slow
Fixed motions	Flexibility for a part family	Full flexibility

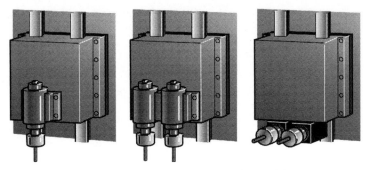

Figure 8.8   Reconfigurable spindle modules.

Preserving the precision of RMs after reconfiguration is a major challenge to their wider use. Many RMTs consist of modules that have been integrated in different ways to create new machine configurations. Each module has its own interface with its own associated tolerances. The combined motions of the cutting tool and the workpiece determine machining accuracy, and so does the relative arrangement of the modules and their interfaces. The overall machine accuracy of the RM is also influenced by its static and dynamic rigidities and the thermal deformations of its elements as well[9].

8.3.3   Arch-type RMT

The arch-type RMT was designed for milling, drilling, and tapping cylinder-head surfaces that are at either 30 or 45° to the main plane, as shown in Figure 8.2. These

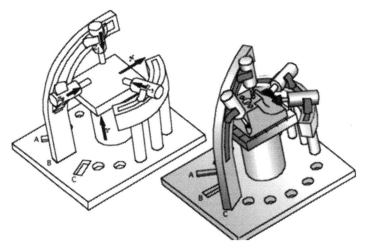

Figure 8.9   Two configurations of a reconfigurable machine tool.

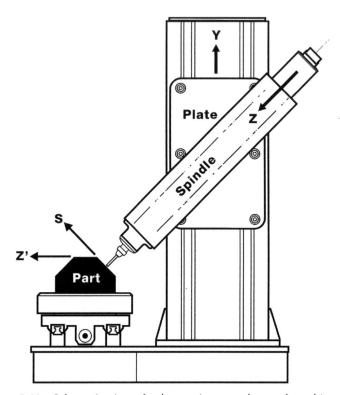

Figure 8.10 Schematic view of a three-axis non-orthogonal machine tool.

tasks were mathematically formulated and input to RMT-design software developed by the Engineering Research Center for Reconfigurable Manufacturing Systems at the University of Michigan. One of the conceptual machine geometries obtained by the software is the RMT shown in Figure 8.10.

Note that if a conventional CNC was used to machine such inclined surfaces, a four- or five-axis machine would be needed. Figure 8.10 shows a new type of "non-orthogonal" machine tool. With only three axes this machine can mill and drill holes on the 45° inclined surface.

Even so, one may argue that it is not economical to build a non-orthogonal machine tool just to operate at 45°. What about other cylinder heads (of the same part family) with a 30° surface? Should we also build a new machine to mill at 30°? Couldn't we have both in one?

We have therefore chosen to develop a three-axis non-orthogonal RMT in which the angle of the Z-axis is adjustable. The conceptual design was developed by the author and is depicted in Figure 8.11. The Z-axis can sweep across an arched plate and be fixed at desired angular positions along the inclined surface. The simple adjusting mechanism (ball screw) that moves the Z-axis spindle around the arch is not servo-controlled and so does not require the continuous tolerance of a regular CNC moving axis of motion.

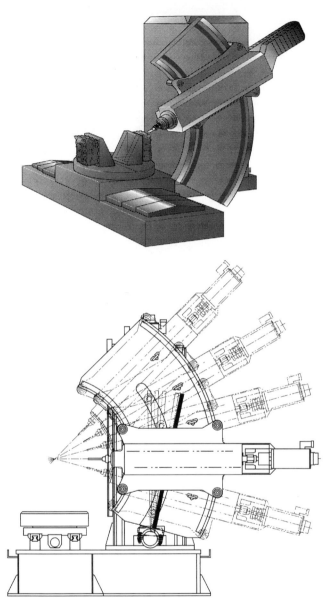

Figure 8.11   Arch-type RMT—conceptual design; the inclined angle can be changed from −15 to 60°.

Because of part family requirements we determined that the RMT should be reconfigurable to six angular positions of the spindle axis ranging from −15 to 60° at steps of 15°. This is shown at bottom of Figure 8.11. The main axes of the machine are: X-axis (table drive horizontal motion), Y-axis (column drive vertical motion), and Z-axis (spindle drive ram and inclined motion).

Figure 8.12 The arch-type RMT at the University of Michigan.

The *XYZ* machine axes comprise a non-orthogonal system of coordinates (except when the spindle is in the horizontal position). Two auxiliary systems of orthogonal coordinates are used to describe the machine, *XSZ* and *XYZ'*, where *S* is an axis parallel to the part surface and *Z'* is an axis perpendicular to both *X*- and *Y*-axis.

The machine is designed to drill and mill on inclined surfaces in such a way that the tool is perpendicular to the surface. With just three servo-controlled axes it performs operations that usually require a four- or five-axis machine. In milling, at least two axes of motion participate in the cut. For example, the upward motion on the inclined surface requires the machine drive to move in the positive *Y* direction (upward) and in the positive *Z* direction (angled downward). When milling a nonlinear contour (e.g., a circle) on the inclined surface of the RMT, the tool motion is likewise the result of combined motion of the *Y*- and *Z*-axes.

An industrial-scale prototype of the arch-type RMT was built in 2002 for the Engineering Research Center for Reconfigurable Manufacturing Systems at the University of Michigan in Ann Arbor. Figure 8.12 shows a photo of the machine (it has a 15 HP spindle). Over 1000 professionals have viewed demonstrations of the machine cutting angular surfaces. Because of limited ceiling clearance, the 60° step was canceled, and the pitch of the spindle axis (the Z-axis) now ranges from −15 to 45°. The time required to reconfigure from one angle to another is less than 2 minutes—a remarkably small interval for precision reconfiguration.

8.4 RECONFIGURABLE FIXTURES

The production-level machining of large or complex parts (such as cylinder heads of engines) requires placing the parts on specially designed fixtures so they can always be deployed in the correct position for the cutting operations. Since most parts have several surfaces to be machined, the conventional solution is to use several fixtures (typically four) over the course of the whole machining operation. When the machining of one surface is completed, the part is released from its current fixture and clamped onto a new fixture for machining the next surface. The cost of a complex fixture is about $30,000. In industry-scale machining systems there may be 50–100 sets of fixtures for every given part. When products change, the fixtures must be changed as well. So, in high-mix machining environments, the investment in fixtures is enormous. A reconfigurable fixture that can accommodate the same part in different orientations, or perhaps be used for more than one part of the same part family, offers enormous economic benefits. Reconfigurable fixtures can also be a benefit for forming and assembly line applications.

To save cost, industry is sometimes using modular fixtures that are based on family of interconnected components that can be assembled to fit various parts of a part family. But these modular fixtures fit only very simple parts. The complex parts in the powertrain industry require fixtures with high degree of reconfigurability.

Several experimental prototypes of reconfigurable fixtures are being considered by industry. One concept is based on a bed of nails principle with adjustable height that was developed for forming[10] as well as for machining.[11] Each nail needs either precise manual adjustment or a small motor and controller to adjust its height. The time consumed in manual adjustment is not practical and neither is the control-based concept requiring an enormous capital investment in motors and controllers, and also making the fixture very large.

The General Motors R&D Center has recently developed an alternative concept for a reconfigurable fixture.[12] The GM reconfigurable fixture consists of hydraulic modular elements that provide the part support and clamping, and a powerful electro-permanent magnetic chuck (base) to support and position the modular elements (Figure 8.13). The permanent magnet holds the hydraulic elements in their designated

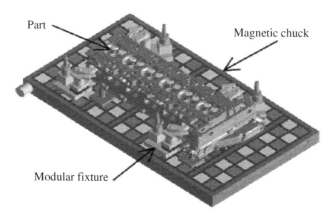

Figure 8.13   A reconfigurable fixture for machining applications—courtesy of GM R&D.

positions even when the electrical power is disconnected. This design solves the challenge of holding non-ferrous (e.g., aluminum) parts directly to a magnetic chuck. The hydraulic power source holding the part is contained in the fixture base, which eliminates the need for hydraulic feed lines and makes this reconfigurable fixture practical.

We close with a practical example of a reconfigurable tool, provided by one of our students.

"In our plant we utilize (in 2005) a Production Adaptive Assembly System (PAAS) tool, which would be considered a reconfigurable assembly machine. Its concept is to be a reconfigurable fixturing system. It is basically a miniature robot that holds parts in proper location while they get welded together. They provide the benefit of being able to build different styles at different dimensional locations (i.e., customization). These modules appear about the size of round kitchen trashcan, and have a computer control that allows them to be moved in three axes. " B. J. Baker

8.5 RECONFIGURABLE INSPECTION MACHINES

The in-process RIM represents a new class of inspection equipment that allows in-line measurements of machined parts. The machine deploys a non-contact measurement system of electro-optical sensors whose location and number are reconfigurable according to the part that is being measured (within its part family). During the inspection process these sensors are fixed and the part moves along an axis-of-motion (or *vice versa*—fixed part and moving sensors) examining the features that are in the sensor range. The RIM rapidly supplies information about the dimensional accuracy and surface quality of each part, and instantly transmits feedback for rapid diagnosis and correction of the manufacturing process. The RIM is applicable to medium- or high-volume production of a whole family of parts, and has a superior advantage where regular switchovers among parts within a family are the practice.

Current Practice: In contrast, current practice in large- or medium-production machining plants involves the use of CMMs for parts inspection. The CMM is a computer-controlled part measurement method utilizing a single mechanical contact probe that moves around the part taking targeted measurements while the part is stationary. It can take up to several hours to complete the inspection of a single, complex part specimen, and so the inspection process is done off-line, usually in a special inspection room. During this inspection, many faulty parts might be produced on the still-operating production line. For example, at a typical rate of two parts per minute over a 2-hour inspection interval, 120 bad parts may be produced before the error is detected.

On some high-production lines, single dimensions are sometimes measured in-process by using dedicated gauges. Each gauge can measure only one dimension, and has to be replaced when the part is changed. These gauges are useful only when the line produces only a single type of parts, and the measured dimension is at a known location on the part.

The RIM: It is composed of a precision conveyor moving the part along one accurate axis of motion within an array of electro-optical devices such as digital or line scanning cameras, and laser-based sensors. The location of each sensor can be changed to fit the geometry of the inspected part. Columns of non-contact electro-optical sensors may be located on both sides of the part, as shown in Figure 8.14, and an additional array of sensors can be positioned above the part. These linear scans can determine surface profile, flatness, parallelism and distance between machined surfaces, distance between machined holes, and other features.

Another approach using the RIM is to move the sensors past the stationary part. In either case the time required to complete the measurement should be synchronized with the normal cycle time of the manufacturing line—typically 20–30 seconds on engine production lines.

In order to adapt the machine for the measurement of a different part of the same part family, the location of the sensors around the machine is reconfigurable. To utilize the RIM reconfigurability, the geometry of the parts on the production line

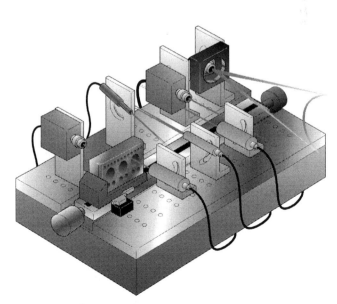

Figure 8.14 A schematic of a reconfigurable inspection machine (RIM).

TABLE 8.4   Inspection Machines

Dedicated	Reconfigurable	Flexible
Contact gauges	RIM	CMM
Very fast	Fast	Very slow
Not flexible	Customized flexibility for a part family	Full flexibility

is known at the outset. Table 8.4 compares the conventional measuring methods with the RIM.

A RIM for measuring surfaces on cylinder heads is shown in Figure 8.15. In this photo two laser-based sensors are shown on one side of the part; three additional laser sensors are located on the other side of the inspected part, as well as an accurate computer-vision system.

RIMs are also useful for detecting and analyzing porosity flaws in machined surfaces. Surface porosity, in the form of tiny voids or pits in the surface of machined castings, can severely degrade the quality of precision-machined components such as engine blocks and cylinder heads. Such voids occur in the casting process when gases are trapped as the casting solidifies. If the void is exposed during machining, it leaves a small pit in the surface.

Depending on where they occur, surface pores can create significant leaks of coolant, oil, or combustion gasses, even though they may be less than 1 mm in diameter. If these pores are not detected, they can cause severe damage to engines and transmissions, and at the very least, consumer could end up with a noisy engine with a shorter usable life. If they are detected in later stages of machining, the unit will be

Figure 8.15   A photo of the RIM with its optical sensors.

scrapped; wasting all of the machining that had been performed up to that point. A RIM equipped with a camera and computer vision software can successfully detect pores at the line speed of 20 seconds.

The following article, taken from the NSF ERC Showcase website[13] shows an implementation of our RIM technology at GM Flint Engine Plant.

 ERC Achievements Showcase

HOME | Site Map | Engineering Education & Centers | ERC Program | ERC Association

Engineering Research Center for Reconfigurable Manufacturing Systems

ERC/RMS Reconfigurable Inspection Machine Installed on GMC Manufacturing Line

Today's automotive engine technology is extremely sophisticated and requires manufacturers to maintain exacting quality specifications to ensure optimum engine performance and reliability. Hence, manufacturers are increasingly employing in-line inspection stations to inspect critical part features on 100% of the parts. In-line inspection minimizes the chances of defective parts reaching the customer and facilitates process control and process improvement. The best applications of in-line inspection are those where the quality is highly unpredictable.

Engine block moves into the inspection station.

One example of such an application is the need for in-line surface porosity inspection systems. Surface porosity is caused by tiny voids or pits at the surface of machined castings such as engine blocks and engine heads. Surface porosity begins in the casting process when gasses are trapped in the metal as the casting solidifies, creating voids in the material. If the void is exposed during machining, it leaves a small pit (i.e., surface pore) at the surface. Although they are typically smaller than 1mm, surface pores can create significant leaks of coolant, oil, or combustion gasses between critical mating surfaces and cause severe damage to engines and transmissions. If such a pore is not detected, the consumer will have a noisy engine with shorter lifetime.

An operator inspects the images of an engine block in which pores were detected, and makes the intelligent decision as to whether the engine block is indeed defective.

As an outgrowth of its Reconfigurable Inspection Machine project, the ERC for Reconfigurable Manufacturing Systems (RMS) at the University of Michigan developed a prototype machine-vision system for in-line surface porosity inspection of engine blocks and engine heads. The system utilizes a specially designed vision system to acquire very high-resolution (300 megapixel) images of the part surface. The high-resolution images are then analyzed rapidly to detect, locate, and measure pores. This technology is very important to engine manufacturers because of the difficulty in objectively measuring the sizes and location of irregularly shaped surface pores at production line rates.

In July 2006, this technology made a significant leap forward. General Motors Corp., an ERC member company, installed an industrial system for in-line surface porosity inspection of engine blocks in Flint, Michigan. The system is based on the technology developed at the ERC/RMS. The inspection system is integrated into the production line, and a conveyor moves engine blocks through the inspection station. Therefore, every part is measured within 15–20s. By using this technology the manufacturer expects to prevent defective parts from reaching the customer and also to collect meaningful data for process improvement.

The integration of RIM systems into production lines enhances productivity and improves the accuracy of production for the manufacturer, and the quality of products going to the consumer.

Below are two professional evaluation of the RIM provided by our former students.

> "RIM brings real-time automated inspection to the plant floor. In addition to raising quality at line rate this can also decrease the time required to reach production level targets during ramp-up. This is extremely valuable to the personalized production paradigm because companies can react more effectively to changing markets." David Matthews
>
> "The use of a CMM is slow and the feedback loop, if something is out of specification or control, is long. In an automotive body shop, the sheet metal parts are critical to the overall exterior fit of a vehicle. But there are only a few parts measured, and that is by shuffling parts back and forth to the CMM room. By the time anyone realizes that anything is out of control, many parts have been made. A RIM could be placed on line, integrated into the manufacturing system, and then part changes could be detected quickly." Cindie Niemann

8.6 OPEN-ARCHITECTURE CONTROLLERS

Designing modular and RMs creates a need for corresponding RM controllers to facilitate that flexibility. Such controllers are based on open-architecture principles. Open architecture allows the adding and swapping of control modules to fit changing, specific applications. IEEE standards define an open system as

> An open system providing capabilities that enable properly implemented applications to run on a wide variety of platforms from multiple vendors, inter-operating with other system applications, and presenting a consistent style of interaction with the user.[14]

Global research efforts have been dedicated to developing open architecture control systems. The three most important initiatives have been: the EU project, OSACA, and its German successor, HÜMNOS; the Japanese initiative OSEC; and the North American OMAC-TEAM project[15]. The OSACA project focused on reference architecture for control systems. The main outcome from OSACA is an object-oriented design as well as specification of a vendor-neutral open architecture for machine control systems. OMAC was an initiative driven by General Motors, Boeing, and NIST to establish a set of Application Programming Interfaces (APIs) to be used by vendors to sell reconfigurable, customized controller products to the aerospace and automotive industries.

Open-architecture systems may include a library of control algorithms (e.g., servos, temperature control, interpolators, etc.) that can be easily integrated into the machine software when needed for a new application.[16] The desired control modules are selected and integrated using a "Control Configurator" for the selected machine and application. The Configurator also checks its real-time constraints. After the experimental execution of the configuration process, control code is generated. This can be carried out according to either vendor-neutral or vendor-specific formats, and converted into PLC or NC code.

TABLE 8.5   Characteristics of an Open Control System

Modularity	Decentralized structures are supported by distributed application modules
Integrability	Integration of hardware and software components that communicate with each other
Scalability	Increased performance by processor upgrade and added application modules
Convertibility	New functionality by adding hardware modules and software application modules
Customization	The ability to exchange control modules to meet new specific applications
Diagnosability	The ability to easily diagnose control software problems after configuration

The system software for an open control system has to contain:[17]

1. An operating system to execute the software module functions.
2. A communication system to enable information interchange between modules utilizing a standard protocol.

The controller's openness is the enabling technology needed to integrate, extend, replace, and reuse hardware and software components in a control system. The open-controller should possess a set of core characteristics (Table 8.5) similar to those for RMs.

The functionality of the system software is derived from the application modules. Integrability leads to the definition of a uniform API that allows modules to be interfaced into any system platform that supports them, as well as changing configurations by repositioning modules in the system. It implicitly demands that system software shield the application from the system hardware. Although on a physical level combined control components depend on the control system platform, the platform itself looks transparent to the user, since a set of uniform APIs is provided for the application software. The API hides all hardware details and offers one homogeneous platform even in distributed control systems.

A specific system platform with these characteristics was designed and implemented by the European OSACA initiative.[18] This software can very easily be ported to different operating systems and it supports real-time features. A wide range of communication networks (such as Sercos, Profibus, Ethernet) is available for the physical coupling of distributed platforms.

Finally, it is important for software modules to correspond to the hardware components of the machine. This means that, using object-based principles, a machine object corresponds to a controller object that runs the control functionality of the machine object.

PROBLEMS

8.1   Which of the six core characteristics are contained in the RMTs depicted in Figures 8.7, 8.9, and 8.12?

8.2 What are the RM design principles that the RIM in Figure 8.14 obeys? Explain.

REFERENCES

1. Y. Koren, F. Jovane, U. Heisel, T. Moriwaki, G. Pritschow, G. Ulsoy, and H. VanBrussel. Reconfigurable manufacturing systems. *CIRP Annals*, November 1999, Vol. 48, No. 2, pp. 6–12.

2. R. Landers, B. K. Min, and Y. Koren. Reconfigurable machine tools. *CIRP Annals*, July 2001, Vol. 49, No. 1.

3. Y. Koren and S. Kota. Reconfigurable machine tool. *US patent* #5,943,750, August 31, 1999.

4. Y. Koren and R. Katz. Reconfigurable apparatus for inspection during a manufacturing process and related method. *US patent* #6,567,162, Issued on May 20, 2003.

5. IMS Report. *Joint International Research Programs into an Intelligent Manufacturing System, International Robotics and Factory Automation Centre* (IROFA), 1990.

6. G. Rogers and L. Bottaci. Modular production systems: a new manufacturing paradigm. *Journal of Intelligent Manufacturing*, 1997, Vol. 8, pp. 147–156.

7. Y. Koren, Y. Moon, and S. Kota.Reconfigurable multi-spindles apparatus. *US patent* #6,569,071, Issued on May 27, 2003.

8. Y. Koren and S. Kota.Reconfigurable machine tool. *US patent* # 5,943,750, August 31, 1999.

9. E. Shamoto and T. Moriwaki. Rigid XY Table for ultraprecision machine tool driven by means of waling drive, *Annals of the CIRP*, 1997, Vol. 46/1, pp. 301–304.

10. K. Youcef-Toumi and J. H. Buitrago. Design of robot-operated adaptable fixtures. *ASME Symposium on Manufacturing System*, Atlanta, Georgia, 1988, pp. 113–119.

11. D. Chakraborty, E. C. De Meter, and P. Szuba. Part location algorithms for an intelligent fixturing system—parts 1 and 2. *Journal of Manufacturing Systems*, 2001, Vol. 20, No. 2, pp. 124–134 and 135–148.

12. C. H. Shen Y.T. Lin, J. S. Agapiou, G. L. Jones, M. A. Kramarczyk, and P. Bandyopadhyay. An innovative reconfigurable and totally automated fixture system for agile machining applications. *Transactions 31st NAMRC*, McMaster University, Hamilton, Ontario, Canada, May 2003.

13. http://showcase.erc-assoc.org/accomplishments/manufacture/rms-07-1-porosity.htm

14. G. Pritschow, Y. Altintas, F. Jovane, Y. Koren, H. VanBrussel, and M. Weck. Open-controller architecture—past, present, and future. A keynote paper. *CIRP Annals*, November 2001, Vol. 50, No. 2, pp. 463–470.

15. Y. Koren, F. Jovane, and G. Pritschow (eds). *Open Architecture Control Systems, Summary of Global Activity*, ITIA Series, Vol. 2. Milano, Italy, 1998.

16. Y. Koren, Z. Pasek, G. Ulsoy, and U. Benchetrit. Real-time open-control architectures and system performance. *CIRP Annals*, July 1996, Vol. 45, No. 1, pp. 377–380.

17. G. Pritschow *et.al.* Modular system platform for open control systems. *Production Engineering*, 1997, Vol. 4, No. 2.

18. W. Sperling et al. *OSACA ESPRIT 6379/9115 Final Report*. FISW GmbH, Stuttgart, Germany, 1996.

Chapter **9**

Reconfigurable Manufacturing Systems

Manufacturing companies in the twenty-first century face increasingly frequent and unpredictable market changes driven by global competition, including the rapid introduction of new products, and constantly varying product demand. To stay competitive, companies must design manufacturing systems that not only produce high-quality goods at low cost, but also allow for rapid response to market changes and consumer needs. Reconfigurability is a novel engineering technology that enables cost-effective, rapid responsiveness to market and product changes. A reconfigurable manufacturing system (RMS), including reconfigurable machines and open controllers, is the cornerstone of this new paradigm.

9.1 THE CHALLENGES OF GLOBALIZATION

To compete globally, the manufacturing plant should stand on three legs: cost, quality, and responsiveness (Figure 9.1). This means that manufacturing plants have three goals: produce at low cost, enhance product quality, and respond to change rapidly and effectively. Responsiveness means the speed at which the plant can fulfill changing business goals and produce new product models.

9.1.1 Cost

No business can compete for long if their products cost more to produce than those of their competitors. Producing at the lowest possible cost and continuing to innovate

The Global Manufacturing Revolution: Product-Process-Business Integration and Reconfigurable Systems
By Yoram Koren
Copyright © 2010 John Wiley & Sons, Inc.

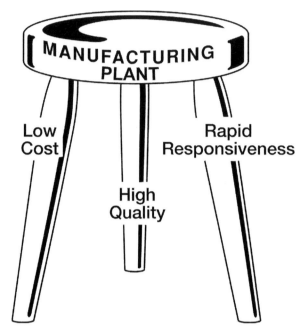

Figure 9.1 Goals of manufacturing plants.

and introduce new products in the competitive global marketplace is an on-going challenge for all manufacturers. Cost and profitability depend on many different factors. Equipment purchases, floor space, operational requirements, and tooling costs are only part of what is entailed in bringing a product online. Another concern for competitive manufacturers is the cost of NOT bringing a product to market. Failing to capitalize on a market opportunity by getting a potential blockbuster product out too late is another way that manufacturers can lose.

As we will show, manufacturing systems that use reconfigurable components and architectures can offer a much greater range of options to manufacturers. Adjustable capacity and flexibility, along with new tools for designing systems and getting production up and running, are a hallmark of reconfiguration design. Timely reconfiguration reduces the time-to-market and provides precisely the quantities needed at the lowest possible cost.

9.1.2 Quality

Making sure that your products are made to the highest quality possible is critical to a manufacturer's success. In manufacturing, there are two areas where product quality can make the difference between success and failure: the quality that your customer sees when they buy the product, and the quality that they will see over time.

The quality your customer sees depends for the most part on the quality of the final assembly. This quality should even exceed customer's expectations. Being aware of the expectations of your customers has always been good advice, but in the era of globalization delivering a product that its quality exceeds expectations is a strategic necessity. Remember, everyone wants to think they got more than their money's worth.

On the other hand, the quality that the customer sees after long use of their product is the feature that keeps customers coming back and builds a brand. Improving the product design through reliability testing, stress analysis, etc. can produce a superior product on paper, but manufacturing is a key to get a consistent quality in every product. Manufacturers must develop production systems that are able to consistently produce every product and part without variation. And when variation occurs, as it inevitably does, it must be corrected at the earliest possible moment to keep from wasting valuable time, energy, and material.

Detecting flaws and removing them from the output product is critical to success but current methods of detecting variation on the production line are frequently too slow to be effective. Quicker, cheaper, more systematized solutions must be implemented. In-line inspection tools improve operational consistency so long as they do their jobs quickly and can be applied to every part produced, instead of merely occasional sampling. That way they can detect and localize errors before large quantities of flawed parts are created and production is wasted. These inspection tools also need to be readily and efficiently reconfigurable to be useful for whole part/product families.

9.1.3 Responsiveness

Responsiveness enables manufacturing systems to quickly launch new products on existing manufacturing systems, and to react rapidly and cost-effectively to:

1. Market changes, including changes in product demand (even after production started).
2. Product changes, including changes in current products, and new product introduction.
3. Government regulations (safety and environment).
4. System failures (keep production up despite equipment failures).

All these changes are driven by aggressive competition on a global scale, more educated and demanding customers, and a rapid pace of change in product and process technology.[1]

Remember: The Speed of Responsiveness is the New Frontier of Manufacturing Enterprises. Although responsiveness is not yet attributed the same level of importance as cost and quality, its impact is quickly becoming an equal imperative. Responsiveness provides a key competitive advantage in a turbulent global economy in which companies must be able to react to changes rapidly and cost-effectively. This can often be done by installing a manufacturing system with modest initial capacity that is designed for adding production capacity as the market grows, and adding functionality as the product changes.

> When analyzing profitability, the value of operational responsiveness should be considered. Responsiveness includes the ability to adjust production volumes efficiently and rapidly change production mix among product variants and models.

Today, new products have very short windows of opportunity to penetrate into the market. The speed at which a manufacturing system is ready to produce a new product at the required quantity and quality is critical to success. Computer-aided design (CAD) has dramatically reduced product development times in the last three decades (Figure 9.2, top); such design innovations are needed for the manufacturing system itself.

The lead time to design and build or reconfigure a manufacturing system, and the time needed to ramp it up should not become a bottleneck to full-volume, high-quality production. If manufacturing system lead time can be reduced, brief windows of opportunity for new products can be captured economically and result in major economic savings. Figure 9.2 (bottom) depicts how rapid reconfiguration of existing manufacturing systems reduces lead time and brings more products to market faster.

In order to produce new products and accommodate changes in existing products, new functions must be added to the manufacturing system through reconfiguration. A well-designed RMS can be converted to consistently accommodate the production of new products for many years allowing for several reconfiguration periods over its lifetime, as depicted in Figure 9.2. To be successful, short ramp-up periods are needed after each reconfiguration to bring the system back on line quickly. This type of reconfiguration requires rapid system convertibility to add new functions.

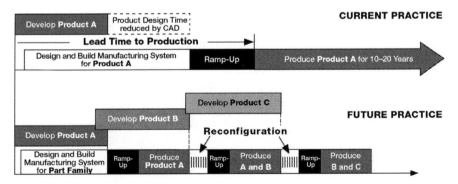

Figure 9.2   Product development time was reduced dramatically by the introduction of CAD systems. However, something equivalent has yet to be done with the manufacturing system (top) itself. Increasing the frequency of new product introductions requires shortening the manufacturing system lead time, enabled through rapid reconfiguration.

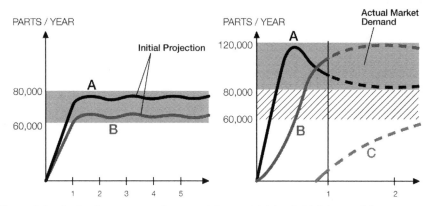

Figure 9.3   Projection compared to actual demand: higher initial demand than expected for both products and Product C is introduced earlier than expected.

In general, two basic types of reconfiguration capabilities are needed in manufacturing systems—in their functionality (as shown in Figure 9.2) and in their production capacity. Adjusting the system production capacity is needed in order to cope with fluctuations in product demand caused by changing market conditions. Figure 9.3 shows how the actual demand for Products A and B can be different from what was planned. This type of reconfiguration requires rapid changes in the system **production capacity**, which is called system **scalability**.

> A responsive manufacturing system is one whose production capacity is adjustable to fluctuations in product demand, and whose functionality is adaptable to new products.

Traditional manufacturing systems are ill suited to meet the requirements dictated by the new, competitive environment. Dedicated manufacturing lines (DMLs), as we have described, are based on inexpensive fixed automation producing a company's core products or parts for a long time at high volume (see Figure 9.4). Each dedicated line is typically designed to produce a single part at high production rate achieved by the operation of all tools simultaneously. When the product demand is high, the cost per part is exceptionally low. DMLs are cost-effective as long as they can operate at full capacity, but with increasing pressure from global competition and over-capacity worldwide, the norm is situations where dedicated lines do not operate at full capacity.

Flexible manufacturing systems (FMSs) can produce a variety of products, with changeable volume and mix, on the same system. However, FMSs consist of expensive, general-purpose computer numerically controlled (CNC) machines and other programmable automation. Because of the single-tool operation of the CNC machines, FMS throughput is much lower than that of a DML. The combination of high equipment cost and low throughput makes the FMS cost per part relatively high. Therefore, the FMS production capacity is usually lower than that of dedicated lines as depicted in Figure 9.4.

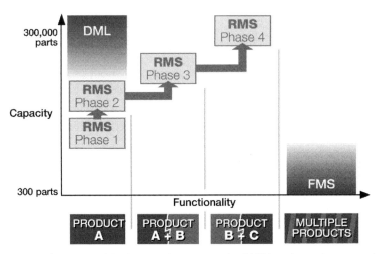

Figure 9.4 Both DML and FMS are static systems; the RMS is a dynamic system that can change capacity and functionality in response to market changes

9.2 RMS—A NEW CLASS OF SYSTEMS

A cost-effective response to market changes requires a new manufacturing approach that not only combines the high throughput of DML with the flexibility of FMS, but also is able to react to market changes by changing the manufacturing system and its elements quickly and efficiently. This is a feature of an RMS whose capacity and functionality can be changed as needed, as illustrated in Figure 9.4.

9.2.1 Japanese Flexible Manufacturing System Complex

In 1977, Japan's Ministry of International Trade and Industry (MITI) initiated the development of a Flexible Manufacturing system Complex (FMC)—a test factory consisting of modular machining units and assembly robots with functionality adaptable to the product to be processed.[2] The project was completed in 1983 with the building of a demonstration factory in Tsukuba, Japan.

The Tsukuba FMC system was designed to produce a whole range of prism-shaped parts within a given envelope and was completely task-driven. The FMC included storage of machine modules in a warehouse when not in use and their assembly on demand to accommodate the product to be produced. Upon completion of each production exercise, the machines were broken back down into their modules and returned to storage. The storage of so many unused machine modules is a waste and unpractical to industry. The demonstration plant continued until 1984 and inspired a whole generation of factory automation in Japan.

This Japanese demonstration plant was impractical and only suitable for small volume production, although it did demonstrate machine modularity and functional convertibility. Even so, this conversion was not done rapidly, or cost-effectively.

Furthermore, the demo plant did not deal at all with capacity changes. By contrast, RMS addresses changes in both functionality and capacity, as well as performing these changes quickly and cost-effectively.

9.2.2 Cost of Capacity

Three features—**capacity, functionality**, and **cost**—define the difference between the three types of manufacturing systems—RMS, DML, and FMS. While DML and FMS are usually fixed at the capacity-functionality plane as shown in Figure 9.4, the RMS is not constrained by capacity or functionality and can change over time as the system reacts to changing market circumstances.

In the system-cost versus capacity plane, the DML is a constant at its maximum planned capacity; a whole additional line must be built when greater capacity is needed. The pure-parallel FMS is scalable at a constant rate (adding machines in parallel), as depicted in Figure 9.5. The RMS is scalable, but at a non-constant rate that depends on the initial design of the RMS and market circumstances.

A critical question is: When is the Right Time to Consider Building a New RMS? It is when planning a new manufacturing system for a part family or a product family line with several variants that are expected to change in the next 10–15 years, and the market is volatile, so it is hard to forecast demand. The new RMS should be designed at the outset for reconfiguration, which will be achieved through:

- Design of the system and its machines for **adjustable structure** that enable system scalability in response to market demands and system/machine convertibility to new products. Structure may be adjusted (1) at the system level (e.g., adding machines), (2) at the machine level (e.g., adding spindles and axes or changing angles between axes), and (3) at the control software (e.g., integrating easily advanced controllers).

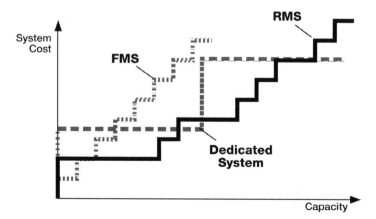

Figure 9.5   Manufacturing system cost versus capacity.

- Design of the manufacturing system around the **part family**, with the customized flexibility required for producing all parts of this part family.

Manufacturing equipment is reconfigurable, and not just flexible, if the answer to the following two questions is positive.

1. Is this manufacturing system or equipment was designed for possible easy changes in its physical structure?
2. Is this manufacturing system or equipment was designed for production or inspection of a particular part family?

9.2.3 RMS—The Best of Both

As we have seen an FMS possess the flexibility needed to switch between the manufacturing of product variants, but is not as cost-effective as DML. By contrast, the DML has high productivity but no flexibility. An RMS embraces the best qualities from both types: a system that not only possesses cost-effective, flexible production, but also has changeable structure (at both the system level and the machine level) so it can handle unexpected market changes.

The DML design focuses on the produced part. If the part is not defined, you cannot design a DML. By contrast, a typical FMS is composed of CNC machines. I was at a technology exhibition in which a small FMS with five CNCs was demonstrated. It was not built to produce any particular part. "You bring the part" they told me "and we will do the process-planning to machine it." Their design focus was to produce multi-axis precise machines. This focus on the machine rather than on the part is one reason for the waste and low production rates of FMS technology.

Borrowing from dedicated lines that are designed around a single part/product, RMS focuses on families of parts, like cylinder heads. Between four-, six-, and eight-cylinder models there are many differences, but they also have many more common features. Focusing on the part family enables the designer to plan a system that accommodates different variations of the same part family with minimum alteration to the production scheme. This approach utilizes the high productivity of DML machine design, and is much more economical than the general functionality of FMS.

An artist's view of the three systems is depicted in Appendix B. As summarized in Table 9.1, a system with adjustable structure and a design focus on a part family constitutes a new class of system—an RMS.

Building a system with changeable structure provides scalability and customized flexibility is focused on a part family and creates a responsive reconfigurable system. The flexibility of RMS, although it is really just "customized flexibility," provides all the flexibility needed to process that whole part family.

9.2.4 RMS Definition

Highly productive, cost-effective systems are created by (i) part-family focus and (ii) customized flexibility that enables the operation of simultaneous tools. The

TABLE 9.1   RMS Combines Features of Dedicated and Flexible Systems

	Dedicated	RMS/RMT	FMS/CNC
System structure	Fixed	Changeable	Changeable
Machine structure	Fixed	Changeable	Fixed
System focus	Part	Part family	Machine
Scalability	No	Yes	Yes
Flexibility	No	Customized (around a part family)	General
Simultaneously operating tools	Yes	Yes	No
Productivity	High	High	Low
Lifetime cost	**Low**	**Medium**	**Reasonable**
	For a single part, when fully utilized	For production at medium-to-high volume parts with variable demand during system lifetime	For simultaneous production of many parts (at low volume) Otherwise—**High**

invention of the RMS is documented in a U.S. Patent (by Y. Koren and G. Ulsoy).[3] The RMS is designed to cope with situations where both productivity and the ability of the system to react to changes are of vital importance.

Each RMS is designed to produce a particular family of parts. The main components of RMS for machining are CNC machines and Reconfigurable Machine Tools (RMTs)[4]—see Chapter 8. To coordinate and operate the CNCs and RMTs, reconfigurable controls integrated in an open-architecture environment are critical to the success of an RMS.

The definition of an RMS is, therefore:

> An RMS is designed at the outset for rapid change in structure, as well as in hardware and software components, in order to quickly adjust production capacity and functionality within a part family in response to sudden changes in market or regulatory requirements.

If the system and its machines are not designed at the outset for reconfigurability, the reconfiguration process will prove lengthy and impractical.

9.3   CHARACTERISTICS AND PRINCIPLES OF RECONFIGURATION

In 1996, the National Science Foundation established an Engineering Research Center for RMSs to explore and describe the enabling technologies that underlay reconfigurable manufacturing. The NSF supported the Center until 2007. The Center has defined a number of principles and characteristics for RMS, and a range of patented innovations that provide the basis for developing new reconfiguration technologies and processes. These enabling technologies and characteristics are discussed below.

9.3.1 RMS Enabling Technologies

FMS and its CNC machines allow flexibility in the production of a variety of parts. The RMS allows flexibility not only in producing a variety of parts, but also in changing the system itself. Note that not only dedicated lines but also flexible systems use fixed hardware and fixed software. In recent years, however, two technologies have emerged that are enablers for reconfiguration: In software— **open-architecture controls** that allow reconfiguration of the machine controller;[5] and in machine hardware—**modular machine tools** that offer the customer more machine options. These emerging technologies enable the design of vastly more responsive systems with **reconfigurable hardware** and **software**, as depicted in Figure 9.6.

Reconfigurable hardware and software are necessary but they are not, by themselves, sufficient conditions for a cost-effective RMS. RMS design must also include an advanced systems perspective that forecasts possible reconfigurations during the operational life of the system with their ongoing economic modeling. Future reconfiguration planning should include system design options combined with possible upcoming reconfigurations of the machines, and the automated part handling and tooling systems, as well as open-architecture controllers. RMS design, therefore, engenders a whole new approach to the design of manufacturing systems—design to meet current needs, but with future perspective.

With such design, the system capacity and functionality can be changed in response to market demand. When the production plan of a new product is added, the system functionality can be adjusted to handle it. We summarize these attributes as:

Exactly the functionality and capacity needed. . . . Exactly when needed.

	Fixed Hardware	Reconfigurable Hardware
No Software	Manual Machines, Dedicated Manufacturing Lines (DML)	—
Fixed Control Software	Flexible Manufacturing Systems (FMS), CNC Machines, Robots, Gantries	**Reconfigurable Gantries** **Reconfigurable Machines**
Reconfigurable Software	Autonomous Guided Vehicle (AGV) Open-Architecture Controller	R M S

Figure 9.6   Classes of machines and manufacturing systems.

Both the systems and their reconfigurable machines must be designed at the outset to be reconfigurable by applying the characteristics discussed below.

9.3.2 Reconfiguration Core Characteristics

Reconfigurable systems must be designed from the outset with hardware and software modules that can be integrated quickly and reliably. Otherwise, the reconfiguration process will be lengthy and impractical. And, like reconfigurable machines, achieving this goal requires an RMS that possesses much the same six key characteristics: Customization, Scalability, Convertibility, Modularity, Integrability, and Diagnosability. These system-level characteristics apply to the design of the whole production system. Ultimately they may even be applied to the enterprise as a whole. We elaborate below on these key characteristics.

Customization: This characteristic distinguishes RMS drastically from that of FMS and DML, and allows for substantial efficiencies in system cost. It enables the design of systems for the production of part families, rather than for single parts (as those produced by DML) or any part (FMS). In the context of RMS, a **part family** is defined as all parts (or products) that have similar geometric features and shapes, the same level of tolerances, require the same production processes, and are within the same range of cost. From a systems point of view, this definition also assumes that most manufacturing system resources are utilized for the production of every member part.

Customization, or customized flexibility, delivers substantial economic benefit by enhancing productivity at low cost. Customized flexibility means that the RMS configuration must accommodate the full range of dominant features of the whole part family. It allows for the greatest commonality of application of multiple tools (e.g., spindles in machining or nozzles in injection molding) on the same machine, thereby increasing productivity at reduced cost without compromising flexibility. When properly designed, the RMS provides the right balance between productivity and general flexibility.[6]

Convertibility: System convertibility is the ability to quickly change system functionality to produce (or inspect) all members of the product family. System convertibility includes also machine conversion. For example, conversion may require switching spindles on a milling machine from a low-torque high-speed spindle for aluminum to a high-torque low-speed spindle for titanium, or manual adjustment of passive degrees-of-freedom changes when switching production between two members of a part family within the same day. System-level conversion includes integrating new machines and extending reach of gantries to expand the range of a system functionality to produce new parts.

Scalability: It is increasingly difficult to predict product demand, providing a compelling reason for why manufacturing systems need to be scalable. Scalability of the system's production capacity is the ability to quickly and efficiently change the maximum production volume possible, and is the counterpart of Convertibility. The Scalability characteristic may require adding spindles at the machine level to increase its productivity, and at the system level changing part routing or adding machines to expand the overall system capacity as the market grows.

Modularity: RMSs need a modular overall structure[7] to meet the requirements of changeability.[8] At the system level, every machine is a module, and many material-handling systems (conveyors, gantries, etc.) are built in a modular structure to facilitate future reconfigurations. In addition, components at the machine level may be modular (e.g., structural elements, axes, controls, software, and tooling). When necessary, modular components, at any level, can be replaced or upgraded to better suit new applications and new market demand.

Integrability: At the machine level, spindles and axes of motions can be integrated to form new machines. At the system level, the machines are the modules to be integrated via material transport systems to form a reconfigurable system. In addition, machine controllers can be integrated into a factory-level control system.

Diagnosability: Diagnosability has two goals in RMSs: noticing machine failures and detecting unacceptable part quality. The second aspect is critical in RMS. As production systems are made more reconfigurable, and their layouts are modified more frequently, it becomes essential to rapidly tune the newly reconfigured system so that it quickly produces quality parts. To this end, reconfigurable systems must also include product quality measurement systems as an integral part. These measurement systems are intended to help identify product quality problems in the production system rapidly, so they can be corrected utilizing control technologies, statistics, and signal processing techniques.

The six core reconfigurable system characteristics are summarized in Table 9.2. Customization, Scalability, and Convertibility are **necessary** characteristics for reconfiguration. Modularity, Integrability, and Diagnosability are **sufficient** characteristics for reconfiguration. The six key RMS characteristics reduce the time and effort of reconfiguration, and thereby enhance system responsiveness. These characteristics can reliably reduce lifetime cost by enabling the system to constantly change during its lifetime, "staying alive" despite changes in markets, consumer demand, and process technology.

9.3.3 Reconfiguration Principles

RMSs operate according to three Reconfiguration Principles that have been introduced by the author. These principles are intended to improve its speed of reconfiguration and consequently its speed of responsiveness to (i) unpredictable external occurrences (e.g., market changes), (ii) planned product model changes, and (iii) unexpected intrinsic system events (such as unexpected long machine failure). The more these principles are applicable to a given manufacturing system, the more reconfigurable that system is.

9.3.3.1 Design Principles of Reconfigurable Manufacturing Systems

> 1. The RMS provides **adjustable production resources** to respond to unpredictable market changes and system intrinsic occurrences:
>   - RMS capacity can be rapidly scalable in small increments.
>   - RMS functionality can be rapidly adaptable to new products.
>   - RMS inbuilt adjustment capabilities enable rapid response to unexpected equipment failures.
> 2. The RMS is designed around **a part or a product family**, with just enough customized flexibility needed to produce all members of that family.
> 3. The **RMS core characteristics** should be embedded in the whole system as well as in its components (mechanical, communications, and control).

The environment of many manufacturing companies is characterized by unpredictable market changes. Changing orders requires altering the output capacity and the processing functions of the manufacturing system. RMSs meet these requirements by rapidly adapting both their capacity and functionality to new situations.

TABLE 9.2 Reconfigurable System Core Characteristics

Customization Flexibility limited to part family	The design of system or machine flexibility limited to just a product family, thereby obtaining customized-flexibility
Convertibility Design for functionality changes	The ability to easily transform the functionality of existing systems, machines, and controls to suit new production requirements
Scalability Design for capacity changes	The ability to easily modify production capacity by adding or subtracting manufacturing resources (e.g., machines) and/or changing the reconfigurable components of the system
Modularity Components are modular	The compartmentalization of operational functions into units that can be manipulated between alternate production schemes to achieve the most optimal arrangement
Integrability Interfaces for rapid integration	The ability to integrate modules rapidly and precisely by a set of mechanical, informational, and control interfaces that enable integration and communication
Diagnosability Design for easy diagnostics	The ability to automatically read the current state of a system and controls to detect and diagnose the root causes of output product defects, and quickly correct operational defects

Implementing the RMS characteristics and principles in the system design enables achievement of the ultimate goal—to create a "**living factory**" that is able to rapidly adjust its production capacity while maintaining high levels of quality from one part to the next. This adaptability guarantees a high long-term benefit-to-cost-ratio on investment in RMSs.

9.4 INTEGRATED RMS CONFIGURATIONS

This section deals with two issues: (a) designing RMS systems that have all six core characteristics and (b) designing RMS systems that incorporate innovative RMTs and reconfigurable inspection machines (RIMs) – both were introduced in Chapter 8 – into the configuration. These two innovations make the RMS more productive and responsive.

Our starting point is the RMS configuration depicted in Figure 9.7. It represents a system already being utilized in the powertrain industry. It is a system of three stages that can produce two different parts simultaneously. A cell gantry serves all machines in a particular stage; it brings parts and loads them on the machines, and takes the finished parts and transfer them to a buffer (the circle in Figure 9.7) located next to the main material handling system. The latter is usually a gantry (called the spine gantry), but it can be also a conveyor, or several AGVs. To balance the system sequence, all stages should have almost the same cycle time. In this figure, the cycle time of each of the two machines in Stage 2 is approximately 1.5 times shorter than the cycle time for the three machines in Stages 1 and 3. (In industry, the set of all machining tasks assigned to a stage is called an "Operation." Usually operations are numbered 10, 20, 30, etc., allowing for the addition of intermediate operations as needed over time, for example, adding Operation 15. However, we prefer the term "stage.")

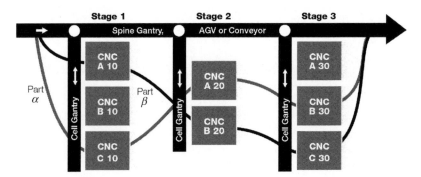

Figure 9.7 Practical RMS configuration with three stages.

The system in Figure 9.7 possesses four of the six core RMS characteristics:

Modularity—At the system level each CNC machine is a module.

Integrability—Machines at the same stage are integrated via cell gantries, which, in turn, are integrated into a whole system by a conveyor, or spine gantries or AGVs. (The circles in Figure 9.7 represent buffers.)

Scalability—It is easy to add machines in each stage without interrupting the system operation for long periods. From a system-balancing viewpoint scalability starts at the stages that are already bottlenecks to reduction of system cycle time.

Convertibility—It is easy to stop the operation of one CNC at a time and reconfigure its functionality to the production of a new type of part.

Scalability and convertibility enhance the overall system performance. The system in Figure 9.7, however, does not yet possess the two remaining characteristics: Customization (i.e., part family customized flexibility) and Diagnosability.

As we have said, implementing customized flexibility is critical to increasing productivity. Introducing this characteristic into a reconfigurable system is key to enhance productivity, but how exactly can it be accomplished? Is there a procedure for implementing such a change in the system?

To begin with, let us assume that the milling tasks on the machined part can be separated from the drilling and tapping tasks and that milling may be assigned to different stages than drilling and tapping (i.e., performed in different stages in the system). If this is done, we are able to integrate the type of RMTs depicted in Figure 9.8 into the modified RMS configuration, shown in Figure 9.9. The RMT in Figure 9.8 is capable of drilling (or tapping) multiple holes simultaneously. It can drill some 10, 20, and even 50 holes in a single stroke—a single motion of the Z-axis. When the part is changed, the spindle head is reconfigured or changed out and replaced.

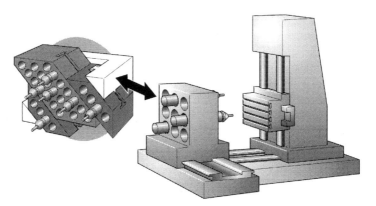

Figure 9.8 A reconfigurable machine tool—RMT.

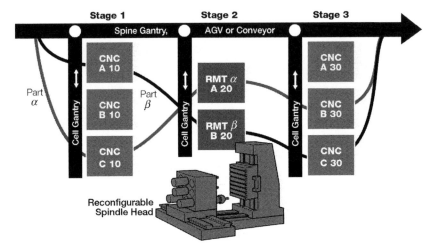

Figure 9.9 RMS with integrated reconfigurable machine tools (RMT).

Figure 9.9 shows an RMS incorporating two specifically designed RMTs in Stage 2. One RMT is capable of producing part α and the other RMT produces part β, both parts at the same time. In a more sophisticated RMT, the spindle heads are on a 90° index table that rotates to fit the part entering for processing, and then there is a need for only one RMT. The index-type spindle head can accommodate up to four different parts and there is no need to employ multiple RMTs.

The configuration in Figure 9.9 possesses five core characteristics, including customization; but how can it also have diagnosability? Diagnosability means that the system has embedded in-process inspection resources, is able to monitor product quality, and detect errors in real time.

To truly have the diagnosability characteristic, RIMs must be integrated into the system in sequence with the part flow, such that they are part of the system configuration, adding one more operation in the sequence. Performing in-process diagnostics has a double advantage: It dramatically shortens the ramp-up periods after reconfigurations, and it allows rapid identification of part quality problems during normal production.

An important issue is what happens if the RIM is down? The last thing that a plant manager wants is for an inspection machine to stall production. The solution—install the RIMs as a separate stage that allows the inspection to be conducted in a contaminant-free environment and can be bypassed if necessary. This solution is depicted in Figure 9.10.

We have now a perfect RMS that possesses all six characteristics. But is this RMS truly perfect? What happens to the bad parts that the RIM tagged to be sent back for reprocessing? Or, what happens if, for example, CNCs B30 and C30 are both down? Is there an alternative to reducing productivity to only 33% throughput in this case?

In order to improve the system responsiveness in these two cases, we can add a return conveyor (or an AGV line, or a gantry) to move the parts backwards, as depicted at the bottom of Figure 9.11. Bad parts can be sent for reprocessing at any stage. In the

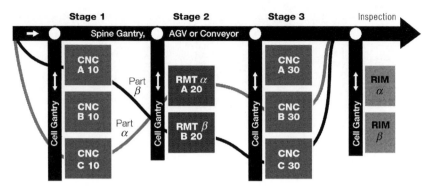

Figure 9.10   RMS with integrated RMTs and RIMs.

case of both CNCs in the third stage being down for an extended period of time, CNC C10 can be reprogrammed to share the load. After the drilling operations at Stage 2, the part can be sent back to CNC C10 to perform the tasks of Stage 3. We have now the ideal RMS—very productive with in-process quality checks, and highly responsive to both customer's needs and machine failures.

9.5 SYSTEM RAPID RAMP-UP

Reducing ramp-up time is critical for converting systems to respond to short windows of opportunity for new products, as well as for scaling existing systems to cope with changing demand. The Ramp-up period is defined as

Ramp-up Period: The period of time it takes a newly introduced system or reconfigured manufacturing system to reach its designed, sustainable, long-term levels of production in terms of both throughput and part quality.

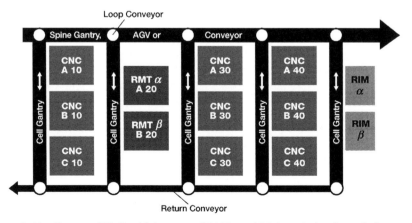

Figure 9.11   Proposed RMS with integrated RMTs and RIMs and a backwards flow-path.

Figure 9.12 Optical measurement of automotive body dimensions.

As production systems are made more reconfigurable, and their functionality and layouts are modified more frequently, it becomes essential to rapidly tune the newly reconfigured system so that it can quickly produce quality parts. The ramp-up process includes embedded stations for dimension verification and diagnostics of the finished parts and products. An example of a measurement station in an auto-body assembly line is shown in Figure 9.12. It is an array of laser triangulation sensors measuring auto-body dimensions on the auto-body assembly line. The measurements are utilized for subsequent error calibration and compensation.

The sensors in Figure 9.12 can detect faults and diagnose problems on the assembly line such as a broken locator or incorrectly programmed robot. If these manufacturing problems are not diagnosed and fixed, they can lead to problems in subsequent assembly, and quality problems with the final product such as wind noise and water leakage.

Rapid ramp-up of a manufacturing system after installation, and after each reconfiguration, is essential to the success of the RMS paradigm. If ramp-up is not done quickly, the reconfiguration advantage is lost. Therefore, reconfigurable systems must be designed to include product quality measurement systems as an integral part of the system (the **diagnosability** characteristic). Systematic methodologies for root-cause analysis of part quality problems combined with rapid methods for on-line part inspection are the key.

The basic engineering steps required are summarized in Figure 9.13. The measurement step requires the selection of type and location of sensors (e.g., part dimensions, axis position, cutting force). The diagnostics step matches that sensor information to a stored model to identify errors and faults. The information is also used to detect and diagnose machine or fixture geometric errors, operational variation,

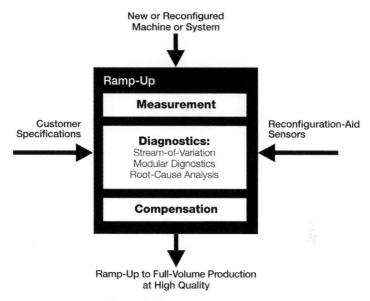

Figure 9.13 Ramp-up process.

and tool breakage. Finally, the machines and processes are adjusted to reduce the errors to the allowed tolerances—this is the compensation stage.

Diagnostic sensors can be embedded at the machine level, and the information sent to the system-level computers. Dimension inspection sensors may be also integrated into the manufacturing system by adding measurement stations, such as the RIM in Figure 9.10, and the lasers in Figure 9.12. The measurement system and the diagnostic methodology should allow for machine and system diagnosability— namely, identifying the sole cause or source of a fault and not merely reporting the errors. The compensation step, taken either automatically or through operator intervention, performs corrective actions (e.g., calibration, adjusting operating parameters, maintenance).

To guarantee a short ramp-up after each reconfiguration, it is necessary to measure both product features and process variables quickly. The measurement system, embedded in the RMS, must rapidly identify the sources of quality problems, and advanced information technologies, statistics, and signal processing technologies correct them in real time.

Real data points from actual production of auto-body assembly have been plotted in Figure 9.14. This figure demonstrates the advantage of the systematic ramp-up process described in Figure 9.13. The benefit is the rapid reduction of the variation (6σ) in critical body dimensions by the use of stream-of-variations* (SoV) methodology.[9] SoV combines engineering process models with statistical analysis to account for how product dimensional variations accumulate as the product moves

---

*The term "Stream of Variations" was coined by Y. Koren.

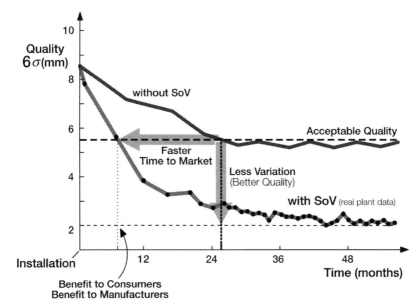

Figure 9.14 Results showing ramp-up time reduction in automotive body assembly.

through a manufacturing system. It can be used, with appropriately selected and placed sensors, to diagnose the root causes of dimensional errors in the production system.[10]

Applying SoV reduces the error ("variation") more rapidly, 15 weeks sooner than normal in this case, and more successfully, reducing auto-body variations from 5 to 2.2 mm. These improvements translate into a significant time-to-market advantage with huge benefits to the manufacturer, and a better product for the consumer (for example, doors that perfectly fit their opening, and trunks that close more accurately).

9.6 HEXAGONAL RMS CONFIGURATIONS

Below we describe a futuristic multi-stage flexibility manufacturing system, which includes a low-cost material handling system and takes up less floor space than a comparable conventional system. For a six-machine cell, the space is smaller by a factor of approximately 1/2.

This new system is composed of hexagonal manufacturing cells, where each cell contains several machines and typically represents an entire operational stage in the system.[11] Typically all machines in the cell (i.e., at the stage level) are identical and their number is calculated to meet the required production capacity (i.e., volume) of the system. Each cell contains up to six identical machines, with each machine installed close to one of the hexagon sides, as depicted in Figure 9.15.

A cell may start with less than six machines; adding machines when needed allows for scaling up the system capacity. Neighboring cells are installed on adjacent sides

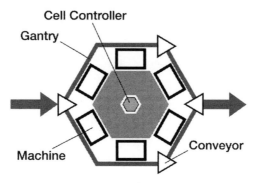

Figure 9.15 Hexagonal manufacturing cell.

of the hexagon in such a way that a honeycomb structure is achieved (see Figure 9.16). This structure allows more connectivity while saving floor space. The gantry tracks (on which the gantries move) of adjacent cells are installed close to each other along the shared sides of the hexagon. The overhead gantry is the material transfer of choice for the honeycomb configuration because it allows access to the machines for service and maintenance.

Each cell has an overhead gantry, equipped with a double gripper that moves along the gantry's hexagonal sides on an upper track and can approach each machine table in the cell. The gantry performs all material handling operations in the cell. The unit has two Z-axes that can move up and down, and each one of these has a gripper at its end, as shown in Figure 9.17. The material handling unit approaches a machine table with one gripper empty and the other holding a part that is ready to be loaded onto the machine. First, the empty gripper is lowered to take the machined part from the machine rotary table, and lifts it out of the way. Then the unit moves slightly along its track and the second gripper, with the new part, is lowered and loads the part on the machine table (this is the position depicted in Figure 9.17). The empty gripper then rises back up and the unit moves away to bring the part that is on the right gripper to a buffer. During all this time the machine continues to operate on a part. When the machining is

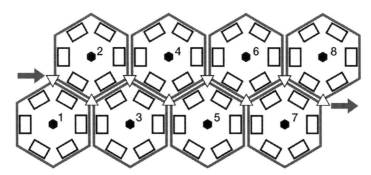

Figure 9.16 Several cells (eight in this example) form a large manufacturing system.

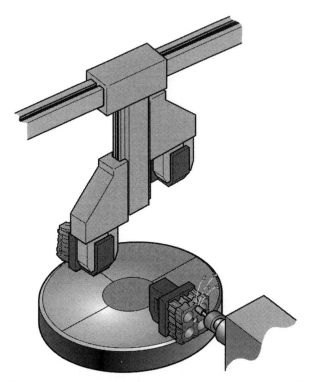

Figure 9.17   The right gripper just picked a ready part and went up; the left gripper is now placing a new part to be machined next.

completed, the table rotates 180° and has a new part to work on, and the finished part waits to be picked up.

The rotary table is a 180° index table. The table carries the new part 180° to place it in the workspace of the cutting tool, and the machine starts its operation. When the operation is done, the table rotates 180° and again the part is swapped out for the next part and is ready to be picked up by the gripper.

The gripper takes the newly machined part and moves it to a triangular loop conveyor that is shared with the cell to which the part is transferred next. The conveyor moves the part to the adjacent cell. The empty gripper returns to a position where it can receive a new part that has to be machined in one of the machines of the original cell.

The hexagonal cell has the optimal shape in terms of **floor space reduction** and enables smooth motions of the gantry. The regular polygon internal angle is $\{180-360/n\}$. The maximum utilization of floor space happens when a regular polygon with n sides ($n > 4$) satisfies the equation:

$$2 \times \{180-(180-360/n)\} = 180-360/n$$

This equation solves the problem: Given two identical regular polygons A and B with one shared (common) side, what is the identical polygon (C) that will have one

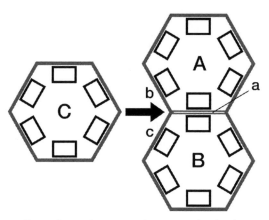

Figure 9.18   From all regular polygons with n>4 only the hexagon (n=6) can fit between two joint polygons, A and B, such that it has two shared sides b and c.

of its sides shared with one polygon (A), and another side shared with one of the sides of the other polygon (B). This is depicted in Figure 9.18. The solution of this equation is $n = 6$. This proves that a manufacturing system composed of regular hexagonal cells occupies the minimum floor space.

In addition to the smaller floor space that is achieved by the honeycomb architecture, it has the advantage that new hexagonal cells can be easily integrated into the existing honeycomb system. Integrating additional manufacturing cells scales up the production capacity and functionality of the whole system.

The honeycomb structure has many potential applications in machining and assembly systems. Personalized design of automobile interiors, as described in Chapter 3, may generate many thousands of variants of auto interiors. The assembly of each component requires specific tools, and may require different assembly times. It is unfeasible to apply a traditional serial assembly line with so complex an assembly program. It is also impractical to assume that personalized production can maintain the pace of a typical line generating a throughput of one car every 50–60 seconds. Floor space will also be a premium in personalize production with so many components being offered.

If the new personalized production paradigm becomes a reality, Ford's serial moving assembly line (invented in 1913) must be replaced by a new approach. A new conceptual system for final assembly of personalized auto interiors is depicted in Figure 9.19. In this system, each small square represents a station where a particular component is being assembled. Each car moves in a route that fits the combination of components that have to be installed. Popular components will require more than one assembly station.

Now, 100 years after the invention of the moving assembly line, and with enabling advances in information technology, and under changing global imperatives, new approaches to assembly need to be developed. We offer this new conceptual system, and other non-serial assembly systems will certainly be developed in the future. In any case, because of the unpredictable demands of the global manufacturing revolution

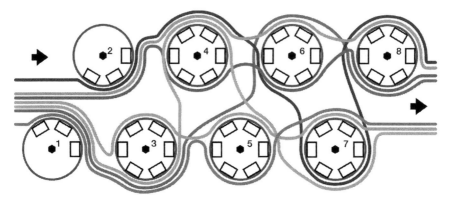

Figure 9.19 Reconfigurable assembly system based on hexagonal configuration.

they all will need to be reconfigurable, enabling freely variable assembly routes to produce the personalized product quickly and at low cost.

PROBLEMS

9.1 A part requires 11 operations to be completed. The processing times, in seconds, are given in the table below.

1	2	3	4	5	6	7	8	9	10	11
20	40	20	15	20	10	30	55	20	20	30

The sequence in which the operations should be executed is given below. (Namely, 3, 4, 5, and 6 can be done in any order after 2 and before 7, etc.)

$$1 \rightarrow 2 \rightarrow \begin{bmatrix} 3 \\ 4 \\ 5 \\ 6 \end{bmatrix} \rightarrow 7 \rightarrow \begin{bmatrix} 8 \\ 9 \end{bmatrix} \rightarrow 10 \rightarrow 11$$

The part is produced on the three-stage system in Figure 9.7. Plan the operation sequence and assign operations to machines such that the cycle time of producing parts is minimized.

9.2 A part requires five (5) machining operations, each to be performed with a special tool. The time needed to complete each operation (including tool changing time) is given in the table. The operations must be performed in the sequence given in the table. (Op. 1, then 2, etc.)

Operation	1	2	3	4	5
Time (seconds)	100	80	60	60	100

Configuration I

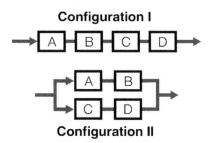

Configuration II

Figure 9.20 Two configurations.

The system includes only four machines, and each machine is equipped with a tool magazine that can hold up to four tools (therefore, five operations cannot be done on a single machine).

(a) Given the two configurations in Figure 9.20, label the operations that each machine should perform to maximize throughput. Calculate the throughput (parts per hour) for each configuration. Which configuration will have a higher throughput (assuming 100% machine reliability)?

(b) Is there another configuration of the four machines that has equal or higher throughput? Draw it and label the operations that each machine is to perform.

(c) Add a fifth machine to each configuration (the two that are given and the one that you proposed in item b) to scale up the system capacity. Draw the three new configurations that you propose, and calculate the new throughput (parts per hour) for each configuration.

9.3 A manufacturer has two options for buying a new production line to produce up to 100,000 products per year: A dedicated line that costs $50 million or an RMS that costs $60 million. The product is sold at a profit of $150 per product. Solve for the three scenarios described below, and draw a graph of profit (or loss) for each case and for each system during 6 years of operation. When does the higher investment in the reconfigurable system become economically justified?

(a) The production is 100,000 products per year, for 6 years, as was expected.

(b) After 2 years of operation the market demand grows to 150,000 units per year. The dedicated line is not scalable and cannot meet the additional product demand. For an additional investment of $15 million, the reconfigurable system can supply the new demand for the next 4 years.

(c) After 2 years of operating the original system, an unpredicted model change is needed (again, requiring 100,000 units per year for the new model; the old one is discontinued). A new dedicated line could be built to produce the new product, or the reconfigurable system can be reconfigured for an additional cost of $10 million, and produce the new model for 4 years.

9.4   Repeat Problem 9.3 when the interest on capital investment is 10% per year. Do you recommend investing in the project?

REFERENCES

1. Y. Koren and A. G. Ulsoy. Reconfigurable Manufacturing Systems. *Engineering Research Center for Reconfigurable Machining Systems (ERC/RMS) Report #1*, The University of Michigan, Ann Arbor, 1997.
2. O. Garro and P. Martin. Towards new architecture of machine tools. International Journal of Production Research, 1993, Vol. 31, No. 10, pp. 2403–2414.
3. Y. Koren and A. G. Ulsoy. Reconfigurable manufacturing system having a production capacity, method for designing same, and method for changing its production capacity. *U.S. patent No.* 6,349,237. Issued on February 19, 2002.
4. Y. Koren and S. Kota. Reconfigurable Machine Tools. *U.S. Patent No.* 5,943,750. Issue on August 31, 1999.
5. Y. Koren, F. Jovane, and G. Pritschow (eds). *Open Architecture Control Systems*, Summary of Global Activity, ITIA Series, Vol. 2, 1998.
6. Similar ideas for computing systems are presented in J. Villasenor and W.H. Mangione-Smith. Configurable computing. *Scientific American*, pp. 66–71, June 1997.
7. G. Erixon. Modularity—the basis for Product and Factory Re-engineering, *Annals of the CIRP*, 1996, Vol. 45/1, pp. 1–4.
8. H. K. Tönshoff, E. Menzel, H. Hinkenhuis, and E. Nitidem. Intelligence in machine tools by configuration. *7th International Conference on Production/Precision Engineering,* Chiba, Japan, 1994.
9. S. J. Hu. Stream of variations theory for automotive body assembly, *Annals of the CIRP*, 1997, Vol. 46/1, pp. 1–4.
10. J. Shi. *Stream of Variation Modeling and Analysis for Multistage Manufacturing Processes.* CRC Press, 2006.
11. Y. Koren and R. Hill. *Integrated reconfigurable manufacturing system. US patent* #6,920,973. Issue on July 26, 2005.

Chapter **10**

System Configuration Analysis

In large manufacturing systems the production is done in many stages. A product is partially processed in one stage and then transferred to the next until all operations are completed. The configuration of a system can facilitate or impede the system's productivity, responsiveness, convertibility and scalability, and also impact its daily operations. Multi-stage manufacturing systems can allow for several operational configurations depending on the way the machines are arranged in the stages, and connected via the material handling system. In this chapter, we offer a method for classification of configurations and use it to compare the attributes of various configuration classes. We will also discuss the configuration of Reconfigurable Manufacturing Systems (RMSs), and present a way to calculate the number of possible RMS configurations based on the number of machines it contains.

10.1 CLASSIFICATION OF CONFIGURATIONS

The first step toward a systematic approach to classifying configurations is to determine the number of possible configurations when the daily demand, Q (parts/day), and the total processing time for the part, t (minute/part), are given. In reality the processing times vary widely depending on the equipment involved; but, to begin with, we assume that it is given.

The Global Manufacturing Revolution: Product-Process-Business Integration and Reconfigurable Systems
By Yoram Koren
Copyright © 2010 John Wiley & Sons, Inc.

Number of Machines	Number of Possible Configurations	Number of RMS Configurations
2	2	2
4	15	8
6	170	32
8	2325	128
10	**35,341**	**512**

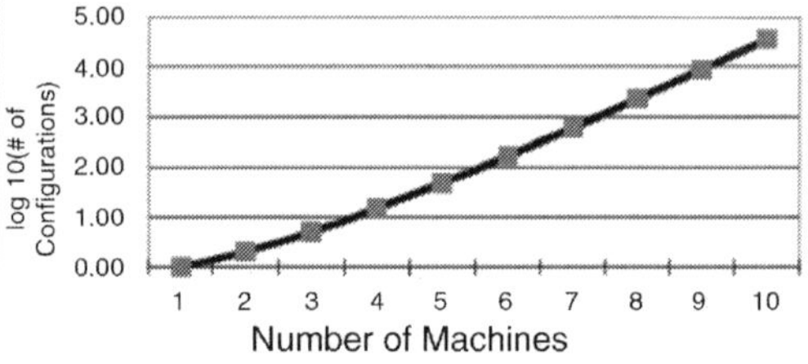

Figure 10.1   Total number of system configurations for different numbers of machines.

The minimum number of machines, N, needed in the system is calculated by the equation

$$N = \frac{Q \times t}{\text{Minutes/day available} \times \text{machine reliability}} \tag{10.1}$$

In the following calculations we assume 100% reliability of all pieces of equipment (i.e., machine reliability = 1). The resulting number of machines calculated by Eq. (10.1) must be rounded to the next larger integer. For example, if there is a need for 500 parts per day and the processing time for each part is 9.5 minutes, for a working time of 1000 minute/day there is a need for at least five machines in the system.

In the general case the total number of configurations for N machines is huge. When plotted on a logarithmic scale, the number of configurations increases almost linearly with the number of machines, as shown in Figure 10.1. We will see later in this chapter that the number of possible RMS configurations is much smaller, as indicated in the table in Figure 10.1.*

Eq. (10.1) yields the minimum number of machines needed to meet the required demand. The next questions are: What is the best way to arrange these machines and how to connect them? Should we arrange them, for example, in a serial line, a pure parallel system, or some combination? Which one of all possible configurations is the most advantageous?

For example, in the case of five machines the total number of configurations that are possible is 48. Figure 10.2 shows 32 of these configurations. As we have seen in Figure 10.1 the number of possible configurations increased exponentially with the number of machines. It is not unheard of in the automotive powertrain industry to have 80 or more machines coordinated into one system. How can one possibly analyze the merits of so many possible configurations?

To begin with, we classify configurations as either symmetrical or asymmetrical, based on whether one can draw a symmetric axis along the configuration. A configuration is then evaluated by its machine **arrangement** and **connections**. For example, configurations a and b have identical machine arrangements (one in Stage 1, two in Stage 2, and two in Stage 3), but they are different because of different connections among the machines—configuration b has cross-coupling between Stages 2 and 3. The type of the material handling system determines the connections

---

*W. X. Zhu, an ERC-RMS Ph.D. student, did the calculation of the number of configurations.

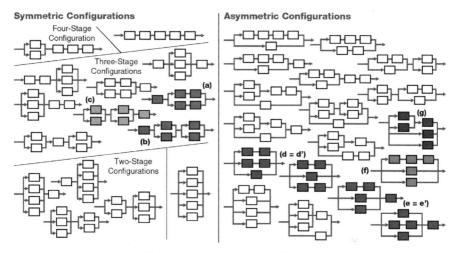

Figure 10.2   Configurations with five machines.

of a configuration. Altogether, a system with five machines may have 16 different symmetric arrangements (13 of which are plotted in Figure 10.2). Fortunately, the designer has to consider only symmetric configurations because:

Only symmetric configurations are suitable for manufacturing systems

Asymmetric configurations add immense complexity and are not viable in real manufacturing lines as will be explained below. The number of possible asymmetric configurations is much larger than that of symmetric configurations—a total of 30 in the case of five machines (18 of them are plotted in Figure 10.2). It is important to note that we define configurations d' and e' as asymmetric (although they have a symmetric axis) because they may be positioned differently (as d and e). Similarly, the two configurations f and g in Figure 10.2 are defined when studying the Reconfiguration Science as asymmetric configurations, although they may be drawn as symmetric.

We would like to explain why asymmetric configurations are usually not suitable for real manufacturing systems. Asymmetric configurations may be sub-classified as (a) variable-process configurations and (b) single-process configurations with non-identical machines in at least one of the stages. Corresponding examples are shown in Figures 10.3a and 10.3b, respectively.

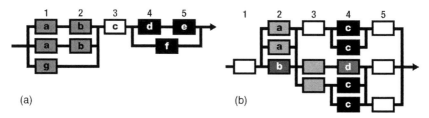

Figure 10.3   Two classes of asymmetric configurations.

Variable-process configurations are characterized by possible non-identical flow paths for the part, and therefore they need a preparation period of several process plans and corresponding setups. For example, in the system depicted in Figure 10.3a possible flow-paths are a-b-c-d-e, g-c-f, g-c-d-e, etc. The executed process plan depends on the flow-path of the part being processed in the system. This is absolutely impractical because: (1) designers will not go to the effort to design multiple process plans for the same part, and (2) different process plans and flow paths increase part-quality problems and make quality error detection more complicated.

In the second class of asymmetric configurations, although the process planning is identical in each flow path, the machines in at least one stage are different. For example, in Figure 10.3b, the machine b in Stage 2 must be two times faster than machines a; machine d in Stage 4 must be two times faster than machines c. (By contrast, in symmetric configurations, the processing times of every machine in a stage are equal.) It is absolutely impractical to mix different types of machines in the same manufacturing stage performing exactly the same sequence of tasks. The system designer should not consider this class of configuration, either, due to that excessive complexity. The conclusion is

> In a real manufacturing context only symmetric configurations should be considered; they are always single-process configurations with identical machines in each stage.

Symmetric configurations may further be divided, into three basic classes as shown in Figure 10.4.

A designer of manufacturing systems should consider only these three classes:

I **Cell Configurations**—Configurations consisting of several serial manufacturing lines (cells) arranged in parallel with no crossovers, as shown as Class I in Figure 10.4, and also shown in Figure 10.5.

II **RMS Configurations**—Configurations with crossover connections after every stage, as shown in Figure 10.6. The part from any machine in stage i can be transferred to any machine in stage $(i + 1)$. All machines and operations in any stage are identical.

III Configurations in which there are some stages with no crossovers. This class includes combinations of the previous two classes.

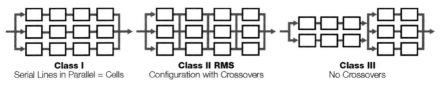

Class I
Serial Lines in Parallel = Cells

Class II RMS
Configuration with Crossovers

Class III
No Crossovers

Figure 10.4 Three classes of symmetric configurations.

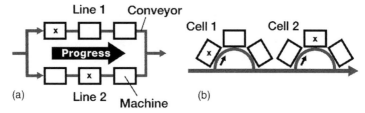

Figure 10.5 Symmetric configuration of Class I—parallel lines, or cells (If the two marked machines fail, the system production stops).

To understand the RMS configuration operations issue, study the sketch in Figure 10.7 of a practical three-stage RMS with gantries that transport the parts. A spine gantry transfers a part to a small cell conveyor; the part moves on the conveyor to a position where a cell gantry can pick it up and take it for processing in one of the machines in its stage. When the part processing is done, the cell gantry returns the part to the conveyor, which moves the part to a position in which the next spine gantry can pick it up for processing in the next stage, and so on.

10.2 COMPARING RMS WITH CELL CONFIGURATIONS

We compare below the two main practical configurations depicted in Figures 10.5 and 10.6 by four criteria: investment cost, line-balancing ability, scalability options, and productivity when machines fail.

Capital Investment: The configurations in Figures 10.5 and 10.6 (or 10.7) have identical machine arrangements—three stages with two machines in each stage—but their connections are quite different. That means that they use different part handling devices, each requiring a different capital investment. The entire part handling system in Figure 10.5 is simpler and has a smaller number of handling devices compared with the RMS in Fig. 10.7. Thus, the capital investment in the RMS configuration is higher.

Line Balancing: A major drawback of the cell configuration compared with the RMS configuration is that it provides less flexibility in balancing the system. For example, if just one product is produced, the processing time in all stages of the cell configuration must be exactly equal to be perfectly balanced. By contrast,

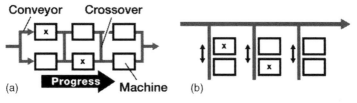

Figure 10.6 Symmetric configuration of Class II—RMS configuration (If the two marked machines fail, the system still has 50% production capacity).

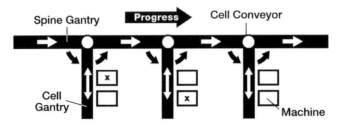

Figure 10.7   A practical Reconfigurable Manufacturing System.

for a balanced RMS configuration only the following relationship needs to be satisfied:

$$t_{s1}/N_{s1} = t_{s2}/N_{s2} = t_{si}/N_{si} \qquad (10.2)$$

where N_{si} is the number of machines in stage i, and t_{si} is the processing time per machine in stage i. Therefore, in RMS configurations the number of machines per stage is not necessarily equal in all stages. The number of machines in the various stages of RMS configurations may be adjusted to provide an accurate line balancing, which consequently yields an improved productivity.

System Scalability: The scalability of the RMS configuration is better by far than that of the parallel line configuration. Adding one machine in one of the stages and rebalancing the system enables adds a small increment of capacity. In the parallel line configuration, a whole additional line must be added to increase the overall system capacity. In markets of unstable demand, scalability is an important advantage of RMS configurations.

Productivity: If machine reliability is low, the RMS configuration offers higher productivity than a parallel line configuration. As shown in Figure 10.5, if machines in two different lines and at two different stages (marked with x) are down, the entire system is down (i.e., throughput $= 0$). Whereas, for an RMS, the same conditions—two machines not working (marked with x in Figure 10.6)—the RMS throughput is still at 50%. So, the RMS is a more productive system from a machine downtime aspect. However, if one of the cell gantries in the RMS is down, the whole system is down. By contrast, systems with parallel lines do not contain cell gantries, and are more reliable from a material handling system aspect. The consequent question is therefore:

When considering reliability, which configuration has higher productivity?

We solved this problem analytically, but showing the full analysis is beyond the scope of this book. In this analysis the number of machines per stage in the RMS configuration is equal in all stages. The RMS configuration has a spine gantry with an identical reliability to the conveyors in Figure 10.5. The analysis calculates tradeoffs between cell-gantry reliability and machine reliability.

As an example we shall show just one typical result in Figure 10.8, which is plotted for a gantry reliability (or availability) of $G_r = 0.96$, and machine reliability of

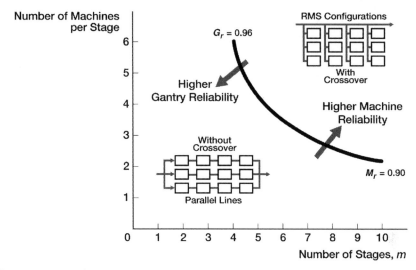

Figure 10.8   Productivity comparison between parallel lines and RMS configurations.

$M_r = 0.90$. Our analysis revealed that there is a borderline based on the machine reliability and gantry reliability (which must always be better than the machine reliability). On the right-top side of the borderline the preferred system is RMS with crossovers. For example, if the system has nine stages with four machines per stage, the RMS configuration will yield higher productivity than parallel-line one. The parallel-line configuration is preferred when, for example, the system has nine stages with just two machines per stage (namely, two parallel lines with nine stages). The better the machine average reliability is (e.g., 0.95), the larger the solution space for the parallel-line configuration (without crossovers), and *vice versa*.

The main conclusions of this analysis are

- In large systems, with a large number of stages and machines per stage, the RMS configuration has higher productivity than the cell configuration.
- If the machine reliability is very high, the cell configuration yields higher productivity than the RMS configuration.

The advantages of each configuration are summarized below.

	Capital Investment	Scalability	Line Balancing	Productivity
Parallel lines	Lower			Higher for high machine reliability
RMS configuration		Much better	Much better	Higher in complex, large systems

10.3 CALCULATING THE NUMBER OF RMS CONFIGURATIONS

We have seen that it is easy to calculate the minimum number of machines N required in the system by solving Eq. (10.1). However, as shown in Figure 10.1, the number of all possible configurations with N machines is enormous. We have conducted a thorough mathematical study of system configurations, and our conclusion is

> **Equations for calculating the number of configurations with N machines exist only for RMS-type configurations.**

The basic equations for calculating the number of possible RMS configurations are given below. The number, K, of possible RMS configurations with N machines arranged in *up to m* stages is

$$K = \sum_{m=1}^{N} \binom{N-1}{m-1} = 2^{N-1} \tag{10.3}$$

The number, K, of possible configurations with N machines arranged in *exactly m* stages is

$$K = \left(\frac{(N-1)!}{(N-m)!(m-1)!} \right) \tag{10.4}$$

For example, for $N = 7$ machines arranged in up to seven stages Eq. (10.3) yields $K = 64$ configurations, and if arranged in exactly three stages, Eq. (10.4) yields $K = 15$ RMS configurations. The mathematical results of these two equations for any N and m may be arranged in a triangular format, known as a Pascal triangle, shown in Figure 10.9.

The method of calculating the numerical value of each cell in the Pascal triangle is as follows. The numerical value corresponding to N machines that are arranged in m stages is calculated by

The value for N machines in m stages = (The value for N−1 machines in m−1 stages) + (the value for N −1 machines in m stages)

For example, in Figure 10.9, the cell of $N = 5$ and $m = 3$ shows 6, which is the sum of $3 + 3$ of the previous line of $N - 1 = 4$ machines with two and three stages.

The triangle also allows the designer to immediately visualize the number of possible RMS configurations for N machines that are arranged in m stages. For example, there are 15 RMS configurations when seven machines are allowed to be arranged in exactly three stages. In addition, the Pascal triangle allows the designer to immediately calculate the number of possible RMS configurations for N machines that are arranged between i and j stages $(i, j < N)$. We will use this information in the following example.

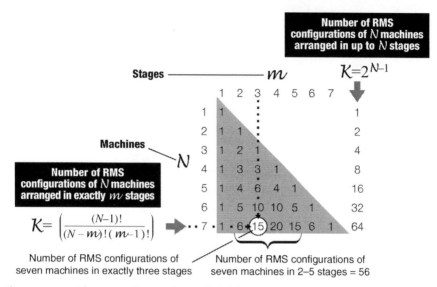

Figure 10.9 The Pascal triangle is helpful in calculating the number of RMS configurations.

10.4 EXAMPLE OF SYSTEM DESIGN

We demonstrate below how the Pascal Triangle in Figure 10.9 can be used in system design. The example deals with designing a machining system that has an RMS configuration.

Raw parts are brought to a machining system after casting. The system contains many CNC machines that perform all machining operations required to finish the part, including milling, drilling, tapping, etc. A typical part of an automobile powertrain system is shown in Figure 10.10. Note that the part has to be machined on several faces, and that there are more than 200 machining tasks required to finish such a part, and so it is impractical to include them all in this demonstration.

For simplicity, we will consider a simpler part that requires work on only two faces. Each face requires a separate fixturing, and therefore the two faces must be machined using two separate setups. Our simplified example requires only five machining tasks

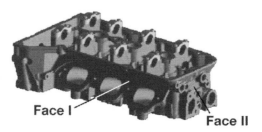

Figure 10.10 An engine part after machining.

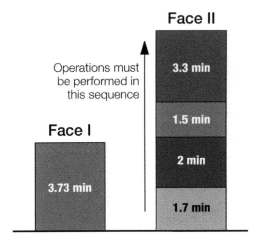

Figure 10.11   Machining times.

to be completed. We will see that even for this simple example, the analysis is tedious and lengthy. However, a methodic approach will be presented to whittle down the range of possibilities, and make logical decisions based on facts and data to find the optimal system configuration.

The problem that we would like to solve is defined below.

10.4.1 Problem

Design a machining system to machine a part that requires $t = 12.2$ *minutes machining time in five machining tasks. The execution times of the five tasks are given in* Figure 10.11. *The required daily volume is* $Q = 500$ *parts/day.*

The working time per day is 1000 minutes. Assume machine reliability 100%

10.4.2 Solution

Producing 500 parts in 1000 minutes requires a cycle time of 2 minutes per part. The first step is to determine the minimum number of machines. Equation (10.1) yields 6.1 machines. But we must round the number to the next integer, which gives us $N = 7$ machines.

According to Eq. (10.3), for seven machines and number of possible stages from 1 to 7, we are presented with 64 configurations to analyze. However, 64 configurations is a large number that can be reduced by considering the specific tasks. Since the part has only five machining tasks, the maximum number of stages can be just 5. The part has two faces and each requires a different setup, and therefore the minimum number of stages must be 2. If we are looking at the Pascal triangle in Figure 10.9, we can see that for seven machines in the range between two and five stages there are only 56 configurations.

But do we still really have to compare 56 configurations? The answer is no!

If the part has two faces, we may divide the system into two sub-systems—one for Face 1 and the other for Face 2—and then design two separate sub-systems. In the sub-system for Face 1 the machining time t is 3.7 minutes per part. According to Eq. (10.1) the required number of machines for the first Face is 2.

$$N = \frac{500 \times 3.7}{1000} = 1.85 \Rightarrow 2 \text{ machines} \tag{10.5a}$$

In the sub-system for Face 2 the machining time t is 8.5 minutes per part. According to Eq. (10.1) the required number of machines for the second Face is 5.

$$N = \frac{500 \times 8.5}{1000} = 4.25 \Rightarrow 5 \text{ machines} \tag{10.5b}$$

Observing the Pascal triangle for these two sub-systems in Figure 10.12 shows only 15 possible configurations (rather than 56): one for Face 1, and 15 for Face 2.

$$1 \times (1 + 4 + 6 + 4) = 15$$

- If the system contains just two stages, there is only one possible configuration: Stage 1 with two machines to work on Face 1, and Stage 2 with five machines for Face 2.
- If the system is comprised of three stages, there are four possible configurations.
- For four stages, there are six possible configurations.
- For five stages, there are four configurations: Stage 1 for Face 1, and four stages for Face 2.

However, the formula for calculating the number of machines, Eq. (10.1), is based on a perfectly balanced system, and here the system is not necessarily balanced. Therefore, several of these 15 possible configurations will not supply the demand of

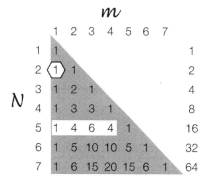

Figure 10.12   Pascal triangle for the example.

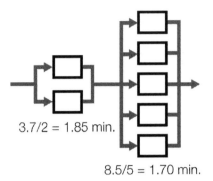

3.7/2 = 1.85 min.

8.5/5 = 1.70 min.

Figure 10.13 Two stages.

500 parts per day. Our next step is to determine which of the configurations will not supply the demand and eliminate them.

For two stages there is only one possible configuration, the one depicted in Figure 10.13. In the first stage, one part is produced every 1.85 minutes (between the two machines), and in the second stage one part is produced (between the five machines) every 1.7 minutes. The first stage is the bottleneck, and dictates the cycle time of the system is $t_{max} = 1.85$ minutes. The number of parts per day is, therefore: $Q = 1000/t_{max} = 540$.

For three stages there are four possible configurations. However, only three of them satisfy the cycle time constraint of $t_{max} \leq 2$ minutes. The three systems are depicted in Figure 10.14. In these three cases the cycle time is $t_{max} = 1.85$ minutes.

The fourth configuration (not shown) has only one machine in the third stage, which becomes a bottleneck with a cycle time of 3.3 minutes, which cannot satisfy the required demand (a minimum cycle time of 2 minutes). Therefore, that configuration is unacceptable.

For four stages there are six possible configurations. However, three of them do not satisfy the cycle time constraint of $t_{max} \leq 2$ minutes and have been omitted from

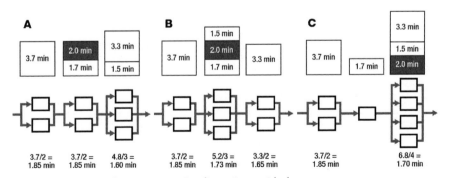

Figure 10.14 Configurations with three stages.

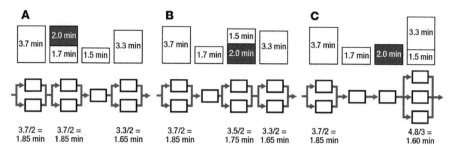

Figure 10.15 Configurations with four stages.

consideration. The three acceptable systems shown in Figure 10.15 all have a cycle time of $t_{max} = 1.85$ minutes. The three omitted configurations have only one machine in the forth stage, which becomes a bottleneck with a cycle time of 3.3 minutes that cannot produce the required demand.

For five stages there are four possible configurations, but only one of them is valid. This one is shown in Figure 10.16. The bottleneck in this configuration is in the third stage, which yields a **cycle time of 2 minutes**. In the other three five-stage configurations, only one machine is placed in the fifth stage, an arrangement that does not satisfy the required cycle time.

We see that because of the cycle-time requirement, the number of configurations is reduced from 15 to 8. Altogether, the number of possible RMS configurations to consider was reduced from 64 to 8. Eight configurations is a manageable number to compare.

In order to make a final decision the designer has to compare at least the following four factors (ranked by importance):

1. System throughput with reliability less than 100% (see next section)
2. Investment cost
3. Scalability—the increment of production capacity gained by adding a machine
4. Floor space, which may be roughly calculated by the configuration length (i.e., number of stages, m) times its maximum width (i.e., the maximum number of machines in a stage).

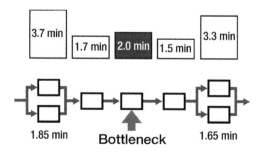

Figure 10.16 A configuration with five stages.

TABLE 10.1   Comparison of Eight Configurations in the Example

Configuration in Figure	Stages m	Floor Space	Throughput at $R = 100\%$	Cost	RANK
10.15	5	10	500	Low	7
10.14A	4	8	540	Med	6
10.14B	4	8	540	Med	5
10.14C	4	12	500	Med	8
10.13A	3	9	540	Med	2
10.13B	3	9	540	Med	1
10.13C	3	12	540	Med	4
10.12	2	10	540	High	3

Gray background = Best ; light gray background = very good result compared with alternatives.

For our example these factors are compared in Table 10.1. The ranking in Table 10.1 is subjective and depends on the weight that the designer (and company) assigns to each factor (cost, scalability, etc). In our opinion, the configuration that the designer would most likely favor (Rank = 1) is the one in Figure 10.13B (we will further clarify this ranking at the end of the next section). By implementing Configuration 10.13B the throughput requirement (500 parts/day) is met and the investment cost (machines and tooling) is acceptable. It has a good scalability factor and will occupy a reasonable amount of floor space.

Important conclusions that we may draw from this example are

1. It is simple to calculate the minimum number of machines N needed in a system based on the total processing time per part and the required daily quantity.
2. The number of possible configurations is bounded by (i) the number of tasks needed on the part and (ii) the number of faces on the part, and it is always smaller than 2^{N-1}.
3. The number of possible RMS configurations is reduced dramatically when considering the daily quantity requirement that must be met.

10.5   IMPACT OF CONFIGURATION ON PERFORMANCE

Differences in configuration can have a profound impact on the performance of the system in terms of throughput (jobs per hour), product quality, capacity scalability, convertibility, and investment and operational costs. A systematic analysis of these performance measures is presented below for different system configurations. For this analysis we assume known machine-level reliability and process capability, as shown in Figure 10.17.[1]

The following performance measures are considered when selecting a system configuration:

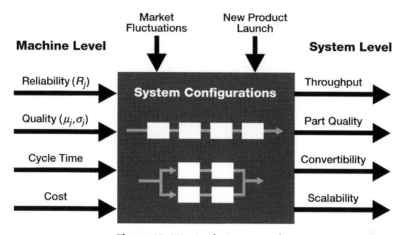

Figure 10.17 Analysis approach.

1. The initial capital cost of the manufacturing system (Chapter 7)
2. Product quality (Section 10.5.1)
3. Throughput, which is dependent on equipment reliability (Section 10.5.2)
4. Capacity scalability (Section 10.5.3)
5. Convertibility—converting the system to production of a new product
6. The number of product types that the system can produce simultaneously.

Analytical or computational tools are necessary to evaluate these performance measures. We will begin with some basic models of performance for a serial and a parallel system with two machines, as shown in Figure 10.18. Each machine in the serial configuration produces one half of the total tasks, and in the parallel configuration, each machine produces the whole set of tasks. Both configurations produce a part every T minutes.

To illustrate the analysis for more complex manufacturing system configurations, we will then compare six configurations, with six machines each (Figure 10.19). We will show that the preferred configurations are either d or e. Configuration b might be selected only for special cases (e.g., where machine #6 performs a special, quick process). If the system has to produce only one or two parts of the same family, we

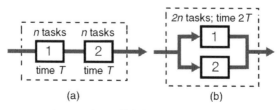

Figure 10.18 Serial (a) and parallel (b) configurations with two machines.

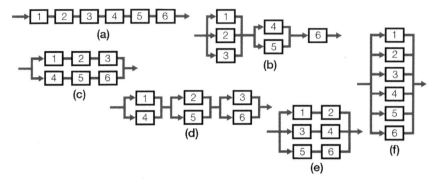

Figure 10.19 Six configurations with six machines.

recommend selecting Configuration d. If the part family is larger than two, we recommend selecting Configuration e, which will be easier to operate when simultaneously producing multiple products.

10.5.1 Product Dimensional Quality

Quality has many meanings. In this chapter we are mainly concerned with the dimensional quality (accuracy) of the machined or assembled product. We define quality here as

Dimensional Quality: Variation of a dimension from its designed intent.

The closer a dimension is to the design intent, the better the quality is.[2] With volume production, the quality of the process can be measured by the mean deviation from the design intent $\bar{y}$, and the standard deviation σ_y from the mean. The second moment from the design intent, $\bar{y}^2 + \sigma_y^2$, can be used as a single measure of the total variation by combining the mean deviation and standard deviation together. This definition is consistent with Taguchi's quality loss function definition. In physical units, the square root, $\sqrt{\bar{y}^2 + \sigma_y^2}$, is used.

Assume that the capability for each machine is given as (μ_i, σ_i^2). For a serial configuration with two machines, if the operation of Machine 2 is dependent on that of Machine 1, then the resulting quality will be given as

$$\sigma_y^2 = \sigma_1^2 + \sigma_2^2 \tag{10.6}$$

For a system with two machines in parallel, each machine will perform all the operations in a single setup. As a result, the standard deviations for the parts from each machine will be small compared with that from a serial configuration. However, because of the two part flow paths, statistical "mixing" exists. As a result, the total variation from the parallel configuration could be larger, depending on the differences in the process means of the two parallel machines. The difference

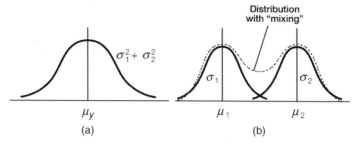

Figure 10.20   Dimensional variation of parts from (a) serial configuration and (b) parallel configuration.

in quality, between serial and parallel configurations with two machines, is illustrated in Figure 10.20.

The mean and standard deviation for parts coming out of a system with parallel configuration (Figure 10.20b) is calculated by the equations

$$\mu_y = (\mu_1 + \mu_2)/2 \qquad (10.7)$$

and

$$\sigma_y^2 = \frac{1}{2}\left(\sigma_1^2 + \sigma_2^2\right) + \frac{1}{4}(\mu_1 - \mu_2)^2 \qquad (10.8)$$

Systems with complex configurations can be analyzed in a similar way. In general, Monte Carlo simulation methodologies can be applied in the analysis by using random numbers to examine the manufacturing process.[3] Given the mean and standard deviations of the machine, fixture, and incoming part variation, the output dimensions of a part or assembly can be predicted using process models.

For the six configurations shown in Figure 10.19, Monte Carlo simulation is used to estimate the dimensional variation from each configuration. Assuming that each machine has a capability of setting the mean to within $\pm 10\ \mu$m, and has a repeatability of 1 μm (one std. dev.). The resulting dimensional variations for the six configurations are summarized in Figure 10.21. As can be seen from this figure, the configuration in Figure 10.19d has the largest quality variation because the number of part flow paths is the highest—8. The serial line (Figure 10.19a) has the best quality because there is only one part flow path and no "mixing" exists.

10.5.2 Reliability and Expected Throughput

The expected, calculated throughput depends on the reliability of the equipment (as well as the processing rate and system balancing). The classical definition of reliability was developed for aerospace and electronic systems. It measures the probability of failure of the system. Similar definitions have been adopted for manufacturing machines and equipment. A handbook developed by the Society of

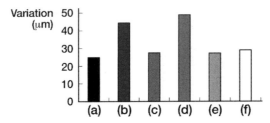

Figure 10.21 Dimensional variation resulted from the six configurations of Figure 10.17.

Manufacturing Engineers (SME) and the National Center for Manufacturing Sciences (NCMS) defines reliability of machinery or equipment as the probability that the machinery/equipment can perform continuously, without failure, for a specified interval of time when operating under stated conditions.[4]

This classical definition of machine reliability cannot be directly applied to calculate manufacturing system reliability because in a parallel configuration, when one of the machines fails, the system can still function at a reduced level (50% of the prior throughput, assuming that the two machines perform identical functions with the same cycle time). (By contrast, in a system that has two identical computers in parallel, if one computer fails, the system can still function at 100%.) Therefore, we use the term **"expected throughput,"** which accounts for the probability of failure and the corresponding throughput associated with each failure mode shown below.

For a system composed of two machines, there are four different system states: no machine fails, one machine fails, and both machines fail. The probability and productivity associated with each failure mode in a serial and a parallel system are shown in Table 10.2, where R_1 and R_2 are the reliability of Machine 1 and 2 respectively.

Therefore, the expected throughput is the sum of the throughputs weighted by the probabilities of the corresponding states.

The synchronous serial line expected throughput is

$$E[P] = 1 \bullet R_1 R_2 + 0 \bullet R_1 (1-R_2) + 0 \bullet R_2 (1-R_1) + 0 \bullet (1-R_1)(1-R_2) = R_1 R_2 \quad (10.9)$$

Eq. (10.9) also expresses the reliability of the manufacturing system.

TABLE 10.2   Expected Throughput for Systems with Two Machines

		Exp. Throughput	
State	**Probability**	Serial	Parallel
No machine fail	$R_1 R_2$	1	1
Machine 1 fails	$R_2(1-R_1)$	0	0.5
Machine 2 fails	$R_1(1-R_2)$	0	0.5
Both machines fail	$(1-R_1)(1-R_2)$	0	0

Nevertheless, to have a more realistic estimate of the system reliability, we have to know the average MTBF (mean time between failures of the machine) and the MTTR (the mean time to repair the machine failure). The expected throughput of a single isolated machine is proportional to the machine reliability R that is calculated by

$$R = \text{MTBF}/(\text{MTBF} + \text{MTTR}) \tag{10.10}$$

where both machine breakdowns and machine repairs occur at random.

For example, if all machines in a synchronous serial line have the same reliability $R = 0.9$, and the line does not have buffers, the system reliability (i.e., % throughput) as a function of the number of machines in the line N is given in the table below.

$N=1$	$N=2$	$N=3$	$N=4$	$N=5$	$N=6$	$N=7$	$N=8$	$N=9$
0.9	0.81	0.73	0.66	0.59	0.53	0.48	0.43	0.39

With six (6) machines, for example, the theoretical system throughput is only 53%.

Asynchronous serial lines throughput is higher than in the table above, and depends not only on the ratio MTBF/MTTR but also on the ratio between the cycle time (CT) and MTBF. The line throughput values were calculated by the ERC/RMS software PAMS for a perfectly balanced line (and no buffers) for a cycle time CT = 10 minutes, and are given in the table below.

MTBF	MTTR	$N=1$	$N=2$	$N=3$	$N=4$	$N=5$	$N=6$	$N=7$	$N=8$	$N=9$
0.9	0.1	0.9	0.893	0.890	0.888	0.887	0.886	0.886	0.885	0.885
9	1	0.9	0.859	0.835	0.820	0.810	0.803	0.797	0.793	0.790
90	10	0.9	0.826	0.767	0.721	0.683	0.651	0.625	0.604	0.585
900	100	0.9	0.819	0.751	0.696	0.645	0.606	0.570	0.539	0.511

The reason for the different values in the two tables is that in the asynchronous line when one machine fails the other machines in the line continue to operate, and the line operation does not stop completely, as assumed by Eq. (10.9). Even when a machine completed the task it holds the part, so it is acting as a temporary buffer, which increases the practical throughput of the line. When MTBF $\gg$ CT, the results are closer to those obtained by Eq. (10.9).

The parallel system expected throughput is obtained by adding the weighted reliabilities of the two machines:

$$\begin{aligned} E[P] &= 1 \bullet R_1 R_2 + 0.5 \bullet R_1 (1 - R_2) + 0.5 \bullet R_2 (1 - R_1) \\ &+ 0 \bullet (1 - R_1)(1 - R_2) = 0.5 R_1 + 0.5 R_2 \end{aligned} \tag{10.11}$$

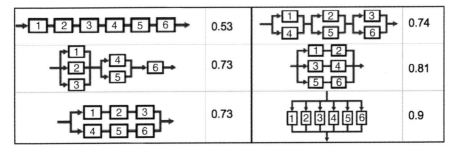

Figure 10.22   The expected throughput of the configurations in Figure 10.19.

For three machines in parallel the equation is $R_1/3 + R_2/3 + R_3/3$. Similar equations are valid for multiple machines in parallel.

Based on the above table, for $R = 0.9$, the expected throughput of the six configurations in Figure 10.19 was calculated and is given in Figure 10.22 (the method of calculating the throughput of configuration d, 0.74, is explained below).

10.5.2.1 Calculating the Expected Throughput In Configurations With Crossover

Calculating the expected throughput in configurations with crossover requires building a binary map with all the possible cases. We will show one example of calculating the expected throughput of the crossover configuration in Figure 10.23.

Each machine can be either up (Up) or down (blank in the table below). For four machines there are $2^4 = 16$ states. The probabilities and the expected throughputs are in the table below. Note that if machines I and III are both down, or if machines II and IV are both down, the system output is 0 (namely, zero expected throughput, $E[P]$).

I	II	III	IV	Probability	Exp. Throughput
Up	Up	Up	Up	$R_1R_1R_2R_2$	1
Up	Up	Up		$R_1R_2R_1(1-R_2)$	0.5
Up	Up		Up	$R_1R_2(1-R_1)R_2$	0.5
Up	Up			$R_1R_2(1-R_1)(1-R_2)$	0.5
Up		Up	Up	$R_1(1-R_2)R_1R_2$	0.5
Up		Up			0
Up			Up	$R_1(1-R_2)(1-R_1)R_2$	0.5
Up					0
	Up	Up	Up	$(1-R_1)R_2R_1R_2$	0.5
	Up	Up		$(1-R_1)R_2R_1(1-R_2)$	0.5
	Up		Up		0
	Up				0
		Up	Up	$(1-R_1)(1-R_2)R_1R_2$	0.5
		Up			0
			Up		0
					0

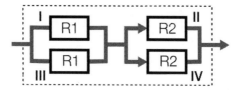

Figure 10.23 Configuration with crossover connection.

$$E[P] = R_1 R_1 R_2 R_2 + 0.5\{R_1 R_2 R_1 (1-R_2) + R_1 R_2 (1-R_1)R_2$$

$$+ R_1 R_2 (1-R_1)(1-R_2) + R_1 (1-R_2)R_1 R_2 + (1-R_1)R_2 R_1 R_2$$

$$+ (1-R_1)(1-R_2)R_1 R_2 + R_1 (1-R_2)(1-R_1)R_2$$

$$+ (1-R_1)R_2 R_1 (1-R_2)\} = R_1 \bullet R_2 + R_1 \bullet R_2 \bullet (1-R_1)(1-R_2)$$

The productivity gain by using the crossover is $\{R_1 \bullet R_2 \bullet (1-R_1)(1-R_2)\}$. For $R = 0.9$ the gain is 0.0081; for $R = 0.6$ the gain is 0.05764.

To calculate the crossover gain there is no need to calculate the whole table; it is enough to calculate only the terms that contribute to the throughput gain, and add them to a calculation performed by using Eqs (10.9) and (10.11).

10.5.3 Comparison of Assembly Systems

Automobile underbodies are assembled by welding operations. The assembly process is as follows: (1) Incoming parts are located using a fixture. (2) Clamps force two parts together; then they are welded in specified locations. (3) Once the welds have been made, the clamps are released and the part springs back.

Traditional assembly systems for automotive underbodies have been designed using serial lines. Each station in the line carries out some welds, and the part is sent to the next station where additional welds are done, and so on until completion. However, advancements in controls have allowed for the implementation of alternative system configurations. Hu and Stecke[5] conducted a thorough comparison of four assembly systems, each composed of four stations: a serial line, a system with four stations in parallel, two parallel lines (two stations in each line), and an RMS configuration (Figure 10.23). The comparison was done for (1) expected relative throughput (i.e., productivity) and (2) quality, which was defined as dimensional accuracy. For the productivity analysis, the reliabilities of the four stations were assumed to be RA = 0.95, RB = 0.90, RC = 0.93, and RD = 0.98. They found that the traditional serial assembly line has the worst performance for both productivity and quality. By contrast, the parallel configuration almost always produced a lower mean deviation than the serial line, but at the cost of higher six-sigma variation (see Figure 10.21). The numerical results of the comparison are shown in Table 10.3.

In each column in Table 10.3 we highlighted the best and second best performers. The results clearly show that serial system of four stations connected in series has by far the lowest throughput. When the four stations are in parallel, the throughput is the

TABLE 10.3   Performance of Four Configurations

System Configuration	Station Complexity	Relative Throughput	Quality	
			Mean Deviation (mm)	6 Sigma of Audited Point (mm)
Serial	Low	0.779	18.40	56.68
Parallel	High	0.940	14.40	59.97
Parallel lines	Medium	0.884	15.85	55.36
RMS configuration	Medium	0.886	14.84	55.45

highest. The RMS configuration has a slightly higher throughput than the two parallel-line configuration. In general, the greater the number of possible material flow paths a system has, the greater its throughput. For example, a serial system has only one flow path, so the system shuts down if only one machine fails. A parallel-line system offers much more redundancy than a serial system, and therefore exhibits a great increase in throughput. The RMS configuration has four flow paths and yields improved throughput.

Nevertheless, in the parallel configuration all the assembly tasks must be done at each station. When assembling a complex product, the number of tools and number of components to be assembled is large, the process becomes too complex, and typically it is impossible to ever actually reach the theoretical maximum throughput.

10.5.4 Capacity Scalability

To adapt to fluctuations in product demand, capacity must be adjusted quickly and cost-effectively. Capacity scalability is the ability to rapidly adjust the production capacity of a system in discrete steps. Even though a system will be reconfigured many times, the initial configuration has a profound effect on the system's adjustment step-size and its cost. For example, if a serial line (Fig. 10.19a) needs to increase its production capacity to satisfy market demand, an entire new line has to be added. The step-size of this addition exactly doubles the production capacity of the system. This addition will be expensive, since there is no guarantee that the extra capacity will ever be fully utilized, risking a substantial financial loss.

System scalability was defined in Chapter 6 as

System scalability $= 100-$ smallest incremental capacity in percentage

Scalability is indicated as the capacity increment by which the system can be adjusted to meet new market demand. The serial line has a minimum production capacity increment of 100% of the system; we define it as scalability $= 100 - 100 = 0\%$. The configuration in Figure 10.19c has a scalability of 50% and that of Fig. 10.19e has a scalability of 67%.

The smallest adjustment steps can be done when the original system is purely parallel (e.g., Figure 10.19f). However, the initial cost of a parallel system is the highest. In parallel configurations each machine must duplicate all operations on the product, and therefore each machine must have more tools and be able to perform more functions. As a result, the cost per additional volume increment is the highest with parallel configurations.

The configuration depicted in Fig. 10.19e (two stages; three machines per stage) might be a compromise. In this case, for example, if a product requires machining on both the upper and side surfaces, Machines 1,3, and 5 might be three-axis vertical milling machines, and Machines 2, 4, and 6 might be three-axis horizontal milling machines. Conversely, in a parallel system, all six machines in Fig. 10.19f must be five-axis milling machines—a system that is much more expensive. The drawback of the system in Fig. 10.17e is that capacity scalability must be performed in steps of 33.3% rather than steps of 16.6% as with the parallel configuration.

The steps of adding capacity in the configurations of Figures 10.19c and 10.19d are even bigger—50%. Figure 10.19b represents a case in which the steps are unequal: an additional 33.3% capacity requires three machines of type 1, 4, and 6; but the next additional increase of 16.6% requires adding only one machine of type 1, and so that increment is not expensive. This configuration might best be applied in cases where Machine 6 performs a brief but specialized operation such as laser welding.

Of course, theoretically, the manufacturer can always add one machine in parallel (a machine that does the whole part processing), to any existing configuration; making the addition an equal match for all configurations. However, this is not recommended in practice, since integration of an exceptional and complex machine into a system that does not otherwise include such machines increases the integration and maintenance costs, and may cause problems in achieving the required part quality.

To compare the six configurations in Figure 10.19, we made cost assumptions summarized in Table 10.4, where the base cost of the machines are all the same, $100,000. But because of the different number of operations required with each machine, the tool magazine capacity and the tooling cost are varied. When we add the scalability cost and its smallest possible increments into the calculation, it becomes evident that Configuration **d** is preferred. (We have not done scalability analysis for Configuration **b** because it is a special case in which the processing time on each machine at the first stage is three times larger than that in the last stage.)

The following example clarifies the option of adding small incremental capacity steps in Configuration **d** in Figure 10.19.

Example: Processing a given part requires 21 machining operations of 30 seconds each (totaling 630 seconds, or 10.5 minutes, needed to machine each part). The required demand is 274 parts per 8-hour shift (480 minutes). Therefore, the required cycle time is 1.75 minutes/part.

(a) Design a scalable system configuration.
(b) After 1 year, the demand has grown, and 320 parts per shift are needed (i.e., reducing the cycle time to 1.5 minutes/part). How many machines should be added, and what is the new configuration?

According to Eq. (10.1) six machines are needed: $274 \times 10.5/480 = 6$. Although the least expensive initial configuration is six machines in a serial transfer line, the preferred solution is the RMS configuration shown in Figure 10.24, in which each machine does seven operations (210 seconds per machine). When the demand grows

TABLE 10.4 Initial System Cost and Cost of Scalability (in $1000)

Configuration	a	b	c	d	e	f
Cost of six machines	600	600	600	600	600	600
Tooling cost per machine	5	20	20	20	25	42
Material handling cost	100	150	120	150	156	162
Total initial system cost	730	870	840	870	906	1,014

Add machines	Add Volume	Scalability Cost					
		a	b	c	d	e	f
One	16.6	–		–	145	–	169
Two	33.3	–		–	290	302	338
Three	50.0	–		420	435	–	507
Four	66.7	–		–	580	604	676
Five	83.3	–		–	725	–	845
Six	100.0	730	870	840	870	906	1,014

to 320 parts/day, according to Eq. (10.1), seven machines are needed. Only this selected RMS configuration yields the optimal solution—adding one machine to Stage 2. One operation is shifted from Stage 1 to Stage 2 (so each machine in Stage 1 operates for 180 seconds), and another operation is shifted from Stage 3 to Stage 2 (so each machine in Stage 2 operates for 270 seconds).

The initial capital investment in the RMS configuration is a bit higher than that in a serial line, but the extra investment is like buying insurance for a future event that is likely to occur. If the event does happen, the system can be easily scaled up and the new demand can be supplied at the minimum additional investment. If the demand is unchanged, a small capital investment (on a more sophisticated material handling system) was lost.

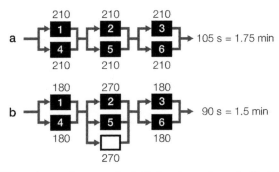

Figure 10.24 When demand grows, the initial system **a** is cost-effectively scaled up to configuration **b** to meet the new demand.

10.5.5 Selecting a System Configuration

As we have said before, in selecting the most appropriate configuration of a production system the designer has to take into account several considerations:

- Initial investment cost
- Expected throughput with reliability less than 100%
- Scalability—the increment of production capacity gained by adding one machine, or a minimum number of machines
- Quality—capability of the system in producing parts with minimal variation
- Number of product variations that the system can produce
- Floor space.

Calculating the system's expected throughput with reliability less than 100% is more tedious than just using the reliability equations. This is because the equations assume a perfectly balanced system, but in reality systems are not balanced. Let us calculate, for example, the throughput for the configuration in Figure 10.16 with machine reliability of 98%.

To have any throughput, Machines 3, 4, and 5 must operate. Only the cases that are in the table below (with Machines 3, 4, 5 up) will yield any production. Note, for example, that if Machine 1 is down, the bottleneck moves from Machine 4 to Machine 2 and the new cycle time for that stage is 3.7 minutes (and not 1.85 minutes). The throughput is the total of the right column in the table—454.8 parts per day (rather than 500 with 100% reliability). For this configuration a reduction of 2% in machine reliability caused a reduction of 9% in the system throughput.

A. Case	B. Event Probability	C. New Cycle Time	D. Throughput	B × D = Adjusted Throughput
1,2,6,7 up	0.868	2	500.0	434.1
1 or 2 up; 6 and 7 up	0.035	3.7	270.3	9.6
1 and 2 up; 6 or 7 up	0.035	3.3	303.0	10.7
1 or 2 up; 6 or 7 up	0.001	3.7	270.3	0.4

For the example in Section 10.4 the throughputs with reliabilities of 0,98, 0.95, and 0.9 were calculated, as well as the scalable throughputs, and they are given in Table 10.5.

The ranking to determine the most appropriate configuration is subjective and depends on the weight that the designer (and company) assigns to each factor (cost, scalability, etc). In our opinion, the configuration that the designer would most likely favor (Rank = 1) is the one shown in Figure 10.14B (on the right). The throughput requirement (500 parts/day) is met with machine reliability of 98%

TABLE 10.5 Comparison of Eight Configurations in the Example

Config. in Fig.	Stages m	Throughput at $R=100\%$ $N=7$ Machines	Scalability Throughput With $N=8$	With $N=9$	Throughput $R=98\%$	$R=95\%$	$R=90\%$	Cost	RANK
10.15	5	500	540	588	455	393	306	Low	7
10.14A	4	540	540	606	500	446	338	Med	6
10.14B	4	540	571	606	500	446	371	Med	5
10.14C	4	500	540	588	467	419	348	Med	8
10.13A	3	540	540	625	512	473	415	Med	2
10.13B	3	540	578	606	**511**	472	414	Med	**1**
10.13C	3	540	588	588	511	470	406	Med	4
10.12	2	540	588	705	522	497	455	High	3

Gray background = 'Best' ; light gray background = very good result compared with alternatives.

(or better). This configuration has a good scalability and reasonable investment cost.

Remember, a serial system is ranked lowest when considering scalability, convertibility and expected throughput with reliability less than 100%. These are the main reasons for not recommending serial transfer lines when demand is uncertain. The more that a system moves from serial toward parallel configuration, the better that it ranks on these three categories.[6] However, as a system moves toward parallel configurations, the system becomes more expensive. The initial cost of purely parallel systems is very high.

It has been shown in this section that the configuration of a system has a profound effect on the performance of the system, including productivity, capacity scalability, and part quality. These features also influence the life-cycle cost of the manufacturing system. This text offers the system designer analytical tools to aid in the selection of the appropriate system configuration. Although the examples given above are from the machining domain, the methodology may be applied to other manufacturing domains as well.

PROBLEMS

10.1 A manufacturing system has to produce three products daily in the quantities given in the table below. Each product requires six manufacturing tasks to be completed. The sequence of the tasks must be done in the order given in the table (i.e., task 1 then 2, then 3, etc.). We assume 1000 minutes per working day.

The manufacturing time in minutes for each task for each product is given in the following table:

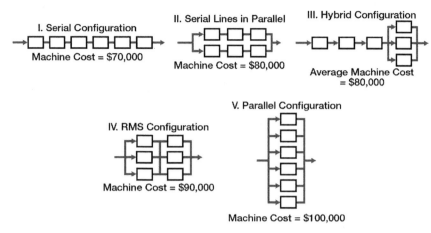

Figure 10.25 Five configurations of Problem 10.1.

Daily Quantity	Product A 200	Product B 150	Product C 150
Task #1	1.5	1.5	1.5
Task #2	1.5	1.5	1.5
Task #3	1.5	1.5	1.5
Task #4	2	1.5	2
Task #5	1	2	2
Task #6	1	1.5	2

The cost of the various machines is given in Figure 10.25. The cost of the material handling system for System I is $120,000; for systems II & III—$200,000; for systems IV & V—$250,000. Assuming that the equipment reliability is 100%, compare the five configurations in Figure 10.25 in terms of (1) investment cost (quantitative results); (2) productivity (qualitative analysis); and (3) producing three products simultaneously (qualitative analysis).

10.2 In the configuration depicted in Figure 10.26, you have to place five machines that have the following reliabilities: $I = 0.5$, $II = 0.6$, $III = 0.7$, $IV = 0.8$, and $V = 0.9$.

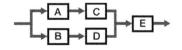

Figure 10.26 Two configurations.

(a) Calculate the expected throughput if $A = I$, $B = II$, $C = III$, $D = IV$, and $E = V$.

(b) Place the machines such that the system expected throughput is maximized (calculate it).

(c) Can you find other configurations of five machines, arranged in three stages, with higher expected throughput? What is the reason that the configuration(s) have higher throughput?

(d) Can you draw a conclusion about planning similar configurations?

10.3 In the configuration in Figure 10.23 the following machine reliabilities are given: $I = 0.5$, $II = 0.6$, $III = 0.7$, and $IV = 0.8$. Calculate the system expected throughput. Is there another placement of the machines that will increase the system throughput?

10.4 In the configuration depicted in Figure 10.23 the part is machined in two operations. In the first stage the operation takes 6 minutes per machine, and in the second stage 5.4 minutes per machine. What is the throughput of the system in parts/hour?

   What is the throughput of the system if the reliability of each machine in the first stage is 0.9, and the reliability of each machine in the second stage is 0.8?

REFERENCES

1. Y. Koren, S. J. Hu, and W. T. Weber. Impact of manufacturing system configuration on performance. *CIRP Annals*, 1998, Vol. 47, No. 1, pp. 689–698.

2. S. J. Hu. Stream of variation theory for automotive body assembly. *Annals of the CIRP*, 1997, Vol. 46/1, pp. 1–6.

3. W. T. Weber. Impact of manufacturing system configuration on performance. *D. Eng. Thesis*, University of Michigan, 1997.

4. T. Faricy. *Reliability and Maintainability*. Society of Manufacturing Engineers (SME) and the National Center for Manufacturing Sciences (NCMS), 1993.

5. S. J. Hu and K. E. Stecke. Analysis of various assembly system configurations for quality and productivity. *International Journal of Manufacturing Research*, July 2009, Vol. 4, No. 3, pp. 281–305.

6. V. Maier-Speredelozzi, Y. Koren, and S.J. Hu. Convertibility measures for manufacturing systems. *CIRP Annals*, August 2003, Vol. 52, No. 1, pp. 367–371.

Chapter **11**

Business Models for Global Manufacturing Enterprises

Globalization has created a new landscape for industry—one of fierce competition, abrupt changes in product demand, and short windows of market opportunity for new products. An important question is how a manufacturing enterprise can introduce new products in a world where competitors have equal opportunities and perhaps can offer similar products? In order to keep up sales and create economic value for one's stakeholders, an innovative industry needs a business model that takes advantage of their company's unique strategic assets. These strategic assets and unique resources should contribute something specific, either in the product, or in the manufacturing strategy, that enables the company to establish a competitive advantage. Manufacturing company must deploy **responsive business models that can rapidly align their strategic resources and supply chains to quickly respond to customer's changing needs and to new market opportunities**.

11.1 EXAMPLES OF BUSINESS MODELS

To clarify the concept of a business model, we start by studying a few well-known examples. In each of these cases the company based their model on a competitive advantage that was aimed at benefiting the customer in a specific way.

11.1.1 Dell Computers

Michael Dell created a company with the highest sales in the industry when he developed a business model that benefited consumers by delivering exactly the

The Global Manufacturing Revolution: Product-Process-Business Integration and Reconfigurable Systems
By Yoram Koren
Copyright © 2010 John Wiley & Sons, Inc.

computer that they ordered directly to their home (or office) in a very short time (about 4 or 5 days between order and delivery).

Each time a customer places an order (usually through the web) and pays for it, Dell assigns a dedicated bar code that accompanies the order until the computer is delivered. This bar code is the heart of the company's competitive advantage. Dell Computers has a complex web-based ordering and information infrastructure connected directly to Dell's assembly factories—a combination of strategic resources that creates a unique competitive advantage.

In the factory, the bar code tag is attached to a tray that travels on a component kitting line of about 10 stations. At each station a laser reads the bar code and instructs a person (or a robot) which part to select and add to the tray. At the end of the kitting line, the tray contains all the parts needed to fill the order in the sequence they go together, and the tray moves to a manual assembly station. The assembly stations are arranged in parallel, each with either one or two persons (see more details in Chapter 6).

From assembly, the computer moves to a software installation station where again the bar code is referenced for automatic software loading that fits the specific order. Software is loaded in parallel (Dell can burn up to 900 computers simultaneously; each taking about 52 minutes on average). From burn, each computer moves on to a testing area. Again, testing is done in parallel stations. The yield is 96% after final verification. Finally each computer is packed into a box. The bar code, now as a label that includes the customer's address, is attached to the box and the computer moves on a conveyor to the shipping area. The total time from kitting to shipping is about 5 hours.

The bar code system, as we see, is the heart of Dell's competitive advantage. It assists in all steps, from building the specific computer to delivering it to the right destination. Dell can also track the production history and customer experience with this single database.

Another key to Dell's competitive advantage is that it is based on product customization. Executing short response times for customer orders is critical to Dell's business strategy, which has been accomplished by its innovative use of their information system.

11.1.2 Examples of Other Business Models

To consider how business models can vary we shall now look at several additional examples from different industries below.

Caterpillar: It is the world's leading manufacturer of construction and mining equipment, diesel and natural gas engines, and industrial gas turbines. This is true despite the fact that Caterpillar's products are more expensive than those of its competitors. Caterpillar products are known to be of higher quality, and customers are willing to spend more on them. Caterpillar's competitive advantage is not only the superior quality of its products, but their comprehensive distribution network, with over 250 dealers worldwide, combined with excellent after-market service that includes high-speed delivery (within 24 hours) of spare parts anywhere in the world. In this example we see that competitive advantage can be created by a combination of otherwise mundane factors.

Personal Computers: Although Apple Computer got an early start in the microcomputer business, IBM quickly reversed Apple's lead when it threw its worldwide distribution network behind the PC. IBM's network for deploying and servicing mainframe computers was transformed into a competitive advantage as the basis of a new business strategy. The IBM distribution network and its well-regarded corporate reputation were strategic assets that provided tangible benefits that helped direct the computing culture of the time.

Cosmetic Products: They are traditionally sold in department stores, with counters and staff dedicated to each brand—one brand per counter. The manufacturer controls all marketing at the counter, including display, sales commissions, and gifts that are frequently provided with the purchase of expensive merchandise. Note that the sale of cosmetics makes up about 20% of store profits.

A New Business Model for Cosmetic Products: Sephora is a French chain of large stores that sells only cosmetic products. Sephora is experiencing a global growth surge just because of the unique way that it displays the merchandise. The products of all manufactures are arranged by category on shelves, rather than by manufacturer in separate locations in the store (see photo, taken by the author). For example, every perfume in the world is arranged alphabetically along the wall in one section of the store. Lipstick is arranged by color with hundreds of products from different manufacturers in direct proximity. This makes it very easy to compare products and prices. The consumer benefits by these direct comparisons and can buy exactly that product that best appeals to them. [Sephora.com].

Printers: They are sold at ridiculously low prices, but refill ink cartridges are very expensive. In this example the economic value to the company is not in the product, but in supplying consumables for the product. Customers benefit in this case by paying less for the product at the time of the initial purchase. This sort of marketing is traditionally referred as the "razor blade" or "cartridge" model.

Jet engines, on the other hand, are not even sold. They are leased to airlines that must sign a long-term maintenance contract with the jet engine manufacturer. The customer—the airline—benefits, since they do not have to buy an expensive product that regularly wears out and must periodically be replaced. The economic value for the manufacturer is in the ongoing contractual relationship. The manufacturer has a lock on their respective client base and the predictable cash flow that results from the maintenance contracts is constant compared to the up-and-down of direct sales. The competitive advantages for the jet engine manufacturers (there are only three in the world: United Technologies, General Electric, and Rolls Royce) are their expertise in producing jet engines and their product's reliability.

Automobiles are sold in dealerships that usually sell just one brand (Cadillac vs. Lincoln) or sometimes two, but of the same manufacturer (Buick and Chevrolet). This approach to displaying merchandise is not particularly for the benefit of the customers that have to do their shopping by traveling to many locations. This business model compares to that of traditional cosmetic products, rather than to the Sephora model.

Domino's Pizza: Domino's Pizza started with just one store in Ypsilanti (adjacent to Ann Arbor), Michigan in 1960. It was the first pizza-producing company to create a new market for fast delivery to the customer's home (30 minutes or free). Today there are more than 7000 stores, including over 2000 outside the United States, with annual sales of nearly $4 billion. It created economic value by addressing just one market need—home delivery—and made its founder a multi-billionaire. The Domino's delivery service required an infrastructure—people, vehicles, and the ability to rapidly produce pizzas—that became their competitive advantage. Of course this business model benefits the customer—the product that they expect is delivered at the right time to the place of their choice. Does the establishment of 2000 stores outside the United States indicate that this delivery model is universal?

Domino's Pizza Israel: November 27, 2003 was a bad day for Domino's Pizza Israel. On this day the Tel Aviv court declared the company's bankruptcy. Domino's Pizza started to operate in Israel in 1990. Their beginning looked very bright. The Domino's Pizza brand name was successfully penetrated into the consumer market in Israel; the company influenced the consumer's habits of home delivery and provided an excellent service. Most of its revenues came from home deliveries. So what went wrong?

There were several reasons. An economic downturn, which in 2002 also affected other similar businesses in Israel, was one cause. During that time, people started to develop a taste for frozen pizzas, for half the price of Domino's. Frozen pizzas eventually became one third of the pizza market. Another reason was the high rental fees that the company paid for stores in prime locations, even though in this type of business the store location is not important—only their telephone number. However, there was a third dominant cause, particular to Israel.

Because of suicide bomber attacks on Israeli stores during 2002, many restaurants started to offer home delivery. All of a sudden Domino's Pizza found itself in a market with thousands of local competitors. Their main strategic advantage—fast home delivery of food—was no longer unique. Domino's Pizza was slow to understand that their market had changed and did not respond to the new conditions in a timely manner. Domino's Pizza Israel needed a new business plan in order to survive, and failed to develop one.

Here are two comments written by our students on this story.

"The example of Domino's Pizza in Israel shows how loosing strategic resources can cause a company to go bankrupt. The only mistake Domino Pizza made was not responding to a change in a timely manner." Ben Kaufman.

"The lessons learned in the Domino's Pizza example follow the ideas of the responsive business model perfectly. Had Domino's had a more responsive business model, it is more likely that they could have adapted to the changes in the market." Andrew Babian.

You Can't afford to be slow . . .

11.2 BUSINESS MODEL OF MANUFACTURING COMPANIES

From this point, we will focus on business models for manufacturing companies, rather than on business models in general. As we described in Chapter 1, manufacturing companies stand on three primary foundations:

- **Design** a range of innovative products that can be customized to meet customers' needs in various world's regions with different cultures and a diverse customer's purchasing power.
- **Make** products cost-effectively by utilizing reconfigurable manufacturing systems that are adaptable to product changes and market demand fluctuations.
- **Sell** products encompassing a variety of personal features in an environment of market changes, by implementing responsive business models that can take advantage of market opportunities.

These three fundamental elements must work in harmony, and they must support each other. For example, if a company produces modular products, the manufacturing system must be designed to produce a family of modular products, and the business model should promote and support the usage of modular products by the consumers. The business model of manufacturing companies must structure their interactions among these three enablers.

Our definition of a business model is:

> **A business model is a strategic approach for creating economic value by utilizing the competitive advantage of the company for enhancing the product value to its customers.**

Customer's Benefits: Business models of enterprises should define who their customers are and explain how to create value for these customers, including how to guarantee long-term relationships with the customers. Customers can benefit from more than just products they can get at low cost, but also by products with characteristics that fit their exact need or by making it easier to select a product of their choice (e.g., Sephora's business model). Customers will also gravitate to vendors who offer first-rate after-sale service. A company that is not concerned with creating value for its customers is opportunistic; it will not exist for a long time, and absolutely will not build a brand name.

Unique product features (differentiating them from competitive products) or a lower price than competing products may create a competitive advantage for one company over another. In order to gain a competitive advantage, a company must utilize its strategic resources and assets to form the foundation of its business strategy.

Strategic Resources: They are those that are essential for the success of the enterprise. In a manufacturing enterprise these resources may be in the product, the process, the manufacturing system operations, and/or ones business assets (e.g., marketing, finance, delivery, service, and human resources).

Strategic assets within a product may include unique features or functions, a novel interface with the user, personalization qualities, aesthetic appearance, etc. The strategic resources of a manufacturing system may include plants designed for cost-effective personalized assembly, high-quality production, manufacturing strategies for high-speed responsiveness to customer's orders, and running at high productivity that reduces cost and, in turn, the product price.

There are also strategic business resources that may be developed. Examples include distributed delivery networks, efficient logistics, superior service, access to capital, buying large quantities of parts at reduced cost, and information infrastructure that links customers directly to the assembly plants (as done by Dell Computers).

The Business Strategy: It is the core of one's business model. This strategy defines the approach and methods by which a company's strategic resources can be applied to create a competitive advantage and generate economic value for a company and its stakeholders (i.e., a larger profit margin). Economic value to one's stakeholders should always be a company objective. Economic value may be also measured by the company's potential, and not only by its current revenue. For example, patents owned by the company or its pre-emptive (first mover) strategies are potential assets.

Figure 11.1 shows the interrelationship between components of the business model and their contribution to both an economic value for the company and benefits to the customers. A variety of other business models that link resources, strategy, and customer's benefit are discussed in the literature.[1] Based on the nature and uniqueness of its **strategic resources** (Section 11.4) and the market scope and segments in which

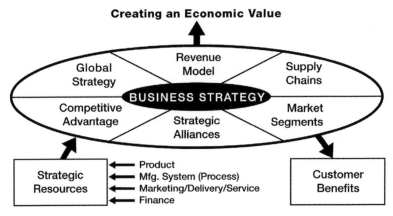

Figure 11.1 The business model flow-chart.

it plans to compete, the company creates its **competitive advantage strategy** (Section 11.3). The competitive advantage of the company must be translated into a **revenue model** that creates economic value.

The issues of **supply chains** and **strategic alliances** are discussed in Sections 11.5 and 11.6. The **Global Strategy**, which we discuss in Chapter 13, includes decision making about factory location and product regionalization. Finally, note that a business model cannot be evaluated independent of the industry type because the customers and the strategic resources depend on the industrial sector.

11.2.1 Business Strategy

The business strategy at the core defines the goal of the business model and the intended approach for achieving one's goal. The business strategy specifies how the firm's strategic resources are translated to market advantage. A successful business strategy must also focus on the value customers get from the product or service.

The business strategy should define:

1. **Market Segments**—market target and scope.
2. **Value Added**—for the customer.
3. **Competitive Advantage**—strategy to gain market advantage.
4. **Strategic Resources**—needed to achieve the competitive advantage.
5. **Revenue Model**—to create economic value as well as future growth strategies.

11.2.2 Target Market Segments

Defining one's target market and scope is the first step in articulating a business strategy. Questions that a market analysis should answer include:

- Who are our current customers, and who might be new customers for the product?
- Which customers should we NOT serve?
- What are the market segments for the product?
- What are the regions of the globe for which our products should be planned?
- What should we do better in these regions than our competitors?
- What are the demographics of the potential customers?

11.2.3 Creating Value for the Customers

Every firm must make an effort to identify ways of creating value for their customers. Because of global competition, a quality product can now be made anywhere in the world. Manufacturing high-quality products is no longer a rare skill that can by itself constitute a competitive advantage or even easily differentiate competitors' products. In a global economy, with rare exceptions (e.g., i-pod), it is hard for an enterprise to gain a competitive advantage based on the product alone. The key to success is the active involvement of the customer in product design and in accommodating the special needs of each customer. "Customers First"—is rule #1 for a successful business in a competitive market.

The challenge, however, is that customer needs are continuously evolving. As the range of available products expands, each customer, private individuals and business customers alike, demands a product that most closely fits their individual needs. Mass production of generic products does not fit today's markets. Mass-customized, regional and personalized products are rapidly taking its place. However, for personalization to succeed, direct interaction with the customers is required, starting with collecting information about their needs, and meeting their satisfaction by letting them be involved in final design of their product.

The business model should state how the customer benefits from the product. Examples include:

- **Match to Customer Expectations**—Manufacturers should evaluate how closely their product fits the customer's personal culture and intended use of the product.
- **Customer Support**—The method by which the firm actually reaches its customers, and what kind of support and service the customer is offered.
- **Pricing Structure**—The pricing method best suited to a particular customer group. An Internet provider, for example, may charge per month or only for the day that the customer uses the service. A telephone company charges for unlimited calls by the month, or per call. A jet engine may be sold, or be delivered at no cost if a long-term maintenance contract is signed.
- **Green**—Embracing green technology and offering "green" products is a new way of creating value for the customers. Companies such as General Electric and Toyota have been at the forefront of "selling green."

11.2.4 Market Opportunity—No One Here Wears Shoes

Even though they may be exposed to the same facts as competitors, manufacturers may fail to recognize a market opportunity or its growth potential. A typical story is about an Italian shoe manufacturer who sends two sales representatives to an African country. After 2 days one salesman sends a fax back to headquarters: "I'm coming back. It's a terrible market. No one here wears shoes!" An hour later a fax arrives from the other salesman: "Send me as many shoes as you can! You won't believe it but no one here wears shoes!"

The market opportunity and its potential growth that are included in a domestic and global strategy analysis should be identified first; only then should the business strategy be developed. An important factor in evaluating a market opportunity is the company's strategic resources. Not every company will have the resources (whether technical or financial) needed to pursue an attractive market opportunity. In these cases, partnership or strategic alliance with another company may be necessary.

"As an additional hindrance to enter the market," writes our student Cheng-Hung Wu, "consider government strategies related to information technology. In Taiwan, the government urges all companies to build standard data exchange systems. Through such a standard protocol, companies can communicate with their suppliers, banks, and customers through a single interface. This will increase the cost and difficulties for foreign competitors to access the market."

11.3 COMPETITIVE ADVANTAGE

An important goal of the business strategy is to define how their competitive advantage benefit's the consumer. After all, the best product in the world will not sell if the consumer does not value it. Since the late 1970s, business strategists have analyzed strategies for gaining competitive advantage. A thorough analysis of how one calculates the cost of production came first. When greater attention started to be paid to customers, strategists realized that just maintaining low-cost production was not the only strategy for gaining a competitive advantage.

Michael Porter was the first to suggest "**Differentiation**" as another major competitive strategy, in addition to cost.[2] In the manufacturing industry, differentiation means that customers are willing to pay more for a product that is different than that of competitors (e.g., the 2000 Prius in the United States). More than just product performance and novel features; manufacturing quality, quick delivery, and product service can also create a basis for differentiation. Porter proposed that companies must base their competition on either low-cost production or by differentiating their products. Since that time, other strategists have shown that these two strategies might sometimes be combined, since there are examples of companies that produce high-performance products at lower costs than their competitors.

Differentiation to the degree of product personalization is a future trend that is emphasized in this book (see Chapter 3). In our opinion, product personalization may be classified as a third distinctive strategy of manufacturing industries (rather than a sub-category of differentiation).

In summary, a competitive advantage is based on at least one of the following categories:

1. **Low-cost Leadership** (Cost and broad scope)
2. **Differentiation** (Uniqueness and broad scope)
3. **Product Personalization** (Uniqueness and narrow scope)

Each of these may constitute a competitive advantage by offering more value than a competitor's product, thereby exciting the customer.

11.3.1 Cost Leadership

Goal: Gaining a competitive advantage by delivering greater value than competitors at lower price in a broad target market

Low-cost manufacturers compete on the basis of purchase price—using the appeal of lower prices to generate more sales of their product. Cost leaders are not always selling inferior products—they only truly provide greater value to customers if they sell identical products at a lower price compared to those of their competitors. This is a good strategy when most buyers use the product in the same way and have common user requirements (e.g., refrigerators). To gain cost leadership, a firm must execute its production and distribution activities in less expensive ways than its competitors do. Low-cost leaders must attract price-conscious buyers in great numbers, and may reduce costs even further by increasing production economies of scale.

Factors that gain cost leadership for manufacturing companies include:

- Higher factory productivity
- Production volumes that achieve economies of scale
- Producing multiple product variants (models) on the same manufacturing system
- Purchasing leverage to reduce supply and sub-assembly costs
- Low-cost labor
- Specialized machines that reduce product manufacturing cost
- Higher productivity contributed by empowered workers
- Lean production technologies
- Close proximity to markets and suppliers
- The firm's experience and knowledge of the market.

Global competition is not going away, and it will continue to suppress product pricing all over the world. However, prices must keep up with costs for the company to continue to function and turn a profit. Smaller profit margins not only reduce a company's stock value, but also constrain capital investment for new products. However, if prices continue to go up, a company will eventually lose its cost leadership position.

A potential alternative is to counter increases in production cost by improving productivity, which enables maintaining product prices. Higher productivity is achieved by running machines faster; productivity can also be improved by reducing manufacturing idle times when switching over to a new product, shortening ramp-up periods for new products, implementing in-process inspection, responding quickly to customer demands, and building efficient supply chains. For this reason, implementing the methods introduced in previous chapters of this book has become critical to industry success.

11.3.2 Differentiation

Goal: Gaining a competitive advantage by delivering a product that is different from those normally available (but still at competitive prices)

Differentiation assumes that customers are willing to pay more for a product that is different from the norm. This differentiation strategy is applicable when customer preferences are too diverse to be satisfied by standard products. However, how does the manufacturer know the desired preferences and value that the variant should have? The solution depends on the customer's perspective. Therefore, utilizing differentiation as a business strategy requires thorough market research of customers' needs and what they perceive as value. Nevertheless, to be profitable, the manufacturer must be able to produce the differentiating features at a comparable cost.

The cost-cutting factors listed in the previous section apply here as well. The product price might be higher than that of competitor's, but customers must still view it as a good value. To achieve differentiation from competing general products, product features might be designed for specific world's regions such that they include qualities specific to the region or its culture. Cultural qualities may include sound, shape, texture, and language embedded in the product. This cultural differentiation can give the product a particular cultural presence so it will be acceptable by potential buyers in that region.

Product differentiation may manifest itself in various ways, as listed below:

- Product distinctiveness
  - Style and features, or attractive packages of multiple features
  - Performance and reliability
  - Interface with the user
  - Market specific to fit a certain customer base
- Service differentiation
  - Information that enables customers to make their product choice
  - Consulting to customers
  - Rapid supply of spare parts
  - Repair speed and repair cost
- Delivery differentiation
  - Distribution network for delivery
  - Speed and method of delivery
  - Logistics at point of delivery
- Image
  - Brand recognition
  - Building reputation

Differentiation is more effective when the differentiating aspects are hard to copy and expensive to provide. Otherwise, clone competitors will appear in no time. This is why sustainable differentiation has to be linked to core competencies.[3] When a company has core competencies that competitors find difficult to match or copy (Caterpillar's service infrastructure for example), then its basis for differentiation is more sustainable and lasts longer. This is especially important when the differentiation is based on new product innovation.

11.3.3 Product Personalization

The differentiation strategy works for customers who value unique features somewhat more than they value price. The ultimate differentiation is product personalization—products that are tailored exactly to each customer's needs. Ideally, since each customer has different needs, each personalized product would be different from all others—a "market-of-one" at an affordable price.

While in cost-leadership strategies the focus is on the product price, in product personalization the focus is on the customer. Because product personalization targets customers who are willing to pay more for products that fit their specific needs, the products may be sold at non-competitive prices. In fact, the uniqueness of each product makes it harder to compare prices, and thereby reduces the customers' sensitivity to prices. This can be a very profitable strategy for manufacturers who know how to produce personalized products cost-effectively and efficiently.

Product personalization requires new approaches to handling variation throughout the enterprise, from product design, through its manufacturing, to delivery and service. The product design unit must concentrate on developing modules for new personalized features that customers will be drawn to and may also perceive as status symbols, which increases their value even further.

The key to producing cost-effective personalized products is highly responsive reconfigurable assembly systems with crossovers between manufacturing stages, rather than traditional serial assembly lines. Customers must be able to place orders directly to the plants (similar to Dell's method) or through dealers that are equipped with scanning and simulation tools to enable them to visualize their personalized product in the dealer's virtual environment.

Although the scope of personalization looks very large at the outset, when it is implemented, the number of possibilities in any given product category is far from infinite, because of space, usage, and safety constraints. However, the personalization strategy reflects more than the product value that the customer gets; it also includes the perceived value by the customer. This perception is a business consideration that can increase sales.

To summarize the business benefits of personalized production, we offer below the perspective of our team.

The full scope of personalization offers far more than a new class of competitive strategy for a single manufacturer. When we were tasked with exploring how personalization might evolve, we discovered that it opens up a whole new economic sector of designing, trading, marketing, and installing personalized components. Once the basic regulations and criteria are established, several new industries will likely evolve to service a growing trend of personalizing one's own products. Beyond the OEMs and traditional supplier base we will need retail-level simulation environments, web-based trade of new and used components as well as service and installation providers to add and subtract components as fast as we can dream them up.—Rod Hill and Tonya Marion.

Table 11.1 summarizes the main differences among the three strategies.

TABLE 11.1   Comparison: Cost Leadership, Differentiation, and Product Personalization

	Cost Leadership	Differentiation	Personalization
Strategy focus	Process innovation	Product innovations	Customer's involvement in product design
Manufacturing system	Dedicated; mass-production plants	Flexible; high-mix plants	Reconfigurable and flexible; buyer-to-plant link
Production strategy	Products made to stock	Products made to order	Products designed and made to order

11.4 STRATEGIC RESOURCES

A company's strategic resources make up the competency nucleus of the business model. For manufacturing enterprises, these resources typically include core products, manufacturing strategy and operations, marketing, finance, and human resources. The strategic resources are essential for defining and creating the competitive advantage that is crucial for the success of its whole business strategy.

> The business strategy should specify how to convert the strategic resources into a competitive advantage.

11.4.1 Strategic Resources in Manufacturing Enterprises

We classify the strategic resources of a manufacturing enterprise into 10 categories. Note that it is very rare for any one enterprise to possess all ten.

1. **Unique Products**, or unique and distinctive features in a common product.
2. **Manufacturing Systems and Processes** are what the firm owns and knows about process technology, including unique process technology, specialized machinery, reconfigurable manufacturing systems, etc.

3. **Manufacturing Strategy** optimizing one's manufacturing assets to produce products and implement operations strategies that are aimed at enhancing responsiveness to change (details are given in the next section).

4. **Low-cost Labor** that yields higher than standard profit per unit of production.

5. **Strategic Assets** are things that the firm owns such as intellectual property, reconfigurable factories, supply chains, databases, reliable equipment, and information systems that link enterprise assets to each other and with customers.

6. **Purchasing Power** enabling a large company to buy supplies at volume discounts.

7. **Skills and Unique Knowledge** encompasses all enterprise's skills, knowledge, and unique capabilities, such as miniaturization, optical systems, unique R&D capabilities, knowledge in designing reconfigurable products, integrated IT, and specific knowledge particular to a market segment.

8. **Access to Working Capital** provides a line of credit that the company uses to pay salaries, buy supplies, etc. (It's a common practice in Europe for a bank to be one of the firm's owners, which enables easier access to capital.)

9. **Strategic Alliances** may be long-standing business collaborations, or the ease of forming new partnerships to complement one's core competencies to address new challenges that it cannot solve on its own.

10. **Geographic Proximity** to one's customer base (especially in supplying personalized goods) or proximity to transportation facilities for fast delivery (e.g., Dell's assembly plants in the United States are located next to airports in Tennessee and Texas; airplanes bring in parts from the Far East, and computers are quickly flown out for distribution in the United States).

Strategic resources are a necessary, but insufficient condition to gain a competitive advantage. For example, a low-labor-cost resource may be wasted if production is not managed efficiently or they lack the adequate skills to deliver the required quality.

11.4.2 Manufacturing Strategy

A company's manufacturing strategy, coupled with its production capability, is its root strategic resource. Skinner[4] described the key role that a manufacturing strategy should have in a corporate framework, and argues that frequently it is missing. The high-level enterprise's business strategy should be developed together with the manufacturing division, and should consider the following issues:

- When to manufacture and when to outsource?
- What quantity is anticipated for each product?
- Should the company rely on auctions (spot markets) for supplies, or develop long-term relationships with suppliers (as Toyota does)?

- How does the company deal with customers both in the first contact and in after-sale service?
- Where can the product be produced to minimize shipping costs, and still maintain control of strategic technology within the company?

Direction for the Manufacturing Strategy must come from the company's business strategy, as depicted in Figure 11.2. For example, if the business strategy is directed toward cost leadership, the manufacturing strategy must do whatever it can to support cost reduction. The moving assembly line manufacturing strategy of Henry Ford is an example of perfect compatibility between Ford's business strategy of cost leadership and the manufacturing strategy of cost reduction. A comparable inconsistency would be if the business unit promotes customized products and the manufacturing division continues to emphasize mass-produced, commodity-type products.

In a production environment of low volume, high mix, with high responsiveness to customer's demands, the role of a manufacturing strategy in the corporate framework is critical. The manufacturing operations must be designed to be adaptable to external factors, such as changes in market conditions and changing customer's requests.

External factors that a manufacturing strategy must consider in coping with changing external conditions, typical in globalization, may include:

- Excess global production capacity in the industry
- New product life cycles becoming shorter across the industry
- Customers demanding more customization options
- Possible mergers, alliances, and takeovers
- Interest rates and credit availability that affect demand
- Labor cost trends globally and locally
- Import/export taxes and currency fluctuations.

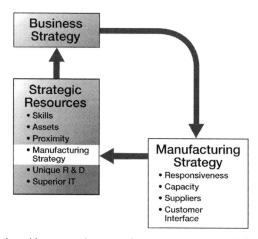

Figure 11.2 The bond between the manufacturing strategy and the business strategy.

Goals of Strategy: The manufacturing strategy needs a set of clear goals that are consistent with the business strategy. Examples of manufacturing strategic objectives are:

- Which product to produce in what factory
- How many of each product should be produced
- How responsive should one be to customers—a strategy that affects lot sizes
- Reduce manufacturing per unit cost
- How quickly to introduce new products to market
- Which factories to close in a case of excess capacity
- How much time and effort should be invested to change factory capacity?

Operations Rules: In the case of a shortage in capacity, the manufacturing strategy should determine rules for operational priority. Examples may include:

- Produce lowest cost products first
- Fill most profitable orders first
- Products that require the smallest production time
- Products with the highest profit/production-time ratio
- Products with least customization
- Produce on a first order in—first order out (FIFO) basis.

Even so, the superseding requirement of every manufacturing strategy is to be responsive to a changing environment. In the twenty-first century, manufacturing systems cannot be based solely on forecasts without concern for changes in customer markets.

Operational Responsiveness: When simultaneously producing multiple product types, a manufacturer will typically employ an optimization sequence that minimizes the time-to-completion (called the *makespan*). Minimizing makespan calls for working with large lot sizes. This operational policy assumes that customer orders will not change once production is started, and that significant disruptions will not occur. However, a customer's needs often change, even after factory operation on the customer's order has begun. We observed just such a production environment in a 1999 visit to Intel's Fab-8 in Jerusalem, which simultaneously produced 40–60 types of silicon wafers. The production makespan of a wafer takes about 6–7 weeks. During this period customers will frequently modify their order quantities; nevertheless, Intel's Fab-8 always supplied the modified ordered quantities on time.

In "lean" environments where customer orders are typically filled directly through new production rather than from inventory, minimizing makespan by operating with large lot sizes is not an optimal strategy. The reason is that producing large lot sizes of one product to minimize makespan may create a shortage for the other product that is produced on the same system. When these other products cannot be supplied at the original due date, manufacturers lose sales, and may lose their customers as well. To avoid such circumstances, we introduced in Section 7.5.2 an algorithm to determine the lot size for Minimizing Irresponsiveness to Customer's Demand.

For all these reasons, the manufacturing system needs to be designed with enough capacity to operate under strategic policies that satisfy customer requirements, even if they are unpredictable. The designed capacity should allow for adjustments in lot size, and tolerate an optimal number of switchovers between products. Having such operational flexibility is a crucial strategic resource in a market where satisfying customer requests is an obligation.

11.5 SUPPLY CHAINS

Manufacturing enterprise supply chains emerged from the trend toward outsourcing in the 1990s. Gone were the days when Henry Ford built his Rouge complex where raw materials such as iron ore, sand, and rubber arrived in bulk and left as finished cars including windshields and tires. Companies now buy components that are not essential to their core business (e.g., steering wheel assemblies or brake pads for cars). The motivation for outsourcers is to reduce capital expenditures and operating cost by focusing on the company's core competencies. The process has evolved so that, instead of just outsourcing single parts, companies now purchase entire modules or sub-assembly (e.g., the entire instrument panels, including audio, air bags, and AC control). A Nissan's truck assembly plant in Canton, Mississippi, for example, receives fully assembled vehicle modules, such as complete axles, front ends, cockpits, exhaust systems, and wheel systems from nearby outside suppliers.[5]

At the same time, the suppliers of these modules depend on another tier of suppliers for the components that make up their modules, and so on. This has resulted in the formation of complex interdependent supply chains of several tiers of suppliers, each supplying parts and components to the next link in the chain. The two critical issues with multi-tier suppliers have always been (1) on-time delivery and (2) controlling the quality of the final product.

11.5.1 Structure and Integration of Supply Chains

A manufacturing supply chain is a network of part makers and sub-assembly producers who coordinate their activities to provide modules to their clients at the right time and in the right quantities all the way up to the final assembly. Supply-chain management requires the coordinated supervision and flow of demand requests from the client company to the suppliers, and delivery of parts and modules back up the chain to the final assembly plant. Effective management of supply chains is critical to the profit of all the companies involved and must be integrated into the manufacturing enterprise business model.

A typical supply chain has several tiers, as diagrammed in Figure 11.3. Each tier must be synchronized into a just-in-time coordination. To ensure this, suppliers use buffers to hold quantities of both incoming parts and outgoing sub-assembly products. With globalization and the unrelenting pressure to reduce cost, second- and third-tier suppliers may be in remote regions of the globe, where labor cost is cheapest. With such global sourcing comes extreme complexity, and consequently critical delays are always possible. Minimizing these delays requires large inventories in buffers, and these in themselves involve considerable cost.

Figure 11.3 shows a simple supply chain for just one final product. Actual supply chain networks are typically far more complex, since lower-tier suppliers may ship parts to the final assembly plants of several manufacturers, even competitors. The challenge for an effective supply chain is in accurately transferring the demand information backwards from the OEM (original equipment manufacturer) through each supplier in the chain, and then responding by transferring parts forward, through the various tiers, to the final assembly plant. The key to success is in accurately transferring both demand (information) and supply (parts) along every tier of the chain, while minimizing overall inventory.

Dell Computers matches supply-to-demand quite efficiently. The success of Dell lies in the effective design of its entire supply chain. The main Dell factory in Nashville has only a 2-hour inventory (observed on our visit in 2004), and timely availability of parts is essential. With such small inventories available, Dell's supply chain must be coordinated and precisely synchronized to meet the end demand (i.e., the customer's personal order).

Dell has two assembly plants in the United States, Nashville, Tennessee, and Austin, Texas. Many parts are common to both plants, but some are unique. On top of it, the end demand is usually stochastic in nature—Dell does not know exactly how many computers and of which type they will need to manufacture at any given time. However, every day, Dell's U.S. management team has to decide how many components to import from Taiwan and China. This adds considerable complexity to the Dell supply chain.

In 2006, General Motors had about 30 vehicle assembly plants in the United States, and Ford had 15. Many components are common to several plants, but many parts and

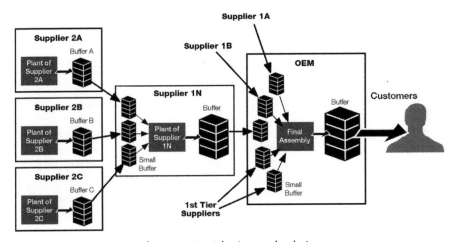

Figure 11.3   A basic supply chain.

all sub-assembly units (e.g., the front instrument panel, which arrives in as a complete unit) are unique to a single plant, although their elements might appear in a number of sub-assemblies throughout the system. Imagine the complexity of a comprehensive GM or Ford supply chain structure.

Synchronizing a supply chain to the ultimate degree is not a simple task. Global sources and supply chains are often not well integrated, and coordination among suppliers is frequently difficult. Constantly vigilant coordination is needed in order to ensure short delivery times and manageable inventories. Transporting parts from a large inventory to the next customer in the chain may reduce delivery time, but, in turn, it increases cost because of inventory holding costs. The more complex the product, more parts are needed, and the total inventory held in the whole supply chain can be enormous.

The right balance between minimizing inventory costs and avoiding delivery delays is essential in supply-chain optimization, especially in industries that serve stochastic, uncertain customer demand. To reduce their costs, suppliers at each tier try to reduce their inventories, both of incoming parts and of those products or sub-assembly that they deliver. However, keep in mind that smaller inventories may cause disruptions in the just-in-time delivery process.

The longer they get, the competing goals of reducing delivery times and decreasing costs make the supply chain process very complex. Sometimes it only takes one link in the supply chain to be out of sync with the just-in-time process, and the entire chain's efficiency is reduced. It is nearly inevitable that customer orders will be delayed from time to time.

There are cases where manufacturing companies have failed to meet the expected performance and results from using supply chains. The main reasons for low performance are:

- **Inventory Levels** at various links of the supply chain; reduced inventory levels save cost, but can increase the impact of supply disruptions in cases of demand surge.
- **Miscalculating** the total delivery costs through the entire supply chain.
- **Low-quality Parts** produced even by just one sub-tier supplier somewhere in the chain reduce the quality of the final product. (One bad part produced by a second-tier supplier for the gas pedal assembly of Toyota cars caused a recall of several million vehicles in January 2010.)
- **Slow Reaction** of the supply chain to market and product changes.
- **Inventory Obsolescence** resulting from unexpected changes in markets and products.

11.5.2 Economic Order Quantity

One of the oldest production scheduling models is called the Economic Order Quantity (EOQ). It represents the level of inventory required to minimize the total of inventory holding cost and ordering cost, and was originally developed by F. W. Harris[6]. Later, R. H. Wilson conducted in-depth analysis of the model.[7] We will use the EOQ to determine the optimal shipping quantity (Q^*) of sub-assembly parts (e.g., car doors or instrument panels) to the final assembly location. This model assumes that the rate of demand is a constant and known (i.e., deterministic). The notation is

- Q = order quantity
- D = daily demand quantity of the part
- P = cost per part
- H = daily holding cost per part (e.g., warehouse space, insurance, etc.)
- C = fixed cost per order (e.g., the cost of a truck carrying the parts, traveling from the sub-assembly location to the final assembly plant)

The total cost per day is

$$\textit{Total cost } (\textbf{\textit{TC}}) = \textbf{\textit{cost of all parts per day}} + \textbf{\textit{shipping daily cost}}$$
$$+ \textbf{\textit{holding daily cost}}$$

where:

Cost of all parts per day = part cost × daily demand quantity, $P \times D$.

Shipping cost is the cost of transportation between locations. The assembly plant has to order D/Q times per day, and each order carries a fixed cost C. The daily cost is $C \times D/Q$.

Holding cost is a cost proportional to the amount of inventory. Since the rate of demand is constant, it is the average quantity in stock between maximum filled stock and empty stock, which is $Q/2$, so the handling cost is $H \times Q/2$. The total cost per day is

$$TC = PD + \frac{CD}{Q} + \frac{HQ}{2}$$

To determine the minimum cost, we set the cost derivative equal to zero:

$$\frac{dTC(Q)}{dQ} = \frac{d}{dQ}\left(PD + \frac{CD}{Q} + \frac{HQ}{2}\right) = 0$$

The result of this derivation is:

$$-\frac{CD}{Q^2} + \frac{H}{2} = 0$$

Solving for Q yields the optimal order quantity Q^*

$$Q^* = \sqrt{\frac{2CD}{H}}$$

Example: A retailer buys a product from a supplier at a cost of $5 per unit. The customer demand for the product is at a constant rate of 100 units per week. The estimated unit holding cost for the retailer is $4 per week. A trucking company delivers the ordered products from the supplier to the retailer and charges $200 per delivery, no matter what the order quantity, Q, is. Determine the optimal order quantity that the retailer should choose in order to minimize the total cost per week (assuming zero delivery lead time). For this order quantity, what is the holding cost and shipping cost per week?

The EOQ model yields

$$Q^* = \text{EOQ} = \sqrt{\frac{2CD}{H}} = \sqrt{\frac{2 \cdot 200 \cdot 100}{4}} = 100 \text{ units}$$

Namely, the retailer should place an order of 100 units, as depicted in Figure 11.4. Note that the graph is not symmetric around the optimal quantity of 100 units.

For $Q = 100$, the holding cost per week is $h\frac{Q^*}{2} = 200$ and the shipping cost is $\frac{C \cdot D}{Q^*} = 200$.

11.5.3 Delayed Differentiation

Global supply chains are often designed with delayed differentiation to better manage a broader variety of products. The common modules of a product (e.g., a computer mother board), or semi-finished products, are assembled in low-labor-cost countries, and shipped to the countries where the final assembly is done and the product is sold. Since the common modules can be included into several final products, the manufacturer can delay the final assembly operation until customer orders are actually placed. The principle of this delayed differentiation strategy is

Make-modules-to-stock and assemble-products-to-order

Figure 11.4 The total cost as function of the ordered quantity.

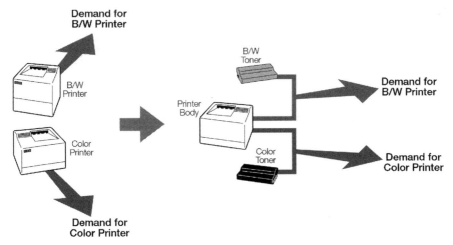

Figure 11.5 Modular design.

Supply chains that include a delayed differentiation strategy save tremendous inventory costs in environments where customer product demand is stochastic. This strategy helps to manage the complexity of adding varieties of products. A simple example is a printer manufacturer who produces two types of printers in its production center in China—a mono (B&W) printer and a color printer. Without delayed differentiation, the company ships both types to its warehouse in the United States. The warehouse must maintain inventory of both printers to meet the product stochastic demand.

With the delayed differentiation strategy, the printer is designed so that the product is decomposed into two components with a common interface: a standard printer body, and a toner module (which can be either for B&W or color toner), as shown in Figure 11.5. Due to the short time it takes to assemble the printer and toner, the warehouse can now keep an inventory of just one common printer body and two different toner modules, and does not assemble these into a final printer until the actual customer order comes in. Since the inventory cost of toners is much lower than that of printer bodies, the total inventory cost is substantially reduced only by delaying the point at which final assembly is completed.

11.5.4 Bullwhip Effect[*]

Typical supply chains consist of several tiers of retailer, wholesaler, and manufacturer. Also, in virtually all industries, consumer demand exhibits some level of randomness. To be able to meet such a demand, every echelon (or level) of the supply chain holds inventories and follows various strategies of order replenishment to maintain the appropriate levels of inventory. Even a moderate fluctuation of demand at the retail level can propagate into a very high variability effect for the manufacturer. This

---

[*]Dr. O. Ceryan wrote the section on Bullwhip Effect.

phenomenon was first noticed by P&G executives who were surprised to observe that diaper orders placed by distributors had much more variation than sales at the retailer stores (level 2). They coined the term "Bullwhip Effect."[8]

Figure 11.6 demonstrates how demand variability may increase as we move from the end consumer sales (level 1) toward the higher echelons of a supply chain: the retailer (level 2), the wholesaler (level 3), and finally to the manufacturer. While the demand from consumer sales is relatively stable with a fluctuation of approximately ± 2 units over time, the retailer's orders to the wholesaler indicate a variance of ± 3 units. As we move further down the supply chain, we observe that manufacturer's orders exhibit a variance of ± 7 units over time.

There are four main causes for the bullwhip effect.

1. **Demand Forecast Updating:** Forecasting is a process of periodic review and response to signals from current demand statistics. When a period's demand is low, a retailer may lower its forecast for the next period. Similarly, if demand increases it can lead to an upward adjustment for next period's forecast. This process, subject to the lead times required for replenishment, increases variability from demand that is observed by the higher echelons of the supply chain.

2. **Order Batching:** In order to reduce various fixed costs associated with order placement, many firms may choose to aggregate the orders into batches. This economically justified behavior often leads to placing bulk orders out of sync with actual demand, and some periods where no orders are placed at all.

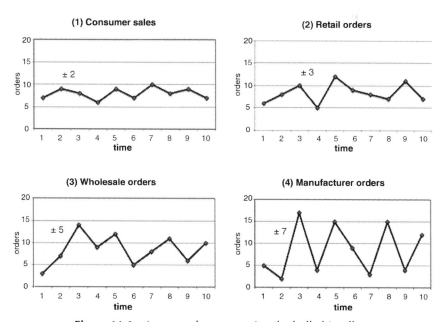

Figure 11.6 An example representing the bullwhip effect.

3. **Price Fluctuations:** Price discounts and special promotions can distort true customer demand in those periods. This can give retailers the incentive for stocking large quantities of inventory in promotional periods. However, when these discounts expire, consumer demand often rebounds below average creating greater variability.

4. **Shortage Gaming:** When demand exceeds supply, manufacturers may ration inventory, leading the consumers to anticipate future shortages and exaggerate their orders out of proportion with their actual demand. Eventually when a shortage subsides, it can lead to order cancellations by the consumer and therefore intensifies variability in the demand process.

Information plays an important role in suppressing the bullwhip effect when establishing supply chains. At least two strategies have been suggested to mitigate the bullwhip effect.

1. **Information Sharing:** Sharing point-of-sale (POS) data through technologies such as electronic data interchange reduces the cost of placing orders and leads to more frequent orders. Using third-party logistic companies, or shipping an assortment of products in a truckload, also lowers the shipping costs associated with frequent order deliveries.

2. **Vendor Managed Inventory:** Centralizing the ordering process for several echelons provides the efficiencies of a single shorter supply chain. An example is where a manufacturer becomes responsible for replenishment of its own products at a customer's retail store, (e.g., P&G is responsible for replenishment of its products that are sold at Wal-Mart).

11.6   RESPONSIVE BUSINESS MODELS FOR GLOBAL OPPORTUNITIES

The manufacturing industry is in an era of turbulence caused by globalization. A responsive business model is one that can quickly adapt to the challenges posed by a market environment dominated by change and uncertainty.

11.6.1   Global Competition Causes Turbulent Markets

The need for responsive business models is driven by a number of recent changes in the global business environment, which include:

- **Global Competition**—Companies in many countries can produce similar products, sometimes cheaper, sometimes better; customers can buy products everywhere.
- **Corporations Become International**—Producing and selling in many countries.
- **Quick Financial Transactions**—Money is transferred by electronic systems.

- **Rapidly Changing Customer Needs**—A global supply higher than demand creates a buyer's market where customers change their preferences at a rapid pace.
- **Increased Customer Purchasing Power**—Globalization has increased customer salaries in developing countries who now can afford to buy almost any product, thereby forcing corporations to introduce products at a higher frequency.
- **Technology Innovations** have led to fierce competition in new product development as well as in implementing advanced manufacturing systems to produce these products.
- **Environmental Regulations** drive "green" products as well as "greener" manufacturing systems and processes.
- **Investment in Production Systems has Decreased** due to the lower cost of high-quality machines, thereby enabling building factories in more countries.
- **Information Technology** and worldwide information networks make communication and information instantaneously and universally accessible.
- **New Design Tools**, especially computer applications, enable the design of new products faster and more efficiently, and it can be done by engineers around the world.
- **Education** in many countries has advanced considerably, globally creating a much larger skilled workforce.

11.6.2 Semiconductor Fabrication

The semiconductor fabrication business is in a turbulence state in the current global environment. Because of the frequent introduction of new technologies and abrupt changes in the number of components used in each end-user product, the semiconductor market is characterized by extreme instability and large fluctuations in demand.

Therefore, semiconductor manufacturers have increasingly shifted away from the traditional business model of carrying out the entire production process in-house aiming toward an outsourcing-based model. Under this new business model, certain parts of the production process are outsourced to silicon foundries and assembly sub-contractors located mainly in Asia. To a certain extent, by shifting to such a production system, semiconductor manufacturers are passing on some of the cyclical business risk associated with market fluctuations to these foundries and sub-contractors.

These sub-contractors have responded by adopting manufacturing equipment that is more reconfigurable and that can respond to fluctuations in the semiconductor market. For example, the semiconductor industry traditionally uses diamond blades to cut the wafers. However, recently the sub-contractor industry started to use laser-cutting technology that can be integrated more cost-effectively into reconfigurable sawing equipment. Laser cutting also has the advantage that it can saw hard materials that are difficult to cut with diamond cutting tools. A reconfigurable laser-based sawing machine can cut both hard and softer wafer materials.

11.6.3 Enterprise Reconfigurability

Enterprise reconfigurability is the ability of an organization to change and adjust itself **internally** and **externally** to accommodate rapid changes in the business world. The driving forces for creating a reconfigurable enterprise are rapidly changing worldwide market opportunities and rapidly changing customers' needs and preferences in various regions on the globe.

At the internal level, the reconfigurable enterprise requires a new organizational structure with a more entrepreneurial team culture and empowerment of the workforce. It also requires communication with customers and better cooperation with suppliers.

At the external level, reconfigurability means the ability of an enterprise to form **strategic alliances** with other organizations in order to gain a competitive advantage. The rationale behind the creation of strategic alliances is that because enterprises cannot change their own core competencies fast enough to take advantage of new market opportunities, they should establish alliances to enhance their competitive edge. Strategic alliances improve an enterprise's ability to reconfigure, and accelerate their responsiveness.

11.6.4 Characteristics of Reconfigurable Business Models

To enable organizations to rapidly create strategic alliances with other organizations, and dissolve them quickly when the partnership is no longer needed, is a challenge that requires the formation of organization-wide reconfigurable business models. With the reconfigurable business model, allied companies can quickly combine resources to share core competency and respond to new market opportunities, as depicted in Figure 11.7.

When new market opportunities emerge and a new core competency is needed, a new strategic alliance might have to be formed. The reconfigurable business model

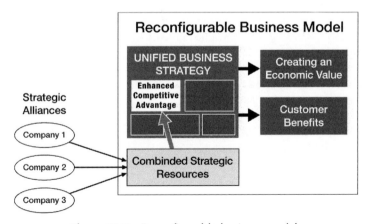

Figure 11.7 Reconfigurable business model.

enables enterprises to focus on new market opportunities more than on the protection of their narrow business turf. However, making decisions about market opportunities is not simple in the case of alliances, because the power to make the decision lies in the hands of several companies rather than those of a single enterprise. Each member company in the alliance evaluates the risk differently including the potential benefits and estimated costs.

For strategic business alliances to be established and dissolved quickly, they should be based on reconfigurable business models that possess the following core characteristics:

Customizable	The alliance structure is customized to make use of a specific core competency to produce a new line of products
Convertible	The alliance's ability to change its mission and convert resources to implement the new mission
Scalable	The alliance's ability to add new companies in response to market changes and mission changes
Modular	A unique strategic resource (a module) that can be integrated into the alliance's current activity
Integratable	The ability to rapidly combine the resources of several firms in the alliance, and use their synergy to compete successfully

11.7 PRODUCT LIFE CYCLE BUSINESS MODEL

The entire product life cycle starts with its conception and design, proceeds through its manufacturing, assembly, sale, and delivery, continues with its use and maintenance, and finally its end-of-life (EOL) stages of disassembly and reuse, recycling, or disposal. To respond to environmental concerns of globalization and reduce the impact of old products at their EOL on the environment, European regulations require recycling of most products, even automobiles. The European end-of-life Vehicles (ELV) Directive, enacted in October 2000, defines new standards for car recycling.[9] It states that manufacturers are responsible for their vehicles from cradle to grave.

About 8 million vehicles are recycled annually in the 15 countries of the European Union (2004 data). However, as a result of the ELV Directive, the actual waste from those ELV vehicles accounts only for about 1% of total waste across the EU member states. This is due to the fact that parts are reused and a high percentage of the materials are recycled or recovered. The reuse and recovery rate of 85% enforced as of January 2006 seems realistic.[10]

These European regulations have a major impact on product design, and they have triggered the search for new business models for automotive companies. Product design must cope with environmental requirements from materials selection to final disassembly for recycling. The intention is to design products with reduced environmental impacts over their entire life cycle, including their disposal and recycling.

The automotive sector is seeking greater revenue vitality in this new business model, and at the same time greater customer satisfaction. One model that aims at achieving these goals is in **Selling Services** rather than selling products.[11] This business model is an expansion of the jet engine service business model or that of vehicle leasing, but it has important consequences on reducing the amount of component produced and disposed.

Selling services rather than products calls for the reuse of **used** components in **new** products along with providing extended maintenance contract. It also implies shorter time between the introduction of new advanced (luxury) product models (extending the life span of the product components) as well as the manufacturing of a smaller number of new components (which supports environmental considerations).

An example of just such a business-engineering reuse model is depicted in Figure 11.8. Let us assume that a car manufacturer has two models that share the same platform, but market segmentation and brand names enable the manufacturer to introduce two models: luxury and standard (e.g., Volkswagen has two super-mini models: the luxury Audi A2 and their standard Polo).

When the luxury product has been used for a while and its performance has deteriorated, and at the same time a new similar product offering better performance is introduced, the customer may wish to change the car. The customer's old car, if not sold to another customer, enters the EOL phase. The business-engineering model in Figure 11.8 shows that in this phase, the product is disassembled, its parts and components that cannot be reused are disposed of, but the other used components are inspected, cleaned for reuse, and assembled into a new standard vehicle.

That is well and good, but would you agree to have used components installed your new car? Probably not! Nevertheless, if the car is on a lease and the manufacturer owns it and guarantees its performance and service, you might agree assuming that the leasing fee is reasonable. In this business model, the cars that customers drive are the property of the manufacturer or leaseholder that sells the service rather than product.[12] In this model, the product design, its manufacturing, assembly, and the business operation are modules that are integrated into a coherent, environmentally friendly enterprise that makes its money providing a service. This comprehensive model is a

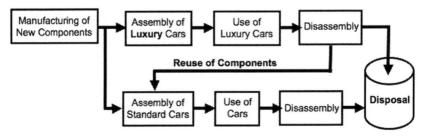

Figure 11.8   Reuse of old components in less expensive products reduces disposal.

good example of the design-manufacturing-business integration that this book advocates (see for example Figure 1.9).

The automotive service-selling business model is not new. It is already being implemented in photocopiers and high-quality printers, where customers pay for photocopying and printing services at their facilities but they do not actually buy the machines.

PROBLEMS

11.1 Can the Sephora model (discussed in Section 11.1) be applied to automobile sales? Does the customer benefit if new automobiles of the same type, but from different manufacturers (e.g., all SUVs, or luxury cars, or light trucks), are sold at one dealership at one location? Is it beneficial to the manufacturer? Is it possible in this directly challenging business model that people determined to buy a certain nameplate will change their mind when shopping in such dealerships?

11.2 For more than a decade, from the late 1980s, Apple's Macintosh computers had an operating system that was much superior to Microsoft's operating system. Still, Apple sales declined, and Microsoft's profits were boosted. What do you think went wrong in Apple's business model?

11.3 A manufacturer has a shortage in its manufacturing capacity (Section 11.4.2). Their forecasting says that the shortage will last for 1 month. The manufacturer produces 200 units per day. Should the manufacturer use the rule "Produce the products with the fewest customization requests first?" Is it a good, long-term strategy?

11.4 A product is composed of five modules provided by five Tier-1 suppliers in a supply chain that has two tiers (Figure 11.9). Each of the first-tier suppliers has 10 second-tier suppliers, where each supplies one part (even though only three suppliers are shown in the drawing). Every supplier in the chain has buffers for

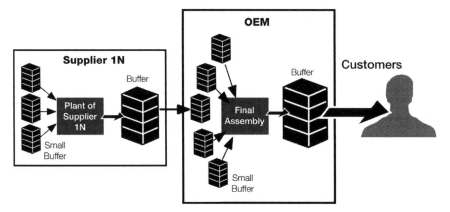

Figure 11.9 The supply chain in Problems 11.4 and 11.5.

inventories (the second-tier suppliers do not have incoming buffers). Each buffer may hold an inventory of up to 100 parts or modules.

If each part that is delivered by the second-tier suppliers costs $10, and each supplier charges for labor and profit 100%, what is the maximum value of all parts and modules held in the buffers of the entire supply chain?

11.5   For the final assembly of their product, an OEM receives parts from five suppliers, as depicted in Figure 11.9. Calculate the optimal order quantity (Q) for the parts shipped by Supplier A and Supplier B. Because of packing constraints, Supplier A can ship quantities in batches of 50s (namely 50, 100, 150, 200, etc.). Supplier B directs its parts to a buffer, which fills gradually at a constant rate. For storing the parts in this buffer the OEM pays holding costs. The cost of each part is $200.

Given:

- $Da = 100$ daily demand quantity of part A
- $Db = 500$ daily demand quantity of part B
- $Ca = \$1480$ cost per order (the cost of a truck carrying the parts from the supplier to the OEM)
- $Cb = \$1000$ cost per order (the cost of a truck carrying the parts from the supplier to the OEM)
- $Ha = \$10$ daily holding cost per part A at the OEM site
- $Hb1 = \$6$ daily holding cost per part B at the OEM site
- $Hb2 = \$4$ daily holding cost per part B at the supplier site

11.6   Read CASE STUDY I—"The Rise and Fail of FriendlyRobotics" and answer the questions at its end.

11.7   Read CASE STUDY II—"He Bet on Botox and Won" and answer the questions at its end.

CASE STUDY I—THE RISE AND FAIL OF FRIENDLYROBOTICS

By Yoram Koren (November 2002)

Abstract

FriendlyRobotics (FR) was an Israeli start-up company, formed in 1995 and worth $120M at its peak, which invented a lawn mower robot that is shown in Figure 11.10. *Time* magazine selected its lawn mower robot as one of the 10 innovative products of the decade. In November 2002, it was sold to the vacuum cleaner company, Hoover, for about a tenth of its former value ($1.5M), before its complete collapse. FR had run out of money to pay the salaries of its employees. How did its promise become such a marketing failure?

The Product: The product concept was that instead of using a hand-driven lawn mower, you turn on your mowing robot and watch it do the work for you. The mowing robot was equipped with sensors to avoid obstacles and a sophisticated navigation system. The robot first scanned the lawn area and self-programmed its path to be

Figure 11.10 The FriendlyRobotics lawn mower robot.

optimal while avoiding obstacles. (The FR product was reviewed by *Consumer Reports* in the late 1990s. Photo—the author tests the FR robot.)

The Strategy

The company's strategy was to develop an automatic lawn mower machine and then sell it to a large U.S., or European company, which would do the marketing and delivery. Venture capital funds invested in FR grew to $30 million. The estimated market for the product is 110 million households in the Western world. The product cost was initially $1000 and dropped later to $600 (as sales declined).

In 2000, FR announced that it signed an agreement with Toro, the largest lawn mower producer in the United States. According to the press, Toro was committed to purchase 100,000 FR mowers within 5 years. The expectations were skyrocketing. FR built large warehouses in the United States, which was a big investment for the company, and it took a loan of $5.5 million from the International Bank. The bank did not hesitate—the contract with Toro was convincing. Nobody paid attention to a small detail in the contract: "The only sanction that Toro will suffer, if it does not fulfill its commitment to purchase and sell 100,000 machines, it would lose its status as a sole distributor."

Toro tried to sell the product through Home Depot, and other store chains, but failed to sell a reasonable number of products. Cindy Love, the U.S. FR president was proud of the fact that FR had been exposed over 70 times on U.S. television—from morning shows to science news. She was confident that the product was "sexy" enough to put on the shelves and that people would buy it. However, that did not happen.

The Drawbacks

The FR mower was more technologically advanced than most consumer products. Its operation was not simple and required considerable knowledge and explanation. The sales clerks of Home Depot were not trained properly and did not have the knowledge or the motivation to learn how to operate this relatively complex product.

In addition, the expectation that pressing a button and the machine will do the work for you was not realistic. The user had to encircle the lawn area with a buried electric cable, which was inserted into the ground to define the lawn's boundaries for the robot. Furthermore, if the robot stopped for some reason, the user had to manually move the 70 lb machine by hand. In addition, the machine's battery had to be charged year-round, even when the robot was not in use. Finally, the robot worked only on flat surfaces and could not negotiate stairs or uneven ground.

Assignment: Analyze the Reasons for the Failure of FriendlyRobotics

In your analysis elaborate on the following points:

- Was this product viable?
- Was its price reasonable?
- Is having a "sexy" product enough to enhance its sales?
- Was the marketing/advertisement method through television shows adequate?
- How would you suggest educating the consumer about this product?
- Was the investment in large storehouses and inventory timely and justified?
- What were the strategic resources of FR?
- If you were the CEO of the company, what would your first steps be in selling this product?

CASE STUDY II—HE BET ON BOTOX AND WON

Based on a story in Business Week (October 13, 2003, pp. 127/128)

David Pyott, Allergan Inc., CEO, has a nearly smooth face and really does not need an injection of his company's wrinkle-erasing drug, Botox. Nevertheless, Pyott underwent a Botox treatment in 2002 to demonstrate that he had no fear of applying it. (Note that Botox is derived from the same paralyzing toxin that causes botulism poisoning.)

Allergan originally purchased Botox in 1991 from an ophthalmologist who was developing it to treat rare muscular disorders such as uncontrollable eye-blinking. Doctors who prescribed Botox had reported its surprising power to erase wrinkles.

However, Allergan was spending virtually nothing to develop the drug for cosmetic use, and Botox was actually ignored by Pyott's predecessor. Before he took the CEO position in 1998, Pyott knew very little about Botox. However, it was Pyott, nonetheless, who decided to put money behind Botox to see what it could do. So in 1999, he boosted spending on research and development 38%, to $135 million— much of it devoted to developing Botox.

Botox, of course, has become a sensation—especially in Hollywood. The word "Botox" was recently added to the Oxford English Dictionary. Pyott's lack of pharmaceutical experience made him an odd choice for Allergan, but his take-charge style captivated the board. Pyott believes Botox can do more than just take a few years off your face. Allergan is testing Botox as a remedy for a host of diseases, including glaucoma, psoriasis, migraines, overactive bladder, chronic back pain, and excessive sweating. Many physicians agree that the ability of Botox to block nerve activity in the areas where it is injected could someday make it a cure-all.

However, the federal government is already concerned that Allergan may be pushing Botox a bit too hard. On June 23, 2003, the FDA warned Allergan that its print ads made overly broad claims about the drug's ability to reduce wrinkles and downplayed potential side effects, which include droopy eyelids, nausea, and respiratory infections.

Assignment: Discuss the Following Issues:

1. In 1999, David Pyott shed off slow-growing products such as a contact-lens solution, and boosted spending on research and development of Botox by 38%.
   - What did he risk by investing all his R&D in a new product rather than in a stable product?
   - Is it a good business strategy to concentrate the R&D efforts of a firm on a single product while reducing the investment in the other firm's products?
2. What are the reasons for the success of the product?
3. Is David Pyott a good a strategic thinker?

REFERENCES

1. G. Hamel. *Leading the Revolution*. Harvard Business School Press, 2000.
2. M. Porter. *Competitive Advantage*. New York Free Press, 1985.
3. A. A. Thomson and A.J. Strickland III. *Strategic Management*. McGraw Hill, 2003, p. 164.
4. W. Skinner. Manufacturing—missing link in corporate strategy. *Harvard Business Review*, May–June 1969.
5. L. Chappell. Nissan's solution: modules. *Automotive News*, March 5, 2001.
6. F.W. Harris. How many parts to make at once. *Factory, The Magazine of Management*, 1913, Vol. 10, No. 2, pp. 135–136, 152.

7. R. H. Wilson. A scientific routine for stock control. *Harvard Business Review*, 1934, Vol. 13, pp. 116–128.

8. H. L. Lee, V. Padmanabhan, and S. Whang. The bullwhip effect in supply chains. *MIT Sloan Management Review*. Reprint 3837, Spring 1997, Vol. 38, No. 3, pp. 93–102.

9. European Union Integrated Pollution Prevention and Control (IPPC), EU, December 2001.

10. European Automobile Manufacturers Association (*http://www.acea.be*).

11. A. Franke and G. Seliger. A new paradigm of manufacturing: selling services instead of products. *Proceedings of 2002 Japan Symposium on Flexible Automation*, Hiroshima, Japan, 2002.

12. M. Shpitalni. Impact of life cycle approach and selling of services on product design. *Proceedings of the Manufacturing 2004 Conference*, Poznan, Poland, 2004.

Chapter 12

IT-Based Enterprise Organizational Structure

It is no wonder that industry, especially manufacturing industry, and the military have quite similar organizational structures. Both of these enterprises represent a considerable investment of money, material, and human resources. Like the military, manufacturing enterprises involve complex webs of organization, including operations, logistics, development, and leadership. For both, leadership is the glue that cements the organization together and makes it effective, or not. In this chapter, we will explore how military command and industrial organization have informed and inspired each other, and how their roles and approaches have evolved to suit changing needs and opportunities both on the battlefield and in the marketplace.

During the 12 years between the First Gulf War in 1991 and the subsequent war in Iraq in 2003, the modern military went through dramatic changes. In both wars the Army's central command developed war plans that were explained to the division commanders. Each division commander gave the instructions to their brigades. From the brigades, instructions were sent down to the battalions, then to the companies within the battalions, and finally to the troops and equipment in the field.

But there was a big difference between 1991 and 2003. In 1991 all the instructions went top-down as commands. In 2003 only the strategic-level instructions describing the overall goals went top-down, and the soldiers in the field were given the authority to make real-time tactical decisions in the battle, as it proceeded. During this 12-year period tanks were equipped with modern technology to fit new battleground conditions. For instance, each tank was equipped with new sensors, such as a global positioning system (GPS), and a digital map of the area on which the exact position of

The Global Manufacturing Revolution: Product-Process-Business Integration and Reconfigurable Systems
By Yoram Koren
Copyright © 2010 John Wiley & Sons, Inc.

each tank or vehicle in the area was clearly marked, even as they moved during battle. Based on this information, tank commanders had as good or better battlefield information than the brigade headquarters, and more importantly, they were empowered to make instantaneous decisions.

The tank commander's decisions were sent to his counterpart tanks and to other units in the area, as well as to the battalion commander, who filtered and organized the essential information and sent it up to the brigade commander. The brigade commander accumulated the information sent from the battalions, processed it, and sent it up to the division headquarters. As a result of this bottom-up information transfer the division commander got a much more accurate picture of the battlefield and could coordinate the overall operations and make intelligent strategic decisions.

The sensor-based knowledge of the battlefield has a twofold advantage:

1. Based on this information, the tank commander knows the exact location of the other tanks in the company and the battalion and can make better tactical decisions during the battle.
2. The brigade and division commanders at headquarters know the exact position of each tank and vehicle in the entire theater of operations, its condition, and ammunition, and therefore can respond rapidly to dynamic situations. The commanders can change the strategic commands as the battle proceeds, channel additional resources, or redirect movements as the situation develops.

Replacing the rigid top-down structure of 1991, the Army implemented a bottom-up approach enabled by advanced information technology. This model is much more responsive to the constantly changing conditions that one experiences in real-time activities. We believe that this new Army approach, based on bottom-up information transfer and information-based empowerment of the workforce, should be the organizational model for manufacturing and industrial enterprises in the twenty-first century.

12.1 TWENTIETH-CENTURY ORGANIZATIONAL STRUCTURE

The main organizing principles of traditional industrial enterprises are multiple levels of hierarchy, and centralization of decision making and control functions. These principles were initially introduced at the end of the nineteenth century, and became standard practice during the first half of the twentieth century. Enterprise organizations during these times were arranged hierarchically, with only limited authority delegated to any one person, who had to report to a superior.

Frederick Taylor, a nineteenth-century mechanical engineer, was the most influential individual on this hierarchical and centralized style of industrial organization. According to Taylor, the organization should be arranged so that each person was responsible to a superior and responsible for subordinates. Taylor created a system that intentionally separated thought and action, and centralized all decision making. In this model, all decisions should be taken as centrally as possible, leaving the rest of the organization to wait for instructions and policy decisions.

According to Taylor, people at the lower levels should not have to think. Employees were not expected to question decisions or to contribute their experience to the decision-making process. Taylor believed that all workers should be told exactly what to do, and in that way their work could be standardized.[1] The term "Taylorism" emerged to describe the rigid top-down hierarchical structure adopted by industry at that time.

The structure of these traditional industrial organizations was modeled along the lines of a military organization of the same era, illustrated in Figure 12.1. At the very top, like the army's division commanders, traditional corporate management has its policy-making vice-presidents. Underneath them are the general managers and directors in industry, the army's equivalent to Major Generals, Colonels, and Lieutenant Colonels (battalion commanders). Then below are the operational managers and supervisors in corporations, as the army's company and platoon commanders in various leadership roles. In traditional organizations, each lower level gets its detailed instructions from the next rank above.

It is, of course, no accident that the organization of manufacturing enterprises mirrors that of the army organization. At the time when the first large industrial organizations were taking shape in the nineteenth century, the army provided the only fully developed model of organization known to work reasonably well, and it was particularly suited to the communications technology of the time.[1]

Taylorism also assumed that people were only motivated by financial reward, and that they were just little more than machines performing predictable operations. These assumptions resulted in a top-heavy management hierarchy. This strictly hierarchical management in which top-down commands are given with minimal bottom-up feedback are adequate for static, non-competitive markets. As operations became more complex, the number of people involved in supervision and planning increased, which made the enterprises even clumsier to respond to changing market conditions.

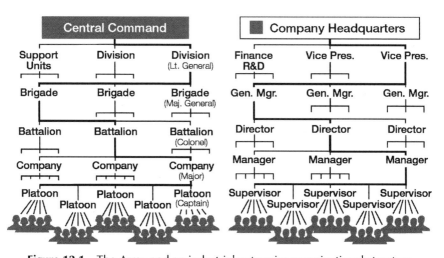

Figure 12.1 The Army and an industrial enterprise organizational structure.

The Taylorism approach of removing initiatives from the people at the bottom of the organizational pyramid, and assuming that they should not be encouraged to think, has been completely abandoned with the implementation of Lean Production methodologies in the last twenty years of the twentieth century. Lean Production empowers even the workers at the lowest level. Now, any assembly line worker can stop the entire line and bring production to a complete halt, when they observe a quality or throughput issue.

12.2 TWENTY-FIRST CENTURY IT-BASED ORGANIZATIONAL STRUCTURE

The constantly changing markets at the dawn of the twenty-first century require a change in the traditional industrial structure. The new market dynamic of shorter windows of opportunity for new products, large fluctuations in product demand, and multiple competitors spread all over the globe requires unprecedented levels of responsiveness by industry. The Taylor Model is no longer relevant, as it works best in environments that are static and stable.

Taylor's top-down model should be replaced by an organization like the Army's new command and control principles described above. To reach the requisite levels of responsiveness called for by the global market, manufacturing enterprises should follow the Army's approach by embedding advanced sensing and information technologies into the organization's decision-making procedures. Remember that by 2003, only the Army's strategic-level instructions were conveyed top-down, and the commanders at the company level were given the authority to make their own real-time tactical decisions. This merger of strategic and tactical decisions was successful because of an IT-based hierarchical organization of advanced sensing and information technology that the Army blended into its organization. The main sensing device for the soldiers was the GPS tracker that each vehicle was equipped with, and enabled its exact location to be traced at all times. Each tank also had a digital map of the area, on which their exact position and every other vehicle in the area was clearly marked and constantly updated. Other sensors monitored and transmitted the vehicle's status: engine condition, ammunition, fuel, etc.

This sensor-based situational awareness has a twofold advantage:

1. The tank commander is aware of the exact condition of other tanks in the close war zone and can make better tactical decisions in real time.
2. The officers at headquarters have data on each vehicle, and can rapidly respond to dynamic situations. The commanders can coordinate tactical and strategic resources or redirect activities as the situation develops.

The combination of these two advantages, which is supported by real-time information system, creates an organization that is much more responsive to the continuously changing imperatives being subjected by external forces. Can these principles transform clumsy enterprise organizations and make them more responsive to changing imperatives being subjected by external market forces?

12.2.1 The Army and the Industry Enterprise

There are many similarities between the operations and logistics of military assets and industrial equipment. An army division is designed around the tank as the primary mission system. Of 8000 or so vehicles in a division, several hundreds may be tanks and the rest are various armored and support vehicles. Manufacturing enterprises may likewise contain some 8000 pieces of equipment (such as AGVs, buffers, etc.) designed primarily around a few hundreds manufacturing machines that perform the main operational tasks (such as machine tools, welding robots, assembly machines, etc.). Similarities between the Army and the manufacturing industry are shown in the table below.

Army	Mfg. Industry
Tank	Machine
Support vehicles	Gantry, buffer
company	Cell
Tank battalion	Mfg. system
50–80 tanks	50–80 machines
Brigade	Factory
$\sim$200 tanks	$\sim$200 machines
Division	Enterprise
1000^+ tanks	1000^+ machines

For industry to model, the Army's high level of responsiveness by mimicking its IT infrastructure-based organization, it has to think of its own operational machinery as equivalent to a tank. Similar to monitoring the tank's operational status, each machine then needs to be able to sense its conditions (e.g., cutting tool wear, machine temperature, etc.) and the quality of parts that it makes and report the essential information to the next level—the cell level. The latter is made up of several machines and supporting equipment and controls.

Like a tank battalion, multiple cells are organized into a manufacturing system that produces parts or assembles products. A factory may contain several manufacturing systems (for machining, for assembly, etc.), and an enterprise often has several factories.

Building an industrial organization that can respond quickly and intelligently to dynamic imperatives requires combining top-down strategic direction with bottom-up tactical decisions done by floor supervisors and managers. This can be accomplished efficiently with information technology that is embedded into all levels of the enterprise controllers, from the machine controller, through the manufacturing cell controller, to the factory supervisory computer.

With this level of information factory managers could make more intelligent decisions when responding to dynamic situations (e.g., market changes, a customer order changes, machine breakdowns, quality issues, and other common incidents that interrupt production). Supplying the right information to a highly skilled workforce and empowering them to make critical decisions in response to unpredictable situations is another way to increase factory productivity.

Contrary to the accepted premise that too many hierarchic levels impede industry responsiveness, we believe that it is not the number of levels that should be reduced. It is rather the size of the functional departments supporting each level in the hierarchy that should be reduced. It is the complexity of these departments that should be simplified by adding information-based tools to allow intelligent decisions at the subordinate levels.

By applying the Army's method of bottom-up information propagation and ample authority delegation to lower levels in the hierarchy, the time to make decisions in the industrial enterprise could be shortened, making it much more responsive to market changes. Furthermore, if industry uses a structure similar to that used by the Army, there would not be a need for as large a number of support personnel at each level of the hierarchy. Reduced personnel combined with rapid decision making will enhance productivity and help the manufacturer remain competitive.

The revolution of the factory and the organization of the enterprise will benefit by

---

- **The sensor revolution, which will add artificial intelligence to the factory**
- **Real-time information, which will be utilized to empower people at all levels**
- **Technology, which will affect the workflow and business intelligence.**

Our proposed sensor revolution raises several subsequent challenges:

1. **Hierarchical Sensing**: Which sensors should be included in the equipment at what level of the factory hierarchy? On the machine itself one may sense broken or worn tools, machine temperature, coolant level, limit-switch status, etc. At the cell level one may monitor the inventory in the buffer, the gantry movement speed, etc. At the system level it is possible to trace the workpieces flow through the system and monitor the level of information traffic throughout the system control network. And, at the factory level—all of these inputs can be rendered into throughput and maintenance data that can provide profiles of the entire plant's operational status.

2. **Management (Top-down) versus Empowerment (Bottom-up)**: How can one reconcile the contradiction between a hierarchical management structure and the empowerment of employees?

3. **Bottom-up Data Filtering**: How can data accumulated at each level be converted into information to be transferred to the next upper level, and eventually to the enterprise itself? This should enable the enterprise commander-in-chief to make intelligent business decisions.

12.2.2 Information-aided Employee Empowerment

Jack Welch (the former CEO of General Electric) was a prominent advocate of employee empowerment in the 1990s. In a speech in 1992 he said: "The way to harness the power of the employees is to protect them, not to sit on them, turn them loose, let them go—get the management layers off their backs, and the functional barriers out of their way."[2] In a 1993 interview with USA Today, Welch said:* " We generally used to tell people what to do, and they did exactly what they were told to do. Now this task (of improving productivity) is to be shared with the men and women on the factory floor, and we are constantly amazed by how much people will do when they are not told what to do by the management." In 1994 he said: "We want everyone to have a say. We want ideas from everyone."*

The Lean Production principle of pushing responsibilities down the organizational ladder and empowering workers on the production floor is another important step in this bottom-up approach. In lean production each team has quality checking responsibilities and can stop the entire production line when a problem appears.

However, Mr. Welch's empowerment philosophy does not emphasize the role of information technology (IT) in empowering the workforce. Applying IT to empower people requires a shift from labor-intensive to brain-intensive operations even at lower levels of the hierarchy, a shift that will affect the skills that both engineers and workers must possess.

In the global manufacturing revolution, employee empowerment is a competitive necessity. But to make the right decisions, the employee must have the right information, and be capable of understanding it. The day is not so far off when all factory employees will have to hold at least a college Associate Degree to do their jobs. Information-aided empowerment of employees, combined with raising their education level, will be critical to increase productivity and profits for factories in the Western world.

Enterprise strategists will also need to contribute to the information-aided organizational structure by looking at issues such as:

- What kind of information is needed to make more effective decisions at various levels of the organization?
- How should the plant manager and the enterprise best reconfigure resources in order to enhance productivity?
- How can information and manufacturing processes support corporation strategy?

This empowering bottom-up approach should also be implemented in the higher levels of the industry hierarchy. Enterprise leaders make intelligent decisions and make them rapidly. This bottom-up, information-rich approach, with technology aiding in empowering people at all levels, is a radical change that will create a less

---

*Quoted in USA Today, July 26, 1993.
*Quoted in Industry Week, May 2, 1994.

corporately conservative industry. It will create an industry that has an entrepreneurial spirit embedded in its structure, a spirit that will be needed to compete in the global environment of the twenty-first century.

The new requirements from the workforce will change the workers skill set. In a speech in Montreal (2003) Dr. Ezio Andreta, Director, Industrial Technologies Research at the European Commission, said: "The next industrial era will be characterized by a new economy based on knowledge. The shift from labor-intensive to brain-intensive operations will modify the jobs and skills required of engineers and the entire workforce."

12.2.3 Organizational Structure for Developing New Products

Whether instructions flow top-down from the executive at each layer of the organization, or from the bottom-up, and employees are empowered, the organizational structure is still a vertically integrated, pyramid-type organization (Figure 12.1 shows examples). There are, however, other organizational structures possible. Two distinctly different organizational structures, currently used for new product development, are the matrix organization and the project-based organization.[3]

Figure 12.2 describes an example of a matrix organization for a manufacturing company that is continuously developing new products. The project leaders and the functional departments have more or less equal power, but the ultimate responsibility to deliver the project's expected deliverables is on the project leader. This structure combines functional skills with resources directed toward common goals more efficiently.

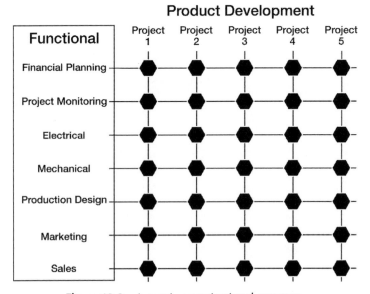

Figure 12.2 A matrix organizational structure.

The project-based organization is commonly found in the movie industry. For each new movie, actors and actresses are selected according to their fit with the movie and its budget. When the project ends, the team is dissolved. This approach is also frequently implemented in the development of new products in large manufacturing companies. For example, people from different functional departments of the organization are brought together into a team to develop a conceptual design for a new product (e.g., a new vehicle). Each person's specialty is in a different area, and the group dynamics and team interactions enable cross-fertilization of ideas and often result in innovative products. Members return to their previous departmental post when the team is dissolved.

12.3 INFORMATION TRANSFER IN MANUFACTURING SYSTEMS

As we have said, enterprise control and management should be modeled along the lines that the Army has demonstrated in recent operations. This premise is explained below.

12.3.1 Control and Management Levels

A typical enterprise for producing discrete products is composed of several levels. At the bottom level is the individual piece of equipment, such as a machine tool, a robot, a part-handling gantry, a fixture to carry the parts, a buffer to hold parts before processing, a rotary index table to assist in part loading into the machine, an ambient temperature sensor, and perhaps an AGV or some other transport device. Each of these pieces of equipment has its own controller; we call it a machine-level controller.

The next level in the hierarchy is the cell level. A cell contains a group of machines that are doing a particular operation as well as all the auxiliary equipment that is needed to complete the operation. An example of a cell may be several robots doing simultaneous welding operations on the same auto-body in an automotive assembly line. Another example may be a group of machine tools in which the part to be machined is transferred from one machine to the next until completion of an operation phase.[4]

An additional example of a cell may be a group of identical machine tools that are machining similar parts in parallel, as well as all their part-handling equipment, as depicted in Figure 12.3. The part-handling equipment may include a buffer to hold parts before processing in the cell, a gantry equipped with grippers to bring parts from the buffer to an indexing table from which parts are loaded into the machine, and the indexing table itself. All these pieces of equipment must work in harmony under the cell controller coordination program.

Next, the cell-level controllers are connected via a network to the system-level controller, as depicted in Figure 12.3. A factory facility may include several manufacturing systems. For example, Ford Motor Co.'s Windsor engine plant

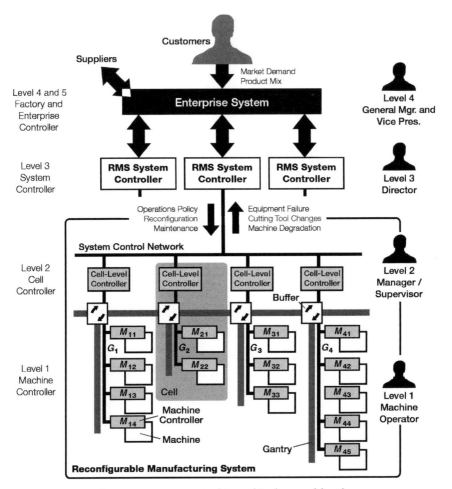

Figure 12.3 Enterprise hierarchical control levels.

contains four RMS machining systems to produce engine parts, with a total of 180 CNC machining centers. (The equivalent in the Army might be a brigade of 180 tanks.) Such a factory may include more than one overall manufacturing activity, say, a machining system that completes final finishing on some parts and an assembly system that combines the parts from the machining system and other sources and assembles them into complete products. A factory may include many combinations of systems, all in one facility.

In our twenty-first-century IT-support model, the enterprise system controller is at the top. It accumulates the customers' orders and coordinate the supply of outsource parts from the various suppliers. It also sends daily product demand requests to all the appropriate factories and manufacturing systems. The customers are at the very top and the entire enterprise structure is built in order to benefit them—providing them with the right product in a timely manner.

We envision that enterprise control will move in the same direction of bottom-up complex information systems that the Army has recently adopted. Similar to the Army's modern tank that sends information about the battleground, the machine M_{ij} in the factory will send information about its conditions to the cell controller and on through the system.

One type of information that a machine-level controller might provide is machine temperature. If the temperature exceeds a certain level, the quality of the part may deteriorate because the machine loses accuracy. For instance, under elevated heating conditions, dimensions expand causing the machine to lose the calibration that it held at normal room temperature. But the machine should not make the decision to stop production by itself. The degree of critical precision should be determined at a higher level of hierarchy (probably at the system level), and that level then communicates instructions as the temperature approaches the critical threshold.

To be effective, however, the machine controller should not send raw data, but convert the data into coherent information before it is sent. In this example, the machine should not send its continuous temperature measurements to the cell controller; it should send just a warning signal when the temperature crosses a certain threshold. The cell controller should monitor all machines in the cell and whether any others have crossed the temperature threshold, and then send appropriate signals to the system-level controller. The latter will make the decision whether to stop production. This decision may be either automatic or done by a person (in the example in Figure 12.3—it is a director's decision).

12.3.2 Coordinating Production

Establishing factory-level IT is essential in coordinating production of several systems. Figure 12.4 shows an example in which engine blocks are sent from casting to a large machining system that machines both V6 and V8 blocks; the machined blocks are then sent to engine assembly. There are two assembly systems, one for V6 engines and the other for V8 engines. When either of these systems has a fatal failure and stops operating, there is no need to continue to supply engine blocks to that system. It is the task of the factory-level IT to coordinate the production of these

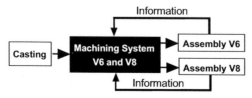

Figure 12.4 Several manufacturing systems are linked in order to produce products.

systems in this case and the upstream and downstream operations in the general case. The shutdown in the assembly system in this example may also be utilized for scheduled maintenance.

12.3.3 Real Experience in Industrial Plants

From the above discussion, one may draw the following conclusions:

- Factory IT should be utilized to empower workers at all levels.
- IT enables blending top-down strategic guidance with bottom-up tactical decisions.
- IT should be embedded into all levels of the enterprise, from the machine controller, through the cell controller, to the factory controller, and above.

Empowering factory employees with timely, relevant information is essential to highly responsive operations and enterprise success. We asked some knowledgeable readers of this book about their experience on the factory floor. Here is a small collection of real-life stories.

"In my company I have definitely seen the rigid top down structure. The motto of our previous Area Manager was 'the easiest thing to do is follow instructions.' That motto led to a group of disenfranchised, unhappy workers that would willingly carry out an incorrect order because we had been beaten down to accept things as they were told to us. I have always felt the need for the bottom-up information propagation and delegation authority at lower levels, but I think that our department has a long road to travel to get out of the old way of thinking." BJ Baker

"Employees must be comfortable about confronting their superiors. Too often, employees don't feel that they can give honest opinions to their supervisors, but this is needed in order for change to occur. The people who are most attuned to which direction a company should move are frequently the people at the bottom. Executives are too far removed from the action and the products to know what should happen day-to-day." Andrea Thomas

"At the plant where I work, we have the technology and the facility to operate as bottom-up organization, but the top-down style is so prevalent in the minds of the old-fashioned management leaders that I wonder if the transition to bottom up will ever actually happen." Andres Babian

"A union environment, such as what is present (2004) in most automotive assembly plants, tends to make this philosophy more difficult to imagine. In the plant that I work in, the union is very particular about making sure that everyone only does the job that they are assigned to. When people are concerned that a union grievance may be written against them, they may be less likely to go beyond the scope of their job. It is possible for someone who finds a quality defect to have a grievance written against him or her if they point it out because their job is not a quality auditor. This philosophy goes against the very idea of empowered employees." Cindie Nieman

---

12.4 IT-BASED MAINTENANCE OF LARGE SYSTEMS

This textbook has already described how large manufacturing systems in factories contain many production machines, material handling, and other pieces of equipment—all of which may break down during normal operation. These systems require (1) regularly scheduled maintenance, (2) repairs of machines that break down and stop operating, and (3) incidental maintenance tasks that, although urgent, require relatively small effort, such as adding coolant or replacing tools. Appropriately coordinated maintenance-scheduling decisions can increase the system productivity if they are done based on information that is transferred comprehensively across hierarchical levels of control and management.

Large manufacturing systems typically have specific personnel to perform these maintenance and repair jobs, each person assigned to a different task depending on his/her skill level and set (e.g., electrician or mechanics). These specialists are typically empowered to do all that is required to sustain production: repair, maintenance, adding coolant, etc. On the factory floor it is hard to assess the impact of a breakdown on the factory throughput and determine what to do first. If an unscheduled event (e.g., a machine breakdown) occurs, or if several events occur simultaneously, which repair job has the highest priority? Which machine failure most seriously endangers the production schedule?

Maintenance crews are frequently facing the challenge of determining the priority of completing their tasks because of the lack of a systematic decision-making system for maintenance. Without comprehending the whole picture, maintenance personnel cannot decide whether they should drop their current job and move to a new problem, or concentrate more resources to speed the completion of the current maintenance job. A solution to this problem can have significant and ongoing benefits to the operation. On top of it there are always conflicts between the production manager, who wants to keep production up no matter what might happen to the production machines, and the maintenance manager.

> "There is often a conflict between the need for production and that for maintenance. Production managers prefer to keep the production system running in order to meet daily production target, while maintenance managers hope to get some sufficient machine time so that adequate preventive maintenances can be performed on the equipment. Resolving this conflict requires the development of advanced decision-making support tools." Professor Jun Ni.

Decision making for effective maintenance of large systems is complex because it depends on several independent sources of information:

- Current "health" status of each machine, and each material-handling device, including: down; running; idling; being maintained; or just about to breakdown
- The current ongoing repair schedule

- The scheduled maintenance plan for the day and the next several days
- The history of each repair, which is a factor in determining a machine's reliability
- The daily production target, and the rate at which it is being accomplished
- Possibility of re-routing of jobs
- The standard system configuration, the given takt time, and optional alternatives.

The system configuration has a profound effect on the maintenance decision-making process. For example, some configurations have identical machines doing identical manufacturing tasks in parallel, as shown in Figure 12.3. If one of these identical machines is already down and in repair, and another of these machines goes down, then the urgency of repair of at least one of them becomes very high. Or, as another example, in the configuration of Figure 12.3, if one gantry is down, the whole system is down, stopping the entire production. In this example, repairing the gantry becomes the highest priority.

The following types of information should be available and should be integrated into a multi-level decision-making system in order to make the appropriate priority choices with the highest impact on productivity.

1. Information from the machine level (Level 1 in Figure 12.3): The "health" status of the machine, as obtained from sensory data that is available from each machine. For example:
   - The machine is down and requires repair (e.g., a broken cutting tool or spindle).
   - The machine has slightly deteriorated and will need an upcoming maintenance action within a certain time horizon (e.g., to change a worn cutting tool, or a worn bearing, or motor shaft).
   - The machine has severely deteriorated and requires an urgent repair within a specified time horizon (e.g., a spindle bearing is wearing out quicker than expected).
   - The machine is healthy and does not require any repair in the planning horizon.
2. Information from the cell level (Level 2):
   - The machine workload: the production volume of each machine during the defined time period (e.g., one day or one shift).
   - The time window available for repair or maintenance in any machine in the cell.
3. Information from the system level (Level 3):
   - The availability of maintenance crews.
   - Spare part inventory.
   - Replacement tools.
   - Routine maintenance scheduling.

- Alternative routing options for the parts produced on the system.
4. Information from the enterprise level (Level 4 or 5):
   - The production requirement (e.g., the mix of products and the number of products to be produced per shift).

Recent research on maintenance decision support tools has made significant progress. Instead of the heuristic rules that are commonly used in today's manufacturing plants for the prioritization of maintenance work-order requests, systematic decisions can be established.[5] These decision-making tools are answering the question raised above "*which repair job has the highest priority?*" by systematically considering the four types of information listed above (especially the production demand, system configurations, the criticality of the impending maintenance or repair requests, and the availability of maintenance crews and their skill sets—electricians, mechanics). This kind of systematic decision-making tools is especially effective to deal with the complex interaction between random production equipment failures and available maintenance resources.

In conventional production system design practice, production bottlenecks are considered only in a static sense or based on steady-state conditions. However, in actual production, the short-term production bottleneck may change from shift to shift or day to day due to the degradation of various production equipment and dynamic fluctuation in buffer status. The identification of transient production bottlenecks answers the question "*which machine failure most seriously endangers the production schedule?*" Answering this question in a systematic way facilitates the maintenance prioritization decisions.[6]

As we said there are always conflicts between the production manager and the maintenance manager. To address this issue of how could one perform systematic equipment maintenance during production without affecting the production throughput at the end of the line, it is necessary to accurately estimate the available opportunity window for maintenance in the midst of production runs. By analyzing the system configuration, current buffer status, and equipment conditions, it is possible to identify sufficient machine time for the preventive maintenance without interrupting normal production schedule.[7]

There is a tradeoff between maintenance personnel staffing levels and the throughput of a production line. The more reactive the maintenance personnel is, the lower the probability that a given repair will be delayed waiting for available personnel. On the other hand, increasing the number of personnel increases the labor costs. Therefore, one important goal of IT-based maintenance systems is to perform adequate maintenance with minimum maintenance crew size. By constructing an optimization formulation, one can solve this maintenance staffing management conflict.[8] The algorithms for solving this issue as well as the one that identifies sufficient machine time for preventive maintenance actions without interrupting the normal production schedule were implemented at General Motors.[*]

[*]Three "BOSS" Kettering awards have been given by General Motors for the successful implementation of the research conducted by Professor Jun Ni and his students Q. Chang and Z. Yang.

The system-level controller is the best one for making effective maintenance decisions. It is positioned where it can receive information from the machine and the cell levels that is sent up to it. These inputs can then be compared to the overall production requirements that are sent down from the enterprise level. Implementing such IT-based maintenance in large manufacturing systems boosts their productivity and increases their reliability and responsiveness to changing operations.

PROBLEMS

12.1 Give an example (preferable from your own work experience) on how supplying the right information to a workforce (at any level) can assist in responding to unpredictable events and/or to increase productivity.

12.2 Which sensors can be included in the equipment at each level (machine, cell, system, factory) of the factory hierarchy (Figure 12.3)?

12.3 What kind of specific information is needed to make more effective decisions at various levels of an organization of a manufacturing company? Give examples.

12.4 Some executives say that the empowerment of employees contradicts the traditional hierarchical management structure. Do you agree?

REFERENCES

1. P. Kidd. *Agile Manufacturing*. Addison-Wesley, 1994, p. 107.
2. R. Slater. *Jack Welch and the GE Way*. McGraw Hill, New York, 1999.
3. G. Morgan. *Creative Organization Theory: A Resourcebook*. Chapter 27, Sage Publications, Newbury Park, 1989, pp. 64–67.
4. Y. Koren. *Computer Control of Manufacturing Systems*. McGraw Hill, New York, 1983.
5. Z. Yang, Q. Chang, D. Djurdjanovic, J. Ni, and J. Lee. Maintenance priority assignment using on-line production information. *ASME Transaction, Journal of Manufacturing Science and Engineering*, 2007, Vol. **129**, No. 2, pp. 435–446.
6. L. Li, Q. Chang, J. Ni, and S. Biller. Real time production improvement through bottleneck control. *International Journal of Production Research*, 2008. DOI: 10.1080/00207540802244240
7. Q. Chang, J. Ni, P. Bandyopadhyay, S. Biller, and G. Xiao. Maintenance opportunity planning system. *Transactions of the ASME, Journal of Manufacturing Science and Engineering*, 2007a, Vol. **129**, No. 3, pp. 661–668.
8. Q. Chang, J. Ni, P. Bandyopadhyay, S. Biller, and G. Xiao. "Maintenance staffing management. *Journal of Intelligent Manufacturing*, 2007b, Vol. **18**, pp. 351–360.

Chapter **13**

Enterprise Globalization Strategies

The pace of globalization is accelerating and shows no sign of reversing course. With the growth of manufacturing capacity in developing countries and advances in communication and transportation, it has become economically attractive for many manufacturing enterprises to consider becoming global. A global company may design a product in one country, buy parts in another country, assemble the product in a third country, and sell it elsewhere. Therefore, we define globalization in the context of this book as:

Globalization is the integration and interdependency of world markets and resources in producing consumer goods and services

Market integration means opening markets of countries around the globe for buying, producing, and selling with minimal government interference, a process that is greatly facilitated when the countries are members of the World Trade Organization (WTO).[1] Government interference might otherwise include import taxes, domestic production subsidies, trade quotas, or import licenses. The absence of government restriction, combined with the low cost and expediency of communication technologies, makes global access to buyers and sellers easy, and generally reduces product and service pricing for consumers.

Market interdependence means that, in order to prosper, local markets are more dependent on markets in other countries for buying, selling, or producing not only the parts and products they need, but also knowledge and R&D capabilities.

The Global Manufacturing Revolution: Product-Process-Business Integration and Reconfigurable Systems
By Yoram Koren
Copyright © 2010 John Wiley & Sons, Inc.

For manufacturing, to a large extent, the pace of globalization is controlled by large enterprises. The successful global manufacturing enterprise typically designs products for different regions on the globe, has manufacturing capabilities in several countries, and sells its products in multiple markets in many countries. Therefore, large manufacturing enterprises in the twenty-first century, whether they like it or not, must prepare strategies for (1) product design that fits multiple cultures and regulations, (2) cost-effective, globally distributed manufacturing plants, and (3) a business strategy that serves a global multi-cultural market. The overall growth of a global manufacturing enterprise depends upon the entire worldwide integration of its successful product development, manufacturing, and business strategy.

13.1 WHY ENTERPRISES BECOME GLOBAL

Globalization enables all enterprises to operate at an international level, a status once reserved for only the very elite. The development of new communications technologies (e.g., undersea fiber-optic cables, high-speed Internet, fax, CD, etc.) and the acceptance of English as the international language for science and business facilitate the integration of international trade and enable the easy exchange of knowledge among the peoples of the world. People can now cooperate more easily; but they can just as easily compete.

Globalization of the manufacturing sector is occurring at an accelerated pace. The removal of trade and financial barriers as well as the reduction of the cost of communications has paved the way to the creation of global "multi-national" enterprises that move not only capital and goods from country to country, but also knowledge and R&D across international borders. Moving products, capital, knowledge, and people across borders creates whole new arenas of security, prosperity, and property rights questions and problems but the benefits are equally compelling.

13.1.1 Benefits for Global Enterprises—Markets Without Borders

Becoming a global manufacturing enterprise has several benefits:

1. **Globalization can reduce manufacturing costs** by building plants in low-labor-cost countries and shipping parts from cost-effective suppliers in these countries to assembly plants in countries where the product is assembled and sold.
2. **Globalization is a new source for enterprise growth** achieved by accessing new markets, enlarging the customer base, and avoiding trade barriers by producing within the new market countries.
3. **Globalization can reduce the business risk** since it may smooth the impact of regional business cycles on the revenues of a global enterprise, thereby spreading the business risk across a wider, more diversified market. (See Appendix C: Business Cycles)

4. **Globalization filters currency exchange fluctuations** because having revenue sources in many different currencies (e.g., dollar and Euro) smoothes currency exchange variations and brings more stability to enterprise earnings.

"Procter & Gamble (P&G) entered the Chinese market in 1989 with its Head & Shoulders shampoo," wrote our graduate student Hui (John) Wang. "Around 1990, P&G at North American had serious financial problems. But at the same time the Chinese P&G profit and market share increased dramatically because of the big market of China. This is the advantage of spreading a business risk by a global enterprise across a diversified market."

Global markets are complicated, however. The global enterprise must carefully monitor currency exchange rates. A company's profit margin, of say for example 9%, in one country can be completely wiped out by an equal fluctuation of 9% in the exchange rate of the country in which products are sold or made. The fluctuations between the dollar and the Euro during the 4 years 2001–2005 were over 40% (on January 1, 2001: Euro/\$ = 0.94; and on January 1, 2005: Euro/\$ = 1.36; a 42% change). So if a German company invested in the United States (or in China, whose currency was linked to the dollar until 2005) in January 2001 and made a 9% annual profit on its investment (totaling 36% over 4 years), it still lost money in Euros in 2005 (assuming that the company cashed in on its investment in 2005).

During the same period, exported commodities from the Euro-financed bloc became 40% more expensive in the dollar-linked financial bloc. Such a financial environment is very dangerous to business, and so investing globally spreads out the risk.

Fluctuations in currency exchange rates can weaken or even eliminate the low-cost advantage of countries like China. China had maintained an exchange rate of 8.28 Yuan to one U.S. dollar for over a decade until 2005. (On July 21, 2005 China finally acquiesced to continuous pressure from the United States, and agreed to detach the Yuan from the dollar. China linked it instead to a basket of foreign currencies.) Before 2005, China's concern was that a higher exchange rate (i.e., fewer Yuan per dollar) would result in a cost advantage to countries like Vietnam, Malaysia, and Thailand, and this could hurt China's growth, increasing their own unemployment rate.

Currency exchange rates can also affect domestic business cycles. When the dollar is weak abroad, U.S. exports to Europe are cheaper, thus more attractive, and their demand increases; U.S. factories work harder to supply the new demand, and the business cycle in the United States climbs out of a slump. Clearly, the four benefits of globalization mentioned above are not independent from one another. However, globalization has also potential risks.

13.1.2 The Risks of Globalization

The pressures on an enterprise to consider globalization are unavoidable, and the benefits often make it worthwhile. However, unless an enterprise plans carefully, the risks and pitfalls of moving into the global arena can erode all of those benefits. A global enterprise must prepare itself by investigating all aspects of its business as it tries to fit into a global template and then it must constantly monitor itself to survive.

1. **Locating Factories Offshore:** Settings up manufacturing operations, especially in "low-labor-cost" and typically developing countries, can have unexpected risks attached that do not arise until the investment is already made. Sometimes the local work rules and ethics of a so-called "low-cost" workforce are so different they can offset much of their cost savings. In some cultures for example, it is customary for workers to take a day off if they feel they have earned enough money in the preceding week. A whole assembly line can be idled even if only a few key workers decide to skip work. In other cultures, work rules limit the number of working hours. In these cases, a surge in demand cannot be met by offering workers an overtime surcharge. Another big issue concerns infrastructure and communications at the overseas plant site. Most of the developing world is struggling with overloaded transportation, communication, and electricity infrastructure. Currently the biggest drags on economic progress in India and China are the capacity and reliability of their power grids, although they are working mightily to improve them. Offshore manufacturing may not be such a simple replacement for domestic production.

2. **Interdependency of World Markets:** The spread and interconnectedness of production, and communication around the world brings about an interlacing of national economies. An economic downturn in one country can quickly affect the economic situation in other nations. The financial crisis that started in the United Stated in September 2008 quickly spread throughout the world. The abrupt downturn in retail purchasing in the United States has caused factories in China to suddenly shut down and send their workers home. In the twenty-first century, the peaks and valleys of business cycles in different countries are linked more than at any other time in history.

3. **Currency Exchange Rates:** We have already discussed how currency exchange rates can have unexpected and devastating impacts on a company's profitability. Currency exchange rates can change dramatically within just a few months, and volatile exchange rates can wreak havoc on complex global supply chains that take years to establish. Exchange rates are often a dominant reason why manufacturers choose to abandon the natural advantages of their

home country, and move operations to the country where their largest markets reside. One of the reasons why Toyota and Honda decided to open automotive plants in the United States was to avoid the hazards of fluctuating exchange rates.

4. **Changing Economic Rules:** In the past, the U.S. government invited its citizens to go shopping to stimulate the economy. This could work in the old economy, when most products were manufactured in the United States. However, in the twenty-first century economic reality, it has had very little of the desired effect, since the money spent is actually used to buy products manufactured overseas. Often, the only contribution to the domestic U.S. economy is in retail sales, shipping, and handling. The bulk of the purchase enriches offshore manufacturers. The new economy cannot be built on spending alone; it must be based on producing goods domestically.

5. **Standards and Norms of Imported Products:** Like infrastructure, product reliability cannot be taken for granted with globalization and neither can quality and product safety. Standards that are part of the landscape of a developed country might be quite rare and difficult to establish in an offshore vendor. Writing quality specifications into an offshore contract are not the same as imposing norms of behavior on the factory floor. For example, if the local workforce sees your standards of hygiene and purity as exotic, accidental contamination of the process will be harder to avoid. If the quality of parts for airplanes and heavy equipment, or the purity of foods and pharmaceuticals is not up to the required standard, disastrous consequences may occur. Increases in inspection, oversight, and control can impact the profitability of an offshore contract as much as any other cause, with the added threat of litigation and liability.

6. **National Sovereignty:** Chief among the risks of globalization are those that challenge a nation's sovereignty over its own conduct and commerce. Globalization impinges on a nation's sovereignty by imposing international rules on the local business landscape. The emergence of institutions such as the WTO, the World Bank, the European Union (EU), and the European Central Bank add constraints that may have been ignored in the past, but are now part of the majority of all trade transactions, especially in manufacturing.

"Another risk of immense globalization is that it broadens the environmental problems. Production was shifted to new countries, and brought with it local environmental problems. But these local problems quickly became global environmental problems. Global problems require global solutions, and it is not possible to solve them with the local mindset of local governments. Therefore, it is a concern that not all countries have accepted the Kyoto protocol."

—Selin Kurnaz, Ph.D., Associate, PRTM (Our former student).

Globalization also encourages the growth of multinational corporations that become less subject to any one country's trade laws, and these can exert economic influence with no oversight but the marketplace. This reduces a country's ability to set its own economic policies since these are all largely market driven and vulnerable to external influences. Governments can no longer expect to manage their economies in isolation, and must increasingly adapt their operations to the pressures and imperatives of the global market. For those countries whose culture evokes a history of industrialization this can come as a serious blow to their identity as well as their prosperity.

To become global, it is not enough to buy inexpensive parts from a low-labor-cost country. The global enterprise needs a global growth strategy that addresses issues such as:

- Which countries are potential new markets? Is the new market large enough to justify adapting products to its regulations and culture?
- Which countries are best for producing products, and which countries are better economically suited for producing the components for these products?
- How can a product be designed to save production cost so that it sells in many countries while minimizing regional modifications?

We will elaborate on these issues and provide some guidelines.

13.2 COUNTRIES OF POTENTIAL NEW MARKETS

Globalization can increase the per capita earning potential in developing countries. This can boost the purchasing power of their population, thereby growing the customer base for new products. This becomes evident when looking at a previous generation of developing countries. In the late 1970s, South Korea, Taiwan, Singapore, and Hong Kong were developing countries. At that time, international manufacturers began building plants in these countries.

As Korea, Taiwan, Singapore, and Hong Kong have shown, the road to prosperity begins with low wages and cheap exports. As skills increase, the value of exported products rises, allowing salaries to increase. Table 13.1 shows the change in salaries in

TABLE 13.1   Salary Growth in Four Countries

	1975 (%)	1995 (%)
South Korea	5	43
Taiwan	6	34
Hong Kong	12	29
Singapore	13	43

these countries as a percentage of U.S. salary during 20 critical years.[2] Accordingly, we have every reason to expect that the wages of knowledge workers in China and India will rise substantially (perhaps up to 30–40% of U.S. levels) within a few years. This already happens (in 2006) in Bangalore, India, where competition for software writers pushed wages up towards U.S./European levels.[3] Such salary increases in such large populations will dramatically change the globalization landscape.

Global enterprises must be prepared for substantial wage increases when planning factories or long-term R&D in China and India. At the same time they have to look at the potential market expansion opportunities there. Expansion into these new markets represents an important positive element of the strategy and the business model for global enterprises.

Table 13.2[4] compares a list of nations with emerging markets (population in millions) and helps enterprise strategists identify growing markets and potential market expansion opportunities. Note that in 2005 it was estimated that only 10% of the populations of China, India, and Brazil had a purchasing power of over $20,000/year. Within a few more years this percentage will probably double and expand to

TABLE 13.2 World's Largest Countries by Population, and Estimates for the Year 2025

Rank	Developed Country	Developing Country	Potential New Market	2004 Population	2025 Estimated Population (in M)
1		China	v	1300	1450
2		India	v	1065	1390
3	United States			293	
4		Indonesia	v	238	280
5		Brazil	v	184	220
6		Pakistan		159	
7	Russia		v	144	130
8		Bangladesh		141	
9		Nigeria		137	
10	Japan			127	
11		Mexico	v	105	130
12		Philippines	v	86	120
13		Vietnam	v	80	110
14	Germany			82	
15		Egypt		73	
16		Turkey	v	69	80
17		Iran		68	
18		Ethiopia		68	
19		Thailand	v	65	70
		South Africa	v	43	37
		Malaysia	v	23	33
Total estimated population in emerging markets in 2025 is					**4050**

The wealthiest 20% of these 4050 million people create an emerging market that is two and a half times larger than the U.S. market. The potential for market growth in these 12 countries (marked by v) is higher than in the mature economies of the United States, Europe, and Australia combined.

perhaps 500 million people, which will create a huge new market for consumer products of all kinds.

Of course political stability, the availability of talent, and the working habits in each country also have to be considered when predicting emerging new markets in these countries. Political stability is usually achieved in democratically empowered countries, but this is not a necessary condition (consider China, for example). In Table 13.2, the symbol **v** indicates, in the author's opinion, 12 countries that have achieved a sufficient level of political stability, and its people have an appropriate work ethic, to establish both a manufacturing base and potential new markets.

The estimated total population (for the year 2025) of these 12 developing countries alone is about **4 billion people**. Assuming that even if only the top 20% of these people have a median income comparable to the U.S. median, it will still represent an emerging market two and a half times larger than the total current U.S. market. The potential for market growth in these countries is far higher than in the mature economies of the United States, Europe, and Australia. Considering this, who will build the products all these consumers will want to buy?

The global opportunities for growth, especially in China, India, Indonesia, Brazil, Russia, and Mexico, are enormous, but the opportunities in these countries come with significant business risks. The dilemma for the global enterprise is that it can neither ignore these opportunities nor disregard the risks.

There are considerable differences in the political system, culture, climate, and geography of these 12 countries, and these differences must be accounted for when preparing a long-term strategy. For example, Indonesia is a Southeast Asian, Muslim country distributed among many islands and located close to the equator. Their needs are likely very different from Russia (Christian, a temperate to arctic climate on one huge country). A major difference between the two is their geography—islands versus one huge landmass—that makes the logistics and distribution systems substantially different (Indonesia is made up of 17,500 islands, and Russia is one country with the largest continuous landmass in the world, comprising 11.5% of the terrestrial earth and spanning 11 time zones). A globally oriented strategy must take into account all these various factors.

In just recent years, the globalization phenomenon has caused a huge shift of wealth and economic power to China and India. Together they make up about half of the world's population, and their integration into the global market has changed the playing field and brought tremendous business opportunities and challenges.

13.3 PRODUCT DESIGN FOR GLOBALIZATION

In all enterprises, strategies for globalization must include three aspects: (1) a business plan built on the four benefits mentioned above in Section 13.1, (2) the strategic location of manufacturing plants, and (3) products that can be customized to fit the requirements of each world market. Products designed for one country may be completely inappropriate for sale in another, and product offerings must always match the culture and needs of the local market. Strategically designed products that can be sold in multiple markets with small changes are critical for the global company. In these designs, the product base platform may be identical, but the add-on modules should be tailored to respond to regional culture and local regulations, and also fit the purchasing power of the target population. Below are examples of how cultural and regional differences can affect product design.

The Japanese buy almost no American cars. U.S. automakers have complained for years that the reason is because of trade barriers imposed by the Japanese government to block foreign companies from competing in Japan. It was not until the late 1980s that a Japanese expert pointed out that the reason was that U.S. automakers tried to sell cars with the steering wheel on the left side (U.S. production), but in Japan automobiles drive on the left side of the road (like in England). To compete globally, U.S. manufacturers must customize their products to fit the regulations and requirements in the destination market.

The world may be "getting smaller" but it is still not reasonable to expect that a single design will serve all potential markets. One size does not fit all. Africa and India, for example, may likely need products with similar basic functionality because large areas of both have similar climate, infrastructure, and topography. However, the purchasing power of those markets and their performance expectations may vary considerably. While a product in India may need certain aesthetic qualities in order to sell, the same basic platform in Tanzania may value reliability or extended range more highly. And neither may be interested in luxury features, common in the USA or Europe, because they put the product out of the price range of their average buyer.

The market for low-cost cars is booming in Brazil, Russia, India, and China (BRIC countries). These low-cost vehicles typically sell for $3000 to $7000. This market grew by about 13% in 2006, and is projected to grow an additional 26% by 2016. Such low prices are possible mainly because of reduced safety standards and the elimination of extraneous features. However, these cars must include interior functions such as storage space, radios, and airflow devices. Interior features for cars in the $3000 range are of course different than for cars in the $5000 or $7000 range. The manufacturer might use design one modular and scalable design to fit the entire price range. However, in all designs, the interior must be aesthetically pleasing and aimed at the particular target market.

Global manufacturers should also be prepared to customize their product offerings to match the life style and culture of their target markets. For example, the size and structure of home appliances depend on living conditions and shopping habits. Apartments in Hong Kong, Israel, and in major European cities (e.g., Paris, Milan) are small, and therefore clothes dryers are commonly installed on top of the washing machine. The typical top loading washing machine in the United States would not fit these markets.

Another example is the size of refrigerators that people buy, which usually depends on the size of the living quarters and shopping habits. Americans tend to have larger homes and do most of their food shopping once a week in supermarkets. In many European cities, the apartments tend to be smaller and there are many neighborhood grocery stores. Europeans do not mind shopping more often and they prefer their foods fresh and not canned or frozen.

To assist in global product development, many enterprises (e.g., GM, Microsoft) have opened global networks for product design. Their goal is only to access the best talents from different countries and to develop real global products. Designers from different cultures think in different ways that can collectively lead to enhanced product design and innovation.

Ordinarily, as products are more customized, their prices should increase. But, sometimes the global market does not allow this to happen. Manufacturers need to appreciate the tradeoff between levels of customization and the manufacturing cost. Microsoft, for example, develops customized, regionalized products to serve its customers in many countries. This is a strategic decision that may not, in itself, generate a profit.

For the most part, customization of their *Office* software means making it operational in languages other than English. However, when the user population of a particular language is small, Microsoft does not profit by that customization. For example, Microsoft offers its products in Hebrew, although the only country in the world that uses Hebrew is Israel with a population of only 7 million people. This customization by itself is not profitable, but it maintains the company's position as a leading global company.

13.4 LOCATION OF MANUFACTURING PLANTS

Where should a global manufacturer locate its manufacturing facilities? If you were a global manufacturer of cell phones, would you consider Finland (the home of Nokia) as the main location for your plant? Should enterprises locate their manufacturing plants in countries with the lowest labor rates or in the countries where the final products will be sold? What other factors should be taken into account when making this decision?

Determining plant location is one of the most critical decisions since "brick and mortar" investments are expensive to build and the hardest to change. Choosing the right location can provide a strategic advantage to the enterprise. In 1999, Ford Motor Company decided to build an advanced engine plant in Windsor, Ontario, Canada, only 5 miles from the United States to Canada border. The engines are shipped from there to automotive assembly plants in Michigan across the Detroit River. The wage rates at that time were lower in Canada than in the United States, but this was not the deciding factor at the time. The main issue was the cost of employee health insurance. Canada has a national health insurance plan, while in the United States health insurance is private, expensive, and a major concern in labor contracts between the employer and the employees.

Historically "the Big-3" automakers have provided generous health benefits to their employees. Mr. Gary Cowger, Group Vice President for Global Manufacturing at General Motors confirms that the price of every car sold in the United States during 2004 included $1200 in health insurance costs for GM employees and retirees. Unlike its main competitor, Toyota U.S. does not have this burden of employee health insurance, and this enhances its competitive advantage. Health insurance coverage and other fixed costs can easily become deciding factors.

Other deciding factors for plant location might be local tax rates, government environmental regulations, and government subsidies for new plant construction. Intel built a Pentium-4 fabrication plant in Israel in 1999 largely because of a government cash subsidy of $600 million against their total investment of $1.8 billion. Ireland, in addition to having an English speaking population, has succeeded in attracting new manufacturing plants by offering low corporate tax rates and large cash subsidies.

Even so, low labor-cost countries such as China, Mexico, and Brazil have continued to be attractive manufacturing sites over the past decade. However, it may not be economical to both produce parts and assemble them to final products in low-cost countries. Refrigerators, for example, should be built close to the target market. Transporting a refrigerator is expensive, particularly when shipping cost is determined by volume (such as transport by sea) rather than weight. Fluctuating fuel prices ($70 for a barrel of oil in September 2005, $140 in April 2008, and $37 in February 2009) also call the remote-site production model into question, and with more volatile the fuel prices, profitability can vary constantly, especially for large products.

Something as simple as poor roads between a plant and a nearby port or airport can delay shipping of products. That's why the most attractive offshore facilities are often those near the most modern export terminals. In China, most industrial development is in cities like Shanghai and Guangzhou that are near the ocean and have modern airports. Reliable transport may be further exacerbated by strikes in the ports and airports, which tend to occur frequently in some countries.

Building automotive assembly plants in the United States is still economical, since the alternative—importing automobiles—is expensive. For this reason, Toyota has invested $13 billion to build automotive assembly plants in Kentucky, Alabama, Texas, Indiana, California, and West Virginia as well as two plants in Canada. These plants have added 190,000 jobs in the United States. As a general rule, final assembly should be done in close proximity to the customers in order to provide timely delivery and reliable service. "Lean sales and service cannot work at all without a production system located in the same area as the sale market," says Lean advocate Jim Womack, et al.[5]

Critical parts for Toyota assembly plant in the U.S. are still imported from Japan and not produced in North America. These critical parts include the seat belt controller, seat belt safety hardware, the airbag assembly including its igniter and controller, special transmission bearings, and small stamped parts made of ultra-high-strength steel. All of these are small, lightweight parts that can be inexpensively shipped by airfreight to Toyota assembly plants in the United States.

Plastro, an Israeli company that builds irrigation equipment, entered the global marketplace in 2000 with major sales to Brazil and Africa. Plastro's competitive advantage is its special dripper; a relatively small but critical part placed at fixed distances along their irrigation pipes. Plastro's solution is to make the pipes, which are simple and take up a lot of space, in Brazil and Africa, but they produce the drippers in Israel and ship them to their target markets. This maintains an economic advantage by keeping production of Plastro's critical components in Israel.

Based on these examples, a useful strategy for global manufacturers may be:

> Produce labor-intensive, mass-produced parts in low-labor-cost countries. Build final assembly plants in the target market country, but keep production of proprietary and critical parts in the home country.

A *unique process technology* can also provide a competitive advantage and should be kept in the home country. For example, Boeing processes critical titanium parts only at its Auburn, Washington plant. This process eliminates ionic contamination and maximizes cleanliness of titanium parts. Boeing's computer-controlled laser and plasma-cutting equipment to accurately cut sheet metal components is a major example of exclusive process technology.

Decisions about planning and adjusting optimal global production capacity can be based upon cost models, stochastic models of market demand, and stochastic dynamic programming methods.[6] These models should take into account the risk of working with overseas factories, as well as issues of production disruptions because of poor local infrastructure.

Our previous student, Rob Rudolf, whose current responsibility includes building manufacturing capacity in the Far East at BorgWarner (a Tier-1 automotive supplier), wrote us:

> Establishing local manufacturing operations in an emerging market can require installing much more capacity compared to serving that same market with imported products from existing operations elsewhere. This additional capital expense can often offset savings in labor wages, at least in the near term.
>
> Reasons for installing extra capacity include reduced machine availability due to the aforementioned condition of electricity and transportation infrastructure. Additionally, an inexperienced workforce and the reduced availability to spare parts can exacerbate downtime. The extra capacity can be used to capitalize on the increased sales opportunities that a local presence affords. (Customers always prefer to buy locally, due to reduced order lead times, having contracts in their own currency, avoiding import duties, etc.) Furthermore, emerging markets have uniquely erratic demand due to their lower per capita incomes (making consumers very sensitive to downturns) and high rate of growth. Scalability is not just a competitive advantage, but a necessity!

"The issue of where to locate manufacturing facilities in a global market is very important," explained our student Mark Ascione. "I worked for a major supplier of large-scale medical devices in the US. When a competing overseas company [in Israel] was acquired, the US parent-company had to transport the product via airfreight to the US, which became incredibly expensive. We found the ocean shipment was considerably cheaper than air transport, despite the extra inventory required to accommodate the longer lead-time. The problem became that increased risk of obsolescent inventory in the US because of drastic changes in customer's orders. If the manufacturing facilities were located in the US, they could provide the customer flexibility they desire without the excess inventory and expensive transport." And Mark asked "Which is better for the company? It's a low-cost production versus flexible supply to customers."

In planning resources, another important question is how one can design manufacturing plants so that production can be quickly shifted from one country to another to take advantage of changing conditions, such as fluctuating currency exchange rates.[7] To be effective, a production shift from country to country must be quickly executed within a several months. To be able to move whole factories, the equipment and production systems must be modular and reconfigurable such that they can be readily shipped to the new location and install there at the required capacity and provides exactly the functionality. When making these kinds of changes, compensation and transition for the workers in the ramped-down plants should also be considered, especially if they ever want them to come back.

13.5 GLOBAL BUSINESS STRATEGIES

Market conditions may vary significantly throughout the world. Producing and selling products globally requires a strategy that smoothes business cycles and currency exchange variations, thereby reducing exposure to some risks. Globalization should be looked upon as an opportunity rather than a threat. The main challenge is in articulating a detailed strategy of spreading the business risks across a wide marketplace, while bearing in mind that the conditions for manufacturing, logistics, and product distribution are different in each country.

13.5.1 Business Model for Globalization

Manufacturing enterprises must design their business models for global operations, which deal with the following issues:

- **Benefit of Globalization:** Will it provide a source of growth, or a short-term competitive advantage based upon low-cost manufacturing or other such factor?
- **Potential Markets:** Which countries are potentially large markets for the company's products? Which large countries are absolutely not potential markets?
- **Product Customization and Regionalization:** Should a product be customized to accommodate the local cultural needs in each country, or should the company sell standardized products? Can a low-cost product differentiation strategy be applied?
- **Global Sales:** What is the strategic approach to building up sales in each target country? What are the estimated expenses? Where should service centers be located? What distribution systems are needed?

- **Manufacturing Plants:** How should manufacturing facilities be distributed? Where should final assembly plants be located, in low-cost countries or in countries where the products are sold? How can the manufacturing plants be designed to facilitate production shifts from one country to another?
- Where should **R&D centers** be located? Should they be distributed in many countries or concentrated in one location?
- **Strategic Alliances:** Which companies and countries might provide strategic alliances?

A thorough analysis of these issues will give the enterprise solid building blocks for developing a global integrated business model.

Building Blocks of Global Business Models

- Value long-term strategies over momentary performance.
- Target countries with the potential for large new markets for your products.
- Match product customization and regionalization to countries and markets.
- Integrate seamlessly global supply chains.
- Locate finishing facilities in large target markets.
- Globalize distribution systems.
- Develop globally strategic alliances.
- Distribute R&D to product target markets where possible to support global product development, as well as to acquire the best global talents.

13.5.2 A CEO's Responsibilities in Globalization—An Interview

There's a bright future for traditional manufacturers that take advantage of global opportunities—depending on how the CEO steers the company.

Background—On May 5, 2006, astonishing news was announced to the manufacturing world: Berkshire Hathaway, Inc. announced the acquisition of 80% of the Israeli firm, Iscar Metalworking Companies (IMC) in a transaction that was valued at $5 billion. IMC manufactures cutting tools for all types of metalworking applications. IMC's products are sold in 61 countries worldwide and manufactured in a global network of advanced manufacturing plants, the largest located in Israel, with additional facilities in the United States, Germany, Italy, India, Korea, China, Japan, and Brazil.

The news was astonishing because Warren Buffett, Berkshire Hathaway's legendary Chairman and CEO, did not decide to buy a hi-tech biotechnology company or an info-technology enterprise, but an ordinary manufacturer of cutting tools for machining operations. Mr. Buffett's implicit message was as stated above: There is a bright future for traditional manufacturing companies that know how to take advantage of global opportunities.

Mr. Buffett explained his reasons for this acquisition: "As a truly international business, IMC is a top performer in its industry, with exposure to European, Asian and Latin American markets, as well as significant opportunities for growth. I have been impressed by IMC's simple and profitable business model."[8] It was announced that IMC would continue to be managed by President and CEO Jacob Harpaz, and that its headquarters would remain in Tefen, Israel.

I personally have known Mr. Harpaz for over 20 years when he first assumed the CEO position at Iscar. At that time Iscar's annual sales were $200 million and it had just one production facility in Israel; in 2006, the annual sales were $1.4 billion. Since IMC is now a truly global manufacturing company with a presence in the world's most dynamic economic regions, and has enjoyed phenomenal growth over the past 20 years, I asked Mr. Harpaz (in August 2006) to share his views on IMC's global strategy.

Q. Did you have a strategic plan or a pre-defined strategy in expanding Iscar from Israel to other countries? Or did it just happen gradually?

J. Harpaz—Iscar recognized international opportunities to acquire new knowledge, **innovative products**, and new production technology. I can't say that there was a pre-defined strategy, but when we recognize new markets or new opportunities we seize the. Our strategic plan is dedicated to products, particularly to tailored-made products, which vary from one country to another.

Q. How did Iscar expand its sales seven times within the last 20–25 years?

J. Harpaz—The expansion in sales is a direct result of extensive efforts in developing **innovative products**. To achieve these goals you need to be creative, think outside the box, and be attentive to the needs of your customers. **Treat your customer as a partner**, teach them how to utilize their machines, reduce their respective production costs, and offer them the opportunity to upgrade the tools in their machines. Our products focus on solving bottlenecks in industry, and we continuously prove to our customers that adopting them will provide the competitive advantage that they are seeking. The expansion is also a result of a series of **acquisitions of niche companies and their unique products**, which together enable Iscar to be a full product line supplier, meaning we offer complete machining solutions.

Q. How do you decide where to locate your factories?

J. Harpaz—In the global environment, industry is acting very dynamically, jobs are moving from one country to another due to cheap labor or other opportunities to reduce production costs. **We need to be close to our customers**, in order to follow up with their needs. Staying close to our customers, guarantees time saving on delivery, and being attentive to their needs. **Decisions about factory location are made based on market size**, the potential that a certain product has, and the market share that Iscar holds in that country. Iscar has also built production facilities in locations in order to penetrate new markets. High import duties for products are also taken as a consideration or as an incentive for setting up manufacturing facilities overseas. Customers also prefer to buy locally—local products. In general, it is important to be close to your customer. **If you are a big player, you are everywhere around the globe**.

Q. Where do you locate R&D? How do you keep your intellectual capital from being taken by your competitors?

J. Harpaz—When you are talking about R&D, it's predominantly brainpower and highly skilled human resources. Therefore, the company needs to keep its own R&D and proprietary technology (its own competitive advantage) protected, controlled, and maintained in the headquarters, with high level of confidentiality. Competition between teams within the R&D department should be encouraged as it inspires more creativity and innovation.

13.5.3 Global R&D Location

The question of where to locate R&D Centers is of a particular interest. Should the research units be situated in low-labor-cost countries, or in countries with a pool of appropriate technical talent? Many companies run low-cost R&D centers; such as IBM and GM, located in Bangalore, India. On the other hand, Samsung has established a major R&D center in Silicon Valley, and they transfer the knowledge gained to their plants in South Korea. Automotive research is concentrated in Michigan. The R&D centers of General Motors, Ford, and Chrysler have been in Michigan for many years. However, from 2005, companies such as Toyota, Nissan Motor, BMW, Volvo Group, Hyundai, and Kia have also built research centers in Michigan. The country of Israel accommodates major R&D centers for computer companies such as Intel, IBM, Motorola, National Semiconductors, and Hewlett Packard. In 2009, HP had 5000 employees in Israel, 1500 of whom were in R&D. This is in line with what Joel Birnbaum, Sr. Vice President of Hewlett Packard, said:[9] "Our trend in the last 5 years is to locate research activities wherever we find the appropriate talent, not by geography or political persuasion."

Many global companies have opened not only factories in China, but also R&D centers. These centers acquire talent at relatively low cost. Microsoft, for example, opened an R&D center in Beijing in 1998 and hired just 1% of all applicants, and at 10% of a normal U.S. salary. The number of R&D centers in China is exceeding exponentially. "At present, over 400 firms out of the FORTUNE 500 have invested in China. The number of R&D centers set up by foreign investors in China has exceeded 700" said China President Hu Jintao in his talk at the 2005 Fortune Global Forum, on May 16, 2005.

Many companies, such as General Motors, Boeing, IBM, Hewlett Packard, and Microsoft, have opened a network of R&D centers in the United States, Europe, China, and India. Global R&D is 24 hour R&D, and the result is that products get to market faster. Because of the time difference, GM R&D in Warren, Michigan can send a problem to GM R&D in Bangalore, India in the late afternoon, and get an answer to their question the next morning, thereby dramatically shortening the R&D lead-time.

This "turbocharged" pace of product and process innovation has become the new standard as product development cycles continue to shorten in the face of global competition.

Many industry leaders think that R&D should be spread globally. "Start-up companies should think global from Day One, and companies should establish R&D centers around the world," said Oracle CEO Larry Ellison in Tel Aviv on August 10, 2007.[10]

"This past summer I worked at the R&D center for Samsung-Rockwell Automation in Shanghai, China," wrote our student, Zack Olds, in 2005. "I worked hand-in-hand with Chinese engineers developing the latest version of Korean PLC software. My responsibility was to write the English version of this software's help manual. I saw first hand the importance of **global R&D centers**. I noticed two benefits of having this global R&D center in China (as opposed to only having it in the US). The first benefit is that we were able to be much more responsive to the Korean's manufacturing needs. A Korean representative was able to quickly fly into our center in Shanghai and explain *exactly how* the Korean manufacturing plant workers like to operate their PLCs certain ways. My second observation was the utilization of cheap, but equally skilled labor. My fellow Chinese engineers at Rockwell-Samsung were very smart and educated in western *team-oriented* ways of engineering. Most of them went to Shanghai JiaoTong University (SJTU) where these skills are emphasized. This results in very good engineers and the ability to pay them much less than American engineers (average engineer with English skills from SJTU made about $6000–$12000/year)."

Although economically it is beneficial to establish R&D centers around the world, some industrial leaders see the shift of intellectual capital to foreign countries as a loss of the most valuable asset that a country may possess, and a threat to economic sovereignty.

13.5.4 Global Invention Potential

When deciding in which country to locate R&D centers, one factor may be the country's invention culture and potential. The magazine Technology Review[11] presented a global invention map with a ranking of countries according to their invention capacity. The ranking is based on the following metrics: (1) the number of patents per million people in 2003; (2) training of scientists and engineers; (3) innovation policies; (4) number and size of technology hot spots located in the country; (5) GDP per capita; and (6) business competitiveness, as well as a few other factors. Based on these metrics the ranking of the invention potential of several countries is given in Table 13.3.

Table 13.3 should be examined with caution. Note, for example, that because GDP per capita is a factor in this ranking, the ranking in the table penalizes countries with very large populations, or wide income disparities, although they already have significant levels of innovation. Counting the number of technology spots penalizes countries with small populations. Israel (population 7 million), for example, is ranked #14 by TR—perhaps too low when considering the following facts:[12]

TABLE 13.3   Ranking of Invention Potential of Countries

Rank	Country	Rank	Country	Rank	Country
1	USA	9	Switzerland	20	South Korea
2	Finland	10	France	21	Italy
3	United Kingdom	11	Netherlands	27	South Africa
4	Japan	12	Canada	40	China
5	Germany	13	Taiwan	42	Brazil
6	Singapore	14	Israel	43	Russia
7	Sweden	15	Australia	44	India
8	Denmark	19	Ireland	46	Costa Rica

- Israel has the largest number of start-up companies, in absolute terms, than any other country in the world after the United States (3500 companies, mostly in emerging technologies).
- In the year 2000, Israel was ranked #2 in the world for venture capital funds, right behind the United States—there was $4 billion available for investment in start-ups and R&D centers.
- Israel is one of the most highly educated countries in the world with the highest number of engineers, scientists, and Ph.D.s per capita (135 per 10,000).
- A number of cutting edge technologies have been developed in Israel, including:
  - The cell phone was developed by Motorola-Israel Development Center.
  - Windows NT software was developed by Microsoft-Israel.
  - The Pentium MMX Chip technology was designed at Intel Israel.
  - Voice mail technology was invented in Israel.
  - The first anti-virus for a PC was developed in Israel in 1979.

13.5.5   Global Supply Chains

A typical global supply chain consists of several links in which demand information flows backwards, and parts and modules are transported forwards. In many cases, labor-intensive parts and their manual sub-assemblies are done in low-labor-cost countries. The sub-assemblies are shipped to final assembly plants that are located in the country in which the product will be sold. In parallel, critical, core parts that are manufactured with proprietary technology are produced in plants in which intellectual property can be kept best as a professional secret, and are also shipped to the final assembly plant. This structure of a supply chain is depicted in Figure 13.1.

One of the biggest advantages of a supply chain is in taking advantage of low labor costs (e.g., in Mexico, China, and Taiwan for products assembled in the United States). The risk, however, is that international shipping requires longer shipping time, and if market demand changes quickly, a delay in shipping part supplies may result in either a loss of sales or excess inventories—both of which lose revenue.

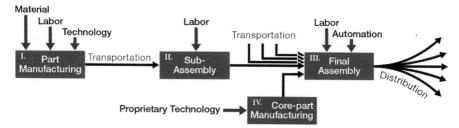

Figure 13.1 Consumer goods are produced in a chain of factories at different locations.

For any global supply chains to be responsive, all suppliers must be connected to the IT system of the OEM. This ensures the information flow needed to match supply with demand at all links of the chain. Nevertheless, because of possible offshore delays, global supply chains are more risky than local outsourcing and local supply chains. Another issue is that changes in products require changes in the supply chain structure. Therefore, industry has started to use reconfigurable supply chains, which optimize the supplier selection.[13]

Global supply chains are often designed for delayed differentiation, which reduces costs when offering a broader product variety. The common modules of a product are assembled in low-labor-cost countries and shipped for final assembly to the countries in which the product is sold. This practice is best implemented to manage the complexity of a growing variety of products and avoid expensive inventories as well as product shortage.

Figure 13.1 shows four types of manufacturing facilities in a supply chain that transform raw material to final products. The global enterprise must carefully consider the location of each of the four classes of facilities depicted in this diagram. Selecting the proper location for factories can minimize the total cost along a global supply chain (including transportation costs). By combining a low-cost strategy (location of factories I and II) with a product differentiation strategy (location of III), a product variety can be offered at low prices.

> If markets change quickly, companies may waste more than they earn by outsourcing through an extended global supply chain—either because of obsolete inventory or due to lack of parts.

13.6 GLOBAL STRATEGIC ALLIANCES

Since the 1990s, companies in many parts of the world have formed global strategic alliances to strengthen their competitiveness.[14] The global market environment, which is assailed by change and uncertainty, is the major reason for their formation. A strategic alliance (also called a Virtual Organization[15]) is a multi-company organizational structure that is formed to enable cooperation between a group of companies or countries. Strategic alliances may come in many forms, from simple joint ventures to complex consortia. The alliance governs the relationship between the member companies.

Strategic alliances may be designed to achieve the following goals:

- **Joint Product Development** by developing new technologies and new products through collaborative research
- **Joint Manufacturing** where sub-systems are produced in different countries to reduce costs and enhance sales
- **Joint Marketing** which helps partners enter new markets or sell a new product
- **Outsourcing Agreements** to take advantage of economies of scale.

Strategic alliances aim at sharing responsibilities and resources and complement individual core competencies in development of new products, or in penetrating new markets. In developing new products, companies risk uncertainty in their technology, especially in novel product technologies. When trying to penetrate new markets, especially if a company decides to locate manufacturing facilities in a new foreign market, it faces uncertainty in its return on investment. The strategic alliance can reduce exposure by sharing the risk among all the members of the alliance.

Sharing the risk in new product development is among the primary motivations for forming alliances, but it is not as important as gaining access to complementary resources, structuring a new growth path and the growing need to operate on a global scale. In most cases, the motivation for forming a strategic alliance is to gain a competitive advantage by accessing new technologies and/or new markets. The number of new strategic alliances has grown rapidly and doubled between the years 1996–2000.[16]

Another motivation for the creation of strategic alliances is that enterprises cannot change their own core competencies fast enough to take advantage of new market opportunities, but they can rapidly establish and disband alliances to gain a competitive edge. In fact, alliances by their very nature can change continuously. When observing these aspects, one may conclude that forming strategic alliances is a tool that enables **enterprises reconfiguration**.

To sum up, the main advantages for companies to form alliances are:

- Generating global growth
- Accessing new core competencies, technologies, and skills
- Expanding into new markets
- Reducing exposure to risk

13.6.1 The Business Strategy for Alliances

A strategic alliance must have an "alliance strategy"[17] a business strategy that defines its mission and structure. It should

- States the goals of the strategic alliance (why it was formed) and its expectations
- Articulates the structure of the alliance and defines its information sharing policy
- Explains the logic of selecting each of the alliance partners
- Spells out the role of each partner and how partners fit into the alliance strategy
- States how risks will be managed
- Enables coordination among the partners
- Defines concrete, common projects, and deliverables
- Articulates how it will manage changes in the market place
- Explains which actions to take in a worst-case scenario in which the alliance fails to accomplish the expected goals.

When a strategic alliance does not have a clear business strategy, it can fail. In 1990, the leaders of Mitsubishi and Daimler-Benz signed a deal in principle to form a strategic alliance in automobile and aerospace technologies.[18] Mitsubishi was particularly interested in Daimler's jet engines and the prospect of building cars with the world's leading maker of luxury cars—Mercedes-Benz. Daimler's main interest was in advanced equipment and space technology, areas in which Mitsubishi excels. The alliance intended to give Daimler access to some of Japan's best innovation, and to give Mitsubishi a foothold in Europe before the integration of the EU in 1992. The capabilities of these companies seemed to be well matched, but this alliance faded quickly because of disagreements about developing automotive technologies. In most cases, choosing an alliance partner that is a competitor rather than a partner with complementary skills, resources, and knowledge will eventually fail due to tension between the partners.

Alliance portfolios can also be important in industries driven by innovation. Pharmaceutical companies, for example, are increasingly using multiple external alliances to complement their internal R&D. They may invest in several small biotech firms and fund several university laboratories that do specialized research on related topics. The reason for such a seemingly fragmented approach is that the chance of success of any single project is low and unpredictable. The portfolio strategy is a way to place multiple bets and hope for a jackpot somewhere among them.[19]

Alliances present major challenges that must be addressed, particularly in cases of joint product development. Among these are: Which company owns the product when the alliance dissolves? And how will the enterprise ensure long-term support of the product?

Personnel issues cannot be overlooked when forming alliances. The partner that is able to place managers in the most key positions in the alliance will probably strengthen its status in the partnership and potentially cause friction with its partners. Cooperative behavior, social interactions, and team building can play an important role in countering this.

Alliances are most useful when the future of a new technology, a new product, or a new market has a high level of uncertainty. In these cases, leading a single company in the wrong direction may end up with a fatal risk. Forming an alliance may be the better approach to share risk. If the future is more certain, a merger or acquisition may be a better strategy. Strategic alliances, mergers, and acquisitions are alternative strategies that manage risk differently.

13.6.2 Examples of Strategic Alliances

We elaborate below on examples of global strategic alliances. In all of these cases, a major challenge was to increase cooperation among the diverse company cultures and organizational structures that were expected to work together and build mutual support for a common goal.

13.6.2.1 United Technologies Corporation (UTC)—Aerospace
In the year 2000, UTC had over 100 alliances around the world. A powerful symbol of their strategic alliance is the Sikorsky S-92, a 19-passenger helicopter, which also has a military version. Sub-assemblies of the Sikorsky S-92 were produced in six countries:

1. **Japan:** Main Cabin by Mitsubishi Heavy Industries
2. **Taiwan:** Cockpit and flight deck by Aerospace Industrial Development Corporation
3. **Spain:** Rotor transmission tailcone and "strongback" composite structure by Gamesa
4. **Brazil:** Landing gear, fuel cells, and gauging systems by Empresa
5. **China:** Vertical tail fin and stabilizer by Jingdezhen
6. **United States:** Sikorsky contributes gearboxes, rotor blades, transmissions, and drive systems, and performs the final assembly in Stratford, Connecticut

In exchange for their participation, UTC has agreements to sell the S-92 in all these countries. It is also interesting to note that the S-92 is powered by engines built by a competitor, General Electric, and not by UTC subsidiary—Pratt & Whitney.

13.6.2.2 The Chiaphua Industries Group—Consumer Products
The Chiaphua Industries Group, located in Hong Kong, produces a diverse range of consumer products (http://www.chiaphua.com/). It has strategic alliances with many U.S. companies in a variety of consumer markets including kitchen and household appliances, healthcare products, cordless power tools, cookware products, etc.

Chiaphua's manufacturing alliances include companies such as Black & Decker, Colgate, Sunstream, etc. New companies and customers are added frequently. Customers' orders may change from month to month depending on the current market forecast. To accommodate the changing production requirements of various companies Chiaphua's manufacturing facilities and capacities are easily convertible, scalable, reconfigurable, and expandable.

Most of Chiaphua's alliance partners provide product designs and Chiaphua builds them. Chiaphua also has customers outside the alliance. The main strategic resource of Chiaphua is its reconfigurable manufacturing systems that can be adapted to produce the various products—order by order—of its outside customers.

Serving as a manufacturing facility for their U.S. partners provides a quick route to increased manufacturing share without the need to establish brand recognition.[20] In return, the western partners provide information on how to tailor products to local markets, so every product Chiaphua manufactures is also a research report on customer preferences and market needs. Chiaphua can then use these insights to study markets more accurately when they enter the market with their own products.

13.6.2.3 Strategic Alliances in the Automotive Industry

There is a general over-capacity in the global automobile industry. One way to deal with this situation is by forming strategic alliances with rival companies. A wave of strategic alliances and acquisitions occurred during the years 1990–2006, all with the objective of reducing cost and expanding market share. Rival companies worked together by sharing production facilities and on joint development of vehicles.

For example, in 1999 Renault of France picked up a 36.8% stake in Nissan Motors of Japan, Ford acquired the passenger car division of Volvo in Sweden, and Daimler Chrysler has paid $1.3 billions for 34% of Mitsubishi Motors in Japan. These examples show how the automotive industry became a global industry at the dawn of the twenty-first century.

13.6.2.4 General Motors Corporation

General Motors Corporation (GM) headquartered in Detroit, Michigan has been a global leader in automobile design and manufacturing for many years. As a multi-national corporation with operations in 32 countries, its vehicles have been sold in 190 nations. GM contributed substantially to the world economy with 388,000 employees globally in 2004.

As part of its global growth strategy, GM had about 500 strategic alliances covering design, manufacturing, and distribution relationships, with companies such as **Fiat Auto** in Italy and **Isuzu** Motors in Japan. GM also has strategic alliances for technology collaborations with **Toyota** Motor Corp. for developing hydrogen fuel cells, and with **Honda** Motor Co., as well as vehicle manufacturing ventures with Toyota and **Renault**. Until early 2006, GM owned 20% of **Suzuki** Motor Corporation and also had a stake in **Subaru** of Fuji Heavy Industries (FHI) in Japan.

GM-Toyota—NUMMI (New United Motor Manufacturing Inc.): In 1984, GM and Toyota opened NUMMI—a 50:50 joint venture in California. For over 20 years, the board of directors was divided 50:50 between GM and Toyota. NUMMI is a $500,000m^2 assembly plant investment that by 2005 was the only automotive plant in California. It produced the Toyota Corolla and Pontiac Vibe subcompact cars on the same assembly line, along with Toyota Tacoma pickup trucks.[21] NUMMI's 2004 production capacity was 245,000 cars and 165,000 trucks.

What could possibly have motivated these two competitors to create such an intimately connected joint venture?

In 1982, Toyota made a strategic decision to penetrate the North America market. The alliance with GM gave Toyota their first experience in operating a manufacturing plant in North America. It was a challenge for Toyota, working with a less disciplined workforce, paying higher wages than in Japan, and incurring other expenses such as employee health and plant insurance. Imposing the "lean manufacturing" technique with union workers posed a challenge for NUMMI from the beginning. The Toyota culture of giving more authority to employees and making them take responsibility for product quality was a new concept in the United States.

At the same time, General Motors made their own strategic decision to introduce those same lean manufacturing techniques known as the Toyota Production System (TPS). The alliance with Toyota gave GM an opportunity to gain first-hand experience in implementing TPS in a real production environment. The pull-type methodology by which the market and customers dictate the production scheduling was absolutely new for GM in the 1980s; GM had to learn how to operate a plant with this new business strategy. For years GM rotated some 15 managers every couple of years to learn lean manufacturing techniques in the real production environment at NUMMI, which has had a significant impact on all GM assembly plants and, in turn, has improved overall GM product quality.

NUMMI has been a successful joint venture for both GM and Toyota giving them both some valuable first-hand experience in each other's operations. Until it pulled out of the alliance in June 2009, GM had the opportunity to continuously monitor the improvements and enhancements of the TPS, and implement them in other GM plants. Toyota evaluated the best practices of GM and estimated the strength of a major competitor.

Conclusions: The examples given above demonstrate how companies have restructured themselves to form strong alliances while achieving remarkable gains. Advanced information technology has been of crucial importance in these cases. Nevertheless, alliances between competitors with similar core business that compete in the same markets tend to be short-lived. The most consistently successful alliances are those in which each partner brings different capabilities (e.g., process capability, specific market access) or different strategic resources to the partnership so that the qualities and resources are complementary, enabling each partner to build upon the its partner's expertise.

13.6.3 Multi-national Strategic Alliances

Countries also form strategic alliances for trade in industrial and agricultural products. These alliances are much more powerful than the strategic alliances between companies and have tremendous influence on global growth. The most notable of these alliances are NAFTA and the EU.

NAFTA: In January 1994, the United States, Canada, and Mexico launched the North American Free Trade Agreement (NAFTA), thereby establishing the world's largest free trade zone. This was an important milestone in promoting the era of globalization. This agreement removed most barriers in North America and brought economic growth to the region. NAFTA has established a strong foundation for future growth and continues to provide a valuable lesson about benefits of trade liberalization. NAFTA has elevated the standard of living for people in Canada and Mexico, but how about the USA? The answer depends on whom you ask. NAFTA has caused a substantial transfer of manufacturing jobs from the United States to Mexico, mainly due to much lower wages, and to Canada due to lower health insurance costs. Altogether, NAFTA has resulted in the loss of many manufacturing jobs in the United States.

Nevertheless, the average annual growth of total trade between the United States, Mexico, and Canada rose to 12% between 1994 and 1999, greatly surpassing the 7% growth in the rest of the world. In just 5 years, the total trade between Mexico, the United States, and Canada rose by 95.5%, reaching more than $590 trillion dollars in 1999. This supports the argument that foreign trade is one of the main engines of economic growth, and that the NAFTA agreement has been a success.

During the 1980s and the 1990s, several automotive assembly plants were transferred from the Mid-West (Michigan, Ohio, and Indiana) to Mexico, which generated a substantial cost savings to the manufacturers. But, how about the product quality? Is the quality of cars produced in Mexico equivalent to those produced in the U.S. quality? "My father is a retired mechanical engineer from Ford and worked on both the Chihuahua engine plant and the Hermosillo assembly plant in Mexico," our student Lisa Hopeman told the class. "Both those plants have 'sister' plants in the U.S. that produce the same product, for the Chihuahua plant the sister plants is Lima, OH. Of those two plants, the one with the highest quality—based on recalls, warranty costs, and inter-process scrape-rate—is the Chihuahua plant. The sister plant for Hermosillo assembly is Wayne assembly plant—both originally made the Escort/Focus. Of those two, the Mexican plant, at Hermosillo has higher quality than Wayne assembly, again based on the same quality factors mentioned before."

"If quality isn't produced in Mexico" continued Lisa, "then the workers are replaced. In Mexico, workers aren't able to hide behind big unions like the UAW in the US, thus it is easier to get fired and people are more careful to keep their jobs. In the US the UAW protects mediocrity."

European Union: In 1957, six European countries (Belgium, West Germany, France, Italy, Luxembourg, and the Netherlands) created the European Economic Community (EEC). The member states removed trade barriers and formed a "common market". In 1967, these European countries established a united Commission and a single Council of Ministers and a European Parliament. The Treaty of Maastricht (1992) introduced new forms of co-operation between the member state governments. By adding this inter-governmental co-operation to the existing "Community" system, the Maastricht Treaty created what is now called the European Union (EU). Economic and political integration between the member states of the EU means that these countries have to make joint decisions on many matters. They have developed common policies in a very wide range of fields—from agriculture to industry and from consumer affairs to economic competition.

The European "Single Market" was formally declared at the end of 1992. Originally the focus was on a common commercial policy for coal, steel, and agriculture. Other policies have been added as the need arose. However, some key policy aims have been modified with changing circumstances. For example, the agricultural policy is no longer to produce as much food as cheaply as possible, but to support farming methods that produce healthy, high-quality food and protect the environment. The need for environmental protection pervades the whole range of EU policies. It took some time for the member states to remove all the barriers to trade, but they now have a truly "common market" in which goods, services, people, and capital can move around freely.

On January 1, 2002, a single European currency managed by a European Central Bank was introduced. The single currency—the "Euro"—replaced national currencies in 12 of the 15 member countries (Belgium, Germany, Greece, Spain, France, Ireland, Italy, Luxembourg, the Netherlands, Austria, Portugal, and Finland).

The EU has taken on some roles that are analogous to those of the federal government in the United States. For example, the EU supports basic research in the EU countries. In 2004–2005, the support for basic research in manufacturing and engineering was much higher in the EU than that of the National Science Foundation in the United States.

BRIC: In 2001, speculation began to consider the possibility that the four largest emerging economies (Brazil, Russia, India, and China) might organize into an alliance that could become the largest single bloc of markets. Such a union would dwarf the EU and NAFTA together in terms of population and land area. China and India would be the dominant global suppliers of manufactured goods and services while Brazil and Russia would be the dominant suppliers of raw materials. Brazil is dominant in soy (a main food staple in China) and iron, while Russia has enormous supplies of oil and natural gas. In February 2005, Russia and China began to explore the feasibility of a strategic alliance not only for defense, but also for trade and energy. In the conceptual plan, Russia would supply oil and gas to China, and China would collaborate with Russia in strategic defense.

The situation became even more complex in the summer of 2005 with Brazil's decision to form an economic alliance with Venezuela, and China and Russia quickly took similar steps. The United States has begun to take countermeasures by trying to bring India and Brazil into U.S. trade alliances. By 2009, the future of BRIC was still evolving and it was not clear to what extent it would succeed in uniting such diverse economies and governments.

In summary, multi-national strategic alliances can enhance a nation's economic growth and the revenues of its largest enterprises. It can have a substantial impact— both positive and negative—on the standard of living of people and migration of manufacturing jobs among countries.

"This chapter touched on our own future in globalization. Millions of engineers graduate each year around the world with the same skills as us in the US. What competitive advantages do we, in the US, have to ensure that we can get a job in this increasingly competitive field?" Thomas Vanasse (a student, 2005).

PROBLEMS

13.1 The table below shows three possible strategies of product development and marketing for a global manufacturing company. Each requires a different investment level, and has corresponding projected sales. For example, for Strategy 1 there is 100% confidence that annual profits will be at least $3 million, and 30% confidence that the profit will be $4 million. The product expected lifetime is 3 years. Which of these strategies is most profitable?

Manufacturer Strategy	Investment	Projected Sales Annual Profits	
		100%	30%
1. Designs exactly the same product for three regional markets	$8 million	$3.0 million	$4.0 million
2. Designs a product for one market, but it can be marginally modified to fit two more markets	$9 million	$3.1 million	$4.3 million
3. Designs three product variants to fit three distinct markets	$14 million	$5 million	$6.5 million

13.2 A company has to make a decision where to locate its manufacturing plant for refrigerators. The refrigerators are sold in the United States. There are three options for the plant location: Columbus, Ohio; Monterrey, Mexico; and Limon, Costa Rica.

The expected average yearly demand is 300,000 units in the east coast and 100,000 units in the west coast. Demand may vary at ±50,000 units according to the discrete probability distributions given below:

Demand	Probability
250,000	0.1
275,000	0.2
300,000	0.4
325,000	0.2
350,000	0.1

The plant will have a capacity of 325,000 units per year. (We refer to this as the high capacity). There may be events such as strikes, infrastructure disruptions, or quality problems, which will lower the capacity to as low as 200,000 units per year. (We refer to this as the low capacity.) The probability of such events occurring is given in the table below.

We assume that we can get revenues of $1000 per refrigerator sold. We can only sell the minimum of the demand and the capacity. For example, if demand turns out to be 275,000 and the capacity that year is 325,000 (high), then we will sell 275,000 for that year. Another example, if the demand for a year is 300,000 and the capacity turns out to be low (200,000), then we will only sell 200, 000 units in that year. Additional cost factors and capacity probabilities are as follows:

Cost Factors	Ohio	Mexico	Costa Rica
Plant investment $	100,000,000	80,000,000	75,000,000
Cost to produce one unit $	750	680	650
Shipping cost per unit $	50	100	120
Probability of high capacity (325,000)	90%	50%	30%
Probability of low capacity (200,000)	10%	50%	70%

What is your recommended location for the plant if the planning horizon is (a) 5 years, (b) 10 years?

13.3   In 2004/2005, the thought at the U.S. Congress was that a stronger Yuan (the Chinese currency) would erase America's trade deficit with China (see Section 13.1). When the United States put pressure on China to devaluate the Yuan, Mr. Wen Jiabao, China's prime minister, argued that China's currency is an issue of China's own sovereignty [*The Economist*, May 21, 2005, p. 11].

Do you think that a stronger Yuan will drastically change the trade deficit of the United States?

Do you agree with Mr. Wen that China's currency policy should be determined by what is best for China?

13.4   Based on the interview with Mr. Harpaz, what are the most compelling reasons to Iscar's global success?

REFERENCES

1. WTO website: http://www.wto.org/
2. World Almanac. *The New York Times*, 2005, p. 149.
3. T. L. Friedman. *The World is Flat*. Farrar, Straus and Giroux, New York, 2005, p. 229.
4. The UC Atlas of Global Inequality. http://ucatlas.ucsc.edu/NY Almanac.
5. J. P. Womack, D. T. Jones, and D. Roos. *The Machine that Changed the World*. Harper-Perennials Publishers, New York, 1991, p. 200.

6. F.M. Asl and A.G. Ulsoy. Stochastic optimal capacity management in reconfigurable manufacturing systems. *CIRP Annals*, 2003, Vol. 52, No. 1, pp. 371–374.

7. A. I. Dashchenko (ed.). *Reconfigurable Manufacturing Systems and Transformable Factories*. Springer-Verlag, Berlin, 2006.

8. http://www.berkshirehathaway.com/news/may0506.html (accessed on May 5, 2006).

9. E. Abele, J. Elzenheimer, T. Liebeck, and T. Meyer. Globalization and decentralization of manufacturing. *Reconfigurable Manufacturing Systems and Transformable Factories*, Chapter 1, A.I. Dachtchenko, Z. Pasek, and O. Dachtchenko (eds). Springer, Germany, 2005.

10. http://www.haaretz.com/hasen/spages/892410.html; Israeli news media

11. Technology Review, May 2004.

12. http://www.ohioisraelchamber.com/membership/israel_facts.htm.

13. C. Chandra and J. Grabiz. Configurable supply chain: framework, methodology and application. *International Journal of Manufacturing Technology and Management*, 2009, Vol. 17, No. 1/2.

14. Y. Doz and G. Hamel. *Alliance Advantage*. Harvard Business School Press, Cambridge, MA, 1998.

15. S. L. Goldman, R. N. Nagel, K. Preiss. *Agile Competitors and Virtual Organizations*. John Wiley, 1994.

16. *Forbes,* May 21, 2001, p. 27.

17. B. Gomes-Casseres.Strategy must lie at the heart of alliances. *Financial Times.* Mastering Management, October 16, 2000, pp. 14–15.

18. D. Sanger. *New York Time,* March 7, 1990.

19. B. Gomes-Casseres. Alliances and risk—securing a place in the victory parade. *Financial Times.* Mastering Risk, May 9, 2000, pp. 6–7.

20. G. Hamel, Y.L. Doz, and C.K. Prahalad. Collaborate with your competitor and Win. *Harvard Business Review*, January 1989.

21. *SME Manufacturing Engineering*, Lean at NUMMI, September 2005, pp. 73–84.

Chapter 14

The Twenty-first Century Global Manufacturing Enterprise

Manufacturing companies, big and small, in Detroit, Shanghai, London, Milan, or Tokyo, are under daily pressure to sustain positive growth, rapidly introduce new products, acquire new market segments and find more customers; and to do all this quickly and cost-effectively. To accomplish this, a company must be positioned to not only increase its productivity, but also shorten its lead time for introducing new products and launching new plants so it can respond rapidly to market opportunities and competitor's actions. The global manufacturing world is going through a sweeping transformation that is speeding up the rate at which business is carried on. Decisions that used to take months must now be made within hours. Every executive decision must consider global consequences and should be done at a greater rate than ever before, and this rate is increasing every year.

How can a company respond to market opportunities faster than its competition? And how can it maintain a substantial growth rate in the face of so much competition? Although there are no certain answers in this uncertain world, a combination of five core elements may be the winning combination for sustained growth in manufacturing. These elements form a remarkably appropriate acronym that is useful to remember—PRIDE.

P—Productivity gains

R—Responsiveness and reconfigurable technology to achieve speedy responsiveness

I—Integration of the product design, manufacturing system, and business model

The Global Manufacturing Revolution: Product-Process-Business Integration and Reconfigurable Systems
By Yoram Koren
Copyright © 2010 John Wiley & Sons, Inc.

D—Design of products for multiple regional markets and personalization

E—Empowerment of the company's workforce with the aid of information technology

We will elaborate below on these five core elements. This acronym also provides a slogan that may be used to identify the goals of a global company:

Take PRIDE in your business!

14.1 P—PRODUCTIVITY

The goal of a manufacturing enterprise is to transform resources into finished products and put them up for sale. To be profitable, this transformation must be done at the highest productivity possible. Higher-level productivity suggests greater efficiency—producing more with the same or fewer resources (people, machinery, money, etc.). Increases in productivity result from better tools, improved technology, and motivated workers.

The tight link between productivity and long-term national economic growth makes productivity a key factor for sustaining expansion in the global economy. A 2001 editorial in the *Economist* about the state of the American economy said:[*]

> "Long-term prospects in America and the rest of the world are driven by productivity. Over the next decade or two, productivity might grow more than twice as fast as it did in the 25 years to the mid-1990s. If **new technologies** really could boost growth in productivity so much, they would go far to justify the strength of Wall Street as a whole. This kind of productivity—with capital and labour held constant—is the true key to a long-term quickening of economic growth."

The key to advancing productivity gains is developing and implementing new manufacturing technologies and optimizing system operations. The multi-stage production line of the mass production system, although invented almost 100 years ago, is a shining example of a technology that enhanced productivity. Delivering high-quality products with the aid of Lean operations methods is another way to improve productivity because it reduces scrape and warranty costs. Introducing computers into industrial operations and systems in the early 1990s boosted productivity. Enhanced productivity is always achieved by reducing costs, delivering high-quality products, producing high product variety at no additional costs, and high speed of responsiveness to changing market conditions (Figure 14.1).

---

[*]*The Economist,* January 6, 2001, p. 72.

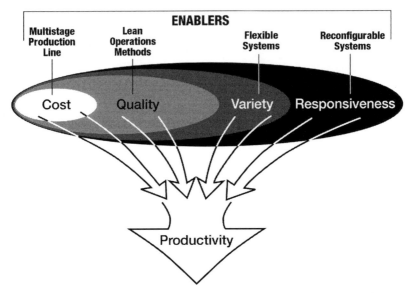

Figure 14.1 Productivity is improved by increasing responsiveness, cutting down costs, and producing a greater variety of high-quality products at low costs.

For manufacturing companies to flourish at the dawn of the twenty-first century, new manufacturing system technologies that enhance productivity must be invented and implemented. Examples include:

- Designing the production system for reconfigurability increases the system longevity in this era of shorter product life cycles, and thereby enhances its average production rate during its entire lifetime. It also shortens the time needed for changing product models or adjusting the output volume to meet market demands.
- Implementing dynamic scheduling adjusts production operations to match changing market demand.
- Shortening ramp-up time after reconfiguration can bring the product up to its designed capacity quickly.
- Launching network-based approaches to factory control increases productivity and assists in efficient maintenance.
- Embedding in-process part inspection machines increases productivity and yield (the percentage of resulting products within quality specifications).

Productivity gains can also be achieved by reducing the life-cycle costs of manufacturing systems, which can be done by reducing equipment and tooling costs, operator training costs, maintenance, etc.

To summarize, increased productivity can be gained not only by cutting expenses but also by higher utilization of manufacturing systems. Higher utilization is achieved by using new technologies to more efficiently launch, operate, and reconfigure the manufacturing system to quickly adapt to new market conditions.

14.2 R—RESPONSIVENESS AND RECONFIGURATION

Responsiveness in industry means the speed at which a company reacts to changing society needs and unanticipated market events as well as the speed at which business decisions are made and executed. Speed is an imperative of the global enterprise. Speed in developing new products, speed in reconfiguring the manufacturing system to produce new products, and speed in taking advantage of new market opportunities. Toyota President Fujio Cho referred to the importance of the firm's speedy reaction to changing markets as "the criticality of speed".[*] In the fierce competition of the twenty-first century it is the speed of responsiveness that will differentiate the thriving company from the unsuccessful one.

> **Responsive manufacturing enterprises deliver the desired PRODUCT, in the correct QUANTITY, at the correct TIME, at the right PLACE**

The rapid reconfiguration of manufacturing systems is critical for responsiveness to market changes. In the past, product life cycles were long and the manufacturing system was built to produce only one product. In the twenty-first century, a single product's lifetime can be so short that it makes the cost of developing a one-product manufacturing system impractical. For example, in the semi-conductor industry the cost of a new wafer fabrication facility may reach $3 billion. Therefore, the design and production of new products must be constrained as much as possible to use existing manufacturing systems with short reconfiguration periods. In the future, these systems will be reconfigured in the normal course of business for the addition of new products, as depicted in Figure 14.2.

A well-designed reconfigurable manufacturing system will go through many cycles of change in its lifetime, producing a whole product family that may last for a relatively long period in one form or another (maybe 15 years or more). It starts by producing Product **A**. After a couple of years, Product **B** is introduced and the system is reconfigured (and rapidly ramped-up) to produce both **A** and **B**. After a few more years, Product **A** is phased out and the system is reconfigured and ramped up to produce Products **B** and **C**, and so on.

A 1998 study done by the National Academies of Engineering identified six Grand Challenges facing manufacturing companies and came up with a ranked list of 10 Priority Research Areas needed to meet these challenges by the year 2020. The highest-ranked Priority Research Area was identified as "**Reconfigurable**

---

[*]*Business Week,* November 17, 2003, p. 116.

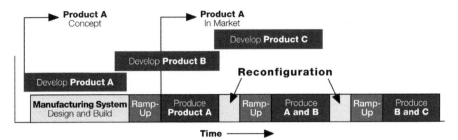

Figure 14.2 The next-generation manufacturing system will produce several products during its lifetime.

Manufacturing Systems," defined as "adaptable, integrated equipment, processes, and systems that can be readily reconfigured for a wide range of customer requirements is a priority technology."[1]

The NAE report went on to emphasize the value of forming "**Reconfigurable Enterprises**" defined as "the ability of an organization to form complex alliances with other organizations very rapidly. The challenge is to reconfigure manufacturing enterprises rapidly in response to changing needs and opportunities. Reconfiguration could involve multiple organizations, a single organization, or the production/process floor of a single organization. The driving factors for reconfigurable enterprises are rapidly changing customer needs; rapid changing market opportunities; and development in process, product, and electronic communications technology."

Rapid responsiveness is crucial to the success of the global manufacturing enterprise in these rapidly changing global market conditions. The product design process must be quick and integrated with the manufacturing system that will produce it, as well as the business strategy that coordinates the supply of products at the right quantities to the right customers. Possessing a flexible system is necessary, but insufficient to compete globally, where the speed of responsiveness to new market conditions creates an opportunity for competitive advantage. Possessing reconfigurable manufacturing systems enables companies to increase their responsiveness because these systems can quickly adjust their production capacity (i.e., volume per product) to match market demand and can be rapidly tooled to produce new products. The reconfigurable manufacturing systems, therefore, provide...

...exactly the capacity and functionality needed, exactly when needed

14.3 I—INTEGRATION OF PRODUCT, PROCESS, AND BUSINESS

A critical factor in sustaining company growth and rapidly responding to market opportunities is the integration of the three basic functions of the manufacturing enterprise:

Design products by product development teams
Make products on manufacturing systems
Sell products by utilizing business strategies.

Traditionally, the marketing, product design, and manufacturing units work successively on the development of new products (Figure 14.3a). Typically, the marketing group in the business unit conducts market research and provides the requirements and specifications for a new product to the design team, together with their predicted sale volume and a target price. Product design then optimizes for performance versus cost tradeoffs, where material cost is given, and with some considerations of design for manufacturing (DFM). The product is then manufactured, and the business unit tries to sell it.

In this traditional approach, profit is calculated by marketing as a function of cost and demand, where demand depends on the price and features of the product. The concern with this approach is that, to maximize profit, marketing might set a list of desirable product features that are too complex and therefore unprofitable to manufacture. It has been common practice for marketing to be disconnected from manufacturing and set target prices without consideration of manufacturing system characteristics. This approach must be changed.

A more effective, integrated approach is depicted in Figure 14.3b. Here, inputs and outputs from each unit are linked to the other two units. With this approach, capacity allocation and manufacturing costs are coordinated with marketing targets during product conceptualization. Furthermore, in order to reduce production lead time and decrease costs, every new product must be produced as much as possible on available machines on an existing manufacturing system that can be reconfigured for the new product. (This is in contrast to the conventional approach that assumes they will be building a new manufacturing system from scratch for the production of each new product.) Although the new approach imposes some additional constraints on the product development team, this is the only way to reduce lead time, decrease cost, and ultimately win the global contest for the customer's pocket.

Also, with this new approach, cooperative efforts between marketing, design, and manufacturing take place during product development instead of much later in the process. The design team analyzes the product features and determines which specifications are unrealistic and must be modified. This is feedback to the business unit, which then must change the product price according to the new specifications. The new price and modified product features may also change the projected demand and production volume targets, which, in turn, will impact the configuration of the manufacturing system.

This approach recognizes the links among the three main enterprise units in the new product development scenario. The details of the design, cost, and

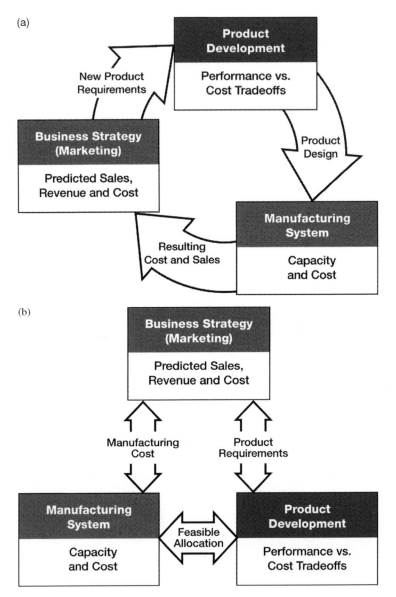

Figure 14.3   (a) A traditional sequential product development process. (b) An integrated, concurrent manufacturing enterprise.

capacity allocation, which are still driven by the profit objective, are handled simultaneously instead of sequentially by design, manufacturing, and business.

To achieve market responsiveness all three elements—the product, the manufacturing system, and the business model—must possess a set of the same five core characteristics that are defined below.

Scalability	The ability to easily scale up or down an existing product size, or an existing production output capacity, or the number of partners in a strategic alliance
Convertibility	The ability to easily transform the functionality of existing products, systems, machines, or business units to suit new requirements
Customization	The ability to design variant products within a product family, or the ability to adapt the customized flexibility of production systems and machines to meet new market requirements; in business—the ability to form a strategic alliance that is customized to a new business opportunity
Modularity	The compartmentalization of operational functions into units that can be manipulated between alternate product, production, or business schemes to achieve the most optimal arrangement to fit a given set of needs
Integrability	The ability to integrate product/production/business phases and modules rapidly and precisely by a set of mechanical and/or informational interfaces

Note that the sixth characteristic, Diagnosability, is applicable to complex customized products (e.g., automobiles) and manufacturing systems, but it is not applied at the enterprise-level business model.

Figure 14.4 depicts graphically the integration (the connection) of the enterprise unit—product, manufacturing system, business—and their common core characteristics. The concept conveyed in this figure indicates the specific way to link them in an integrated

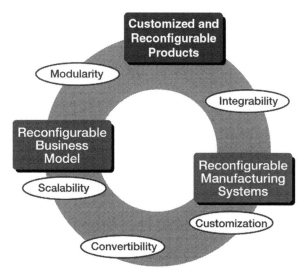

Figure 14.4 The set of core characteristics needed to form a reconfigurable enterprise is common to the product, the system, and the business models.

product–process–business approach that utilizes reconfigurable business models, combined with the design of regional customized, or reconfigurable products, produced on reconfigurable manufacturing systems, to enhance the speed of enterprise responsiveness.

The integration and links between product design, the manufacturing system, and business requires a set of methodologies including concurrent product design for manufacturing (DFM), designing the product for service, building supply chains, and methods for handling the logistics of product variety. Creating tools that enable a business to sustain long-term relationships with their customers is an important goal of the manufacturing enterprise. The customer is the focus of all three units of the manufacturing enterprise: product design for the customer, making high-quality, cost-effective products for the customer, benefiting the customer by providing good service, and developing enduring relationships with the customers to build a brand name.

14.4 D—DESIGN FOR THE GLOBAL MANUFACTURING PARADIGM

With the ever-increasing competition of globalization, customers have more power and their preferences can be satisfied to a higher degree, at an affordable price, than ever before. In the global manufacturing paradigm, this product design trend has two aspects:

1. **Products designed for multiple world markets, matching the customer's purchasing power, needs, and culture in specific regions.**
2. **Personalized products tailored specifically to individual customer's needs and preferences, targeting a market-of-one.**

When designing products for various global markets, the goal is to design a line of products with similar basic functionality (e.g., washers and dryers), but different features to fit different price ranges and living conditions. Global products are customized to make them fit the customer's purchasing ability, to the customers' culture, needs, and preferences, as well as to the country's regulatory environment The products should be designed so they can be manufactured in factories that are globally distributed, which makes product design more challenging than ever before. It has to match the available local manufacturing capacity as well as the purchasing power, culture, and regulations of the population in the target country. Developing products whose prices fit the purchasing power of customers in target countries and regions opens new markets and expands regional sales.

The personalized product category is aimed at more wealthy customers who desire a higher degree of attention to their personal needs than just purchasing sets of customized options offered by manufacturers. This trend toward personalized production can be done economically only if products become more modular, and are designed with open architecture for mechanical, electric, and information interfaces. This approach enables a two-stage design of personalized products:

1. Design of the product architecture and range of modules by the manufacturer. Then the product is contracted and sold.

2. Design of the personalized product—selecting and arranging modules by the customer. Then the final product is assembled for the individual customer.

With this two-stage approach the sale precedes both the final design and the manufacturing and final assembly, which brings about a substantial economic advantage to the manufacturing enterprise. When this approach is adopted by the auto industry and mechanical-electrical open-architecture standards are established, dozens of small new companies will start to produce special modules (such as dog baskets and storage cabinets), which will evolve to several new industries. Instead of just trading used cars, people will start to trade used modules as their needs change and they want to update and remodel their existing cars. Because this personalized production business model is beneficiary to both the manufacturers (that are being paid before the product is built) and to the customers (who are getting exactly the product that they need), and because it will generate new industries that produce innovative modules, it could be a giant booster to the local economy.

A second type of personalized design products contains non-modular products that are made to fit some dimensional measures of the customer's body. Examples include shoes (as described in Chapter 3), the internal foam of bicycle helmets,[*] and the grips of tennis rackets that can be made to fit the player's hand.

Personalized production entails a new business model, requiring closer interaction than ever before among the product development, the manufacturing systems, and the business unit, with a focus on the customer who is at the center.

14.5 E—EMPOWERMENT OF THE WORKFORCE

Perhaps the most important asset that makes a manufacturing company great is **motivated people**. The instructions and expectations from the employees, however, must be reasonable. The king, in the book *"The Little Prince"* by Antoine De Saint-Exupery, explains this point very well:

" If I ordered a general to fly from one flower to another like a butterfly, or to write a tragic drama, and if the general did not carry out the order that he had received, which one of us would be in the wrong?" the king demanded. "The general or myself?"

"You," said the little prince firmly.

"Exactly. One must require from each one the duty that each one can perform," the king went on. "Accepted authority rests first of all on reason. ...**I have the right to require obedience because my orders are reasonable.**"

---

[*]Professor Jack S. Hu initiated the personalized bicycle helmet project.

The old industrial culture that was characterized by "I'm the boss. Do what I say and don't use your brain!" is over. Leading manufacturing companies are striving to develop a culture in which every employee cares about the company and feels some sense of ownership.[2]

To accomplish this goal, however, it is not enough to motivate employees to think about the consequences of their actions. Employees must have **information** that enables them to make intelligent decisions and help them to be responsible for the outcome of their actions. For example, by having the right information about the operating status of the manufacturing system and the daily production targets, employees on the production line can help find new opportunities to enhance productivity and improve product quality.

Employees at all levels must have reasonable instructions and be empowered with the authority to make critical judgments. But making critical decisions requires skills, information, and knowledge. Information technology, when planned correctly, distributes knowledge where it is needed and when it is needed. Knowledge combined with the loyalty of employees and their dedication to the success of the company can foster a strong competitive advantage.

At the higher levels of an organization, when giving timely information, managers can think about modifying products and ways to better satisfying customer's needs. This will enhance customer satisfaction and increase the company's competitive edge.

Striving toward **information-based empowerment** encourages an entrepreneurial spirit in the company. This spirit, combined with a greater sense of ownership, speeds up the company's responsiveness to unpredictable situations, increases productivity, and creates a momentum of rapid innovations in the company's product and process.

14.6 THE DILEMMA OF GLOBALIZATION

We elaborated on the five core elements of PRIDE. Implementing PRIDE on a global scale will sustain enterprise growth. But there are sometimes political conditions and global economic situations that occur because of globalization and may still put the future of a manufacturing enterprise at risk. These situations are sometimes beyond the control of the enterprise. We offer below some discussion on these issues as well as on the dilemmas surrounding globalization.

Like it or not, globalization is here to stay. Is globalization a good trend? The answer depends on who is being asked. If you are an employee that was laid off because his job was transferred overseas to a low-wage producer, you may strongly oppose globalization. If you are an entrepreneur who formed a successful start-up with global sales, you may praise globalization—it offers you a higher degree of freedom than an individual has ever had before. If you are Bill Gates (don't worry, you're not), and in 1998 you opened a research center in Beijing where you employ the brightest computer scientists in China (just 1 position for 100 applications) and pay them 20% of the corresponding U.S. salaries, you embrace globalization. On the other hand, if you are the CEO of Delphi (a $30 billion company supplying automotive parts that applied for bankruptcy in October 2005) and you cannot compete with low-wage countries, you will probably curse globalization.

14.6.1 Political, Economic, and Social Aspects

Globalization is essentially driven by large global enterprises that try to increase their profits. These global enterprises, which are mostly rooted in the more advanced industrial countries, typically do not care about the social justice problems they may create, nor are they structured to solve the social issues that globalization can cause, especially in the United States and Europe.

The shipping of jobs from the United States to low-wage countries (both simple manufacturing jobs and high-quality jobs in engineering and specialty services) is one of the biggest problems facing the United States at the dawn of the twenty-first century. Because of globalization U.S. industry lost 3 million jobs in just 5 years— 2000–2004, with the U.S. automobile industry losing 200,000 jobs during that period. As a result, the state of Michigan and especially some of its small towns, which depend on the auto industry, continue to suffer an economic crisis. People who are not working are not paying taxes, and consequently the state and towns struggle to support the basic functions (including education) that they are obligated to provide.

Lou Dobbs of CNN is one of the most vocal opponents of globalization. In 2005, he devoted many of his CNN evening programs to the evils of globalization. In his book, *Exporting America,* he tells the story of Galesburg, Illinois that was home to a Maytag factory that provided 1600 jobs.[3] After the NAFTA agreement was ratified, Maytag decided to transfer the factory to Reynosa, Mexico, cutting their labor costs by 15:1. Maytag did not have a choice; without the transfer of the factory to Mexico, the company could no longer compete against cheaper refrigerators that Asia was importing to the United States. But with the closure of the Maytag factory, unemployment in Galesburg went up to 20%. This had a devastating effect on the entire town and community. Not only were 20% of the households in this town unable to pay their taxes because they were not working, Maytag also stopped paying taxes. To make matters worse, workers stopped spending money in local stores, which affected the whole local community. As a result the town itself could not even offer the basic services that it is required to provide its citizens.

But the hardship caused by globalization is not only an issue in the United States. Our student, Steve Pratt from Adelaide in South Australia, wrote to us in January 2006: "I live in Adelaide where two of the four Australian auto-manufacturing plants are located: GM Holden and Mitsubishi motors. As a result, Adelaide has a high dependency on manufacturing with not only the auto plants, but also the components suppliers that support these plants. The city's growth has been directly linked to the car plants. But Australia now struggles to compete with the low cost countries of Asia, and therefore must find efficiencies in other areas."

Despite the numerous sad stories of people whose jobs were "offshored" and consequently were hurt by globalization, many experts believe that globalization is good for the United States as a nation, and eventually it will lead to economic growth. It is for this expressed reason that president Clinton signed the NAFTA agreement in 1994. In the 2000 World Economic Forum, he said: "Fifty years of experience shows that greater economic integration and political cooperation are positive forces." Thomas Friedman discusses the globalization dilemma and concludes: "America as a whole will benefit more by sticking to the basic principles of free trade, as it always has, than by trying to erect walls."[4] In spite of the problems, we, as consumers, enjoy the low prices of entertainment equipment, appliances, computers, printers, and other devices imported from Asia and other low-labor-cost countries.

There is no getting around the fact that globalization is a complex phenomenon full of contradictions. Analyzing globalization is key to understanding the big changes that occur, on both global and national scales. We believe that in order to comprehend the situation and form a position about globalization, we have to look at arguments from four viewpoints:

- The United States (or other Western countries) as a nation (economic and political arguments)
- The global manufacturing enterprise in an industrial country
- The community or town in the United States (social arguments)
- The private consumer and citizen in the United States and other Western countries

The pros and cons of globalization from these four points of view are listed in Table 14.1.

One outcome of globalization is that Western countries that produce high-tech products import the parts for these products from low-cost countries. A study conducted in Germany in 2002 indicated that the value share of imported parts in products produced in Germany and then exported was 39%.[5] This confirms that global outsourcing that Western companies are implementing is a contributor to low-cost exports and the increasing wealth of these countries.

Globalization also contributes to a lower inflation rate, as pointed out by Alan Greenspan (U.S. Federal Reserve chairman, 1987–2005). "Greenspan would point to large pools of labor in Asia that have come online over the past two decades as the reason for the a slowdown in the increase of labor costs and the resulting fall in the rate of inflation."[*]

George Soros (a billionaire who has created several foundations dedicated to supporting open societies) said on the issue of free market ideology: "Markets are amoral. But society cannot function without some distinction between right and wrong. The globalization of markets without corresponding strengthening of our social arrangements has led to a very asymmetrical social development."[6]

If we look at the global scale (not included in Table 14.1), it is true that while globalization has increased the standard of living of hundreds of millions of

---

[*]*U.S. News & World Report,* November 7, 2005, p. 61.

TABLE 14.1 The Broad Impact of Globalization—Political, Economic, and Social Aspects

United States	Global Enterprises	U.S. Communities	U.S. Citizens
Rationale for Globalization—The Opportunities			
Opportunity for national economic growth	Market expansion into new countries	U.S. entrepreneurs enrich the community by flourishing and paying local taxes	New jobs created by entrepreneurship; new specialty jobs and expertise are created
Reduced inflation pressure, because of lower-priced products	Lower-cost manufacturing increases profit	Capital investment from overseas is invested in U.S. towns	Consumers enjoy lower prices and greater purchasing power
Spread of American values and culture; world-wide cohesion promotes peace	Access to best talent worldwide	Universal agreement on basic cultural values reduces the power of terrorist groups	Product quality and selection improves due to global competition
Rationale against Globalization—The Threats			
Larger trade deficit, caused by loss of production, may greatly devaluate the dollar; United States is headed for decline in its economic power and standard of living	Companies fail because of low-wage competition	Companies pull out of towns, or go bankrupt, stop paying taxes; employees no longer pay taxes and become a drain on social support	People lose their jobs in manufacturing and services, including high-paying jobs (e.g., engineering, medical assistants)
Loss of jobs increases total unemployment compensation, which increases the deficit	Loss of sovereignty over standards and market norms makes it difficult to maintain quality	The gap between rich and poor enlarges; the middle class is diminishing	Low-skilled workers earn lower wages; highly skilled workers may be forced to relocate globally
The United States no longer produces goods necessary for national security	Off-shore supplies can be cut, causing whole industries to shut down	Society may suffer if critical goods are not available when crisis occurs	The standard of living of America's citizens declines

people in many countries (especially India and China) and reduced the income inequality in poor countries by providing jobs, especially to unskilled workers, globalization does not work for all countries. Globalization has actually done nothing yet for Africa's countries. And although it is true that globalization has reduced the income gap between rich and poor countries, at the same time it has widened the gap more between countries that participate in globalization and those that do not. Theoretically globalization offers equal competitive opportunity for all countries. But in practice it disproportionately favors China and the richer countries.

So, globalization does not work for all. It operates according to the globalization rules set by three institutions: The World Trade Organization (WTO), the International Monetary Fund (IMF), and the World Bank (WB).[7] The most advanced industrial countries formed these institutions, and they set the globalization rules so that the financial interests of their countries would be pursued above any others. These institutions, as well as the global enterprises they serve, do not care how many people have actually been made worse off because they lost their jobs. This is the main reason for large demonstrations at the meetings of the WTO in Seattle (in 1999), the IMF in Prague (2000), and the WB meeting in Washington DC (in 2001). More equal spreading of the wealth across the globe is still a problem that should be addressed.

14.6.2 The Role of Policymakers

Globalization, when pursued to fulfill just the financial interests of the few, may create poverty rather than higher standard of living. The free market ideology that guides these international institutions (WTO, WB, and IMF) has limits—it does not result in social justice. What is needed is a more balanced and humanistic approach to globalization, an approach that better balances the personal economic security of people with the financial health of large enterprises. The big question is how to do it. U.S., European, and Japanese enterprises that have enjoyed globalization should participate in finding solutions to these problems, and they should do it jointly with policymakers.

Globalization, indeed, has many facets—economical, technological, and cultural. It, like all of nature, creates not only winners but also losers—both among individuals and nations.

- The integration of markets means that people of one country can consume the products of other countries, and through the Internet and TV people know more about the lives of people in other countries more than ever before. Unquestionably, globalization is affecting the daily lives of people all over the world, which, in turn, affects not only their economic status but also their cultural habits. We are, therefore, witnessing a wide-ranging transformation of human life in unprecedented ways.
- Moving existing manufacturing plants to low-labor-cost countries causes people to lose their jobs; globalization, therefore, can have a devastating effect on the lives of many well-to-do individuals in developed countries.

- Many people are also concerned about the growth of an international "monoculture", dominated by the West, which seems to threaten the disappearance of national, cultural, and religious traditions. This is a very dangerous misunderstanding that may cause devastating reactions to the economic transactions of global trade.

- Developing countries, especially in Africa, see globalization and its consequent trade liberalization as an unfair trading system that increases the gap between industrialized and developing countries. They interpret that their poverty has actually increased because of globalization and protest the unfairness in tariffs that industrialized countries put on their products (often their agriculture, which is most likely what they have to export).

- Globalization undermines the ability of governments to raise taxes on imports, and as a consequence they cannot provide services for their citizens.

Government policymakers are constantly whipsawed between two opposing positions regarding free trade versus protectionism in the global economic environment. Should government press for a purely free-trade position and trust the marketplace to provide all the most positive results for the economy? Or, should we use protectionist tariffs to defend the local workforce from foreign labor? Experience has shown that neither option offers a complete solution, and in fact, in the long run, both may create bad consequences, such as recession and inflation.

It is the responsibility of policymakers to find ways to make globalization work better for the individuals who are left behind because of changes in international trade, and to reduce the inequality for the developing countries.

14.7 WHERE ARE MANUFACTURING ENTERPRISES HEADED?

We started this book by defining globalization as a revolutionary approach of integrating world markets and nations, which are becoming very dependent on each other.

Globalization is the integration and interdependency of world markets and resources in producing consumer goods and services

For manufacturing enterprises the integration of world markets has created new conditions:

- Fierce competition on a global scale
- Global product supply being much greater than demand
- Increased customers' purchasing power
- Rapid changes in customer needs and demands
- An accelerated pace of product and process innovations that spread rapidly

- International environmental awareness that brings about stricter regulations imposed by governments (e.g., fuel efficiency, collecting used products for disassembly).

These conditions cause new challenges for the global manufacturing enterprise.

- Abrupt changes in product demand
- Frequent product changes and new government regulations
- Short windows of market opportunity for new products
- Increased product variety, moving toward a market-of-one.
- Precise coordination of global resources, through multi-tier supply chains, to build products for lowest cost and in close proximity to customers.

How can manufacturing enterprises create a competitive advantage in this turbulent environment, and how can they justify their size? Will the manufacturing enterprises in developed countries become much smaller? Will they disappear?

Analyzing previous manufacturing paradigms might help in developing new strategies. Figure 14.5 summarizes the transitions between three major manufacturing paradigms in the last 100 years related to the changing needs of customers and market climates. It illustrates how the market influences the invention of new types of manufacturing system, and how desire for richer product variety drives the product architecture and the business model that enterprises implement.

Currently the global manufacturing paradigm points at two directions: personalized production and regionalized production for multiple world regions. The latter, perhaps more critical to the economic success of the enterprise, requires the development of product architecture that can be tailored to address specific cultural and regional needs. This product architecture enables the design of products with multiple functions that can fit the culture, government regulations, climate, and needs, as well as the purchasing power of various target markets on the globe. To accomplish this, manufacturing enterprises must develop a global strategy that considers which product variants to develop for which regions on the globe, in which countries to locate factories, and how to integrate their global supply chains.

And the same imperatives that drive personalization and regionalization—the competitive global market and economy, and the globally integrated society that desires to maintain individual national cultures —force the invention of new products and new manufacturing technologies.

In July 2009 Charles M. Vest, the president of the National Academy of Engineering, wrote:[1] "We must turn our attention to unleashing technological innovation to create products and services that *add actual value*. As a nation we must refocus on *the real economy*, and that will require a reenergized innovation system to generate new knowledge and technology." The real economy is one that produces something that adds value, and not the one that sends people shopping, buying stuff that they cannot afford and do not need. Therefore, manufacturing will

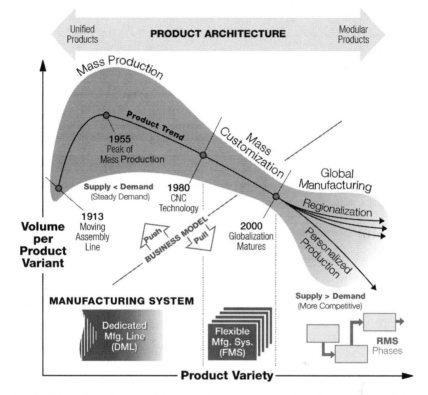

Figure 14.5 Paradigms and their product, process, and business characteristics.

always remain a major means by which wealth is created for any society. The manufacturing enterprises cannot disappear.

But the manufacturing industry as a whole is going through a major transformation that requires enterprises to comprehend the new frontier in manufacturing technology and strategy, and to develop new ways of thinking. They have to be restructured and strategically directed, which will eventually yield a growing economy and wealthier society.

The new frontier for the manufacturing industry is in achieving faster responsiveness to market changes as well as to customers' requirements. To accomplish this goal, manufacturing enterprises have to be designed for frequent reconfigurations in their structure, in their global resources and supply chains, as well as in their factories. The manufacturing strategies of the twenty-first-century enterprise should be designed with the options to be rapidly modified exactly when needed.

We offer below a set of 10 strategic planning rules for global manufacturing enterprises that will help them to prosper in the turbulent global economy. Implementing these rules will result in a growing global economy and a larger number of manufacturing jobs.

---

*NAE Member Newsletter, July 2009.

Strategic Rules for Global Manufacturing Enterprises

1. **Global Strategy:** The manufacturing enterprise must develop a global strategy that determines issues such as which products to develop, for which regions on the globe, where to locate factories, how to integrate global supply chains, and how to boost productivity with the same global resources. The enterprise should develop business strategies for emerging markets, such as Brazil, Russia, India, and China.

2. **Integration of Product–System–Business:** The global manufacturing enterprise must apply a systems approach in which product design is integrated with the manufacturing system that will produce it and with the business plan that sells it.

3. **Rapid Responsiveness:** The key to global success is faster responsiveness to customers' needs and market changes that is built into their business strategy as well as into their manufacturing system.

4. **Reconfigurable Manufacturing Systems:** The global manufacturing enterprise must possess reconfigurable manufacturing systems whose capacity can be easily changed to adapt to market demand, and its functionality can be cost-effectively adapted to introduce new products with short lead times.

5. **Innovative Products:** The engine for a successful enterprise is a stream of innovative products introduced within short lead times. Nurturing an enterprise culture of creativity is imperative for continuous innovation.

6. **Products Fit for Regional Markets:** The product design and its functions should fit the culture, regulations, climate, and purchasing power of the targeted market customers. To reduce cost, develop from a common base (platform) and differentiate modules as necessary.

7. **Personalized Products:** An emerging market in industrialized countries is created around cost-effective personalized products—ideally, each product will be made exactly for an individual customer's needs (a market of one).

8. **Empowerment with Information:** The enterprise must provide real-time continuous information to employees and empower them to make decisions; empowerment sustains a momentum for rapid innovation in both the product and the manufacturing system.

9. **Critical Parts and Final Assembly:** A cost-effective manufacturing strategy that also protects intellectual property is to build assembly plants in the target market country but keep production of critical parts at home.

10. **Strategic Alliances:** Combine the skills and resources of alliance partners to develop innovative products at the highest quality and lowest costs.

Globalization has brought many new players to the field from various world regions that impact each other. Consequently, globalization has created a more complicated world with economic turbulence that affects companies and individuals alike. At first, small and medium-size companies felt the fierce competition and small market turbulence. When the market turbulence increased, it started to impact the large global enterprises as well. Eventually these waves of turbulence will become bigger and have a stronger effect on the entire world economy. They will impact not only the careers of factory employees but also the living conditions of millions around the world.

By the 1990s, the United States built a highly productive, low-inflation economy that generated unprecedented wealth, jobs, and earnings. The foundation of this economy was the manufacturing industry. But globalization has changed the playing field and resulted in a reduction in the strength and size of the manufacturing sector. This reduction impacts the entire U.S. economy, as well as the economies of Europe and Australia. The twenty-first-century new industries in the United States and Europe are focused on manufacturing solar panels, wind turbines, and batteries. But these industries will shortly migrate to China, which suffers from polluted air and rivers and desperately needs these energy-generated technologies. By contrast, personalized production will also reside close to the customers, and has the potential to regenerate the economy.

Is it possible to regain the U.S. and European economic success of the 1990s by strengthening the manufacturing industry by the government and implementing the above strategic rules by the industry itself. Governments must understand that the foundation of a strong economy is still in the manufacturing of new products. The service economy can survive only when it is based on this solid foundation. But creating a strong economy requires another change; in the twenty-first century manufacturing enterprises must be dynamic entities that continuously change in response to unpredictable market turbulences. To make them dynamic and responsive, industries should implement the 10 strategic rules at a global scale, as well as the five "PRIDE" principles.

Globalization is here, and it will stay. New technologies will intensify globalization even more. Therefore, in the global era, enterprises will have to coordinate their resources across national borders and reconfigure quickly to accommodate unpredictable market, cultural and political changes. Rapid responsiveness, new products design for globalization, reconfiguration technology, and seamless integration among the business and engineering facets are the imperative challenges of the revolution in global manufacturing, challenges that when met will bring wealth and prosperity to the global manufacturing enterprises of the twenty-first century.

It is not the largest enterprise that'll survive nor those that have experienced leadership, but the ones most responsive to change

REFERENCES

1. J. Bollinger et al. *Visionary Manufacturing Challenges for 2020*. National Academy Press, Washington D.C., 1998, p. 30.
2. R. F. Bruner et al. *The Portable MBA*. John Wiley & Sons, New Jersey, 2003.
3. L. Dobbs. *Exporting America*. Warner Books, New York, 2004.
4. T. L. Friedman. *The World is Flat*. Farrar, Straus and Giroux, New York, 2005, p. 227.
5. R. Buderi. *Engines of Tomorrow: How the Worlds Best Companies are Using Their Research Labs to Win the Future*. Simon & Schuster, 2000.
6. G. Soros. *On Globalization*. PublicAffairs, New York, 2002.
7. J. E. Stiglitz. *Globalization and its Disconnect*. Norton & Company, 2002.

Computer Controlled Milling Machine in 1973

CNC–AC milling machine (McMaster University, Hamilton, Canada, May 1973)

Yoram Koren invented and built the world's first adaptive control (AC) of a milling machine, integrated with home-built CNC. The control computer of both the CNC and the AC was Hewlett-Packard HP-2100. It was a 16-bit computer with a memory of 4096 words (4 K), with cycle time of 1 microsecond and 16 I/O slots that were used to send signals to the three control loops and obtained signals from a sophisticated force sensor mounted on the spindle (the force sensor was designed by Professor J. Tlusty).

This CNC–AC system was demonstrated at the 1st NAMR Conference, at McMaster University. Hamilton, Canada, May 14–16, 1973. The AC algorithm may be found in Chapter 8 of the book Computer Control of Manufacturing Systems, McGraw Hill, 1983. The algorithm of the CNC interpolator was published at: Koren, Y.: Interpolator for a CNC system. IEEE Trans. on Computers. Vol. 25, No. 1, pp. 32-37, January 1976.

Appendix **B**

Three Types of Manufacturing Systems

Dedicated Manufacturing Line
Machining (or assembly) stations arranged sequentially in a line, where
each station is capable of performing a given, unchangeable task.

**Flexible
Manufacturing System**
A system consisting of
programmable CNC
machines and robots.
The system is easily
changeable to production
of new products.

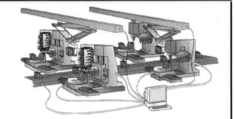

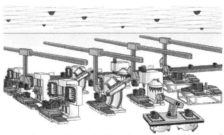

Reconfigurable Manufacturing System
A mix of CNCs and RMTs, where each cell is serviced by an overhead gantry and can be
expanded to increase capacity with additional CNCs. If variation errors are detected by a
RIM at the last stage, parts can be returned up stream with an AGV.

Artist Rodney Hill

The Global Manufacturing Revolution: Product-Process-Business Integration and Reconfigurable Systems
By Yoram Koren
Copyright © 2010 John Wiley & Sons, Inc.

Appendix **C**

Business Cycles

All market economies regularly go through cycles of recession (when output declines and unemployment rises) and expansion (when output and employment rise). These "business cycles" are one of the most important factors determining not only the profit of manufacturing companies but also the socioeconomic conditions of the people. Two important questions are why there are business cycles and what are the indicators that may predict them.

Business cycles are a complex phenomenon that depends on the amount of money available as well as on the relationship between demand and supply. *A business cycle starts to rise* when demand for products increases, and then factories accelerate their production. Because sales are rising, when demands are nearing full factory capacity, companies decide to build new factories and to order new manufacturing equipment. And if demand rises further, factories accelerate production even more, etc.

. . . Eventually the cycle has to turn down

Sales stabilize.

Factories reduce production, and stop ordering new equipment.

Undesired inventories built up.

People stop buying so much and sales fall.

The economy starts to go downwards.

The Global Manufacturing Revolution: Product-Process-Business Integration and Reconfigurable Systems
By Yoram Koren
Copyright © 2010 John Wiley & Sons, Inc.

There are 10 indicators that help in predicting changes in business cycles:

1. New orders of consumer goods and materials.
2. Orders for new factories and new equipment.
3. Number of new private housing, measured by the number of building permits.
4. Average length of workweek of production workers in manufacturing companies.
5. Weekly unemployment insurance claims.
6. Interest rate.
7. Money supply—the ease of getting credit (e.g., to buy cars, to pay salaries, etc.)
8. Percent of manufacturing companies receiving slower delivery from their suppliers.
9. Index of stock prices.
10. Index of consumer expectations.

The first three indicators represent commitments to economic activities in the near future. The combination of the above 10 indicators can predict the end of the bottom of a business cycle (i.e., end of a recession) about 5 months in advance, and predict the end of the business cycle peak about 9–10 months in advance. The building of a new factory, however, takes more than 10 months. Therefore, building new plants and ordering expensive equipment present a serious challenge that manufacturing companies are facing before deciding on expansion. Assuming that business cycles occur at different times at different regions of the globe, opening a new factory for products that can be easily shipped from one country to another (e.g., hard disk) is less of a dilemma than in the cases where it is expensive to ship high-volume products between countries (e.g., cars, engines, etc.).

Appendix D

Term Project: Project Description and Requirements

PRODUCT DEVELOPMENT IN A COMPETITIVE GLOBAL ENVIRONMENT

This project is a team project (3–5 students per team) which has three goals:

1. Design innovative products for mass customization and personalization.
2. Utilize flexible and reconfigurable manufacturing systems to produce the products.
3. Establish business strategies to sell your new products.

General Requirements

- **Create a company that will produce and sell a family of mass-customized products**.
- **Identify a product** whose market share could be significantly increased if designed with variants that fit various customers' needs (i.e., mass customization or personalization).

    Past examples of products selected by students: wheelchairs, bicycles, car seats, watches, backpacks, sport equipment, sunglasses, skate boards, office furniture, chairs, golf clubs, etc.

The Global Manufacturing Revolution: Product-Process-Business Integration and Reconfigurable Systems
By Yoram Koren
Copyright © 2010 John Wiley & Sons, Inc.

- **Design a manufacturing system** that produces the product cost-effectively. Select equipment, draw factory layout diagrams, estimate capacity, etc.
- **Elaborate on a business model** that will sell your product.
- **Submit three reports**: two intermediate reports (on the product and on its manufacturing), and a final, comprehensive report.

Detailed Requirements

1st Report: Product Design and Market Analysis
This report should cover the following items:

1. **Describe Your Product, and Explain the Rationale of Selecting it**
   - Elaborate on the advantages of your product and its fit to mass customization or personalization markets.
   - Elaborate on the desired features that differentiate your product from similar competing products.
   - Search patent databases (see at the end of this section) and report on similar inventions.
2. **Describe the Market of your Product and the Customers**
   - What is the total market value of products of this type?
   - What is the market share that you expect to capture?
   - Who are your customers?
3. **Provide Sketches and Specifications of the Product**
   - Elaborate on key design ideas allowing cost-effective variations of your product (e.g., modularity).
   - How many variations can customers choose from?
   - Can you classify components of the product as strategic and non-strategic?
4. **Why Would the Customers Buy Your Product?**
   - What needs do the customers have that your product offers?
   - Can you conduct a small market survey to prove your claims?
   - How do you know that your planned price is right?
   - What differentiates your product from your competitors?

2nd Report: The Manufacturing System
This report should elaborate on the design of the production system and cover the following points:

1. **Production System Description and Investment Cost**
   - Describe the system type and its configuration and floor layout as well as the type of equipment needed.

- Elaborate on equipment flexibility and reconfigurability.
- Explain how the system can manufacture the different product variants.
- Estimate the investment cost for the equipment and the facility (get quotes for equipment).

2. **System Performance**
   - Determine the production time per product and the throughput of the system.
   - Elaborate on convertibility issues (changing between product models to satisfy customer's needs).
   - Elaborate on production capacity and scalability issues (adding capacity).

3. **Transferring Customer's Needs to the Manufacturing System**
   - Discuss how current customer needs will be translated into the production of customized products by the manufacturing system.
   - Estimate the time from order to delivery to the customer.
   - If relevant to your product, discuss special equipment and methods that enable the measurement or estimate of customer requirements (e.g., particular size of jeans) for the customized product.

4. **Self-manufacturing Versus Outsourcing**
   If you use outside suppliers to supply components (outsourcing)—explain why and elaborate on the issue of just-in-time delivery of these components.

BUSINESS TOPICS IN THE FINAL REPORT

The final report and its oral presentation are based on the previous intermediate reports and, in addition, should include the following business-related topics:

1. **Competitive Advantage**
   - Market analysis.
   - Do you compete on cost leadership, product differentiation, or personalization? Explain.

2. **Creating Value for the Customer**
   How do the customers benefit from your product?

3. **Strategic Resources**
   - List and explain your resources. Are they unique?
   - Elaborate on your core competency that can create the competitive advantage.

4. **The Business Strategy**
   - Market target and scope; global growth strategies.
   - How are your strategic resources helping you to define the business strategy?
   - Marketing strategies; rapid response to customer orders and needs.

- Using the web and information technology in marketing and responding to customers.
- Product distribution and delivery methods.
- Outsourcing and supply chains.

5. **Selecting the Location of the Production Facility** Compare possible locations such as the USA (where?), China, India, Central America, Mexico, etc.

6. **Company Organization**
   - The organization structure of the company; number of employees; the decision-making authority.
   - The workforce size and skills.
   - Possible strategic alliances and cooperation with partnering companies.

7. **Financing**
   - Plot a chart of your projected sales (for best and worst scenarios) versus expenses (investment and operational) projecting forward up to 7 years; discuss break-even points. How much money do you plan to raise to start your company?

FINAL REPORT FORMAT

Cover Page (title, student names, date, group number)
Table of Contents
Executive Summary (1 page)

1. **Vision and Rationale** for selecting the product (company goals, how to achieve the goals)
2. **The Product** (describe your product and its uniqueness; based on the 1st report)
3. **Manufacturing System and Infrastructure** (based on the 2nd report)
4. **Competitive Advantage** (elaborate on your competency that creates a market advantage)
5. **Business Model** (market analysis, creating value for customers, strategic resources, the business strategy, responding to customers, supply chains, outsourcing, etc.)
6. **Management and Organizational Structure**
7. **Basic Financial Plan** (estimate investment and operational costs vs. sales in worst- and best-case scenarios for the first 7 years)
8. **Summary**
Attachments

The final report size is limited to 30 pages, not including product and plant layout drawings.

Submit:

- One hard copy of a nice, bounded booklet
- An electronic copy (MS Word) on a CD.

For the 1st report you should look for similar concepts and ideas at patent databases.

Patent Databases

U.S. Patent Office:	www.uspto.gov/web/offices/pac/doc/general/
IBM:	www.patents.ibm.com/
European:	www.epo.co.at/index.htm

Author Biography

Yoram Koren
Paul G. Goebel Professor of Engineering
Director, NSF Engineering Research Center (ERC) for Reconfigurable
Manufacturing Systems
The University of Michigan College of Engineering, Ann Arbor, Michigan

Professor Yoram Koren is internationally recognized for innovative contributions to robotics, flexible automation, and reconfigurable manufacturing systems. He is credited with conceiving of the reconfigurable manufacturing paradigm and as a pioneer in establishing flexible automation, particularly computer numeric control and adaptive control of machine tools, as a research field and educational discipline. He is a member of the National Academy of Engineering, and his innovations have helped establish the University of Michigan as a premier institution for advanced manufacturing research.

Professor Koren is the founding director, in 1996, of the Engineering Research Center (ERC) for Reconfigurable Manufacturing Systems (RMS), sponsored by the National Science Foundation. During 12 years of NSF sponsorship, the Center—comprised of 20 professors, 10 investigators, and 25 companies—received $48 million in funding, and graduated 220 Masters and 70 Ph.D. students.

Tools developed at the ERC-RMS, using Professor Koren's designs and principles, have already made their way to factory floors improving their productivity and part quality. The Center has held three Reconfigurable Manufacturing Conferences with participants from 40 countries, and conducts outreach, including school demonstrations with a portable manufacturing lab, building museum exhibitions, and spearheading programs to increase participation of underrepresented minorities in the field.

According to Google Scholar, 9,000 papers have cited professor Koren's work (280 publications, 14 U.S. patents 3 books, and 20 reports). He is the author of three award-winning books that have been translated into French, Japanese, and Chinese. This current textbook, *The Global Manufacturing Revolution*, was written for the Global Manufacturing graduate course at the University of Michigan.

Some of his earlier accomplishments include the 1973 development of the world's first computerized real-time adaptive controller for a milling machine, (see Appendix A), long before computers were commonly used in industrial applications, as well as the 1993 development of a mechanical snake robot whose movement was remarkably true to life.

Professor Koren has won numerous prestigious manufacturing awards, including the Merchant Medal of ASME & SME, the Society of Manufacturing Engineering Gold Medal, the William T. Ennor Manufacturing Technology Award, and the Japan-U.S. Hanasufa Outstanding Investigator Award on Flexible Automation. He received the UM College of Engineering Excellence in Research Award in 1992 and the Attwood Award in 2008. He was the first holder of the Edmond J. Safra Distinguished Visiting Professor Chair at the Technion – Israel Institute of Technology.

Author Index

Subject Index

The Global Manufacturing Revolution: Product-Process-Business Integration and Reconfigurable Systems
By Yoram Koren
Copyright © 2010 John Wiley & Sons, Inc.

WILEY SERIES IN SYSTEMS ENGINEERING AND MANAGEMENT

Andrew P. Sage, Editor

YACOV Y. HAIMES
Risk Modeling, Assessment, and Management, Third Edition

DENNIS M. BUEDE
The Engineering Design of Systems: Models and Methods, Second Edition

ANDREW P. SAGE and JAMES E. ARMSTRONG, Jr.
Introduction to Systems Engineering

WILLIAM B. ROUSE
Essential Challenges of Strategic Management

YEFIM FASSER and DONALD BRETTNER
Management for Quality in High-Technology Enterprises

THOMAS B. SHERIDAN
Humans and Automation: System Design and Research Issues

ALEXANDER KOSSIAKOFF and WILLIAM N. SWEET
Systems Engineering Principles and Practice

HAROLD R. BOOHER
Handbook of Human Systems Integration

JEFFREY T. POLLOCK AND RALPH HODGSON
Adaptive Information: Improving Business Through Semantic Interoperability, Grid Computing, and Enterprise Integration

ALAN L. PORTER AND SCOTT W. CUNNINGHAM
Tech Mining: Exploiting New Technologies for Competitive Advantage

REX BROWN
Rational Choice and Judgment: Decision Analysis for the Decider

WILLIAM B. ROUSE AND KENNETH R. BOFF (editors)
Organizational Simulation

HOWARD EISNER
Managing Complex Systems: Thinking Outside the Box

STEVE BELL
Lean Enterprise Systems: Using IT for Continuous Improvement

J. JERRY KAUFMAN AND ROY WOODHEAD
Stimulating Innovation in Products and Services: With Function Analysis and Mapping

WILLIAM B. ROUSE
Enterprise Tranformation: Understanding and Enabling Fundamental Change

JOHN E. GIBSON, WILLIAM T. SCHERER, AND WILLAM F. GIBSON
How to Do Systems Analysis

WILLIAM F. CHRISTOPHER
Holistic Management: Managing What Matters for Company Success

WILLIAM B. ROUSE
People and Organizations: Explorations of Human-Centered Design

GREGORY S. PARNELL, PATRICK J. DRISCOLL, AND DALE L. HENDERSON
Decision Making in Systems Engineering and Management

MO JAMSHIDI
System of Systems Engineering: Innovations for the Twenty-First Century

ANDREW P. SAGE AND WILLIAM B. ROUSE
Handbook of Systems Engineering and Management, Second Edition

JOHN R. CLYMER
Simulation-Based Engineering of Complex Systems, Second Edition

KRAG BROTBY
Information Security Governance: A Practical Development and Implementation Approach

JULIAN TALBOT AND MILES JAKEMAN
Security Risk Management Body of Knowledge

SCOTT JACKSON
Architecting Resilient Systems: Accident Avoidance and Survival and Recovery from Disruptions

JAMES A. GEORGE AND JAMES A. RODGER
Smart Data: Enterprise Performance Optimization Strategy

YORAM KOREN
The Global Manufacturing Revolution: Product-Process-Business Integration and Reconfigurable Systems

Printed in Poland
by Amazon Fulfillment
Poland Sp. z o.o., Wrocław
29 November 2020

7310d6b4-ddb6-46af-83d1-e2b79be8e891R01